LIBRARY OF HEBREW BIBLE/
OLD TESTAMENT STUDIES

564

Formerly Journal for the Study of the Old Testament Supplement Series

Editors
Claudia V. Camp, Texas Christian University
Andrew Mein, Westcott House, Cambridge

Founding Editors
David J. A. Clines, Philip R. Davies and David M. Gunn

Editorial Board
Alan Cooper, John Goldingay, Robert P. Gordon,
Norman K. Gottwald, James Harding, John Jarick, Carol Meyers
Patrick D. Miller, Francesca Stavrakopoulou,
Daniel L. Smith-Christopher

APPROACHES TO THE "CHOSEN PLACE"

Accessing a Biblical Concept

Rannfrid Irene Thelle

t & t clark

Published by T&T Clark International
A Continuum imprint
The Tower Building, 11 York Road, London SE1 7NX
80 Maiden Lane, New York, NY 10038

www.continuumbooks.com

Visit the T & T Clark blog at www.tandtclarkblog.com

© Rannfrid Irene Thelle, 2012

All rights reserved. No part of this book may be reproduced, stored in a retrieval system, or transmitted in any form or by any means, electronic, mechanical, including photocopying, recording, or otherwise, without the written permission of the publisher, T & T Clark International.

The Scripture quotations contained herein are from the New Revised Standard Version Bible, copyright 1989, by the Division of Christian Education of the National Council of the Churches of Christ in the United States of America, and are used by permission. All rights reserved.

Library of Congress Cataloging-in-Publication Data
Thelle, Rannfrid I., 1966-
  Approaches to the "chosen place" : accessing a biblical concept / by Rannfrid Irene Thelle.
    p. cm.
  "A Continuum imprint"--T.p. verso.
  Includes bibliographical references.
  ISBN-13: 978-0-567-46807-9 (hardcover : alk. paper)
  ISBN-10: 0-567-46807-0 (hardcover : alk. paper) 1. Jerusalem in the Bible. 2. Temple of Jerusalem (Jerusalem) 3. Bible. O.T. Deuteronomy--Criticism, interpretation, etc. 4. Bible. O.T. Former Prophets--Criticism, interpretation, etc. 5. Bible. O.T. Kings, 2nd, XXII-XXIII--Criticism, interpretation, etc. 6. Deuteronomistic history (Biblical criticism) 7. Josiah, King of Judah. I. Title.

BS680.J37T44 2012
296.4'82--dc23

ISBN: HB: 978-0-567-46807-9

Typeset and copy-edited by Forthcoming Publications Ltd. (www.forthpub.com)
Printed and bound in the United States of America

To my husband,
Stuart Lasine

Contents

Acknowledgments	xi
Abbreviations	xiii

Chapter 1
INTRODUCTION	1
The "Chosen Place" in the Book of Deuteronomy	1
The Place of the "Chosen Place" in Scholarship on Deuteronomy	3
The Dating of Deuteronomy	4
A Religious Reform under King Josiah	9
A Deuteronomistic Author, Source and Historian	11
Approaching the "Chosen Place"	21
The "Chosen Place" in Deuteronomy, the Pentateuch and in the Former Prophets: Outline of the Content of the Chapters	23

Chapter 2
CHOSEN PLACE AND CHOSEN CITY	27
The "Centralization Formula": Some Remarks on Scholarship	28
The Chosen Place in Deuteronomy	30
Brief Comment on the Contents of Deuteronomy	30
The Place which YHWH Your God Will Choose	30
The Expanded Form with the Mention of Tribes	33
The Expanded Form with the Name: Put His Name There (לשום שמו שם)	36
The Expanded Form with the Name: To Let His Name Dwell There (לשכן שמו שם)	38
A "Centralization Formula" in Deuteronomy?	39
Joshua 9:27	40
The Chosen City, Jerusalem	41
"For the Sake of Jerusalem, which I Have Chosen"	42
References to Jerusalem, the Chosen City, in Regnal Summaries	45

2 Kings 23: "I Will Reject this City That I Have Chosen"	47
1 Kings 8: A House for YHWH's Name in the Chosen City	48
Can One Speak of Centralization in Kings?	52
The Chosen City in Chronicles	53
Conclusions	53

Chapter 3
"CENTRALIZATION" IN DEUTERONOMY 12

	57
Centralization and Chosen Place in Scholarship on Deuteronomy 12	58
A Reading of Deuteronomy 12	59
Deuteronomy 11:30–31	59
Deuteronomy 12:1–7	60
Deuteronomy 12:8–12	68
Deuteronomy 12:13–28: Laws Governing Sacrifice, Gift Offerings, and Non-Sacrificial Slaughter	72
Deuteronomy 12:20–28	76
Deuteronomy 12:29–31: Warning Against Idolatry	78
Centralization Affirmed	79

Chapter 4
"JERUSALEM" IN THE FORMER PROPHETS

	81
Jerusalem in Joshua, Judges, and 1 Samuel	82
Jerusalem in 2 Samuel	82
The "City of David" in 2 Samuel and Kings	83
Sense of Place in 2 Samuel 7	85
Jerusalem in 2 Samuel	87
Ornan's Threshing Floor in 1 Chronicles 21	88
Jerusalem in the Book of Kings	89
Summary and Conclusions	93

Chapter 5
THE CULTIC CONTEXT OF THE "CHOSEN PLACE"

	95
The Pentateuch	97
The Sanctuary	97
The Altar	100
The Ark	106
Sacrificial Cult	108
Festivals	109
Ritual Purity	109
Vows and Gifts	110
The Sabbath in Deuteronomy	110

Further Comments on Cult, Ritual and the Cult Site in Deuteronomy	111
Summary	112
Sinai, Horeb, and Moab	112
Cult and Ritual in the Former Prophets	113
Joshua	114
Judges	117
Samuel	122
Kings	124
Conclusions	126

Chapter 6
"CENTRALIZATION" AND THE STORY OF JOSIAH'S REFORM:
IS DEUTERONOMY 12 CENTRAL TO JOSIAH?

	129
Scholarship on Josiah's Reform: Some Remarks	130
2 Kings 22: The Book-Finding Story	134
Huldah's Oracle: What Does It Say About the Contents of the Book?	136
The Covenant Renewal Ceremony in 2 Kings 23:1–3	139
Josiah's Reform in 2 Kings 23:4–20	140
The Account of the Reform	140
The *bamot*	142
The Account of the Reform, Continued	146
Is Deuteronomy 12 Central to Josiah?	150
2 Kings 23:4–20 as "Centralizing" Reform?	152
Josiah's Passover	155
Passover in Deuteronomy	157
What Is So Deuteronomistic About Josiah's Passover?	160
Passover in the Former Prophets	161
Reform Narratives in Kings	162
The Chronicler's Passover: The "True" Deuteronomistic Passover?	162
Josiah's Centralized Passover: Enough to Make it Deuteronomistic?	165
Summary and Discussion	166
Conclusions	168

Chapter 7
DIVINE ELECTION AS A PRINCIPLE OF AUTHORITY

	170
Election in the Pentateuch	170
The Election of Israel in Deuteronomy	171
Israel as Chosen, the Duty to Keep the Law, and YHWH's Rescue from Egypt	175

Election of "Place" in Deuteronomy	178
Divine Election in Other Parts of the Bible	181
The Chosen King and the Chosen City	182
Israel as Chosen	184
Conclusion	185

Chapter 8
KINGS REVISITED:
KINGSHIP IN DEUTERONOMY AND THE FORMER PROPHETS

	186
Descriptions of Kings and Kingship in the Former Prophets	187
References to Kingship in "Premonarchic" Narratives	187
The Establishment of the Monarchy in 1 Samuel	187
The Portrayal of Kings in Samuel and Kings	190
The Evaluation of Kings in Samuel and Kings	193
Saul, David, and Solomon	194
Kings Who Do Evil	195
Kings Who Do Good: Hezekiah and Josiah	196
The Law of the King in Deuteronomy 17:14–20	197
Discussion of Kingship in Scholarly Debate: An Illustration of the Problems	200

Chapter 9
CONCLUSIONS

	204
Final Thoughts	208

Bibliography	213
Index of References	228
Index of Authors	238

Acknowledgments

While I am solely responsible for the choices I have made in writing this book, a number of people and institutions deserve a mention of thanks for their support, participation, and encouragement. Work on this book began during my period as a post-doctoral fellow at the University of Oslo, the Faculty of Theology (2000–2005), and I thank my colleagues for providing a stimulating and supportive work environment. Travel grants from the Norwegian Research Council enabled trips to Cambridge and Jerusalem to collect research material at the initial stage. I worked on the book also during my two-year stint at Luther College in Decorah, Iowa; however, most of the writing was done in Wichita, Kansas, which has been my home since 2007.

I want to express my gratitude to Claudia Camp, who, from the very first time we met in Cambridge in 2003, has encouraged and supported this book project. I thank both her and Andrew Mein for accepting the book for publication in the Library of Hebrew Bible/Old Testament Studies series.

Along the way, a number of people have read the various drafts of my work. In particular, I want to thank Martin R. Hauge for reading parts of my manuscript and providing valuable feedback during a crucial stage of writing. Hans M. Barstad read the entire manuscript as the process neared its completion and provided useful suggestions, for which I am truly grateful.

Most of all, I want to thank my husband, Stuart Lasine, who has read most parts of the book at various stages. His always pertinent and thought-provoking questions, acute and astute textual observations, and unfaltering stylistic suggestions have greatly improved the end result, although, again, I am solely responsible for it. One of the bonuses that comes from working in the same field, our household conversations about biblical texts and issues have been the greatest source of inspiration for this project in its final, and decisive, phase. In the deepest appreciation of this scholarly support, and for making life so wonderful, I dedicate this book to him.

ABBREVIATIONS

AB	Anchor Bible
ABD	*Anchor Bible Dictionary*. Edited by David Noel Freedman. 6 vols. New York, 1992
AnBib	Analecta biblica
ANET	*Ancient Near Eastern Texts Relating to the Old Testament.* Edited by James B. Pritchard. 3d ed. Princeton, 1969
AOAT	Alter Orient und Altes Testament
ATANT	Abhandlungen zur Theologie des Alten und Neuen Testaments
ATD	Das Alte Testament Deutsch
BBB	Bonner biblische Beiträge
BeO	*Bibbia e oriente*
BET	Beiträge zur biblischen Exegese und Theologie
BETL	Bibliotheca ephemeridum theologicarum lovaniensium
BFCT	Beiträge zur Förderung christlicher Theologie
Bib	*Biblica*
BJRL	*Bulletin of the John Rylands University Library of Manchester*
BKAT	Biblischer Kommentar: Altes Testament
BR	*Bible Review*
BTB	*Biblical Theology Bulletin*
BWANT	Beiträge zur Wissenschaft vom Alten und Neuen Testament
BZ	*Biblische Zeitschrift*
BZAW	Beihefte zur ZAW
CBQ	*Catholic Biblical Quarterly*
CRBS	*Currents in Research: Biblical Studies*
EdF	Ertrage der Forschung
FAT	Forschungen zum alten Testament
FOTL	Forms of the Old Testament Literature
FRLANT	Forschungen zur Religion und Literatur des Alten und Neuen Testaments
HAT	Handbuch zum Alten Testament
HSM	Harvard Semitic Monographs
HTR	*Harvard Theological Review*
HUCA	*Hebrew Union College Annual*
ICC	International Critical Commentary
IEJ	*Israel Exploration Journal*
ISBL	Indiana Studies in Biblical Literature
JAOS	*Journal of the American Oriental Society*

JBL	*Journal of Biblical Literature*
JBR	*Journal of Bible and Religion*
JNES	*Journal of Near Eastern Studies*
JNSL	*Journal of Northwest Semitic Languages*
JQR	*Jewish Quarterly Review*
JSOT	*Journal for the Study of the Old Testament*
JSOTSup	Journal for the Study of the Old Testament: Supplement Series
LCL	Loeb Classical Library
LD	Lectio divina
LHBOTS	Library of Hebrew Bible/Old Testament Studies (Formerly Journal for the Study of the Old Testament: Supplement Series)
NCB	New Century Bible
NRT	*La nouvelle revue théologique*
OBO	Orbis biblicus et orientalis
Or	*Orientalia*
OTS	*Oudtestamentische Studiën*
SBAB	*Stuttgarter biblische Aufsatzbände*
SBL	Society of Biblical Literature
SBLDS	SBL Dissertation Series
SBLMS	SBL Monograph Series
SBS	Stuttgarter Bibelstudien
SBT	Studies in Biblical Theology
SJOT	*Scandinavian Journal of the Old Testament*
TDOT	*Theological Dictionary of the Old Testament*. Edited by G. J. Botterweck and H. Ringgren. Translated by J. T. Willis, G. W. Bromiley, and D. E. Green. 8 vols. Grand Rapids, 1974–
Them	*Themelios*
ThR	*Theologische Rundschau*
TynBul	*Tyndale Bulletin*
VT	*Vetus Testamentum*
VTSup	Vetus Testamentum, Supplements
WBC	Word Biblical Commentary
WMANT	Wissenschaftliche Monographien zum Alten und Neuen Testament
WUNT	Wissenschaftliche Untersuchungen zum Neuen Testament
ZABR	*Zeitschrift für altorientalische und biblische Rechtsgeschichte*
ZAW	*Zeitschrift für die alttestamentliche Wissenschaft*

Chapter 1

INTRODUCTION

The "Chosen Place" in the Book of Deuteronomy

Deuteronomy is the only book in the Bible which contains the command that the Israelites must bring all their sacrifices, gifts, and offerings to "the place which YHWH your God will choose."[1] Moses tells the people that when they enter the land, they are to conduct all of their feasts at this un-named chosen place, and also practice judgment there. The command is elaborated extensively and is integrated into all of the legislation having to do with cultic practice, but no explanation is given for it. It is simply stated and repeated in various ways. Nevertheless, most modern readers find this command to be crucial and significant; for some, it is innovative, programmatic, or even revolutionary.[2]

---

1. Deut 12:5, 11, 14, 18, 21, 26; 14:23, 24, 25; 15:20; 16:2, 6, 7, 11, 15, 16; 17:8, 10; 18:6; 26:2; 31:11.
2. M. Weinfeld applied the term "revolutionary" several times to the group he called the Deuteronomists. Weinfeld wrote extensively throughout his career on the idea of a "Deuteronomic school" located in the scribal circles of Israel's monarchy, which was inspired by the ancient Israelite sapiential tradition; see, e.g., *Deuteronomy 1–11: A Commentary: A New Translation with Introduction and Commentary* (AB 5; New York: Doubleday, 1991), 37; "Deuteronomy's Theological Revolution," *BR* 12 (1996): 38–41, 44–45. B. M. Levinson highlights what he calls the "innovation" of the writers of Deuteronomy in their "programmatic" reinterpretation of ancient Israelite legal traditions; see *Deuteronomy and the Hermeneutics of Legal Innovation* (New York: Oxford University Press, 1997). N. Na'aman refers to Deuteronomy as "revolutionary and innovative," in "The Law of the Altar in Deuteronomy and the Cultic Site Near Shechem," in *Rethinking the Foundations: Historiography in the Ancient World and in the Bible, Essays in Honour of John Van Seters* (ed. S. L. McKenzie and T. C. Römer; BZAW 294; Berlin: de Gruyter, 2000), 141–61 (146). Writing from a literary point of view, R. Polzin makes the same assertion; see *Moses and the Deuteronomist: A Literary Study of the Deuteronomic History, Part I: Deuteronomy, Joshua, Judges* (New York: Seabury, 1980), 9. The impression that the reform program of Deuteronomy is thought of as "revolutionary"

Once one recognizes that the command to bring all sacrifices to, and celebrate feasts at, the "chosen place" is a distinctive feature of Deuteronomy, a number of fundamental questions arise. Why does this command make such a strong impression on readers of Deuteronomy? What role does this regulation play within the book, and how does it relate to cultic regulations pertaining to the sanctuary, the cultic personnel and the feasts in Exodus, Leviticus, and Numbers? More broadly, what role, if any, does Deuteronomy's idea about the chosen place play in the events reported the Former Prophets, Chronicles, Ezra, and Nehemiah? Questions such as these are not only legitimate but crucial, once we recognize the distinctiveness of Deuteronomy's concept of the "chosen place" and its influence on how readers understand other biblical books.

When I turn to past scholarship on the idea of YHWH's "chosen place," what strikes me most is how the understanding of this idea has been constricted by its intimate association with a few basic practices of historical-critical research. These are practices such as dating and literary criticism (*Litterarkritik*), which dominated the agenda in the formative period of academic biblical research. As I will specify in more detail shortly, scholars assigned the idea of YHWH's "chosen place" a crucial role in historical-critical reconstruction of textual history and of ancient Israelite history. This role has, in turn, shaped scholarship and how we as trained scholars read any biblical text from the Pentateuch or Former Prophets. It has shaped our presuppositions and questions to a greater extent than we might be aware of, and has made it difficult to speak about the "chosen place" in other ways.

Approaching Deuteronomy's "chosen place" in the twenty-first century, one must ask several challenging questions. In what specific ways has past research mapped out the path toward the biblical concept of "chosen place"? How has it restricted and shaped (and how does it continue to shape) the body of knowledge that has been amassed? Even more importantly, can the biblical evidence actually sustain the role which that concept of the chosen place has been made to play in scholarship?

---

is exemplified also by P. T. Vogt in the opening sentence of *Deuteronomic Theology and the Significance of Torah: A Reappraisal* (Winona Lake: Eisenbrauns, 2006), 1, and the literature cited there.

It would seem that in order to interpret Deuteronomy as innovative or revolutionary, the literary chronology established by the documentary hypothesis would have to be taken as a given. Wellhausen argues throughout for the transitional role that Deuteronomy represents, representing something new and different from an early, Israelite form of religion, that gradually later developed (or degenerated, he might have thought) into Judaism, represented by the "priestly" writings.

1. Introduction

A fresh study of the "chosen place" must primarily focus on close inspection of the complex literary connections between Deuteronomy and Exodus, Leviticus and Numbers, and between Deuteronomy and the books of Joshua, Judges, Samuel, and Kings. In addition, however, any study of the cult site in Deuteronomy will also have to take into account, at least to some extent, the wealth of critical scholarship on the role of the "chosen place," both in Deuteronomy and in the various renderings of what might be summarized as the Deuteronomistic History hypothesis.

The Place of the "Chosen Place" in Scholarship on Deuteronomy

Beginning with W. M. L. de Wette's *Dissertatio* in 1805, Deuteronomy was seen as stemming from a distinct source. The fourth of de Wette's six arguments for this distinction was the feature of limiting cultic activity to one divinely chosen place.[3] Since this early time in critical biblical scholarship, the study of the "chosen place" has been influenced by the desire for this concept to serve as a main argument for designating

---

3. The full title is *Dissertatio critico-exegetica qua Deuteronomium a prioribus Pentateuchi libris diversum, alius cuiusdam recentioris auctioris opus esse monstratur* ("A critical-exegetical discussion which shows that Deuteronomy is a work that differs from the first books of the Pentateuch, and is the work of another, later author"), and was defended for the degree of philosophy at the University of Jena in 1805; available in a reprint in the series Opuscula theologica (Berlin, 1830). De Wette developed this small dissertation, published when he was only 25 years old, further in the subsequent *Beiträge zur Einleitung in das Alte Testament. I. Kritischer Versuch über die Glaubwürdigkeit der Bücher und Gesetzgebung* (Halle, 1806); II. *Kritik der israelitischen Geschichte. Erster Teil: Kritik der mosaischen Geschichte* (Halle, 1807; repr. Darmstadt: Wissenschaftliche Buchgesellschaft, 1971). It was in the course of arguing for the distinctiveness of Deuteronomy, and as an argument for its date to the seventh century B.C.E., that de Wette pointed out, *in a footnote*, the possible connection between Deuteronomy and Josiah's reform, an argument he later refined in several publications; cf. J. W. Rogerson, *W. M. L. de Wette: Founder of Modern Biblical Criticism: An Intellectual Biography* (JSOTSup 126; Sheffield: JSOT, 1992), 39–42.

For a summary of de Wette's *Dissertatio*, and the development of the arguments in the *Beiträge*, see Rogerson, *W. M. L. de Wette*, 40–42, and for an analysis of its intellectual context and impact on subsequent biblical studies, see 42–63. For more on de Wette and his fundamental influence on all subsequent biblical studies, see R. Smend, *Wilhelm Martin Leberecht de Wettes Arbeit am Alten und am Neuen Testament* (Basel: Helbing & Lichtenhahn, 1958), and, in English, *From Astruc to Zimmerli: Old Testament Scholarship in Three Centuries* (trans. Margaret Kohl; Tübingen: Mohr Siebeck, 2007), 43–56 (esp. 48–49, on the *Dissertatio*).

Deuteronomy as different from the rest of the Pentateuchal material. Most scholars have followed de Wette in emphasizing cultic "centralization" as distinctive to Deuteronomy.[4] Subsequently, scholarship on the "chosen place" in Deuteronomy has been situated primarily within the context of developing source-critical, tradition-critical and redaction-critical expositions of the composition of Deuteronomy and of the Former Prophets. Since the late 1970s, the larger discussions involving challenges to the documentary hypothesis[5] have also impinged on the understanding of the "chosen place" in Deuteronomy, to varying extents. In general, these larger questions have set the parameters for research in various ways and have held power over the scholarly discourse on the "chosen place."

Three sets of positions in scholarship have converged to play a particularly dominating role in shaping the discussion on the "chosen place": (1) the dating of Deuteronomy to the seventh century and its separation from other books of the Pentateuch, (2) the idea of a religious (deuteronomistic) reform under King Josiah, and, (3) the idea of a deuteronomistic author, school, or movement connected in some way to those who were responsible for this reform, or who were later inspired by it, and who wrote or successively edited a unified historical work conveniently termed the Deuteronomistic History (DH). I will briefly refer to these discussions to illustrate their crucial importance for the study of the "chosen place." These well-established positions are now seriously under question, on many fronts. Nevertheless, this scholarly discourse continues to dictate the discussion. I will therefore introduce questions which point toward the need for new approaches.

The Dating of Deuteronomy
The dating of some form of Deuteronomy to the seventh century has been fundamental in scholarship. W. M. L. de Wette, for one, proposed that the book that Hilkiah found in the temple (2 Kgs 22:8) was some

---

4. Almost all commentaries on Deuteronomy and books of the "Introduction"-genre, both classic and more recent, make this point, e.g. S. R. Driver, *A Critical and Exegetical Commentary on Deuteronomy* (3d ed.; ICC; Edinburgh: T. & T. Clark, 1903; repr. 1978), 138; Weinfeld, *Deuteronomy 1–11*, 37–44; R. D. Nelson, *Deuteronomy: A Commentary* (OTL; Louisville, Ky.: Westminster John Knox, 2002).

G. von Rad is one of the few who objected to the emphasis on cultic centralization as a distinguishing characteristic or theological center of Deuteronomy, *Deuteronomy: A Commentary* (OTL; Philadelphia: Westminster, 1966), 64; trans. of *Das fünfte Buch Mose: Deuteronomium* (ATD 8; Göttingen: Vandenhoeck & Ruprecht, 1964).

5. On the documentary hypothesis, see below.

form of Deuteronomy.⁶ Even though de Wette was simply reiterating a long tradition,⁷ his identification is considered by many as an "Archimedean point" in the history of biblical literature.⁸ The identification of the ideas about centralization found in Deuteronomy with Josiah's reform has formed the basis for both the understanding of compositional history of the Pentateuch and for the history of the ancient Israelite religious institutions.

In developing the insights of de Wette, Vatke, Reuss, Graf, and other scholars, Julius Wellhausen formulated the classic documentary hypothesis.⁹ In his work with the biblical texts, Wellhausen was struck by the

---

6. The literature on this is vast. J. A. Montgomery and H. S. Gehman, eds., *A Critical and Exegetical Commentary on the Book of Kings* (ICC; Edinburgh: T. & T. Clark, 1950; repr. 1986), 543–44, list some of the literature from the early twentieth century. A major compilation of literature can also be found in J. M. Paul, *Het Archimedisch Punt van de Pentateuchkritiek: Een historisch en exegetish Onderzoek naar de Verhouding van Deuteronomium en de Reformatie van Koning Josia (2 Kon. 22–23)* ('s-Gravenhage: Uitgeverij Boekencentrum B.V., 1988).

7. The identification of Deuteronomy (or the whole of the Torah) with the book found by Hilkiah in 2 Kgs 22 was an ancient tradition. It was the idea that Deuteronomy was not an ancient book written by Moses, but a document contemporary with King Josiah that made such a breakthrough with de Wette, and that provided crucial tools for the complete reconstruction of ancient Israelite history at a time that was witnessing the breakthrough of modern history writing.

8. E.g. Weinfeld, *Deuteronomy 1–11*, 16; see also his 1967 article "Deuteronomy: The Present State of the Inquiry," *JBL* 86 (1967): 249–62 (249–50). On the ancient roots of the identification of Hilkiah's book, see J. M. Paul, "Hilkiah and the Law (2 Kings 22) in the 17th and 18th Centuries: Some Influences on W. M. L. de Wette," in *Das Deuteronomium: Entstehung, Gestalt und Botschaft* (ed. N. Lohfink; BETL 68; Leuven: Leuven University Press, 1985), 9–12. See further, Paul, *Het Archimedisch Punt*. Although I disagree with its main conclusions, this work contains perhaps the most extensive bibliographic review on the connections between Deuteronomy and "Josiah's Reform" throughout the history of interpretation. O. Eissfeldt also uses the term "archimedischen Punkt" in designating the position of Deuteronomy within Pentateuchal criticism; see Eissfeldt, *The Old Testament: An Introduction: Including the Apocrypha and Pseudepigrapha, and Also the Works of Similar Type from Qumran: The History of the Formation of the Old Testament* (trans. Peter R. Ackroyd, from the 3d German ed.; New York: Harper & Row, 1965). This usage has caught on and is quoted in many subsequent publications.

9. First developed fully by Wellhausen in his 1876/77 *Die Composition des Hexateuchs* (later combined with a 1878 study of Judges, Samuel and Kings and published as *Die Composition des Hexateuchs und der historischen Bücher des Alten Testaments* in 1899) and the 1878 *Geschichte Israels I* (the proposed second volume never appeared, and the book was reprinted in 1883 as *Prolegomena zur Geschichte*

fact that "cultic centralization" was not a concern of the prophets in either the prophetic books or in the Former Prophets until late in the monarchic period. It was this observation that led him to date Deuteronomy to the seventh century and the priestly law to the sixth century.¹⁰ The idea of "cultic centralization," a term used by Wellhausen, is thus a centerpiece in the dating scheme that held the main ground of scholarship until quite recently.¹¹

The dating of Deuteronomy has consistently been one of the most important tasks connected to the study of this book, in particular because the "secure" date assigned to it provided a benchmark for the relative chronology of other biblical sources.¹² As one of the key criteria for

---

Israels, the title by which it became a classic). The *Prolegomena* was translated into English in 1885 and has since been reprinted numerous times. For a discussion of the immediate response to the *Prolegomena*, see Smend, *From Astruc to Zimmerli*, 96–98.

A seventh-century date for Deuteronomy, or some form of it (*Urdeuteronomium*) was maintained by de Wette (although he dated the priestly source *before* Deuteronomy, unlike what came to be the consensus), K. H. Graf, and J. Wellhausen; see also S. R. Driver, *An Introduction to the Literature of the Old Testament* (Gloucester, Mass.: Meridien, 1956; repr. 1972 by arrangement with World Publishing; first published 1897), and Driver, *A Commentary on Deuteronomy*, xliv–lxv; K. Budde, "Deuteronomium und die Reform König Josias," *ZAW* 44 (1926): 177–224.

See the discussion summarizing the seventh-century consensus in scholarship in the mid-1980s in G. J. Wenham, "The Date of Deuteronomy: Linchpin of Old Testament Criticism. Part One," *Them* 10, no. 3 (1985): 15–20, and Wenham, "The Date of Deuteronomy: Linchpin of Old Testament Criticism. Part Two," *Them* 11, no. 1 (1985): 15–18.

10. De Wette, unlike what became the later consensus, had dated the priestly law earlier than Deuteronomy.

11. Since Wellhausen's formulation of the classic documentary hypothesis in the JEDP-order, countless source-critical studies on the Hexateuch have seen the light of day. Many expositions of the Documentary Hypothesis and its reception and influence exist; see, e.g., E. Nicholson, *The Pentateuch in the Twentieth Century: The Legacy of Julius Wellhausen* (Oxford: Oxford University Press, 1998), 3–92; B. S. Childs, *Introduction to the Old Testament as Scripture* (Philadelphia: Fortress, 1979), 109–27; R. N. Whybray, *The Making of the Pentateuch: A Methodological Study* (JSOTSup 53; Sheffield: JSOT, 1987; repr. 1994).

12. Although the seventh-century dating of Deuteronomy has been challenged periodically, it has survived for 200 years, and is the majority consensus in America. After some time during which the scholarly consensus established itself, the question of date became a matter of debate especially in the 1920s. One of the results was a symposium of the *Society of Biblical Literature* in 1928, at which diverging opinions were debated, published in *JBL* 47 (1928): 291–379. See the third of these articles,

1. Introduction

posing a dating scheme for the compositional history of Deuteronomy, the concept of the "chosen place" and the way it has been viewed and understood has been tightly bound to any dating discussion involving this book. For the context of the study of the "chosen place," this is significant. As a crucial dating criterion, the "chosen place" also became a key for the reconstruction of ancient Israelite history and religious history. This is particularly evident in the reconstructions of a reform of "cult centralization" under Josiah.

G. Dahl, "The Case for the Currently Accepted Date of Deuteronomy," 358–79, for a summary of the majority consensus and its arguments from the time of de Wette up to the time of its publication.

In addition to conservative and fundamentalist scholars who continued to defend a Mosaic origin of Deuteronomy, proponents of an early date from a critical perspective include Th. Oestreicher, *Das deuteronomistische Grundgesetz* (BFCT 27/4; Gutersloh: Gutersloher Verlagshaus, 1923); Oestreicher, "Dnt 12.13f im Licht von Dtn 23.16f," *ZAW* NF 2 (1925): 246–49; and A. Welch, *The Code of Deuteronomy: A New Theory of Its Origin* (London: J. Clarke, 1924); Welch, "When Was the Worship of Israel Centralised at the Temple?," *ZAW* NF 2 (1925): 250–55. Welch argued that most of Deuteronomy was older than the time of Josiah and did not demand centralization, but was concerned with the battle of Yahwism against Baalism. For a contemporary critique of the arguments for an early date (mainly Welch's), see J. A. Brewer, "The Case for the Early Date of Deuteronomy," *JBL* 47 (1928): 305–21.

Although it did not receive much attention, later dates were proposed from the beginning of critical research; for a summary of these, see L. B. Paton, "The Case for the Post-Exilic Origin of Deuteronomy," *JBL* 47 (1928): 322–57. The most influential arguments for a late date have been posed by, e.g., G. Hölscher, "Komposition und Ursprung des Deuteronomiums," *ZAW* 40 (1923): 161–255, who argued that Deuteronomy had to be later than 500 B.C.E, and was never put into practice, also arguing that many parts of 2 Kgs 22–23 were from a late deuteronomistic editor (see the critique of Hölscher in Paton, "The Case for the Post-Exilic Origin," 329–32); G. R. Berry, argues for a late date of Deuteronomy in "The Date of Deuteronomy," *JBL* 59 (1940): 133–39, and thinks that the code found in the temple was the Holiness code. See an overview of this in C. Houtman, *Der Pentateuch: Die Geschichte seiner Erforschung neben einer Auswertung* (Kampen: Kok Pharos, 1995), 279–342; and W. Baumgartner, "Der Kampf um das Deuteronomium," *ThR* 1 NF (1929): 7–25.

A different source of support for a seventh-century date came with the publication of the Neo-Assyrian vassal treaties in 1958, and the argument that the book of Deuteronomy was fashioned on these as a literary genre. R. Frankena, "The Vassal Treaties of Esarhaddon and the Dating of Deuteronomy," *OTS* 14 (1965): 122–54. E. Otto has argued in several studies on the basis of Neo-Assyrian legal texts that parts of Deuteronomy should be dated to the seventh century. His argument is synthesized in his *Das Deuteronomium: Politische Theologie und Rechtsreform in Juda und Assyrien* (BZAW 284; Berlin: de Gruyter, 1999). The "Cross school" (see

If one begins to question the criteria and methods used to date biblical texts, it becomes a major challenge to disentangle and rearrange the historical reconstructions informing the understanding of the idea of the "chosen place" from the various shifting positions and arguments about dating. An even more radical question is: What can be said about the "chosen place" if we do not possess criteria for dating the texts

below) has been most influential in North America, and most current text books, for example, reflect the seventh-century consensus.

In Europe, the tendency toward a "later" date is more pronounced. Most recently, E. A. Knauf, "Observations on Judah's Social and Economic History and the Dating of the Laws in Deuteronomy," *Journal of Hebrew Scriptures* 9 Article 18 (2009): 2–8, proposes a sixth-century date; see also P. R. Davies, "Josiah and the Law Book," in *Good Kings and Bad Kings* (ed. L. L. Grabbe; LHBOTS 393; European Seminar in Historical Methodology 5; London: T&T Clark International, 2005), 65–77, who dates Deuteronomy to the fifth century. The trend toward an emphasis on the later date to some extent coincides with the tendency to focus more on final forms of the text and to abandon the endeavor of reconstructing earlier stages of the text. However, the practice of reconstructing stages of redaction or *Fortschreibung* of the text is still widely in practice; see, e.g., T. C. Römer, *The So-Called Deuteronomistic History: A Sociological, Historical and Literary Introduction* (London: T&T Clark International, 2005); and R. G. Kratz, *Die Komposition der erzählenden Bücher des Alten Testaments* (Göttingen: Vandenhoeck & Ruprecht, 2000), available in English translation by J. Bowden, *The Composition of the Narrative Books of the Old Testament* (London: T&T Clark International, 2005). R. E. Clements argues for an exilic date for Deuteronomy on the basis of the changes to the cult brought about by the destruction of the temple; see Clements, "The Deuteronomic Law of Centralisation and the Catastrophe of 587 B.C.E.," in *After the Exile: Essays in Honour of Rex Mason* (ed. J. Barton and D. J. Reimer; Macon, Ga.: Mercer University Press, 1996), 5–25.

The followers of the "Göttingen school" (see below) have normally chosen an exilic date for their several redactions, although some form of Deuteronomy is considered to pre-date the exile.

Not directly related to dating, but a topic that is related to different methods of diachronic study, the concept of *Fortschreibung* has come to be used in a way that seems to replace the traditional concept of redaction criticism. See a discussion and critique of the practices of *Literarkritik–Redaktionskritik* and *Fortschreibung* in N. Lohfink, "Fortschreibung? Zur Technik von Rechtsrevisionen im deuteronomistischen Bereich, erörtet an Deuteronomium 12, Ex 21,2–11 und Dtn 15,12–18," in *Das Deuteronomium und seine Querbeziehungen* (ed. T. Veijola; Schriften der Finnischen Exegetischen Gesellschaft 62; Helsinki: Finnische Exegetische Gesellschaft; Göttingen: Vandenhoeck & Ruprecht, 1996), 127–71. A recent discussion of scholars' attempts to elucidate the practices of ancient legal writing can be found in J. Stackert, *Rewriting the Torah: Literary Revision in Deuteronomy and the Holiness Code* (FAT 52; Tübingen: Mohr Siebeck, 2007).

precisely?[13] In reading texts related to "chosen place," the present study will not make any assumptions about "centralization" as a dating criterion, and no chronology will be assumed. As a first step toward disentangling it from the dating debate, I will ask: What does the "chosen place" look like when viewed without its role as a dating criterion?

A Religious Reform under King Josiah
There is an established understanding in scholarship that the narratives involving Josiah in 2 Kgs 22–23 reflect historical efforts to "reform the cult" according to the prescripts of Deuteronomy, or that Deuteronomy was composed during this period to justify the reforms of Josiah (some scholars include Hezekiah).[14] In either case, the historicity of a reform is assumed. Scholars who argue that Deuteronomy was not the law book found by Josiah nevertheless presuppose that a religious reform took place, and that it influenced Deuteronomy.[15] Even scholars who see the text of 2 Kgs 22–23 as basically fictional, or date it and/or Deuteronomy to a later period, usually relate it to a historical development that occasioned the need for such a story.[16] Archaeological material has been used in various ways also to argue for a reform of "cult centralization" either in the time of Hezekiah or Josiah.[17]

---

13. The problem of dating Deuteronomy is a whole field in its own right and a critical analysis of that history of scholarship would no doubt yield an insightful perspective on our field in general. Often, it might be correct to say that those who favor an earlier dating usually accept the idea of "later additions," but place more value on "original" strata or sources, such as the concept of an *Urdeuteronomium*. Correspondingly, those who have assigned a later dating have tended to focus on a more final form of the text. Even most late-date advocates will concede that the author has used earlier sources and edited them, the exception being perhaps J. Van Seters (see references to his works below).

14. A convenient summary and discussion of the positions on this can be found in L. K. Handy, "Historical Probability and the Narrative of Josiah's Reform in 2 Kings," in *The Pitcher is Broken: Memorial Essays for Gösta W. Ahlström* (ed. S. W. Holloway and L. K. Handy; JSOTSup 190; Sheffield: Sheffield Academic, 1995), 252–75. The extent to which this is still a burning issue is clearly expressed in R. Albertz's article, "Why a Reform Like Josiah's Must Have Happened," in Grabbe, ed., *Good Kings and Bad Kings*, 27–46.

15. For more details and examples of scholars who propose that something other than Deuteronomy was found, see the discussion of 2 Kgs 22:8–10 in Chapter 6.

16. For a summary, see, e.g., Römer, *The So-called Deuteronomistic History*, 49–56.

17. E.g. M. Weinfeld, "Cult Centralization in Israel in the Light of a Neo-Babylonian Analogy," *JNES* 23 (1964): 202–12. Using archaeological data, the "time of Hezekiah" has also been proposed by some scholars as the time when cult

Through its identification with the book found by Josiah, therefore, the book of Deuteronomy—including its emphasis on the "chosen place"—has functioned as a key to the literary history of the Bible. This in turn has provided a cornerstone for the reconstruction of ancient Israelite history. These assumptions are deeply linked with the dating issue described above.[18]

centralization took place; see, e.g., I. Finkelstein and N. A. Silberman, "Temple and Dynasty: Hezekiah, the Remaking of Judah and the Rise of the Pan-Israelite Ideology," *JSOT* 30 (2006): 259–85. As a response to the latter, D. Edelman, "Hezekiah's alleged Cultic Centralization," *JSOT* 32 (2008): 395–434, offers a critique of various attempts to explain the reason for Hezekiah's cult centralization as a political move in the face of the "Assyrian crisis."

The idea of Hezekiah's reform as historically "reliable," building on 2 Chr 29–31, was long quite stable in research, though it has been criticized and builds on a few highly influential articles that establish the reliability of Chronicles as a source. See e.g., W. F. Albright, "The Judicial Reform of Jehoshaphat," in *Alexander Marx Jubilee Volume On the Occasion of His Seventieth Birthday: English Section* (ed. S. Lieberman; New York: Jewish Theological Seminary, 1950), 62–69; H. N. Richardson, "The Historical Reliability of Chronicles," *JBR* 26 (1958): 12; H. H. Rowley, "Hezekiah's Reform and Rebellion," *BJRL* 44 (1961): 395–431 (404). See the criticism already in L. K. Handy, "Hezekiah's Unlikely Reform," *ZAW* 100 (1988): 111–15.

18. This highlights, once again, the degree to which the "chosen place" has been researched and debated within specific, limiting, parameters. A clear expression of this situation is that H. D. Preuss, in his history of research on Deuteronomy, begins the whole book with a chapter on 2 Kgs 22–23 and its connection to Deuteronomy; see "2 Kön 22/23—Die Kultusreform des Josia, der Buchfund und das Deuteronomium," in *Deuteronomium* (EdF 164; Darmstadt: Wissenschaftliche Buchgesellschaft, 1982), 1–12. This book provides an excellent overview of the literature on Deuteronomy up to 1982. It should be mentioned that there was something of a lull in the focus on 2 Kgs 22–23 between the big debate of the 1920s (see above, on dating), and the late 1950s, see the summary of this, plus a detailed review of H.-D. Hoffmann's and H. Spieckermann's contributions (for full citation of these works, see Chapter 6) in N. Lohfink, "Recent Discussion on 2 Kings 22–23: The State of the Question," in *A Song of Power and the Power of Song: Essays on the Book of Deuteronomy* (ed. D. L. Christensen; Sources for Biblical and Theological Study; Winona Lake, Ind.: Eisenbrauns, 1993), 36–61. Significantly, when O'Brien writes his bibliographic survey in 1995, he chooses the same format at Preuss, also beginning with a section on 2 Kgs 22–23 and then proceeding to the "centralization of the cult," in M. A. O'Brien, "The Book of Deuteronomy," *CRBS* 3 (1995): 95–128. See also the "concise historical overview" of E. Eynikel, *The Reform of King Josiah and the Composition of the Deuteronomistic History* (OTS 33; Leiden: Brill, 1996), 7–31.

One exception to the usual line of argument is R. Kratz, who does not connect the dating of Deuteronomy to Josiah's reform, but thinks the connection between the

The "chosen place" texts have been made to bear a heavy burden in the enterprise of textual and historical reconstruction, particularly in light of the fierce debates of the 1980s and '90s on historical methodology.[19] In this book I will not argue for or against any particular position about the relationship between Deuteronomy's "chosen place" and Josiah's "reform." My focus will be on the role played by the concept of the "chosen place" in the received text.[20] In these terms, the key question is this: What picture might emerge if we look with fresh eyes at the relevant biblical texts, bracketing out the set of scholarly assumptions which have become the optic through which we ordinarily view them?

A Deuteronomistic Author, Source and Historian
Following from the assertion that Deuteronomy distinguishes itself from the other books of the Pentateuch and constitutes a separate source, scholars began to identify deuteronomistic redactions of other books.[21]

---

two is secondary. He argues for the possibility of both a seventh-century date and an early exilic date for *Urdeuteronomium*, but leans toward the latter; Kratz, *The Composition of the Narrative Books*, 131–32. In general, I appreciate his openness to more than one possibility and his willingness to propose more than one possible solution to historical-critical questions. In my opinion, this is the only way we can work with biblical texts, the historical situations of which we really know so little.

19. A summary of the discussion and debates, with extensive bibliography, can be found in H. M. Barstad, *History and the Hebrew Bible: Studies in Ancient Israelite and Ancient Near Eastern Historiography* (FAT 61; Tübingen: Mohr Siebeck, 2008).

20. The point of departure for the analysis is the MT.

21. Beginning, right after de Wette, with the suggestions of, variously, C. P. W. Gramberg, Karl-Heinrich Graf, Heinrich Ewald, and A. Kuenen; see the survey of T. C. Römer and A. de Pury, "Deuteronomistic Historiography (DH): History of Research and Debated Issues," in *Israel Constructs Its History: Deuteronomistic Historiography in Recent Research* (ed. A. de Pury, T. C. Römer and J.-D. Macchi; JSOTSup 306; Sheffield: Sheffield Academic, 2000), 24–141 (35–40), and after the documentary hypothesis was established, in, e.g., Driver, *Introduction*, 166–68, 170–71, 185; R. H. Pfeiffer, *Introduction to the Old Testament* (New York: Harper & Brothers, 1941/48), 304–6, 315, 333–36, 365–68, 410–12. Scholars writing after Noth's thesis was published (see below) who continued to favor a source-critical approach are G. Fohrer, *Introduction to the Old Testament: Initiated by Ernst Sellin, Completely Revised and Rewritten by Georg Fohrer* (Nashville: Abingdon, 1968); trans. of *Einleitung in das Alte Testament* (Heidelberg: Quelle & Meyer, 1965), 202–3, 212–13, 225, 229–36; Eissfeldt, *The Old Testament*, 255, 266, 280, 299–301.

The idea of a deuteronomistic redaction of the prophetic books began to be investigated also around the end of the nineteenth century, exemplified by B. Duhm's *Das Buch Jeremia* (HAT 11; Tübingen: J. C. B. Mohr [Paul Siebeck], 1901). Duhm did not place much value on the "late," "deuteronomistic" additions to the prophet

With this activity, the label "Deuteronomist" began to be used. In the late nineteenth and first part of the twentieth centuries, source-critical studies operated with various understandings of deuteronomistic[22] redactions of the books of Judges, Samuel, and Kings. This development was considered separately from the development of the books of Genesis through Joshua, because of the dominant source-critical view that the book of Joshua was part of a Hexateuch. Martin Noth's thesis about the Deuteronomistic History would change this completely.

Since the reception of Martin Noth's work,[23] the idea of a unified "Deuteronomistic History" has gained ground and has dominated the

---

Jeremiah's *ipsissima verba*, and did not comment much on these. A shift of focus from the prophet's own words to the ideas of the redactors later led to the hunt for widespread deuteronomistic redaction of prophetic books. Inspiration also came from tradition-historical studies. For example, W. L. Moran pointed out the importance of the language of covenant in Deuteronomy in "The Ancient Near Eastern Background of Love of God in Deuteronomy," *CBQ* 25 (1963): 77–87. Similar language was noticed in Hosea and Jeremiah in particular, and attributed by some scholars to a deuteronomistic redaction of these books. See, e.g., W. H. Schmidt, "Die deuteronomistische Redaktion des Amosbuches: Zu den theologischen Unterschieden zwischen dem Prophetenwort und dem Sammler," *ZAW* 77 (1965): 168–93; H. W. Wolff, *Joel und Amos* (BKAT 14; Neukirchen–Vluyn: Neukirchener, 1985); W. Thiel, *Die deuteronomistische Redaktion von Jeremia 1–25* (WMANT 41; Neukirchen–Vluyn: Neukirchener, 1973), and Thiel, *Die deuteronomistische Redaktion von Jeremia 26–52* (WMANT 52; Neukirchen–Vluyn: Neukirchener, 1981).

22. In spite of efforts to make distinctions, between, for example, what pertained to and was influenced by Deuteronomy as "deuteronomic" and that which had to do with a later "school" as "deuteronomistic," the labels have been confusing and have not been used uniformly throughout the history of research. The labels have been applied to sources, redactions, and authors. Source critics tended to speak of "deuteronomic" redactions. I am going to use the one term, "deuteronomistic," throughout this study, with the knowledge that it was not used uniformly by scholars.

23. M. Noth, *Überlieferungsgeschichtliche Studien* (Schriften der Königsberger Gelehrten Gesellschaft. Geisteswissenschaftliche Klasse 18; Königsberg: Wissenschaftliche Buchgesellschaft, 1943); available in English in two separate volumes, as *The Deuteronomistic History* (2d ed.; JSOTSup 15; Sheffield: JSOT, 1991); and *The Chronicler's History* (JSOTSup 50; Sheffield: JSOT, 1987); trans. of *Überlieferungsgeschichtliche Studien* (2d ed.; Tübingen: Max Niemeyer, 1957).

Noth's work was published in 1943, during WWII in Königsberg, then still a part of Germany, and was not widely known until after the second printing in 1957. Two other works from around the same period independently confirm Noth's major claims, although these are much less widely known: A. Jepsen, *Die Quellen des Königsbuches* (Halle: Niemeyer, 1953); and I. Engnell, *Gamla testamentet: en*

discourse "until this day." The historian was named "Deuteronomist" by Noth because he believed that this writer combined the law of Deuteronomy and other sources to form one ideologically unified work consisting of the books of Deuteronomy, Joshua, Judges, Samuel, and Kings. After Noth's work became known, countless renderings and reconstructions of the compositional history of a unified work of history encompassing some form of the books of Deuteronomy–Kings have been put forth.[24] In spite of some dissenting voices,[25] and although it was modified in countless ways, Noth's thesis was widely received and became one of the most established axioms of biblical research.

As it had been crucial to the dating of Deuteronomy and in distinguishing it as a distinct source, "cultic centralization" has been fundamental to the concept of a Deuteronomistic History. M. Noth takes as a given that "Josiah's law is the same as the basic text of Dt."[26] He argues that "only the demand in the Deuteronomic law that there should be only one place of worship (Deut 12:13ff.) and the various requirements directed against the continuation of Canaanite cults and rituals, that is, specifications concerned with cult, came to the forefront and had a disproportionate effect on the actions of Josiah." He goes on to claim that all of the law was important to Josiah, even though the biblical record does not specify it. The important point for Noth is that the Deuteronomist "adopted it in the introduction to his history...[and] thus came to assign to the law a crucial role, regarding it as a norm for the relationship between God and people and as a yardstick by which to judge human conduct, a "legal" conception of the factors which determined the course of history." This comes at the very end of the book and, surprisingly, the content of the law code of Deuteronomy is not discussed very much at all

---

traditionshistorisk inledning, I (Stockholm: Svenska Kyrkans Diakonistyrelses Bokförlag, 1945).

24. Of the many summaries introducing the DH hypothesis, see, e.g., Römer, *The So-Called Deuteronomistic History*, 13–41; see also the more detailed Römer and de Pury, "Deuteronomistic Historiography," with the presentation of the recaption of Noth's thesis (55–62); another summary can be found in J. G. McConville, "The Old Testament Historical Books in Modern Scholarship," *Them* 22 (1997): 3–13; see also T. Veijola, "Deuteronomismusforschung zwischen Tradition und Innovation (III)," *ThR* 68 (2003): 1–44.

25. Among those who did not accept Noth's thesis were O. Eissfeldt and G. Fohrer; see, e.g., Eissfeldt, *Old Testament*; and Fohrer, *Introduction*, esp. 193–95. Fohrer's criticism was mainly of the idea of a single author for the books of Joshua–Kings as a comprehensive work. He recognizes deuteronomistic redactors (even writers, for Kings).

26. By "Dt" he means Deuteronomy. This and the next two quotations are all from Noth, *The Deuteronomistic History*, 124.

in the main part of the book. It is an underlying assumption, supported by the observation that the Deuteronomist put it at the beginning of his work. The various forms of the DH hypothesis all involve a crucial consideration of the idea of "cultic centralization."

Scholarship has gone in two main directions in developing the Deuteronomistic History hypothesis since the time of M. Noth. The first direction has been called the "double redaction" or "block" hypothesis. This direction disagrees with Noth by dating a first version of the DH to the seventh century, and proposing a second redaction in the exilic period.[27] The second direction accepts the exilic dating of Noth, but adds more and more redactional layers. This direction disagrees with Noth mainly in his claim of a single author, with very few additions.[28] Finally,

---

27. The first to propose a double redaction was actually Heinrich Ewald, in a series of studies published from 1843 to 1859; see Römer and de Pury, *Deuteronomistic Historiography*, 35–38. After Noth, it is the direction often labeled the "Cross school" that has maintained this idea, by developing the ideas put forth by F. M. Cross in the tenth essay of *Canaanite Myth and Hebrew Epic: Essays in the History of the Religion of Israel* (Cambridge, Mass.: Harvard University Press, 1973), 274–89, and is represented by the works of scholars such as R. D. Nelson, *The Double Redaction of the Deuteronomistic History* (JSOTSup 18; Sheffield: JSOT, 1981); and G. N. Knoppers, *Two Nations Under God: The Deuteronomistic History of Solomon and the Dual Monarchies* (2 vols.; HSM 52–53; Atlanta: Scholars Press, 1993–94), in the US, and J. A. Soggin, *Introduction to the Old Testament: From Its Origins to the Closing of the Alexandrian Canon* (trans. J. Bowden; rev. ed.; OTL; Philadelphia: Westminster, 1977), 205; H. Weippert, "Das deuteronomistische Geschichtswerk: Sein Ziel und Ende in der neueren Forschung," *ThR* 50 (1985): 213–49; and R. Rendtorff, *Das Alte Testament: Eine Einfürung* (Neukirchen–Vluyn: Neukirchener, 1993), in Europe. Rendtorff later became an advocate of a canonical reading of the Old Testament/Hebrew Bible; see his *Theologie des Alten Testaments: Ein kanonischer Entwurf* (2 vols.; Neukirchen–Vluyn: Neukirchener, 1999–2001).

A similar idea as the "double-redaction" theory was also advocated by one of Noth's critics, G. Fohrer, who, although he did not accept the idea of a unified work of history, argued for a similar development for the book of Kings, namely that it was written by "deuteronomistic authors," writing a first edition shortly after 622 B.C.E., and a supplementor who wrote during the time of the exile, but did not know of its end (around 561 B.C.E.); see Fohrer, *Introduction*, 229–36.

28. R. Smend began this direction, often referred to as the "Göttingen school," when he distinguished another redactor, separate from Noth's Dtr into the first, basic historian DtrH (H = historian), who was preoccupied with the law, and called it DtrN (N = nomistic redactor); see R. Smend, "Das Gesetz und die Völker: Ein Beitrag zur deuteronomistischen Redaktionsgeschichte," in *Probleme biblischer Theologie: G. von Rad zum 70. Geburtstag* (ed. H. W. Wolff; Munich: Kaiser, 1971), 494–509. Smend agreed with Noth about dating the DH to the exilic period, and so disagrees with the "Cross school" in terms of dating. Following Smend's model, scholars such

one might also say that another tendency is that of a shrinking DH, which agrees with Noth's basic thesis of one single author in the exilic period, but considers many blocks of text to be later additions.[29]

In general, the idea of a unified deuteronomistic work of history came to replace the source-critical understanding of the genesis of the books of the Former Prophets.[30] After a couple of decades, the discussions that began to undermine the classical documentary hypothesis started to have an impact also on the DH hypothesis. Discussions about the relationship between the DH and the Pentateuch have led to more theories about the growth of texts and their redactions into larger units.[31] However, the

as W. Dietrich, *Prophetie und Geschichte: Eine redaktionsgeschichtliche Untersuchung zum deuteronomistischen Geschichtswerk* (FRLANT 108; Göttingen: Vandenhoeck & Ruprecht, 1972); and T. Veijola, *Die ewige Dynastie: David und die Enstehung seiner Dynastie nach der deuteronomistischen Darstellung* (Toimituksia - Suomalaisen Tiedeakatemian, Annales Academiae Scientiarum Fennicae: Sarja-Ser. B 193; Helsinki: Suomaleinen Tiedeakatemia, 1975), developed further criteria for distinguishing more redactional layers, including a DtrP (prophetic redactor). See, for more details and examples, Römer and de Pury, "Deuteronomistic Historiography," 67–72, and also the analysis of the ideological suppositions behind these models, 72–74.

29. J. Van Seters, *In Search of History: Historiography in the Ancient World and the Origins of Biblical History* (New Haven: Yale University Press, 1983). In this and multiple later works he is in basic agreement with Noth in seeing the deuteronomistic historian as a single author in the exilic period, but argues that what he calls the "Court History" of 2 Sam 10–20 and 1 Kgs 1–2, and the Elisha narratives, were later, post-deuteronomistic additions. Another example of a similar position is the work of S. L. McKenzie, *The Trouble with Kings: The Composition of the Books of Kings in the Deuteronomistic History* (VTSup 42; Leiden: Brill, 1991).

30. As mentioned above, already during the heyday of source criticism, scholars had been speaking about a deuteronomic/istic redaction of several biblical books, the books of Judges and Kings in particular (see n. 21, above). When source criticism ceased to be the dominant method in biblical scholarship, tradition criticism and redaction criticism took over as the main approaches to the books of Deuteronomy and the books of Joshua, Judges, Samuel, and Kings.

Form criticism never was as influential in the study of these books as it was in the study of the Prophets or Psalms. An early example of the use of form criticism, however, was Otto Eissfeldt, who tried to combine source criticism and form criticism in his massive *Einleitung*. A significant, more recent example is C. Westermann's work, in particular, *Die Geschichtsbücher des Alten Testaments: Gab es ein deuteronomistisches Geschichtswerk?* (Neudrucke und Berichte aus dem 20. Jahrhundert 87; Gütersloh: Kaiser Gütersloher Verlagshaus, 1994).

31. For an exposition of the concept of the Primary History, also referred to as the Enneateuch, see K. Schmid, "Buchtechnische und sachliche Prolegomena zur Enneateuchfrage," in *Auf dem Weg zur Endgestalt von Genesis bis II Regnum: Festschrift Hans-Christoph Scmitt zum 65. Geburtstag* (ed. M. Beck and U. Schorn;

book of Deuteronomy was ignored to some extent by the Pentateuchal studies which focused narrowly on the first four books, the Tetrateuch.[32]

Another development is the more recent tendency in Pentateuchal research to date the Yahwist to a much later date than in the original documentary hypothesis.[33] Among other things, this has led to new discussions regarding the relationship between the "Yahwist" and the "Deuteronomist," even to the point of equating the two, or posing that the Yahwist had been influenced by the Deuteronomist.[34] Although these

---

BZAW 370; Berlin: de Gruyter, 2006), 1–14, and the literature he cites. See also the other contributions in this volume. As an example of the impact of these concepts on the study of Deuteronomy and the role of Deuteronomy in understanding the larger compositions, see, e.g., F. García López, "Deuteronomio 31, el Pentateuco y la Historia Deuteronomista," in *Deuteronomy and Deuteronomic Literature: Festschrift C. H. W. Brekelmans* (ed. M. Vervenne and J. Lust; BETL 133; Leuven: Leuven University Press, 1997), 71–85; T. C. Römer, "Deuteronomium 34 zwischen Pentateuch, Hexateuch und deuteronomistischem Geschichtswerk," *ZABR* 5 (1999): 167–78; H.-C. Schmitt, "Dtn 34 als Verbindungsstück zwischen Tetrateuch und deuteronomistischen Geschichtswerk," in *Das Deuteronomium zwischen Pentateuch und deuteronomistischem Geschichtswerk* (ed. E. Otto and R. Achenbach; FRLANT 206; Göttingen: Vandenhoeck & Ruprecht, 2004), 180–92; and, in the same volume, T. C. Römer's article specifically on Deut 12, "Cult Centralization in Deuteronomy 12: Between Deuteronomistic History and Pentateuch," 153–67, and other contributions to that volume. A work focusing on the book of Kings within this framework is E. Aurelius, *Zukunft jenseits des Gerichts: Eine redactionsgeschichtliche Studie zum Enneateuch* (BZAW 319; Berlin: de Gruyter, 2003). A synthesis of various observations along these lines has been presented by Kratz in his *Die Komposition der erzählenden Bücher*, 2000.

32. As pointed out by H.-C. Schmitt in, "Das Spätdeuteronomistische Geschichtwerk Genesis I–II Regnum XXV und seine theologische Intention," in *Theologie in Prophetie und Pentateuch: Gesammelte Schriften* (ed. U. Schorn and M. Bütt; BZAW 310; Berlin: de Gruyter, 2001) 277–94 (277).

33. The first to argue this, in different ways, were H. H. Schmid, *Der sogenannte Jahwist: Beobachtungen und Fragen zur Pentateuchforschung* (Zurich: Theologischer Verlag, 1976); R. Rendtorff, *Das überlieferungsgeschichtliche Problem des Pentateuch* (BZAW 147; Berlin: de Gruyter, 1977), available in English, *The Problem of the Process of Transmission in the Pentateuch* (JSOTSup 89; JSOT, 1980); and J. Van Seters, *Abraham in History and Tradition* (New Haven: Yale University Press, 1975).

34. M. Rose, *Deuteronomist und Jahwist. Untersuchungen zu den Berührungspunkten beider Literaturwerke* (ATANT 67; Zurich: Theologischer Verlag, 1981); the thesis of E. Blum of a composition that includes most of the traditional J and D into one work he calls KD should also be mentioned; see *Studien zur Komposition des Pentateuch* (BZAW 189; Berlin: de Gruyter, 1990). For an overview, see O. Kaiser, "The Pentateuch and the Deuteronomistic History," in *Text in Context: Essays by Members of the Society for Old Testament Study* (ed. A. D. H. Mayes;

discussions reverse the understanding of the relative dating of the material assigned to the traditional sources, the date of Deuteronomy seems to have remained constant. Even though these discussions would seem to impact the role of the "chosen place" in scholarship, it has not done so to any real extent. In the most recent discussion, the Pentateuch and other biblical texts have been seen as the product of a "debate," beginning in the exilic period, between two major "schools of thought" or "milieus," the "priestly" and the "deuteronomistic."[35]

The very idea of a DH has also been subjected to increasing criticism, as has the usefulness of the terminology associated with this hypothesis.[36]

Oxford: Oxford University Press, 2000), 289–322; and Nicholson, *The Pentateuch in the Twentieth Century*, 95–101, 132–60. An illustration of the most recent situation in scholarship on the "Yahwist" is represented by collections such as T. B. Dozeman and K. Schmid, eds., *A Farewell to the Yahwist? The Composition of the Pentateuch in Recent European Interpretation* (SBL Symposium Series 34; Atlanta: SBL, 2006), and the discussion, "What Happened to the Yahwist? Reflections after Thirty Years: A Collegial Conversation Between Rolf Rendtorff, David J. A. Clines, Allan Rosengren, and John Van Seters," in *Probing the Frontiers of Biblical Studies* (ed. J. H. Ellens and J. T. Greene; Princeton Theological Monograph Series; Eugene, Ore.: Pickwick, 2009), 39–66.

35. This way of framing the issue seems to be a variant of the idea of a "nomistic" redaction of the DH, but also involves ideas about the formation of the Pentateuch; cf. E. Blum's idea of a work combining a D-composition and a P-composition, *Studien zur Komposition des Pentateuch*. See, e.g., Römer, *The So-Called Deuteronomistic History*, 178–83, who speaks of the Pentateuch as a result of a "historical compromise" between the "priestly" and the "deuteronomistic" schools; in a different take on the same idea, E. Otto argues for a "post-priestly," scribal reworking of the Tetrateuch and Deuteronomy, which formed a prototype of later rabbinical writing, in, e.g., "Scribal Scholarship in the Formation of Torah and Prophets: A Postexilic Scribal Debate between Priestly Scholarship and Literary Prophecy—The Example of the Book of Jeremiah and Its Relation to the Pentateuch," in *The Pentateuch as Torah: New Models for Understanding Its Promulgation and Acceptance* (ed. G. N. Knoppers and B. M. Levinson; Winona Lake, Ind.: Eisenbrauns, 2007), 171–84. See also E. Ben Zvi, "Towards an Integrative Study of the Production of Authoritative Books in Ancient Israel," in *The Production of Prophecy. Constructing Prophecy and Prophets in Yehud* (ed. D. V. Edelman and E. Ben Zvi; London: Equinox, 2009), 15–28. Ben Zvi's more open approach to the production of biblical books allows, I think, for a more flexible model that can accommodate the many idiosyncrasies of individual biblical books and texts more successfully than many past models. The problem with the model is its heavy reliance on the context of *literati* and their activity in the Persian period, although this also seems more flexible and open than the concept of an endless sequence of "deuteronomistic" and "priestly" schools.

36. E.g. R. E. Clements, "The Former Prophets and Deuteronomy: A Re-examination," in *God's Word for Our World*. Vol. 1, *Biblical Studies in Honor of Simon*

A major problem is the whole question of criteria for "deuteronomism." Even from the above short survey, it is quite clear that the phenomenon of "deuteronomism" is so pervasive, yet is described in so many different ways, that the idea of a "Deuteronomist" stands in danger of having lost its meaning.[37] The distinctiveness of an author/editor/supplementor who plays many different roles, stands in danger of being lost and the term "deuteronomistic" made to mean so much that it may become all but empty.[38] Often, the connection of the criteria to Deuteronomy or a Deuteronomist has become almost impossible to identify.

As we have already seen, the revisions of Noth's thesis in various directions are already a testimony to its problems. One main argument goes against the unity of the work; another is that the work does not constitute a "history."[39] In addition, some scholars have questioned the

---

John De Vries (ed. J. H. Ellens et al; JSOTSup 388; London: T&T Clark International, 2004), 83–95; H. Rösel, "Why 2 Kings 17 Does Not Constitute a Chapter of Reflection in the 'Deuteronomistic History,'" *JBL* 128 (2009): 85–90.

37. Already in the nineteenth century, the term "Deuteronomist" was being used in more than one way, and did not always seem to have any clear link to the book of Deuteronomy, or the conceived source Deuteronomy. The various types of redaction activity assigned to "Deuteronomist/s" were not necessarily coordinated with one another either, creating confusion and disconnects for later scholars. About one hundred years ago Sigmund Mowinckel, in describing what he called the *source C* of the book of Jeremiah (much of what was Duhm had defined as Deuteronomistic), identified its authors with the "canonizers." The main difference between his time and the last 30–40 years, of course, is the value assigned to these "later" phases of composition (Mowinckel had a low view of them, whereas they more lately have been viewed with increasing interest); see Mowinckel, *Zur Komposition des Buches Jeremia* (Videnskapsselskapets skrifter II. Hist.-filos. Klasse. 1913, No. 5; Kristiania: Jacob Dywad, 1914).

38. I am not interested in criticizing what might be called "pan-deuteronomism" in the way that Raymond Person warns against; see R. F. Person, Jr., *The Deuteronomic School: History, Social Setting, and Literature* (Studies in Biblical Literature 2; Atlanta: SBL, 2002), 13–15.

39. For example, E. Sellin and G. Fohrer, because they preferred to see deuteronomistic redactions of individual books and did not accept the idea of a unified history (see nn. 25 and 27, above). Similarly, A. Weiser did acknowledge a deuteronomistic environment, but maintained that each book had its own distinct history and that there was no unified DH; see A. Weiser, *Einleitung in das Alte Testament* (6th improved ed.; Göttingen: Vandenhoeck & Ruprecht, 1966); E. Würthwein and C. Westermann both published studies in 1994 urging against the idea of a history, Würthwein, "Erwägungen zum sog. deuteronomistischen Geschichtswerk: Eine Skizze," in *Studien zum deuteronomistischen Geschichtswerk* (ed. E. Wurthwein; BZAW 227; Berlin: de Gruyter, 1994), 1–11; Westermann, *Die Geschichtsbücher*. Originally defended as a doctoral thesis in 1989, E. Eynikel's redaction critical

1. *Introduction* 19

existence of what has been called the "deuteronomistic movement."⁴⁰ In spite of the periodic criticism of and objections to the concept of the DH and even its pronounced demise,⁴¹ the number of reaffirmations of the DH hypothesis in response to such criticism is a testimony to the fact of its survival.⁴² The number of publications on various aspects of a DH and the deuteronomistic redactions of biblical books is overwhelming, and the "Deuteronomistic History" has become an ingrained part of

---

analysis of 2 Kgs 23 brings him to conclusions similar to Westermann's, in that there was no *one* overriding deuteronomistic redaction, and therefore no one unified DH, until the distinct, individual books were "fused...into a single whole," Eynikel, *The Reform of Kings Josiah*, 363–64. See also E. A. Knauf, "Does 'Deuteronomistic Historiography' (DH) Exist?," in Römer and de Pury, eds., *Israel Constructs Its History*, 388–98.

40. E.g. N. F. Lohfink, "Gab es eine deuteronomistische Bewegung?," in *Jeremia und die "deuteronomistische Bewegung"* (ed. W. Gross; BBB 98; Weinheim: Betz Athenäum, 1995), 313–82.

41. By e.g. Childs, *Introduction to the Old Testament*, 235–38.

42. Some illustrations of the debate that is bringing up serious questions concerning the DH include the anthology edited by T. C. Römer, *The Future of the Deuteronomistic History* (BETL 147; Leuven: Peeters, 2000), with supportive contributions such as S. L. McKenzie, "The Divided Kingdom in the Deuteronomistic History," 135–45; J. Van Seters, "The Future of the Deuteronomistic History: Can It Avoid Death by Redaction," 213–22; and R. Albertz, "In Search of the Deuteronomists: A First Solution to a Historical Riddle," 1–17; and critical contributions such as H. L. Rösel, "Does a Comprehensive 'Leitmotiv' Exist in the Deuteronomistic History?," 195–211; and A. G. Auld, "Prophets Shared—But Recycled," 19–28; and the anthology edited by L. S. Schearing and S. L. McKenzie, *Those Elusive Deuteronomists: The Phenomenon of Pan-Deuteronomism* (JSOTSup 268; Sheffield: Sheffield Academic, 1999), with essays such as R. Coggins, "What Does 'Deuteronomistic' Mean?," 22–35; Auld, "The Deuteronomists and the Former Prophets, or What Makes the Former Prophets Deuteronomistic?," 116–26; see also a summary of the status quo in S. L. McKenzie, "Postscript: The Laws of Physics and Pan-Deuteronomism," 262–71; an anthology from the German-speaking environment that represents this tendency is, M. Witte et al., eds., *Die deuteronomistische Geschichtswerke: Redaktions- und religionsgeschichtliche Perspektiven zur "Deuteronomismus"-Diskussion in Tora und Forderen Propheten* (BZAW 365; Berlin: de Gruyter, 2006). A monograph that seeks to rectify but also rehabilitate the DH is M. A. O'Brien, *The Deuteronomistic History Hypothesis: A Reassessment* (OBO; Freiburg: Vandenhoeck & Ruprecht, 1989). A more recent monograph that reaffirms the DH is J. C. Geoghegan, *The Time, Place, and Purpose of the Deuteronomistic History: The Evidence of "Until This Day"* (BJS 347; Providence, R.I.: Brown Judaic Studies, 2006), 96–118. R. D. Nelson, who developed his 1973 dissertation on the double redaction hypothesis in a 1981 work, continues to argue for it; see Nelson's "The Double Redaction of the Deuteronomistic History: The Case is Still Compelling," *JSOT* 29 (2005): 319–37.

biblical studies parlance and of textbooks.⁴³ Even some of the attempts to assess it critically and present an alternative theory or method choose not to shed the terminology.⁴⁴ The idea of a DH is not only surviving; it is alive and kicking.⁴⁵ Although things might change in the near future, this

43. The most comprehensive recent history of research is the already mentioned 2000 publication of Römer and de Pury (above). See also Veijola, "Deuteronomismusforschung zwischen Tradition und Innovation (III)." Römer's *The So-Called Deuteronomistic History* has a summary of research and selected bibliography (13–43). In the rest of the book he provides his own reconstruction of the composition or development of the DH, which is a kind of comprehensive model that attempts to make use of all the available data and to reconcile various models. His model proposes three stages of redaction in Deut 12, corresponding with three major redactions in the pre-exilic, exilic, and post-exilic periods, creating a combination of the "Cross" and "Göttingen" models. Römer also attempts to "fix" the lack of correlation between layers in Deuteronomy and the DH, as pointed out by both Levinson, *Deuteronomy and the Hermeneutics*, 153, and E. Otto, "The Pentateuch in Synchronical and Diachronical Perspective: Protorabbinic Scribal Erudition Mediating Between Deuteronomy and the Priestly Code," in Otto and Achenbach, eds., *Das Deuteronomium zwischen Pentateuch*, 14–35 (25 and literature in n. 42).

44. E.g. K. Noll, "Deuteronomistic History or Deuteronomic Debate? (A Thought Experiment)," *JSOT* 31 (2007): 311–45, declares that "…what we have in the Former Prophets is a conversation with the book of Deuteronomy. What we do not have is deuteronomism." Yet, he continues to employ the term "deuteronomistic" in his essay to characterize specific themes or topics he discusses, sometimes in quotation marks, sometimes without (e.g. 327, 334, 338, 339, 340, 341, 343), confusing at least one reader (me). Ingrid Hjelm, *Jerusalem's Rise to Sovereignty: Zion and Gerizim in Competition* (JSOTSup 404; Copenhagen International Seminar 14; London: T&T Clark International, 2004), 10–15, critiques the circularity of the arguments for dating and textual chronology and points out some aspects of how redaction and form criticism are dependent on the expectations of the scholar.

Another illustration of the extent to which the idea of a unified work encompassing Deuteronomy, Joshua, Judges, Samuel, and Kings, has become accepted is how the label DH is employed even by scholars who choose a literary, synchronic approach. For example, R. Polzin chooses Deuteronomy, Joshua, Judges, Samuel, and Kings as a literary whole, refers to the writer as the "Deuteronomist," and proceeds with a literary, synchronic, structuralist-type analysis. In the first of a trilogy, *Moses and the Deuteronomist*, 12–24, Polzin cities heuristic concerns as the reason for retaining the term "Deuteronomistic history," maintaining the fact that historical criticism has not provided any agreement about the composition of the DH as the reason he chooses a literary approach.

45. Or, as R. R. Wilson put it, "we are left with a picture of pan-Deuteronomist of epidemic proportions," in, "Who Was the Deuteronomist? (Who Was Not the Deuteronomist?): Reflections on Pan-Deuteronomism," in Schearing and McKenzie, eds., *Those Elusive Deuteronomists*, 64–82 (77), concluding that there is a possibility that everyone is now the Deuteronomist, and, if that is the case, nobody is the Deuteronomist.

is the context of present scholarship,[46] posing specific challenges for any new study of the idea of the "chosen place" in Deuteronomy, because of its "centrality" in the scholarly constructions.

In several ways, the present book illustrates how the study of the "chosen place" is the victim of a captivity of sorts.[47] The scholarly tradition and the paradigm within which the "chosen place" has been discussed and explored, determine, to a large degree, what can be said about it. We must therefore ask how we might begin to describe the biblical concept of the "chosen place" without becoming ensnared by issues such as the dating of Deuteronomy, in the idea of a historical religious reform in the time of Josiah, or the ways in which this concept has been made to play a pervasive role in the various forms of the DH hypothesis. What do we find if we approach the "chosen place" without looking at the texts through these optics?

Approaching the "Chosen Place"

In this book I am going to present some discoveries about the concept of the "chosen place" by undertaking a selective probe of texts clustering around this idea. I am going to lay those results out. Cumulatively, I believe that this will provide material for the case that Deuteronomy and the books of the Former Prophets are quite distinct works. These works disagree on certain issues, do not know of or ignore each other on some issues, and are in various ways in strong tension with each other. Overlap in vocabulary may even sometimes be quite misleading, as we will see in the case of the "chosen place" and "chosen city." These aspects need more attention, and should not be ignored or interpreted in a way so as to fit in with a "grand hypothesis," whatever that may be.

As pointed out at the opening of this chapter, the legislation about the "chosen place" in Deuteronomy sparks questions about its function within the book itself, in relation to other legal corpora and in relation to the books of the Former Prophets. In exploring the connections between Deuteronomy and other biblical books, some of these connections seem to contradict the idea of a Deuteronomistic History. Some of the discoveries

---

46. As illustrated by the title of one of the panel sessions at the 2010 IOSOT Congress in Helsinki, "What Is 'Deuteronomistic'?," with one of the papers entitled, "The (Still) Elusive Deuteronomist(s)," presented by S. L. McKenzie, and the continuously thriving sessions on the DH in the Society of Biblical Literature.

47. The year 2013 marks the seventieth anniversary of Noth's publication, and of course the "chosen place" had then already been under the control of others for quite a while before that.

cannot be explained by it. And yet other connections seem to call for explanations that go beyond what a reasonable variant of the DH hypothesis can bear. Some connections are hard to explain in any way we know how at the moment. Through the present exploration, I am trying to do justice to some of those observations that sparked the idea of the DH hypothesis, even though I have ended up not being satisfied with the traditional explanations.

In spite of claims that "centralization" is particular to Deuteronomy, this strict distinction needs moderation and discussion. It is true that Deuteronomy alone explicitly refers to the "place that YHWH will choose." However, as scholars have always acknowledged, the idea of a central cult site is also incorporated and presupposed, though perhaps not distinctly articulated, in Lev 17–26, the so-called Holiness Code.[48] The understanding of the sanctuary reflected in the legislation of Exodus, Leviticus, and Numbers also implies a "centralized" understanding.[49] However, the Wellhausian legacy of disregarding what was seen as "late" legal material, combined with the priority placed on the "origin" of traditions, led to a downplaying of the priestly legislation which has impacted scholarship up until quite recently.[50] The situation is complex, and raises the need to remind ourselves of the broader Pentateuchal context of Deuteronomy's laws of centralization.

The question of what role an idea of a "chosen place" or centralized cult site plays in the Former Prophets is perhaps even more complicated. I mentioned above that Pentateuchal scholarship has developed along the consensus that Deuteronomy was significantly *different* from the other

---

48. For a very useful overview of scholarship on the relationship between Deuteronomy and the Holiness Code, see C. Nihan, "The Holiness Code between D and Some Comments on the Function and Significance of Leviticus 17–26 in the Composition of the Torah," in Otto and Achenbach, eds., *Das Deuteronomium zwischen Pentateuch*, 81–122.

49. Wellhausen made this point very clearly, *Prolegomena zur Geschichte Israels*, 34, 99. Usually brought up within discussions of literary dependence or compositional growth of the Pentateuch, the fact that some type of centralization is also present in other books of the Pentateuch is often underplayed in discussions of the uniqueness of Deuteronomy.

50. The situation has changed in the last few decades, and increased attention has been credited to the relationship between priestly legislation and Deuteronomy. In fact, the interest in what has been referred to as *Fortschreibung* reflects a recent upgrading of how the material is evaluated, that used to be denigrated as "late," "judaizing" and reflecting a "process of decay." Methodologically, however, there is not much difference in how the textual material is divided up. The difference lies in the value attached to the texts.

books of the Pentateuch and that the idea of a single, central cult site, as advocated in Deuteronomy, has been one of the main features of that difference. With the relationship between Deuteronomy and the Former Prophets, however, the situation is the opposite, and it is the *links and connections between them* that have been emphasized. This is in many ways warranted by the nature of the texts, but the drive in scholarship to develop overarching models to explain the compositional history of texts poses significant challenges to any attempt at a fresh exploration.

As I mentioned earlier, my project involves a kind of reading of select texts "with fresh eyes," pointing out features of the text as they appear, without being pre-shaped by scholarly assumptions. In a sense, I will be describing the textual territory, pointing out features and oddities as I go. I hope to be able to expose some of the features that have been overlooked, become blurred, or explained away, particularly in diachronic readings whose purpose is to recreate the literary history of the books or readings that try to fit the texts into one of the proposed literary and/or theological schemes such as the "Deuteronomistic History." My readings are "final-form" readings in the sense that I begin by reading the texts in the forms that they are now available to us in the received text. I do keep in mind an awareness that the text has grown and changed, and am open to observing signs of the diachronic history of the text. In other words, while I do not think that it is possible to account for a text's genesis, I do not necessarily try to make sense of every part of it within a final-form synchronic reading.

In order to address the textual issues that warrant attention, I have felt the need to carve out a spot from which I can take into consideration, whenever appropriate, both discussions that take place within the redaction-critical paradigm involving the DH hypothesis and discussions that have issued around the more literary approaches. Even though I am not primarily asking diachronic historical questions, any new insight gained about the texts through my readings must necessarily also reflect on classical issues of date, authorship, textual history, and relative chronology. My observations, therefore, though not intended to contribute to these issues directly, might end up doing so indirectly.

The "Chosen Place" in Deuteronomy, the Pentateuch and in the Former Prophets: Outline of the Content of the Chapters

This study will begin with the book of Deuteronomy and follow its literary contexts, both by following what appears to be the narrative chronology between Numbers and Joshua and by exploring contexts identified through intertextual echoes or the occurrence of identical and similar linguistic and thematic motifs. We begin in Chapter 2 by surveying the appearances of the "chosen place" in Deuteronomy. This idea is prominent in the book, in a specific form which is all but unique. The "chosen place" in Deuteronomy leads us to explore another chosen place, the "chosen city" in Kings. Scholars have almost unanimously taken this idea in Kings to be a kind of implementation of the concept of "chosen place" found in Deuteronomy.[51] As Chapter 2 will highlight, however, the concept of the "chosen place" functions in an entirely different way in Deuteronomy than the "chosen city" does in Kings.

Chapter 3 follows with a close reading of Deut 12, the chapter that first announces the command to sacrifice only at the "chosen place." The reading of this key text will help to present the workings of the "centralization law" within the book of Deuteronomy. This literary, synchronic reading will make reference to the scholarly debates that have been constitutive of the discussion of the "chosen place."

Chapters 4 and 5 both contain fairly wide-sweeping surveys. Chapter 4 explores the construction of "Jerusalem" in the Former Prophets. One of the questions that will be pursued is how the idea of "chosen city" plays a role in the discussion of centralization as a "deuteronomistic" idea. The ideas of the "chosen city," and Jerusalem as the place that a "house of YHWH" comes to be built, are brought together in the course of a lengthy and convoluted narrative in a seemingly tangential, although surprisingly subtle, way.

Chapter 5 provides an overview of the phenomena of ritual cult, the cult place and the sanctuary in the Pentateuch and in the Former Prophets. This will allow us to lay out the wider context for Deuteronomy's specific understanding of cult in its two primary contexts, the Pentateuch and the Former Prophets. One purpose of this is to be able to see more clearly how Deuteronomy is distinct from, but also connected to, the rest of the legal material in the Bible. Another purpose is to trace specific connections to the Former Prophets on topics of ritual and cultic practice. Too often, "centralization of the cult" becomes a slogan that is quite abstract and not really stringent enough to make appropriate comparisons between actual texts. In particular, the importance of the sanctuary in the legislation of Exodus–Numbers will be contrasted with the paucity of references to the sanctuary in Deuteronomy. We will also consider the centrality of the temple in Kings and the connections between the temple-building account in 1 Kgs 6–8 and Exod 25–40. The descriptions of the

---

51. E.g. H. Weippert, "'Den Ort, den Yahweh erwählen wird, um dort seinen Nahmen wohnen zu lassen': Die Geschichte einer alttestamentlichen Formel," *BZ* 24 (1980): 76–94.

sacrificial cult and of various cult sites in the Former Prophets will also be mapped out, in order to gauge their significance for the centralization issue, and to gain an appreciation of the role of cult in these books.

Building on the broad surveys of Chapters 4 and 5, Chapter 6 will focus on the Josiah narrative of 2 Kgs 22–23 and its connections to Deuteronomy. This has been a key text for all of the various constructions of the DH hypothesis. In particular, I interrogate the assumptions that underlie the claim that Josiah's reform was "Deuteronomistic" and that the passover was celebrated according to the "Deuteronomistic" ritual in Deut 16. The assumptions that support this claim come, overwhelmingly, from the identification of the book found by Hilkiah as some form of Deuteronomy but also from a projection of the Chronicles version of the text onto the Kings version. In fact, Josiah's reform can be understood perfectly within the book of Kings and its theme of royal reform, and, far from being a "centralizing" reform, it is a reform of cultic purging and defiling. This reading will provide an opportunity to gain insight into the concerns of the Josiah narrative and its particular concern of cultic cleansing, and also to readdress some of the ongoing debates that have shaped the scholarly discussion of these texts.

Chapter 7 will explore election as a principle of authority in Deuteronomy. The rhetorical power of Moses' speeches in Deuteronomy has been the focus of several studies.[52] One rhetorical strategy that has not received due attention involves the idea of divine election. The rhetoric of election may contribute to the perceived power of the idea of centralization. The chosenness of the place gives it a divine authority that makes it unassailable. The workings of the authority of divine election in Deuteronomy will be compared with other parts of the Pentateuch and to the role played by divine election in underpinning the authority of the Davidic monarchy in Samuel and Kings.

In Chapter 8 the concept of kingship as it is portrayed in the books of the Former Prophets will be compared and contrasted with the law of the king in Deut 17. After concentrating so closely on the idea of the "chosen place" and cult centralization, the new focus of this chapter provides a counterpoint. As yet another topic on which there is tension between Deuteronomy and books of the Former Prophets, kingship provides another illustration of ways in which the traditional explanations using the DH hypothesis fail to account adequately for the textual data. The chapter ends with some thoughts about the wider implications of this conclusion for future research.

---

52. See Chapter 3 n. 1.

While abandoning the DH hypothesis may prove liberating and open new avenues for approaching the "chosen place," paying close attention to how these texts *have* been read[53] may also prove key to understanding other parts of the canon. There has often been confusion between how texts have been read and what has been attributed to texts as their intention or purpose. In other words, descriptions of ways in which texts have been read (reception history) or ways in which they can be read together with other texts (e.g. by conflating Kings and Chronicles) should not be confused with authorial intent. This book will ask primarily about how the concept of "chosen place" is constructed as a textual phenomenon in Deuteronomy and the Former Prophets, instead of asking about the texts' intention (and thus about the writers, their time, and their identity). Through this focus, this book will also show, for example, that Chronicles is more "Deuteronomistic" than the DH.

53. Bernard Levinson's work on the development of biblical and ancient Near Eastern law is important in this regard. The most important point is the idea of the reinterpretative hermeneutics, or inner-biblical exegesis. The main problem with the method is that it assumes a fair amount about texts that that we do not possess anymore, but that have been reconstructed from existing texts. We only have the texts that were kept, even though probably also others sought to replace them. For example, how can we know what the covenant code that the writers of Deuteronomy used looked like? Further, how do we know what form of the DH the writer of Chronicles might have used as his source?

Chapter 2

CHOSEN PLACE AND CHOSEN CITY

The phrase "the place which YHWH your God will choose" appears 21 times in Deuteronomy and once in the book of Joshua. The reference to Jerusalem or "the city" as chosen by YHWH appears nine times in the book of Kings and eight times in Chronicles.[1] These phrases have been collectively referred to by scholars as the "centralization formula." In various ways, the appearance of this formula in specific texts has constituted basic material for conclusions about "cult centralization" as a deuteronomistic concept.

This chapter will survey the occurrences of these phrases.[2] At the outset, the term "election phrase" will be used to speak of the phrases, rather than the term "centralization formula." I prefer to use a more open term, one that does not assume either a concept of "centralization" or the notion of a formula, until after the investigation has been undertaken. The term "election phrase" is thus better suited, since it is merely descriptive and does not denote a function or designation that is specific.

Of the books of the Pentateuch, only Deuteronomy contains this type of reference to a chosen *place*.[3] A survey of the 21 occurrences in the book of Deuteronomy will function so as to pin down the type of literary contexts they appear in and what the meaning and function of the phrase might be within Deuteronomy. Next, the occurrences in Kings will be surveyed and their characteristics noted. The question towards the end of

---

1. Deut 12:5, 11, 14, 18, 21, 26; 14:23, 24, 25; 15:20; 16:2, 6, 7, 11, 15, 16; 17:8, 10; 18:6; 26:2; 31:11; and Josh 9:27; 1 Kgs 8:16, 44, 48; 11:13, 32, 36; 14:21; 2 Kgs 21:7; 23:27; 2 Chr 6:5, 6, 34, 38; 7:12, 16; 12:13; 33:7.

2. The idea of divine election also appears in biblical literature with reference to objects other than "place," for example, "Israel," "king," or "priests." Chapter 7 will survey the idea of divine election more comprehensively, whereas in this chapter the scope is restricted to the idea of a chosen *place*, whether it is named, unnamed, or referred to as "the city."

3. In fact, the verb בחר with YHWH as the subject rarely appears in the books of Genesis–Numbers, as will be further explored in Chapter 7.

the chapter will be: How do the concepts of *chosen place* and *city chosen by* YHWH distinguish themselves from one another, and how do they relate to each other?

The "Centralization Formula": Some Remarks on Scholarship

As mentioned above, scholars have referred to the election phrase (when it refers to a place) as the "centralization formula."[4] Based on its various forms, many studies of the "centralization formula" have concentrated on reconstructing the history of the formula and its development in the book of Deuteronomy. A finding that is significant for the present study is Helga Weippert's demonstration that different forms of the "formula" appear in what scholars consider as being the same redactional layer. A chronology of the development of the formula is therefore impossible by redaction-critical criteria alone, according to her.[5]

In a different type of analysis, Norbert Lohfink has shown that numeric and aesthetic principles may underlie the variations and that the short form is an abbreviation of the longer one that recalls the full form when heard.[6] Lohfink concludes that the very stereotypic and short centralization formula has this form because it refers to something well known and already established. Eleonore Reuter also thinks that the short form is an early form. Her main point is to show that the "centralization formula" belongs to the earliest stratum of Deuteronomy, thus supporting the traditional date of the core of Deuteronomy to the middle of the seventh century.[7]

---

4. The term "centralization" has its background in modern theories of social and political organization. J. Wellhausen uses it with respect to Deuteronomy in his foundational *Prolegomena*, 74, 98. S. R. Driver does not use it in his 1902 commentary, however. This term becomes an established key word for the distinctiveness of Deuteronomy's view of cult and the cult site, but it is not always clear that it is understood in the same way by scholars. A critical study of the ways in which scholars have used and understood this term would no doubt be useful.

5. Weippert, "Den Ort, den Jahwe erwählen wird," 79. I think her observation about the difficulty of reconstructing the development of the formula is crucial, but I do not share her confidence as she goes on to use contextual information to argue for a historical development, claiming a development from the "short" to the "long" versions of the formula.

6. N. Lohfink, "Zur deuteronomischen Zentralisationsformel," *Bib* 65 (1984): 297–328.

7. E. Reuter, *Kultzentralization: Entstehung und Theologie von Dtn 12* (BBB 87; Frankfurt: Hain, 1993), 189. Reuter's study contains a detailed history of research on the idea of cult centralization, 18–41.

Others have tried to argue that although the formula is indeed early, it was originally meant to be understood distributively, so that it had also referred to cultic places other than Jerusalem, such as Shechem.[8] The point of some studies has been to show that Deuteronomy depends on Northern traditions,[9] and to explain why Deuteronomy also refers to the building of an altar at Shechem (Deut 27:1–8).[10] In spite of much work on tracing the history of the "centralization formula," there is no consensus on its development. Perhaps a focus on how it works rhetorically within the book of Deuteronomy would be more helpful.

Although past studies do not reach a unanimous conclusion, they do, however, have one thing in common. Scholars have related the references to the "chosen place" in Deuteronomy to the references in Kings and Chronicles to the "chosen city," and have, since the time of Noth, understood the relationship between them within the parameters of some understanding of the DH hypothesis.[11] Scholars have taken the references to the "chosen city" or "Jerusalem, which I have chosen" to be indicating an implementation of Deuteronomy's idea of "chosen place." The references in Kings are understood to constitute a development or an accommodation of the existing formula in Deuteronomy. Helga Weippert specifically develops this idea, maintaining that the references in Kings stem from the hand of a redactor at the time of Josiah.[12] The general consensus is that the "centralization formula" refers to the same concept

---

8. Welch, "When was the Worship of Israel Centralised?," and Welch, *The Code of Deuteronomy*; Oestreicher, "Dnt 12.13f im Licht von Dtn 23.16f," 246–49. See also the summary in B. Halpern, "The Centralization Formula in Deuteronomy," *VT* 31 (1981): 20–38 (22–23), and H. Seebass, "בחר bachar," *TDOT* 2:73–87 (80). On the discussion of Deut 12:14, see below.

9. E.g. von Rad, *Deuteronomy*; E. W. Nicholson, *Deuteronomy and Tradition* (Philadelphia: Fortress, 1967), and "The Centralisation of the Cult in Deuteronomy," *VT* 13 (1963): 380–89, which also depends heavily on a historical interpretation of double campaigns into Judah of Sennacherib in 702 B.C.E. and 688 B.C.E.; G. J. Wenham, "Deuteronomy and the Central Sanctuary," *TynBul* (1971): 103–18.

10. Arguing this text is a later insertion, is, among others, Na'aman, "The Law of the Altar in Deuteronomy," 141–61; see the discussion of Deut 27 in Chapter 4.

11. This goes for the occurrences in Kings in particular. The consensus that Chronicles is younger and used Samuel–Kings as a source has framed the understanding of the phrase in Chronicles. For a different perspective on the chronological relationship between Kings and Chronicles, which argues that they both used a common source, see A. G. Auld, *Kings without Privilege: David and Moses in the Story of the Bible's Kings* (Edinburgh: T. & T. Clark, 1994).

12. See, e.g., Weippert, "Den Ort, den Jahwe erwählen wird," 81–87. She argues that the editor of the book of Kings, for example in the evaluations in the kings, takes the idea of cult centralization from Deuteronomy for granted.

both in Deuteronomy and in Kings, or that the "deuteronomistic" author of Kings was adapting or applying the idea of centralization from Deuteronomy when writing about the "chosen city" in Kings. The findings of my study will challenge this view.

The Chosen Place in Deuteronomy

Brief Comment on the Contents of Deuteronomy
In the book of Deuteronomy, the expression "the place which YHWH your God will choose," appears, with some variations, 21 times.[13] The expression appears in legislation about cultic gifts and sacrifices, about religious festivals, and in laws about offices of authority. The texts in question can all be found in the main central corpus of Deut 12–26, with the exception of one (31:11). The core of Deut (chs. 12–26) consists of legal material governing religious ordinances such as sacrifices, festivals, and the tithe (mainly 12:1–16:17), and religious officials (17:17–18:22), and also laws governing city of refuge and murderers (19:1–13; 21:1–9), the justice system (19:15–20), warfare (ch. 20), slaves (ch. 15), civilian law (21:10–25:19), and other matters. According to the narrative framework of Deuteronomy, these laws are given as a divine speech held by Moses to the Israelites as they are standing on the east bank of the Jordan Valley in the land of Moab. They are given as laws that the Israelites are to keep when they enter and settle the land "which YHWH, the God of your fathers has given you to possess." In the book of Deuteronomy, the divinely chosen place is not named.

The Place which YHWH Your God Will Choose
The election phrase, as it pertains to a place, appears in a basic form and three expanded forms. The basic form is:

המקום אשר יבחר יהוה

"the place which YHWH your God will choose."

This syntactical unit is formed form the noun מקום in the determinate form plus the addition of the attributive אשר־יבחר יהוה. Occasionally, but not always, אלהים or אלהיך is added. The verbal mode of בחר is imperfect and denotes a future action when understood within the narrative framework of Deuteronomy.[14] The phrase implies that the main

---

13. See n. 1 of the present chapter.
14. The Samaritan Pentateuch differs from the Masoretic tradition in that it uses the perfect mode of the verb. The Samaritan textual tradition thus communicates the idea of a place that has already been chosen. We know of the historical controversy

distinguishing characteristic of the place is that it will be chosen by YHWH. The election phrase appears in the basic form eleven times in Deuteronomy, twice in Deut 12, once in the law about the tithe, once in the law of firstlings, three times in the festive calendar in ch. 16, twice in laws about the justice system, once in reference to the duties of the Levites and, finally, in reference to the command to read the law once every seven years (31:11). As we can see, the occurrences are spread out throughout the first half of main legal body and occurs only once outside chs. 12–26.

The first seven occurrences of the "basic form" concern cultic legislation. They occur between chs. 12–16 in Deuteronomy, the section that mainly contains cultic laws.[15]

1. Deut 12:18, on the tithe, firstlings, votive gifts and freewill offerings:

> …these you shall eat in the presence of YHWH your God at the place which YHWH your God will choose (במקום אשר יבחר יהוה אלהיך בו), you and your son and…

2. Deut 12:26, on sacred donations:

> But the sacred donations that are due from you, and your votive gifts, you shall bring to the place which YHWH will choose (אל־המקום אשר־יבחר יהוה).

3. Deut 14:25, on the tithe, if the place is too far away:

> …then you may turn it into money. With the money secure in hand, go to the place which YHWH your God will choose (אל־המקום אשר יבחר יהוה אלהיך בו).

4. Deut 15:20, on the firstling of the herd and flock:

> You shall eat it, you together with your household, in the presence of YHWH your God year by year at the place which YHWH will choose (במקום אשר־יבחר יהוה).

in early Judaism, where the Samaritans claimed Gerizim over Jerusalem as the legitimate cult site. In this light, it becomes particularly significant that the Masoretic tradition maintains the openness of the text and does not yield, so to say, to the temptation of making Deuteronomy read more easily as having a specific place in mind.

15. The biblical citations in English are from the NRSV. In most instances, however, "the LORD" has been substituted with "YHWH" and the verse number indication ordinarily follows the Hebrew text.

5. Deut 16:7, on the passover sacrifice:

And you shall cook it and eat it at the place which YHWH your God will choose (במקום אשר יבחר יהוה אלהיך בו); the next morning you may go back to your tents.

6. Deut 16:15, on the festival of booths:

Seven days you shall keep the festival to YHWH your God at the place which YHWH will choose (במקום אשר־יבחר יהוה); for YHWH your God will bless you in all your produce and in all your undertakings, and you shall surely celebrate.

7. Deut 16:16, on appearing before YHWH at the appointed times:

Three times a year all your males shall appear before YHWH your God at the place that he will choose (במקום אשר יבחר): at the festival of unleavened bread, at the festival of weeks, and at the festival of booths. They shall not appear before YHWH empty-handed.

The above excerpts all deal with cultic legislation. The offerings, the festivals, the tithe, anything that is commanded, should be carried out *at the place which* YHWH *your God will choose*. The formula is repeated again and again, until it becomes almost as a mantra, clustered in particular in the texts of Deut 12 and 16, texts that involve rules about the sacrifices and the passover festival.

There is more to be said about each of these texts and their wider literary contexts. At the present moment, I am simply listing the occurrences to get an idea of what type of contexts in which they can be found. In the next chapter a re-reading of Deut 12 will present an analysis of the workings of the election phrase in its context, and Chapter 6 will return to discuss Deut 16.

The remaining four occurrences of the basic form of the centralization formula are found in texts that deal with the justice system and religious duties.

8 and 9. Deut 17:8–10, in the case of a difficult judicial decision:

If a judicial decision is too difficult for you to make between one kind of bloodshed and another, one kind of legal right and another, or one kind of assault and another—any such matters of dispute in your towns—then you shall immediately go up to the place which YHWH your God will choose (אל־המקום אשר יבשחר יהוה אלהיך בו), where you shall consult with the Levitical priests and the judge who is in office in those days;

they shall announce to you the decision in the case. Carry out exactly the decision that they announce to you from the place which YHWH will choose (מן המקום ההוא אשר יבחר יהוה), diligently observing everything they instruct you.

10. Deut 18:6–7, on Levites who come to "the place":

If a Levite leaves any of your towns, from wherever he has been residing in Israel, and comes to the place which YHWH will choose (אל־המקום אשר־יבחר יהוה) (and he may come whenever he wishes), then he may minister in the name of YHWH his God...

11. Deut 31:11, on the public reading of the law:

...when all Israel comes to appear before YHWH your God at the place that he will choose (במקום אשר יבחר), you shall read this law before all Israel in their hearing.

These excerpts deal with how to carry out justice and with religious duties. The important message is that these things must be carried out *at the place*. The arbitration of difficult juridical cases that could not, we assume, be decided in the gates (השארים), are to be taken to "the place which YHWH will choose." Both Deut 17:8–10 and 18:6 assume a priestly, Levitical office, and an office of judge (see also Deut 26:3, which assumes a priestly office). The above texts show that centralization involved more than specifically sacrificial and ritual cultic duties. It involved the organization of the justice system and the priesthood as well. These are aspects that have not received as much attention as the specifically cultic aspects, in discussions of "centralization" in scholarship.[16]

The Expanded Form with the Mention of Tribes
The election phrase is found in three expanded forms. In the first of these, there is a reference to the tribes of Israel. We find this twice in Deuteronomy.

---

16. For more on these aspects, see, among others, R. R. Wilson, "Israel's Preexilic Judicial System," *JQR* 74, no. 2 (1983): 229–48 (246–47); Y. Suzuki, "Deuteronomic Reformation in View of the Centralization of the Administration of Justice," *Annual of the Japanese Biblical Institute* 13 (1987): 22–58 (33–36), and the literature cited there; Levinson, *Deuteronomy and the Hermeneutics*, 98–143; T. M. Willis, *The Elders of the City: A Study of the Elders-Laws in Deuteronomy* (SBLMS 55; Atlanta: SBL, 2001).

Deuteronomy 12:5 outlines how to perform cultic acts:

> But you shall seek *the place which YHWH your God will choose out of all your tribes as his habitation to put his name there* (המקום אשר־יבחר יהוה אלהיכם מכל־שבטיכם לשום את־שמו שם לשכנו). You shall go there, 6. bringing there your burnt offerings and your sacrifices, your tithes and your donations, your votive gifts, your freewill offerings, and the firstlings of your herds and flocks.

Deuteronomy 12:14 specifies where to perform cultic acts:

> But only at *the place which YHWH will choose in one of your tribes* (במקום אשר־יבחר יהוה באחד שבטיך)—there you shall offer your burnt offerings and there you shall do everything I command you.

As one can see, in 12:5 the formula includes also the phrase "to put his name and make his habitation there" (לשום את־שמו שם לשכנו), a combination of another two phrases (see below on these additional phrases). Deuteronomy 12:14 contains the simple election phrase plus the reference to tribes. In 12:5 the expression is מכל־שבטיכם, "from among/out of all of the tribes," which is identical to what we find in all other cases; see below. The phrase that stands out as unique and has caused quite a lot of discussion is in Deut 12:14, with the phrase באחד שבטיך, "in one of your tribes." This phrase has been understood by many scholars as originally indicating a distributive sense—that it did not refer to one place exclusively, but that it referred to the deity as choosing one place at a time.[17] However, even the proponents of the view that it was originally understood distributively concede that in the present context, an exclusive place is meant.

---

17. Discussions about the interpretation of this phrase in literary criticism have been a key part of dating and providing a chronology for the development of the idea of centralization. Oestreicher, "Dtn 12,13f. im Licht von Dtn 23.16f," and Welch both argue that באחד שבטיך should be translated as meaning a choice of one out of any of the tribes, and should be understood distributively, that is, that it could be referring to more than one place, successively. In other words, it does not limit the choice to one tribe. For a discussion of these arguments, see Welch, "The Problem of Deuteronomy," 296–300. See also Halpern, who discussed this subject in, "The Centralization Formula in Deuteronomy," 21–23. He thinks that an early form of the phrase might have been interpreted distributively and later altered by someone advocating centralization. See J. G. McConville's critique of this view in "Time, Place and the Deuteronomic Altar Law," in J. G. McConville and J. G. Millar, *Time and Place in Deuteronomy* (JSOTSup 179; Sheffield: Sheffield Academic, 1994), 117–20. See also the discussion in Reuter, *Kultzentralization*, 65–67. In general, too much has been made of the difference between the two expressions, especially when it has been made a criterion of literary-critical dating of different parts of the text.

The LXX of Deuteronomy renders the two phrases in question identically, ἐν μιᾷ τῶν (φυλῶν), thus fudging or harmonizing the differences when it comes to this expression. The Codex Vaticanus renders πόλεων where the Alexandrinus has φυλῶν in 12:5 and the Alexandrinus has πόλεων in 12:14. So, while the expression causing so much discussion in the MT is harmonized in the LXX, the object ("tribe"), which is identical in the two instances of MT is also found rendered as "city" in the LXX.

In its present MT context the reference to tribes in these two occurrences indicates that the place which YHWH will choose will be in a part of the land belonging to one of the tribes, although the exact meaning of the phrase seems to be difficult to pin down in the context of Deuteronomy. Elsewhere in Deuteronomy, the notion of election "from among the tribes of Israel" is found in Deut 18:5, where it refers to the Levites, who have been chosen to "stand and do service in the name of YHWH." The tribe of Levi receives some attention in Deuteronomy. In 29:20 we find the notion of YHWH singling out for punishment "from all the tribes of Israel" anyone or any entity that does not uphold the covenant. In these contexts, the reference to tribes seems straightforward.

In the narrative material of the Hebrew Bible outside of Deuteronomy, reference to the election "from among/out of the tribes of Israel" is found eight times. Seven of these concern references to the election of the city of Jerusalem, which will be discussed in the next part of this chapter (1 Kgs 8:16; 11:32; 14:21; 2 Kgs 21:7). These texts associate the election of the city closely with the election of David and with the one tribe that Solomon was allowed to keep. The election of Samuel as priest is also referred to as an election "from among/out of all of your tribes" (1 Sam 2:28), and is somehow paralleled by Deut 18:5.

The reference to choosing "from among the tribes of Israel" touches on a complex of motifs that puts the references in Deuteronomy in touch with a whole set of connotations, as expressed in larger narrative complexes such as the election of David and Jerusalem in 2 Sam 7 and the partition of the kingdom in 1 Kgs 11. The appearance of these cross-contextual motifs is perhaps one phenomenon contributing to what might tend toward an indiscriminate identification of the idea of centralization in Deuteronomy with what is probably more correctly identified as an ideology of YHWH's election and protection of Jerusalem, in the book of Kings (see more on the references from Kings, below). For now, we simply note that the reference to tribes is one of the existing expansions of the election phrase in Deuteronomy.

The case of Deut 12:5 needs a further comment. This is the first occurrence of the election phrase in Deuteronomy, and it occurs only here in this fully expanded form. It would seem that this serves a rhetorical and stylistic purpose. The first time that the idea of the "chosen place" is announced, at the very beginning of the legal core of Deuteronomy, the full election phrase is used, with all of the additional phrases. In this way, whenever even a part of it appears, the whole of it will be recalled by the reader/hearer.

The Expanded Form with the Name: Put His Name There (לשׂום שׁמו שׁם)
The election formula may also be expanded by addition of one or both of another two phrases: (1) "the place which YHWH your God will choose to put his name there" (לשׂום שׁמו שׁם, 12:5, 21; 14:24), and (2) "the place which YHWH your God will choose to make his name dwell there" (לשׁכן שׁמו שׁם, 12:5, 11). In these additional phrases it becomes clear that YHWH has a purpose for choosing the place: to put or allow his name to dwell there. For the present purposes, I will regard both phrases as expressing a claim about a divinely elected place for the purpose of practicing worship, justified by an understanding about the divine presence.[18]

---

18. The literature on the meaning of the phrases "to put his name" and "make his name dwell" is quite extensive. Several scholars have understood Deuteronomy as demythologizing an ancient concept of YHWH as present on earth by insisting that YHWH is present in heaven, but that his name "dwells" on earth; see, e.g., G. von Rad, "Deuteronomy's 'Name Theology' and the Priestly Document's 'Kabod' Theology," in *Studies in Deuteronomy* (SBT; London: SCM, 1953; repr. 1963); trans. of *Deuteronomium-Studien* (rev. ed.; Göttingen: Vandenhoeck & Ruprecht, 1948), 37–44. M. Weinfeld develops the idea of demythologization into a major part of Deuteronomic ideology (e.g. *Deuteronomy and the Deuteronomic School*, 191–209); see the review and critique of the idea of demythologization in J. Milgrom, "The Alleged 'Demythologization and Secularization' in Deuteronomy," *IEJ* 23 (1973): 156–61, and Weinfeld's reply in "On 'Demythologization and Secularization' in Deuteronomy," *IEJ* 23 (1973): 230–33. Tryggve N. Mettinger has done extensive work on "name theology" and ideas about divine presence, with an understanding reflecting the history of religions approach, where he interprets the development of a name theology as a response to the destruction of the temple and the collapse of an earlier "Zion-Sabaoth theology" of YHWH's royal presence in Jerusalem. See, for a summary of his position, Mettinger, "The Name and the Glory: The Zion-Sabaoth Theology and Its Exilic Successors," *JNSL* 24 (1998): 1–24. In a detailed study of the language of the "centralization formula," M. Keller outlines what he considers to be a specific "shem"-theology in Deuteronomy and the DH, which resulted from the crisis of the exile, *Untersuchungen zur deuteronomisch-deuteronomistischen Namenstheologie* (BBB 105; Weinheim: Beltz Athenäum, 1996). See also, for the alternative view that Deuteronomy expresses, overall, an

One detail to note is that the expanded form that mentions the "name" is found exclusively in connection with sacrificial legislation and not, for example, in connection with the justice system, the king, or the reading of the law. The same is the case for the addition of the phrase mentioning tribes, above. It is only when "the place" is referred to by the "basic form" that activity other than sacrificial or cultic festivities are described (see above). This might be coincidental; at least I am not sure at this point what it could mean.

The phrase "put his name there" (לשום שמו שם) occurs three times as an expansion of the election formula, in reference to the *place*.

1. Deut 12:5, see above.

2. Deut 12:21, on non-sacrificial slaughter:

> If the place where YHWH your God will choose to put his name (המקום אשר יבחר יהוה אלהיך לשום שמו שם) is too far from you, and you slaughter as I have commanded you any of your herd or flock that YHWH has given you, then you may eat within your towns whenever you desire.

understanding of God as immanent and present, I. Wilson, *Out of the Midst of the Fire: Divine Presence in Deuteronomy* (Atlanta: Scholar's Press, 1995), who by way of a conclusion, points out that, "the significance of the divine Name in relation to the "chosen place" calls for further investigation," 217.

On the contrast between the two phrases, it has been claimed that the term שכן is associated with a more transitory existence, associating the term with a lifestyle involving tents, whereas the term שום indicates a more permanent existence. This may be true, but it seems that in the present context, there is no distinction between the two.

The broader Near Eastern literature can be helpful in illuminating possible ways of understanding the biblical usage, for example as implying some form of conquest, e.g. the Amarna Letters, in *ANET*, 488. The most recent review of the ancient Near Eastern material in relation to the so-called name-theology is S. Richter, *The Deuteronomistic History and the Name Theology:* l'shakken shemo sham *in the Bible and the Ancient Near East* (BZAW 318; Berlin: de Gruyter, 2002), with extensive history of research, 11–36. She refutes the older consensus represented by von Rad and also subsumed in Mettinger's work, and argues against the so-called name theology, quite successfully, as far as I can see; instead, she sees the phrase as representing YHWH's conquest of the Promised Land and his claim on it. See also J. Van Seters' critique of Richter's work in "The Formula *lᵉšakkēn šᵉmô šām* and the Centralisation of Worship in Deuteronomy and DH," *JNSL* 30 (2004): 1–18. The ancient Near Eastern material is also discussed in Wenham, "Deuteronomy and the Central Sanctuary"; R. de Vaux, "Le lieu que Yahvé a choisi pour y établir son nom," in *Das Ferne und Nahe Wort: Festschrift Leonard Rost zur vollendung Seines 70. Lebensjahres...* (ed. R. Maas; Berlin: Töpelmann, 1967), 219–28.

3. Deut 14:24–25, on the tithe:

> But if, when YHWH your God has blessed you, the distance is so great that you are unable to transport it, because the place where YHWH will choose to set his name (המקום אשר יבחר יהוה אלהיך לשום שמו שם) is too far away from you, then you may turn it into money.

Again, these occurrences are found in the chapters that deal with cultic legislation, in the same contexts as the appearance of the "basic form" of the election phrase, in Deut 12 and 14. The fact that a new element has been added to the reference to the chosen place does not, curiously enough, seem to add that much to the meaning. A set of connotations to the idea of "the name" may be set in motion by reference to it, but the election phrase still remains vague, and its usage is more like a slogan than something specific and contingent.

The Expanded Form with the Name: To Let His Name Dwell There (לשכן שמו שם)

The six occurrences of the phrase with the additional phrase לשכן שמו שם can also be found mostly within the three chapters dealing with cultic legislation, namely chs. 12, 14, and 16. One occurrence is found in the final chapter of the main legal body, ch. 26, and concerns the sacrifice of the first fruits.

1. Deut 12:11, on the legitimate place of sacrifice:

> ...then you shall bring everything that I command you to the place which YHWH your God will choose as a dwelling for his name (המקום אשר־יבחר יהוה אלהיכם בו לשכן שמו שם): your burnt offerings and your sacrifices, your tithes and your donations, and all your choice votive gifts that you vow to YHWH.

2. Deut 14:23, on the tithe and firstlings:

> In the presence of YHWH your God, in the place that he will choose as a dwelling for his name (במקום אשר־יבחר לשכן שמו שם), you shall eat the tithe of your grain, your wine, and your oil, as well as the firstlings of your herd and flock, so that you may learn to fear YHWH your God always.

3. Deut 16:2, on the passover:

> You shall offer the passover sacrifice to YHWH your God, from the flock and the herd, at the place which YHWH will choose as a dwelling for his name (במקום אשר־יבחר יהוה לשכן שמו שם).

4. Deut 16:6, on the passover:

> But at the place which YHWH your God will choose as a dwelling for his name (אל־המקום אשר־יבחר יהוה אלהיכם לשכן שמו שם), only there you shall offer the passover sacrifice, in the evening at sunset, the time of day when you departed from Egypt.

5. Deut 16:11, on the feast of weeks:

> Rejoice before YHWH your God—you and your sons and your daughters, your male and female slaves, the Levites resident in your towns, as well as the strangers, the orphans, and the widows who are among you—at the place which YHWH your God will choose as a dwelling for his name (במקום אשר יבחר יהוה אלהיכם לשכן שמו שם).

6. Deut 26:2, on the first fruits:

> …you shall take some of the first of all the fruit of the ground, which you harvest from your land that YHWH your God is giving you, and you shall put it in a basket and go to the place which YHWH your God will choose as a dwelling for his name (אל־המקום אשר יבחר יהוה אלהיכם לשכן שמו שם).

Once again, we note that it is significant that all of the different versions of the election phrase, the so-called centralization formula, appear in the same texts, and are mainly clustered in chs. 12, 14, and 16, with scattered references in chs. 15, 17, 18, 26, and 31.

A "Centralization Formula" in Deuteronomy?

The secondary literature has tended to use the term "centralization formula" to speak of what I have been referring to as the "election phrase." My point in using this term has been to differentiate between the idea of election and the idea of centralization. In much of the scholarly discussion, the distinction between these two seems to be fudged in a way that is reductive. I will be exploring how the idea of divine election is employed in Deuteronomy to give authority to the idea of centralization, especially in the discussion of this in Chapter 7. It is necessary to distinguish between centralization as an idea of cultic organization that Deuteronomy advocates, and divine election as a means to give authority to that idea.

The election phrase is found in cultic regulations about offerings, the tithe and gifts, the passover and other feasts, about the justice system and the king, and about the reading of the law. The character of the references to the chosen place in Deuteronomy points clearly in the direction of what can be considered a formula, the survey has shown. The references to the chosen place do not have the characteristic of a narrative recounting of an act of election. There is, so to speak, no founding narrative of YHWH's election of "the place." Rather, being chosen figures as an attribute of "the place," something that identifies the place. The frequent reference to a divinely chosen place as a kind of *fait accompli* gives a weight and authority to the idea as something that is not to be questioned, and, as such, it is very convincing. Further, the way in which the concept of the divinely chosen place figures in the laws in Deuteronomy has the consequence that cultic activity is localized at a certain point around which everything else is ordered, and which has consequences for other areas of life, such as the justice system. As a temporary conclusion, therefore, it seems that the term *centralization of the cult* is appropriate in order to characterize the insistence upon the divinely chosen place as the "place" for cultic activity, certain judicial activities, and specific religious duties in Deuteronomy. Beyond this textual characteristic, it is difficult to deduce any significance for historical, contingent information about the "place."

Joshua 9:27
In Josh 9:27 we find the following piece of information:

> But on that day Joshua made them hewers of wood and drawers of water for the congregation and for the altar of YHWH, to continue to this day, in the place that he should choose (אל־המקום אשר יבחר).

What about this text? It follows the pattern of the Deuteronomy texts and it is the only occurrence outside of Deuteronomy of a reference to "the place that [YHWH] will choose." Joshua 9:27 is identical in form to the type of "basic form" that we find in Deuteronomy, except that the subject, YHWH, is not specified following the attributive אשר יבחר, but assumed. Like Deuteronomy, it does not name the place, but speaks of the undesignated "place that he will choose."

In designating the Gibeonites as slaves for the Israelites, this text connects reference to the *altar* of YHWH with the concept of the chosen place, never mentioned explicitly in connection with the election phrase anywhere in Deuteronomy. The altar is mentioned in connection with the election formula in Deuteronomy once (12:27). However, it is not in the same syntactical unit, and the altar and the election formula are associated by context only. As a whole, the altar, or even a sanctuary, is not a primary concern of the "centralization" texts of Deuteronomy (see Chapter 5).

2. Chosen Place and Chosen City   41

This occurrence of the election phrase in Joshua provides one connection between the books of Deuteronomy and Joshua. Somewhat similar to Deuteronomy, the idea of a "chosen place" is taken for granted in this Joshua text. Like Deuteronomy, it is not elaborated on and seems almost kind of happenstance. Thus, whereas certain commands of Deuteronomy are narrated as being specifically implemented by Joshua in the book of Joshua, there is no narrative of setting up a sanctuary or cult site at "the place which YHWH will choose." "The place" is mentioned almost incidentally here in 9:27, and is almost superfluous in the context. It functions more as a slogan.

However, there are other connections between Joshua and Deuteronomy concerning the establishment of the sacrificial site on Mount Ebal and the covenant renewal ritual prescribed in Deut 27 and narrated in Josh 8. Further, a cult center is established in Joshua, when the Israelites set up the tent of meeting at Shiloh (Josh 18:1). But those texts do not refer to the "chosen place," nor do they contain any reference to "as YHWH had commanded by Moses," as we find in other parts of Joshua. These cultic texts of Joshua will be explored further in Chapter 5.

Questions can be asked already at this point. If the idea of "cult centralization" is one of the key features of Deuteronomy that manifests itself in the so-called DH, one might expect there to be some more consistency both in how the election phrase is employed in the books of the Former Prophets and in how events involving a central cult site are recounted in the narrative. Instead, there is confusion from the outset, with a seemingly insignificant mention of "the place which YHWH will choose" in Josh 9:27, the careful retelling of the building of an altar that is not referred to as the "chosen place" in Josh 8 (or Deut 27), and the central role envisioned for Shiloh, which is also not referred to as the "chosen place" in Joshua. Someone who has read about the DH hypothesis and understands there to have been a consistent "Deuteronomistic historian," may have expected a little bit more thorough editing, or at least some more explanation of features that do not fit in.

The Chosen City, Jerusalem

The divine election of a place is referred to nine times in the book of Kings. Six of these are found in two key texts; first, there are three references to the chosen city in Solomon's prayer at the inauguration of the temple in 1 Kgs 8, and second, there are three references to Jerusalem in the narrative of the division of the kingdom in 1 Kgs 11. The remaining three are found in the summary of the reign of King Rehoboam in

1 Kgs 14, in reference to the "house of God" that Manasseh desecrated with the image of Asherah in 2 Kgs 21, and in 2 Kgs 23:27, an oracle of judgment against Jerusalem.

Basically, we find in Kings (and Chronicles) an expression such as, "Jerusalem, the city that YHWH has chosen." The reference serves to identify Jerusalem or "the city" as chosen by YHWH, and consists of an attributive clause with the verb in perfect mode. In Deuteronomy, we find the expression "the place which YHWH will choose...," or something similar. It is vague and contains the imperfect mode of the verb, distinguishing it from the straightforward attributive sentence in Kings. While it may be correct to determine both of these as formulaic in some way, the meaning and function of the formula in Kings turns out to be quite different from that of Deuteronomy.

The focus in this part of the investigation will be on the immediate environments of the election phrase, in its respective textual contexts. This will help us to see that we are dealing with texts that are quite different from the cultic legislation in which the election phrase appears in Deuteronomy. However, the investigation will also serve to bring up the need for an extended look at the bigger picture of several of these texts.

"For the Sake of Jerusalem, which I Have Chosen"

Some of the references to Jerusalem as chosen in the book of Kings serve to support a rationale for less harsh divine punishment. The first use of this type of reference is in 1 Kgs 11:13. In a divine speech recorded as being spoken directly to Solomon, YHWH says he will take Solomon's kingdom away from him, because he had turned away and followed other gods. YHWH adds:

> I will not, however, tear away[19] the entire kingdom; I will give one tribe to your son, for the sake of my servant David and for the sake of Jerusalem,[20] which I have chosen (למען ירושלם אשר בחרתי).

The grammatical structure of the election phrase here is a proper noun with an attributive clause, with the verb in the perfect. The whole is an adverbial phrase. The phrase refers to an act that has taken place, and the attributive phrase confirms that Jerusalem is identified as the city that has been chosen by YHWH. This is the form that is most typical of the book of Kings.

---

19. The word here is אקרע. LXX has λάβω, which would give אקח, "take."
20. The LXX and Syriac versions also contain τὴν πόλιν, "the city," which harmonizes with 1 Kgs 11:32, 36; 14:21, and 2 Chr 12:13.

In this text, Jerusalem as a city chosen by YHWH means that its status as elected grants protection to the royal house. David, YHWH's servant, and Jerusalem, his chosen city, serve as protection for Solomon. For the sake of David, Solomon will be spared and the punishment deferred to his son. And for the sake of David and Jerusalem, YHWH will keep one tribe, let one tribe survive. Immediately, we are plunged into a whole set of concepts involving the promise made to the house of David, and the connections between this promise and the idea of a chosen city.

Prior to this narrative event, the accounts of the inauguration of the temple and Solomon's prayer in 1 Kgs 8 have established the connections between the election of David, the building of the temple, and YHWH's choice of Jerusalem as the chosen city. These connections are intricate and complex, and are discussed separately below. In the narrative of the division of the kingdom (1 Kgs 11), the status of David and Jerusalem as *elected* by YHWH serves as the rationale for partial redemption, and for protection of this city and this royal house.

First Kings 11:13 is part of a larger narrative that, just like Deut 12 and 16, contains several different forms of the election phrase. First Kings 11:13 is the only occurrence in the historical literature that is in what we have been referring to as the basic form, with no additional phrases.[21] The election phrase occurs two more times in 1 Kgs 11. Further on in the narrative, we find the story of the prophet Ahijah and the parable of his mantel. In a divine speech spoken through the prophet Ahijah, YHWH says to Jeroboam, King Solomon's adversary who rebelled against him:

> He then said to Jeroboam: Take for yourself ten pieces; for thus says YHWH, God of Israel, "See, I am about to tear the kingdom from the hand of Solomon, and will give you ten tribes. One tribe will remain his, for the sake of my servant David and for the sake of Jerusalem, the city that I have chosen out of all the tribes of Israel (למען ירושלם העיר אשר בחרתי בה מכל שבטי ישראל)." (1 Kgs 11:31–32)

The speech goes on to justify the punishment. Solomon followed other gods and did not keep YHWH's rules and regulations. Apostasy is the cause for punishment. The ideology is completely in line with that of 1 Kgs 11:13. Jerusalem as a city elected by YHWH serves as a deterrent against his punishment. The addition to the election phrase here of "out

---

21. As we saw above, the fact that one finds several versions of the formula within what scholars have determined to be the same redactional layer is one of the features that made it very difficult to date the evolution of the formula or to date the growth of the texts on literary-critical grounds; see, among others, Weippert, "Den Ort, den Jahwe erwählen wird," 81–82.

of all the tribes of Israel" seems natural in this context in a different way than it did when tribes were mentioned in Deuteronomy. The whole discourse is about the division of the kingdom along the lines of tribes. The idea that Jerusalem was chosen "out of all the tribes" thus forms part of the justification for why Solomon gets to keep this tribe.

The same logic is continued further on in the same speech. On the narrative plane, it is interesting to note that what the readers find out about the whole of Ahijah's speech in 1 Kgs 11:31–39 is spoken to Jeroboam only, out in the open country. How does Solomon find out about this and know to try to kill Jeroboam (11:40)? YHWH also says through Ahijah to Jeroboam:

> Nevertheless I will not take the whole kingdom away from [Solomon] but will make him ruler all the days of his life, for the sake of my servant David whom I chose and who did keep my commandments and my statues; but I will take the kingdom away from his son and give it to you—that is, the ten tribes. Yet to his son I will give one tribe, so that (למען) my servant David may always have a lamp before me in Jerusalem, the city where I have chosen to put my name (בירושלם העיר אשר בחרתי לי לשום שמו שם). (1 Kgs 11:34–36)

In this segment it is particularly the privileged status of David that serves to minimize the punishment. The status of David and the status of Jerusalem are linked closely together by the repetition of the election phrase. The status of David and the status of Jerusalem curb the harshness that the punishment potentially could have had. Solomon's son does not lose the whole kingdom, because David and Jerusalem are chosen by YHWH. Jeroboam is promised future protection and even his own dynasty if he listens to YHWH and follows him, like David did (11:37–38).

In the three cases of 11:13, 32, and 36, YHWH speaks in the first person about "Jerusalem, which [he] chose." In each case, the election phrase has the same grammatical structure. The mention of tribes is added in 1 Kgs 11:32 and the mention of the dwelling place for the name in 11:36.[22] Significantly, the syntactical structure emphasizes that one tribe was saved, that Solomon was not entirely destroyed, because of (למען) the chosen city, Jerusalem, and because of David. Verse 39 is probably to be read as a summary of the whole speech, though it might not at first sight be quite clear to what למען זאת is referring.

---

22. The mention of "tribes" as an addition to the election phrase is found also in 1 Kgs 11:32; 14:21; 2 Kgs 21:7–8; 2 Chr 12:13; 33:7. The mention of Jerusalem as the dwelling place for the divine name is found also in 1 Kgs 14:21; 2 Kgs 21:7; 23:27; 2 Chr 12:13; 33:7. In 1 Kgs 8:16, Jerusalem is not specified.

These examples show that the election phrase in Kings underlines the status of Jerusalem as *protected*. The strong link to the privileged position of David is crucial in these examples. This is also consistent with the prayer of Solomon in 1 Kgs 8, which refers to a *city* chosen by YHWH, as we shall see further below.

References to Jerusalem, the Chosen City, in Regnal Summaries
In 1 Kgs 14:21 and 2 Kgs 21:7–8, the election phrase serves to identify Jerusalem in the context of the presentation of the reigns of two kings of Judah. It seems as if the idea that the city is divinely elected can be understood as a part of the regular description and identification of Jerusalem, and serves as a means to clarify the identity of the city as privileged. It functions, in a way, as a kind of tag or slogan associated with the city. The first one is found in the formulaic summary of the reign of King Rehoboam, son of Solomon.

First Kings 14:21 reads:

> ...and he reigned seventeen years in Jerusalem, the city that YHWH had chosen out of all the tribes of Israel, to put his name there (בירושלם העיר אשר־בחר יהוה לשום את־שמו שם מכל שבטי ישראל)...

This occurrence is composite, mentioning tribes and including the reference to the "putting" of the name. In ways similar to Deut 12:5, the expanded phrase might serve to recall the full set of references even in cases when they are not mentioned. In 1 Kgs 14:21, the election phrase has been built into the formulaic summary of the king's reign as a way of identifying Jerusalem as the chosen city and all that this entails. Interestingly, Rehoboam is the king who inherited the one tribe that was not taken away from Solomon in the narrative of the partition of the kingdom (1 Kgs 11:32). He is the first king who receives the punishment for the sins of Solomon, but also the king whose throne is saved "for the sake of" the chosen city and David.

There are no other examples of Jerusalem being identified in this way in the regnal summaries in Kings until we get to Manasseh in 2 Kgs 21. Yet, somehow, perhaps this epithet of Jerusalem as the chosen city rings in the ears of the readers/hearers when the next regnal summaries are heard.

Second Kings 21:7–8 reads:

> The carved image of Asherah that he had made he set in the house of which YHWH said to David and to his son Solomon, "In this house, and in Jerusalem, which I have chosen out of all the tribes of Israel, I will put

my name forever (בבית הזה ובירושלם אשר בחרתי מכל שבטי ישראל אשים את־שמי לעולם); I will not cause the feet of Israel to wander homeless any more out of the land that I gave to their ancestors, if only they will be careful to do according to all that I have commanded them, and according to all the law that my servant Moses commanded them."

In a list of all the evil things that Manasseh did (2 Kgs 21:3–9) the "house of YHWH" is mentioned twice. First, in v. 4, "He built altars in the house of YHWH, of which YHWH had said, 'In Jerusalem I will put my name'." In other words, the temple or house of YHWH is fully identified with Jerusalem here. Jerusalem is the place specified for the "putting of the name." The identification of temple and Jerusalem is reinforced again in v. 7, where another evil of Manasseh is listed; he places an Asherah figure in the temple. Here the narrator identifies the place that Manasseh sets the Asherah as "the house of which YHWH said…" The focus is very much on the characteristics of this house of YHWH. To flesh out what is special about this house, something YHWH is to have said in the past to David and Solomon more than two centuries earlier is quoted, "In this house, and in Jerusalem, which I have chosen out of all the tribes of Israel, I will put my name forever." What is special about the temple is that YHWH had declared to David and Solomon, the kings of the "Golden Age," that he had chosen Jerusalem, and that he would put his name there (at the house/Jerusalem).

This passage builds on and cements further the association of Jerusalem as YHWH's chosen place with the idea of the house of YHWH as the dwelling place of the name of YHWH. It is ironic in the present context and serves to contrast with the list of evils attributed to Manasseh. In this summary evaluation of Manasseh's reign the logic of YHWH's protection of the temple for the sake of David and for the sake of Jerusalem, his chosen city, is tested. Because of all of his evil deeds, Manasseh will bring disaster on Jerusalem and Judah (2 Kgs 21:11–15). The protected status of the city is now threatened because the king has not kept the law and has instead misled the people. In the earlier occurrences, we noticed that despite the sins of Solomon, Jerusalem was protected "because of David," and because Jerusalem had been chosen by YHWH. Now, this idea of protection has been eroded because of the sins of Manasseh. This helps to prepare for when the final destruction of Jerusalem eventually does occur, in spite of its protected status.

Solomon was protected from punishment even though he worshipped other gods, "for the sake of David" and for the sake of Jerusalem. His son Rehoboam, who received the punishment due Solomon, was also not fully punished but received one tribe, "for the sake of David" and Jerusalem. However, by the time of Manasseh, his sins seem only to increase in depravity when contrasted with the promise of YHWH to David and Solomon about the "house for his name." Manasseh has desecrated this house, and the promise to David and Solomon will no longer protect it.

In Chronicles, the text that is parallel to Kings is all but identical (2 Chr 33:1–8). However, the major difference is in the larger context, where Manasseh turns to YHWH after being exiled to Babylon, and returns to Jerusalem to become a classic "good king" (33:12–20). He builds edifices, strengthens the army, and carries out cult reforms. Because of this, the meaning of the threat against the chosen city is an immediate one in Chronicles, one that Manasseh averts by his pious turnaround, whereas in Kings it becomes a threat to Jerusalem in the future that Manasseh could not rectify, because of his sins.

2 Kings 23: "I Will Reject this City That I Have Chosen"
Second Kings 23 contains the final occurrence of an instance, like in the Manasseh narrative, where the understanding of the chosen city as *protected* is turned around and instead becomes the grounds for punishment. This is also the final occurrence of the reference to the chosen city in the Former Prophets. Whereas we can classify the utterances in 1 Kgs 11 discussed above, and in the prayers of King Solomon (see below) as promises or reassurances of protection, the judgment speech in 2 Kgs 23:27 plays on this promise and turns it around, turning it into a threat of destruction.

Second Kings 23:27 reads:

> YHWH said, "I will remove Judah also out of my sight, as I have removed Israel; and I will reject this city that I have chosen, Jerusalem (את־העיר הזאת אשר־בחרתי את־ירושלם), and the house of which I said, My name shall be there (ואת־הבית אשר אמרתי יהיה שמי שם)."

This text contains the other side of the coin of the ideology espoused in texts such as 1 Kgs 11. In a speech of judgment, the divine threat of leaving or destroying Jerusalem becomes the ultimate threat and punishment. Of course, this is also what finally happens, according to the biblical texts. YHWH turns on the city which he chose, and destroys the house that he had erected for his name.

This text also refers to the chosen city in conjunction with a reference to the "house built for your/my name," as we have seen consistently above. These texts all associate the chosen place with the house built for YHWH's name to dwell there. As we will see in the next section, this connection between the concepts of divine election and a house for YHWH is established by the narrative of 1 Kgs 8.

1 Kings 8: A House for YHWH's Name in the Chosen City

In the narrative chronology, 1 Kgs 8 is the first context in which the election phrase is found in Kings. It appears in the prayer of Solomon at the inauguration of the temple (1 Kgs 8:22–54), the prayer which follows the temple-building narrative that began in 1 Kgs 6:1. The prayer is preceded by a blessing performed by King Solomon.

First Kings 8:15–16 reads:

> He said, "Blessed be YHWH, the God of Israel, who with his hand has fulfilled what he promised with his mouth to my father David, saying, 'Since the day that I brought my people Israel out of Egypt, I have not chosen a city from any of the tribes of Israel in which to build a house, that my name might be there (לא־בחרתי בעיר מכל שבטי ישראל לבנות בית להיות שמי שם); but I chose David to be over my people Israel."

This text emphasizes the election of David. It is, in effect, the book of Kings' recounting of the founding of the Davidic dynasty. Solomon recounts how David had planned to build "a house for the name of YHWH, the God of Israel" (8:17). He then goes on to tell of how YHWH, though he praised David for the idea of building him a house, nevertheless told him that his son Solomon would be the one to build this house. It is quite amusing how the divine reassurance that it was right of Solomon to build the temple is laid in the mouth of Solomon himself. It is part of a blessing directed at YHWH, for having fulfilled his promise of having a temple built for himself. So, Solomon is speaking words of YHWH which praise him, Solomon. This must be a great example of the mutual praise of unassailable leaders.

The point of significance for our present context is the phrase "chosen a city..." We learn that no city had been chosen by YHWH during all the time from the time of the Exodus up until now. By this "non-telling," the text communicates that the idea of YHWH choosing a city is something fundamental. It is almost a negative "founding" story about the election of Jerusalem.

However strong the concept of Jerusalem as chosen comes across as being in the Hebrew Bible, there is no other such "founding" narrative anywhere in the narrative texts. In fact, it is in the poetry of certain Psalms (such as Ps 132) and in specific prophetic texts that the idea of the election of Jerusalem and its special status is expressed most clearly.[23]

---

23. For more on the ideological "construction" of Jerusalem in the Former Prophets, see Chapter 4, and on the use of divine election in some Psalms, see Chapter 7.

In 1 Kgs 8, the reference to YHWH's (non-)election of a city up to the narrative present implies significance as the place chosen for the building of the temple, a "house for the name of YHWH." In Kings, this is the first time that the idea of Jerusalem as chosen and the idea of a "house for YHWH" are brought together. In the book of Samuel, the narratives concerned with the idea of building a temple, a house for YHWH (e.g. 2 Sam 7), do not employ the terminology of election. Second Samuel 7 speaks of the founding of the house/dynasty of David and a house/temple for YHWH, but there is no mention of Jerusalem. In fact, the references to Jerusalem in 2 Samuel consistently signify the city as David's home base for his military campaigns and are used almost exclusively as a logistical term. But with this speech by Solomon, referring back to the promises of YHWH to David, the connection between the idea of Jerusalem as chosen and the idea of temple is established. Two ideas are thus brought together in this text: the idea of Jerusalem as chosen, not found in Samuel, and the idea of a temple for YHWH, introduced in 2 Sam 7 but mentioned nowhere else in Samuel.

The connection between the concept of YHWH choosing a city and the idea of building a temple for his name is strengthened through the appeal to David as a figure of authority, by virtue of *his* chosen-ness. In a way, the connection between chosen place and temple appears as a matter of fact through this retrospective telling, even when told in the negative (i.e. YHWH has not chosen a city, implying that now he has or will). The next two occurrences of the election phrase, found in the prayer of Solomon itself, which begins in 1 Kgs 8:23, then have the effect of further cementing the link suggested here.

As will be discussed more fully in Chapter 4, ideas about the privileged status of David and the location of Jerusalem for the "house" of YHWH are ideas that are found in Samuel and that are brought together more fully in Kings. The question for now is: Does Kings make any kind of reference to fulfilling a requirement of Deuteronomy?

Even though the election phrase is similar to the type we find in Deuteronomy, and contains the same type of expansions, the concern communicated here seems entirely different from that in Deuteronomy. We are not dealing with centralization of cult here, we are dealing with the election of Jerusalem as a special city where YHWH will be present and guarantee its protection. And we are dealing with the very close connections that are spun between the concepts of the election of David and his "house" and YHWH's protection of it, and the concept of Jerusalem as a city that is chosen by YHWH for the building of a house for YHWH. The theme of David's election is associated, through repetition, with the building of the temple, building on texts such as 1 Kgs 5:3–5 and 6:12–13. The commissioning of Solomon to build the temple in 1 Kgs 5:3–5 also has motif associations with Deut 12:10, which we shall turn to below.[24] First Kings 6:12–13 ties the building of the temple together with the call to heed YHWH's laws and ordinances and the promise to David of staying with Israel. In 1 Kgs 8:16 the idea of election of the city is explicitly associated with the building of the temple, in a type of parallelism with the election of David.

As for the reference to the chosen city itself, the phrase could here be seen as a composite phrase made up of several parts. It includes the reference to election out of all the tribes, plus a kind of rationale for the election: "in order to build a house that would be for my name." Again, the reference to tribes in this context perhaps makes more narrative sense than those in Deuteronomy, since it can be understood as a fairly straightforward reference to the twelve tribes of Israel from the time of the Exodus up to now.

Continuing on into the prayer of Solomon we find two references to the "chosen city," in the sixth and seventh petitions.

First Kings 8:44–45 reads:

> If (כי) your people go out to battle against their enemy, by whatever way you shall send them, and they pray to YHWH toward the city that you have chosen (העיר אשר בחרת בה), and the house that I have built for your name, then hear in heaven their prayer and their plea, and maintain their cause.

The next petition of Solomon's prayer takes the case of if the people have sinned, and have been sent into exile and captivity, and then recognize their sin and repent, and then,

> ...pray to you toward their land, which you gave to their ancestors, the city you have chosen (העיר אשר בחרת בה), and the house I have built for your name; then hear in heaven your dwelling place their prayer and their plea, maintain their cause. (1 Kgs 8:48–49)

Just as 1 Kgs 8:15–16, these two excerpts explicitly associate the chosen city with the house built for YHWH's name. The connection between the concepts of election of a city and a house for YHWH is firmly established by the temple building narrative and by the prayer of Solomon. Associations circulate around a city, Jerusalem, chosen by YHWH as the dwelling place for his name, which guarantees protection for those who invoke him.

---

24. See Chapter 3.

In 1 Kgs 8:16 we saw a narrative form of the election phrase formulated in the negative ("I have *not* chosen…"). YHWH is recalling that he did not choose any city. In the prayers, the references seem more formulaic or slogan-like. We might say that the "tag" of "the city that I have chosen" becomes established in this narrative.

The prayer of Solomon has a theology which is quite consistent and in which some form of *centralization* is clearly present.[25] There is, for example, the idea that a prayer uttered in the direction of the "house for the name of YHWH" will be heard and answered by YHWH. The world of Israel, as it is reflected in this prayer, is certainly ordered around this "house for YHWH's name." Interestingly, the prayer is more concerned with protection against danger and the consequences of sin (war, drought, famine, exile) than with cultic activity or festivals. Importantly, Solomon does offer sacrifices at the temple as a part of the inauguration. The prayer of 1 Kgs 8:23–53, which is where this feeling of "centralization" is expressed most clearly, does not specify the sacrificial cult. The blessing of the assembly, following the prayer, does speak generally of keeping the "commandments, statutes, and ordinances," of which the sacrificial cult must be considered a significant part (8:56–61). This is interesting when comparing with the "centralization formula" in Deuteronomy, where the idea of the chosen place is very closely tied to legislation about the sacrificial cult and the festivals and other sacred duties. In Kings, the association of "chosen city" and cultic activity is more tangential, and the explicit connection has to do with the building of the "house for YHWH's name."

---

25. The text of Solomon's speech 1 Kgs 8:22–53 has often been considered one of the typically deuteronomistic texts reflecting a theology of a transcendent God. The idea of transcendence has been considered a deuteronomistic trait that distinguishes it from what is considered to be a priestly theology of immanence. This idea has accompanied, for example, Weinfeld's analysis of Deuteronomy and the deuteronomistic school as representing a process of demythologization and secularization. There are many problems with this analysis, though it is not possible to discuss them fully here. See M. Weinfeld, *Deuteronomy and the Deuteronomic School* (Winona Lake, Ind.: Eisenbrauns, 1992), 190–209, and the literature cited above.

The dichotomy of transcendence and immanence is also behind the idea of name theology. It has been claimed that in order to accommodate the idea of transcendence, "Deuteronomists" developed the idea of the Name taking its presence in the temple instead of YHWH's *kabod*, or the idea of his presence in the temple. See n. 18 above on the name theology. I feel that the dichotomy of transcendence and immanence is not easily applicable to the biblical world view.

In 1 Kgs 8 the presence of YHWH's name and the temple as a point of orientation for communication with YHWH in heaven and on earth are at the forefront. In this context, Jerusalem as the chosen location of the house of YHWH receives importance as a point of orientation of YHWH's protection and a reminder of his promises.

Can One Speak of Centralization in Kings?
The conclusion after the investigation of the election phrase in Deuteronomy was that it clearly suggested a concept of what could be termed "cultic centralization." The question at this point is: Are the texts that we have examined in Kings referring to cult centralization? Does the reference to the status of Jerusalem as elected in the book of Kings carry with it the implication that cultic practices are forbidden elsewhere? Is cult centralization the burning issue in the texts we have examined thus far in Kings? I think we can say: Not clearly. In Kings, the idea of the chosen city does not seem to denote the same concept as that to which the references to a divinely chosen place in Deuteronomy point. The references to YHWH's election of Jerusalem in Kings do not occur in contexts occupied with the idea of cultic centralization; rather, they seem to be a testimony to an ideology of YHWH's protection and the privileged position of the house of David.

This is not to say that there is no connection between the ideology of the "chosen city" as expressed in the text we have examined in this chapter and specific ideas about the place of worship and the idea of forbidding specific cultic practices. The "chosen city" texts we have looked at are all keenly concerned with the idea of a "house for YHWH," as we have seen. And the narrative about the building of the temple is framed by references to cultic practice at other locations. For example, 1 Kgs 3:2–3 and 3:4 refer to the people and Solomon worshiping at "high places" in Gibeon, and 1 Kgs 11 account Solomon's building of cult sites for his foreign wives. These connections will be explored more fully in the chapters to follow. For now, however, we can say that these connections, which are contextual and tangential, do not allow us to conclude that the election texts in Kings are advocating "cultic centralization."

What we can safely say at this point is that if the book of Kings does advocate a centralization of the cult, it is not argued explicitly in these texts about the chosen city. This stands in contrast to the explicit focus on centralization in the Deuteronomic texts containing the election phrase. Deuteronomy's focused message about the place for cultic practice is explicitly connected to the election formula, while this is not the case in Kings.

2. Chosen Place and Chosen City 53

The Chosen City in Chronicles

When we compare the answers to the prayer of Solomon in 2 Chr 7:12–16 with that of 1 Kgs 9:3 we notice some differences. In Kings, the *house* is "consecrated" and the name is "put here forever." In Chronicles, YHWH says that he has "chosen this place for myself as a house of sacrifice (בית זבח)" (2 Chr 7:12), and the house has been chosen and consecrated so that "my name may be there forever" (2 Chr 7:16). This is an example of one of the major differences between Kings and Chronicles in the texts that concern the chosen city. It seems that Chronicles is much more concerned with the sacrificial cult and its identification with Jerusalem than is Kings. Where the "chosen city" is mentioned in the inauguration prayer of Kings, however, there is no reference to ritual cult.

Chronicles is more concerned with the cult than Kings, and thus perhaps exhibits stronger links to Deuteronomy's emphasis on cultic practice connected with the "place that YHWH will choose." A word of caution should be brought in here, however, because the reason for the Chronicler's emphasis on the cult might have more to do with the Chronicler's own agenda than his understanding of texts that he may or may not have received. This also pertains to the role of the king as understood in Chronicles, which profiles the king in the role of a cult leader much more clearly than Kings. On this issue, of course, Deuteronomy is completely different, and does not see a cultic role for the king at all. On the connection between cult and "place," however, it is interesting to note that on an issue often described by scholars as being a mark of deuteronomistic theology or ideology, Chronicles is more "deuteronomistic" than the "deuteronomistic" book of Kings.

The election phrase that appears in the evaluation of the reign of Rehoboam is rendered in a formulaic way also in 2 Chr 12:13. The differences between Kings' version and Chronicles' here are interesting, though they do not relate specifically to the election phrase. Rather, the differences are with respect to the order of events in the story and the weight given to the piety of Rehoboam in his career. This is something which we do not find in Kings (cf. also the Manasseh story).

Conclusions

The reference to the divine election of a place is put to different uses in Deuteronomy and in Kings. We find some of the same motifs and intersecting language, including the mention of "tribes" and the expansions with the addition of "to put his name there" and "to make his name dwell there." We even find the same type of variation in the way that these expansions are used in the election phrase. That is, one finds variations with respect to the expansions of the election phrase within the same short passage, for example, in Deut 14 and in 1 Kgs 11. However, despite overlapping language, what it means that a place is *chosen* is clearly different in the two corpora.

In Deuteronomy, the election phrase occurs mostly in texts dealing with cultic legislation and a few dealing with other religious duties. As we shall see more clearly in the next chapter and in Chapter 7, the election phrase serves to underpin the place of cultic activity with an authority that the idea of divine election accords it. The "centralization formula" grounds itself in that authority which is associated with the concept of divine election, to *authorize* cultic centralization. In Deuteronomy, one can rightly speak of the election phrase as a "formula." The attributive phrase "...that YHWH will choose" becomes a tag of a sort, and supports the scholarly nomenclature of "centralization formula."

In Kings, the election phrase is not associated explicitly with a place for cultic activity. Instead, it is associated with the privileged status of David and the idea of a sanctuary for YHWH, a "house for his name." The city that YHWH has chosen is granted special protection because of David. This context for the idea of the divinely chosen city brings us into touch with a whole complex of narrative and poetic biblical texts at which we will be looking more closely in the course of this book.

Further, it is not completely appropriate to speak of a "centralization formula" in Kings. The references to the elected city are not easily classified as formulaic, but more importantly, the election phrase is not primarily focused on "centralization" as an organizational dynamic. There might be what we can call a stereotypic phrase, or tag, but it should not be called a "centralization formula."

Since it seems quite clear that the idea of Jerusalem as the chosen city in Kings is concerned with a different set of ideas than the idea of the "chosen place" in Deuteronomy, the question arises as to how the relationship between these two sets of texts should best be described. In order to attempt such a description, more investigation is needed. It is necessary to untangle the debates and investigate texts separately.

This brings us first to the need for a focused reading of the Deut 12 in order to reappraise the election phrase in its primary literary context. The reading presented in the next chapter will attempt to gain a sense of the dynamic of Deuteronomic legislation involving the "chosen place." It will also provide the opportunity to gain an awareness of the distinctiveness of Deuteronomy's rhetoric, for the purposes of subsequent comparisons with other Pentateuchal texts and narratives from the Former Prophets.

Our preliminary conclusion at this point is that, based on the texts containing the election phrase, the book of Kings does not propagate a dogmatic centralization. If this is so, the advocates of the idea that the "deuteronomistic idea of cult centralization or reform" is a crucial component of the "Deuteronomistic History" must be using a different set of texts to argue this. On closer inspection, it turns out to be true that other texts have played a role in arguing for a "deuteronomistic idea of cult centralization or reform." This brings us to the narratives about Hezekiah and Josiah. These texts (2 Kgs 18–20 and 22–23) have been understood to relate episodes of cultic reform in Judahite history, or to have been composed in order to legitimize the program of reform understood to be offered in Deuteronomy. The relationship of these narratives to Deuteronomy stands at the heart of much scholarship, and needs to be reexamined. A guiding question, for now, might be: Do these narratives contain a Deuteronomic form of centralization? After the separate investigation of Deut 12 and the surveys of Chapters 4 and 5, we will be in a better position to explore this question, and Chapter 6 will return to examine 2 Kgs 22–23.

The need to reexamine key texts is warranted, not only because Deuteronomy and Kings seem to be using the election phrase in different ways, but also because the findings raise the question of whether the distinctions between the two literary bodies in the understanding of the chosen place and chosen city have been fully appreciated in scholarship. Partly because of the scholarly assumptions regarding dating and the almost universally accepted understanding that Kings is dependent on Deuteronomy in some way, most explanations do not take into account the clear difference between Deuteronomy and Kings with regard to the election formula.

A specific topic that will be pursued concerns the question of why Deuteronomy is not at all concerned with a house, temple, or even altar of YHWH. Deuteronomy never mentions a house built for YHWH and does not contain any command to build a sanctuary, contrary to the legislation of Exodus through Numbers, where it is such a major component (Exod 25–40; Num 2; 4; 10). An altar is never specified in Deuteronomy, with the exception of Deut 12:27. In fact, Deuteronomy does not seem interested at all in temple or sanctuary.

In contrast to this absence of the sanctuary in Deuteronomy, the most consistent expansion of the election phrase in the historical books is one that incorporates the idea of a "house built for YHWH" as a "dwelling place for his name." In the book of Kings, the idea of a place for the name of YHWH is explicitly tied to the idea of a "house," a temple or sanctuary of some kind. In the book of Samuel, the promise of a house for YHWH is associated with the promise of a house for David (in Samuel, the phrase "dwelling place for YHWH's name" is not used). In Kings, the idea of Jerusalem as a city that YHWH has chosen is very closely tied to the concept of a "house built for YHWH," a concept that runs throughout the book of Samuel and Kings. This discrepancy between Deuteronomy and Samuel–Kings is another lead to follow from our quick survey of the election phrase in the two corpora, and provides further rationale for the survey presented in Chapter 5. But first, the next chapter will focus on Deut 12, and will "listen in" to this core text concerning the "chosen place" in Deuteronomy.

Chapter 3

"CENTRALIZATION" IN DEUTERONOMY 12

In Deuteronomy, as Chapter 2 showed, the election phrase occurs mainly in cultic legislation, clustering in chs. 12, 14, and 16. Deuteronomy 12 lays out the laws governing sacrifice, gift offerings, and slaughter. The election formula is found tightly woven into these laws, appearing in Deut 12:4, 11, 14, 18, 21, and 26. In Deut 16 it appears in the laws about the passover and the festival of unleavened bread (16:1–7), the festival of weeks (16:9–12), and the festival of booths (16:13–15), and in the law about men having to appear before the priest (16:16–17). The tithe, firstlings and other sacrifices that are listed in Deut 12 are detailed further in 14:22–26; 15:19–20, and 26:1–2. Finally, the centralization formula appears in connection with ordinances dealing with officials, such as the judges (17:8–10), the Levites (18:6–7), and in connection with the reading of the law in 31:10–11.

The previous chapter also revealed that Deuteronomy does not have a specific command concerning the "chosen place." The election phrase consistently appears in subordinate sentences and never as a main clause. Yet, especially in ch. 12, it comes across to most readers as the most significant feature of the legislation. In fact, one of the most intriguing questions about the command to carry out religious duties at "the place" is that no explanation is ever given for it in Deuteronomy. There is no etiology, no story behind it. The insistent command to practice religious activities at the designated, divinely chosen place is, rather, a given, an axiom, a fundamental. It is presented in a way that seems not to leave room for questions from a pious reader. The question for us, however, is how this effect achieved in the "centralization" texts. We will seek the answer through analysis of the literary context and the function that the "centralization" concept plays within the different laws in Deuteronomy, using ch. 12 as an example.

Centralization and Chosen Place in Scholarship on Deuteronomy 12

As I pointed out in Chapter 2, most studies of the election phrase and the concept of centralization in Deuteronomy have focused on historical reconstruction, including textual and compositional history and the history of Israelite religion. For these studies, the primary purpose is often not so much to understand the textual dynamic of Deuteronomy itself, but the development of legal tradition, the textual history or the history of religious ideas. Some studies have explored "centralization" and how that is constituted in the book of Deuteronomy from a rhetorical point of view.[1]

Another discussion concerning the "chosen place" in Deut 12 that has been quite lively throughout the history of interpretation regards the identification of the place. As a matter of principle, this discussion does not concern us all that much. Clearly, the text of Deuteronomy itself does not identify or name the place, so this text was not concerned with identifying the place. This fact should not be controversial, in spite of all the speculation about what the writers of Deuteronomy may have had in mind, whether it was one place, a succession of places, or different

---

1. It is interesting that one of the earliest explorations of Deuteronomy as rhetorical speech, G. von Rad's *Studies in Deuteronomy* (trans. D. Stalker; SBT 9; London: SCM, 1953), 27, in which he reads the book as the result of Levitical preaching, is one of the few studies that downplays the significance of centralization in the book of Deuteronomy.

In 1979, S. A. Kaufman published a lengthy article arguing that the structure of Deut 12–26 was based on the Decalogue, "The Structure of the Deuteronomic Law," *MAARAV* 1 (1978–79): 105–58. These ideas were developed further especially by G. Braulik; see, e.g., Braulik, ed., *Bundesdokument und Gesetz: Studien zum Deuteronomium* (HBS 4; Freiburg: Herder, 1995); "Die Ausdrücke für 'Gesetz' im Buch Deuteronomium," *Bib* 51 (1970): 39–66; "Die Abfolge der Gesetze in Deuteronomium 12–26 und der Dekalog," in Lohfink, ed., *Das Deuteronomium*, 252–72; *Die deuteronomischen Gesetze und der Dekalog: Studien zum Aufbau von Deuteronomium 12–26* (SBS 145; Stuttgart: Katolisches Bibelwerk, 1991); *Studien zum Deuteronomium und seiner Nachgeschichte* (SBAB 33; Stuttgart: Katholisches Bibelwerk, 2001). See Lohfink's critique of Braulik's thesis about the arrangements of the legal material based on the Decalogue in "Die These vom 'deuteronomischen' Dekaloggang—ein fragwürdiges Ergebnis atomistischer Sprachstatistik," in *Studien zum Pentateuch: Walter Kornfeld zum 60. Geburtstag* (ed. G. Braulik; Wien: Herder, 1977), 99–109.

An example of a rhetorical study of a part of Deuteronomy is T. Lenchak, *Choose Life! A Rhetorical Critical Investigation of Deuteronomy 28:69–30:20* (Rome: Pontificio Istituto Biblico, 1993).

places envisioned by different authors/redactors/traditions behind the present text. Later readers, tradents, and interpreters have thought different things about this question.[2] The fact that the Samaritan Pentateuch consistently has the perfect mode of the verb בחר shows that this alternative textual tradition made a definite choice, whereas the MT tradition remains continuously open to YHWH's future choice. While it is true that other parts of the MT tradition do name Jerusalem as a city that YHWH has chosen (Kings), and also refers to past choices of YHWH (Shiloh, in Ps 132 and Jer 7), in reading Deuteronomy I am suggesting that we as readers remain true to the openness of the text on this question.[3]

A Reading of Deuteronomy 12

Deuteronomy 12–26 consists of legal material governing religious ordinances such as sacrifices, festivals, the tithe, and religious officials, and also laws governing murderers, warfare, slaves, the royal house, and other matters. According to the narrative framework of the book of Deuteronomy, these laws are all given as a long speech held by Moses to the Israelites as they are standing on the east bank of the Jordan Valley in the land of Moab. The laws are given as laws that the Israelites are to keep when they enter and settle and possess the land "which YHWH, the God of your fathers gives you" (Deut 11:31).

Chapter 12 is thus the first chapter in the main central core of the book of Deuteronomy. We find the "centralization" command five times in Deut 12: vv. 4–7, 10–14, 17–18, 21, 26–27. Paying attention to the literary context of each of these, this chapter will provide a presentation of the meaning of "chosen place" as it is constructed in this chapter.

Deuteronomy 11:30–31

Deuteronomy 11:31–32 forms a transition and introduction to the laws and statues of Deut 12,

> When you cross the Jordan to go in to occupy the land that YHWH your God is giving you, and when you occupy it and live in it, you must diligently observe all the statutes and the ordinances that I am setting before you today.

---

2. See the survey in McConville, "Time, Place," 90–104, which covers the main discussions and identifications from the biblical literature, through ancient to modern interpretations.

3. Another testimony to the openness of the MT and perhaps also to the impulse to concretize this in other traditions is the Temple Scroll's use of the word מקדש in the place of מקום when it uses the formula.

Any audience that has read or listened to Deuteronomy from the beginning will by this point have heard this hortatory command to keep the commandments many times already (e.g. 4:1–2, 5–6, 9, 40; 5:1, 31–33; 6:1–3, 6, 17, 24–25; 7:11; 8:1, 11, 19–20; 10:12–13; 11:1, 8, 13, 22, 26–28). This is one of the most important messages of Deuteronomy. Sometimes it seems as if the content of the commandments comes across as less important than the message that they have to be kept. The whole tone of Deuteronomy produces a type of urgency to do according to the commands of YHWH.[4]

In addition to serving as a formal introduction to the core legislation, Deut 11:31–12:1 announces the point in time from which the laws have validity. The laws will be valid when the Israelites have entered the land.[5] The introductory verses in Deut 11:31–12:1 thus introduce the conditions that will apply to the implementation of the laws. Deuteronomy 26:1 introduces the last chapter of the legal core also with a reference to the time when they will have entered the land.

Deuteronomy 12:1–7

The opening of Deut 12 introduces what is to follow as "the laws and the ordinances," thus introducing the main body of legislation in the book of Deuteronomy:

> These are the statutes and ordinances (אלה החקים והמשפטים) that you must diligently observe in the land that YHWH, the God of your ancestors, has given you to occupy all the days that you live on the earth. You must demolish completely all the places where the nations whom you are about to dispossess served their gods, on the mountain heights, on the hills, and under every leafy tree. Break down their altars, smash their pillars, burn their sacred poles with fire, and hew down the idols of their gods, and thus blot out their name from their places. You shall not worship YHWH your God in such ways. But you shall seek *the place which YHWH your God will choose out of all your tribes as his habitation to put his name there*. You shall go there, bringing there your burnt offerings and your sacrifices, your tithes and your donations, your votive gifts, your freewill offerings, and the firstlings of your herds and flocks. And you shall eat there in the presence of YHWH your God, you and your households together, rejoicing in all your undertakings in which YHWH your God has blessed you. (Deut 12:1–7)

---

4. For more on how this sense of urgency is achieved, and on the concept of divine election in Deuteronomy, see Chapter 7, below.
5. Similar references to a time in the future when Israel will keep specific laws in "the land" are found in Exod 12:25; 13:11; Lev 14:34; 19:23; 25:2; Num 15:2, 18; Deut 17:14; 18:9; 26.1.

3. "Centralization" in Deuteronomy 12

The chapter opens with the same authority as the beginning of Deuteronomy, אלה הדברים ("These are the words..."). A mood of solemnity thus prepares the audience that something of great portent is about to be announced. After several lengthy speeches[6] recapitulating Israel's history of disobedience, their rescue from Egypt by YHWH, and countless admonitions to heed his word, his commandments, his statutes and ordinances, the reader/audience is finally going to hear what the content of these commandments are.[7] The very lengthy introductions as they now stand do not only provide the narrative framework of Moses speaking on the plains of Moab, but also in fact contribute to heightening the tension of the marginal experience by repeatedly delaying the feeling of reaching the real meat of the issue, the laws themselves.

If we pause to take a look at the syntactical build-up of Deut 12:1, we will find a feature that is characteristic of the style of the authors of Deuteronomy. The verse is composed of the introductory clause, which states that what follows are the statutes and ordinances, and a string of relative clauses:

אלה החקים והמשפטים
אשר תשמרון לעשות בארץ
אשר נתן יהוה אלהי אבתיך לך לרשתה כל־הימים
אשר־אתם חיים על־האדמה

The statutes and ordinances (החקים והמשפטים) are introduced as laws that the Israelites are to observe when they enter the land. The land is further qualified as the land that YHWH has given to their fathers to possess. And this bestowal is further qualified in time: they have been given it all the days that they live upon the earth.

This string of phrases accomplishes many things in addition to introducing the main body of legislature. In simultaneously introducing one of the main conditions for the practice of the law, namely the possession of the land, this introduction connects the worship of YHWH very closely to the promises of land and possession. YHWH has given the land for them to inherit, to possess.

This description of Israel's ownership of the land stands in stark contrast to the description of the "nations" in Deut 12:2, who are described as the "nations who you shall dispossess" (הגוים אשר אתם ירשים אתם). The same verbal root, ירש, is used for both Israel's possession of the land

---

6. The rhetorical style of Deuteronomy has been noted for its several speeches, which some have called "sermons." See, e.g., von Rad, *Deuteronomy*, 23–27; Weinfeld, *Deuteronomy and the Deuteronomistic School*, 10–58.

7. The Decalogue has already been heard, but the main legal core is now being introduced.

and the dispossession of the nations. The issue of the inheritance and ownership of land thus becomes central in defining the relationship between the Israelites and the "nations," and this relationship becomes an inherent part of the legislation. And it is through the use of a relative clause that it works to string together these very important relational definitions. As we shall continue to see, the technique of identifying important "players" on the scene with a qualifier beginning with אשר is a very significant feature of Deuteronomy.

Even before the instruction about what to do with the nations and their religious sites begins, the Israelites are already qualified as the possessors of the gift of land that they will receive from YHWH, and which will mark the time from which YHWH's law will have validity.

Deuteronomy 12:2–3 contains the very first instruction in the central body of legislation in Deuteronomy. It is the first command that the Israelites are supposed to carry out when they enter the land. The instructions spell out: (1) what the Israelites are to do—destroy (אבד תאבדון) the cult sites; (2) who those cult sites belong to—the nations; (3) who those nations are—the ones who Israel will dispossess; and (4) what went on at those cult sites—those nations worshipped their gods there, on the mountains on the heights and under every green tree. Verse 2 defines the Israelites' relationship to the nations through what the Israelites do to them. As we pointed out, the relative clause introduced by אשר defines a key relationship. The "nations" are described as those nations that Israel will dispossess (אשר אתם ירשים אתם את־אלהיהם).

After this has been made clear, a string of verbs follows, in short, almost hacking phrases:

Israel shall:

אבד תאבדון	utterly destroy	their places (v. 2)
נתצתם	destroy	their altars
שברתם	break, shatter	their *matzevot* (מצבת)
תשרפון	burn	their *asherim*
תגדעון	hew down	their molten images (פסילי אלהים)
אבדתם	destroy	their names

from that place.

All of the verbs in Deut 12:2–3 denote destruction, violence, and breaking, tearing, and cutting down. These verses, with their forceful, violent verbal arsenal, form a great contrast to the preceding sentence, which was a nominal sentence. The commands are formulated in the positive, that is, they are "You shall…" commands, which contribute to the forcefulness of these verses. The heirs to YHWH's land will dispossess "the nations" when they carry out the first acts that YHWH commands, namely to destroy and wipe out their religious sites and objects, totally and without exception.

A significant point in Deut 12:2–3 is the emphasis on the "places" of the nations that are to be destroyed. Deuteronomy 12:2–3 opens and closes with reference to "all the places" (כל־המקמות) and to "that place" (המקום ההוא). All of the places of the nations, which are to be dispossessed, are to be destroyed completely. And the names of their gods are to be destroyed from *that* place.

These two verses contain many of the important motifs that dominate the rest of Deut 12. The mention of the place of worship, the name of *their* gods, and the way of defining the relationship between the Israelites and the nations in terms of ownership (possession and dispossession) all contribute to setting the stage clearly. The tenor of urgency is upheld, and the legislation is bound up with the shaping of Israel's identity as the recipients of YHWH's inheritance, with all that it entails in terms of obedience to the instructions and correct worship.

In Deut 12:1 both the singular and plural second person address appear in the same sentence. The fluctuation between persons in Deuteronomy often referred to as the *Numeruswechsel* has been a subject of literary-critical study in the past.[8] The appearance of both forms in the same sentence here at the very beginning of Deut 12 is yet another example of how the features and motifs that will appear throughout the chapter are introduced in the first few verses.

We now move on to Deut 12:4. This short sentence, לא־תעשון כן ליהוה אלהיכם, "You shall not do so to YHWH your God," forms the transition from the commands to destroy the nations, to how the Israelites are to worship YHWH. The command not to do *so* (לא־תעשון כן) must in this case be taken to refer to the previously described behavior. It thus

---

8. As first analyzed by C. Steuernagel, *Der Rahmen des Deuteronomiums. Literar-kritische Untersuchung über seine Zusammensetzung und Entstehung* (Halle: Wischan & Wettengel, 1894), and W. Staerk, *Das Deuteronomium: Sein Inhalt und seine literarische Form: Eine kritische Studie* (Leipzig: Hinrichs, 1894). The versions are also very unstable regarding the singular or plural forms of the second person pronoun. While this fluctuation between second and third person was used for decades in order to argue for different source strata in Deuteronomy, the idea that the phenomenon reflects stylistic devices of a single author has been advocated from the start, and recently by N. Lohfink and G. Braulik. For an overview of the phenomenon, see C. T. Begg, "1994: A Significant Anniversary in the History of Deuteronomy Research," in *Studies in Deuteronomy in Honour of C. J. Labuschagne on the Occasion of His 65th Birthday* (ed. F. García Martínez et al.; Leiden: Brill, 1994), 1–11.

explicitly sets the commands that follow in contrast to the acts they are to carry out toward the nations. The short sentence of Deut 12:4, "You shall not do so to YHWH your God," refers to these actions in commanding that the Israelites shall *not* do this to YHWH their God. In addition to being a command in its own right, Deut 12:2–3 serves the function of being like a contrast to the following legislation about how the Israelites should correctly worship YHWH. The commands about what the Israelites are required to do against the nations in eliminating their cultic existence are used as a foil and a contrast to how they are supposed to act toward YHWH *their* God. The contrast is continued in the legislation Deut 12:4–7, where the Israelites are given the commands for how they are to worship when they enter the land.

The first sentence immediately following is:

כי אם־אל־המקום
אשר־יבחר יהוה אלהיכם מכל־שבטיכם לשום את־שמו שם לשכנו
תדרשו ובאת שמה

But to the place
that YHWH your God will choose out of all of your tribes as his habitation
to put his name,
you shall seek, and there you shall go.

Following this short transitional sentence we then come to the first instruction pertaining to Israelite worship. The set-up of the text above attempts to point out that the emphasis in this instruction is on *the place*. The way in which the sentences are constructed allows for this projection of the place as a kind of temporary dramatic climax. The qualification of the place as "the place which YHWH your God will chose out of all of your tribes as his habitation to put his name," becomes almost secondary compared to the emphasis achieved by the juxtaposition of the two sentences "You shall not do so to YHWH your God" and "But to the place…" The qualification of "the place" as YHWH's chosen place functions almost as a parenthesis at this stage. It is a subordinate sentence that does not necessarily demand real attention at this point.

Whereas this might be the case purely syntactically, however, the qualifying clause about the chosen place is crucial at this point. It is introduced in its fullest form the first time that it appears, bringing in all the motifs that will appear later, thus announcing the concept of the chosen place at the very outset as something natural, a given, something that does not need explanation, substantiation, or further comment.[9] The idea

---

9. See the previous chapter for the mention of the different forms of the centralization formula. Deut 12:5–7 is usually considered the last of the centralization laws

of the divinely chosen place is thus simply slipped in, and the fact that it does not necessarily demand attention syntactically allows it to pass by undetected, so to say, and without questioning. It slips into the subconscious.

The verbs of action in Deut 12:5 are "seek" (דרש) and "go" (בוא). The actions are verbs of motion, directed towards *the place*. In initiating movement toward one point, these verbs set the stage for the construction of *centralization*. The movement from a periphery toward a center is initiated here, and will continue to gain force throughout Deut 12.

It is quite an odd contrast that is set up between Deut 12:2–3 and 12:5–6. The first has only verbs of destruction in a strong position, as we observed above. The second has verbs of motion, in a secondary, latter position in the sentence, standing in stark contrast to the verbs of destruction to strike the nations in the verses preceding it.

Although motifs of place and name of God appear in both sentences, the nature of the motifs in 12:2–3 contrasts with that of 12:5–6. First there is the contrast between "*all the places* where the nations which you shall dispossess served their gods, on the high mountains and on the hills and under every green tree" and "the place which YHWH your God has chosen." Then there is the contrast between the command to obliterate the names of the gods of the nations from all of their places in 12:3, and the reference to the place which YHWH will "put his name," in 12:5:

והבאתם שמה
עלתיכם וזבחיכם
ואת מעשרתיכם ואת תרומת ידכם
ונדריכם ונדבתיכם ובכרת בקרכם וצאנכם

Deuteronomy 12:6 lists up what the Israelites will bring *to* the place: they will bring (בוא, Hiphil) their burnt offerings and sacrifices, their tithes and their donations, their votive gifts, their freewill offerings, and the firstlings of their herds and their flocks. The obvious feature of this list is the emphasis that is put on the act and the place, "and *there* you shall bring." There is no interest on the part of the author/speaker at this point to explicate further the acts of sacrifice, how they should be carried out, or who shall do what. It seems as if the legislators considered it unnecessary to chronicle the details of the actual cultic acts.[10] The message in the

---

to be added to ch. 12, see, e.g., Römer, *The So-Called Deuteronomistic History*, 56–65, who considers vv. 2–7 to be probably from the Persian period, and cites support from the "Göttingen School" (p. 63). Scholars with different determinations of the dates of texts agree on the relative lateness of 12:2–7.

10. The explanation for this could either be that one should assume that Deuteronomy also assumes another code to supplement it, or that it considers the practice

commandment is that all these things on the list should be *brought to that place*.[11] With the next verse, one gets the impression that it is all a family affair. The only official who is mentioned is the Levite, but he is not prescribed any specific role.

When v. 7 is added, the feeling that we are in a completely different territory than either Exod 25–40 or the meticulous cultic legislation of Lev 1–7 grows even stronger:

ואכלתם־הם
לפני יהוה אלהיך
ושמחתם
בכל משלח ידכם
אתם ובתיכם
אשר ברכך יהוה אלהיך

There are another two commands here: *there you shall eat*, and *you shall rejoice*. The focus on the *place* continues through into this verse, with the specification of the adverb שם. The Israelites are to eat there, before YHWH, and to rejoice in all that their hands have done, and with their whole household, whom YHWH has blessed them with.

At the same time, another contrast could be pointed out between vv. 2–3 and vv. 4–6. In designating the objects that are to be destroyed, vv. 2–3 give a description of a cult site that is quite specific, even though the terms are generic. The "places" of the "nations" exist on "mountain tops," "high hills," and "under leafy trees," they have altars, are populated with stelae, *asherim*, and have molten figures. In contrast, the "place" to which the Israelites are commanded to bring their sacrifices, is completely non-descript and has no objects. It is not even specified that the "place" should not have these things, as we do find in Deut 16:21–22. However, Deut 12:27 does reveal that an altar is assumed. The contrast between Deut 2–3 and 4–7 is stark, nevertheless.

Deuteronomy 12:7 ends with a description of YHWH as the one who has blessed them with gifts. The reason given for the command to perform the religious duties at *the place which YHWH chooses*, is that when they do this, they shall rejoice, be happy, be blessed (Deut 12:7). The promise of rejoicing is the reason given for the command. They shall do these things—and rejoice. As we shall continue to see below, the

---

of these sacrifices and acts as otherwise known. It could also be that it did not consider the details of the performance of the actual cultic acts particularly interesting or important.

11. The same feature is found in the other places that regulate the offering of firstlings: Deut 15:19–20 and 26:1–2.

command to rejoice in the blessings of YHWH is a crucial component of the rhetorical technique of the book of Deuteronomy.[12]

To summarize the law of Deut 12:2–7, the emphasis of the rhetoric here is: you shall *not* do as they do, but do such and such. The "they" is defined by referring to the acts that the Israelites are to carry out against *them*, the nations, as commanded in Deut 12:2–3. These are all acts of violence: to destroy, cut down, break, shatter and burn. This way of defining the relationship draws a line between "them," the nations, and "you," the Israelites, between *their* religion and the Israelites' religion, *their* places and the *place which YHWH chooses*, the places of the names of *their* gods, and the place of YHWH's name.

The first command to the Israelites regarding worship is that they shall seek out and go to the place which YHWH will choose. This is set in deliberate contrast to the command to destroy the places of the nations. Finally, there is the positive command to eat and rejoice, activities that are to be carried out *at* the *place*. The content of the positive commands in Deut 12:5–7 circles around the concept of *the place*, with the focus on bringing the cultic gifts to the place, and on the act of eating there, at the place. There are a number of verbs of motion: seek, go, bring— all related to the *place*. The centralization formula itself thus seems to remain in the center even though it is syntactically subordinate throughout. All of the movement in the text serves to draw up a movement toward the center for Israel.

Deuteronomy 12:2–7 contains almost all of the motifs that we will find in the rest of Deut 12: the chosen place, the emphasis on doing the cultic acts at *the place*, the listing of the cultic acts, the command to eat and rejoice, and the mention of the household. With the "centralization" formula in its most extensive shape, and the mention of all of the acts that in later occurrences will be included, these verses are like an initial summary, introducing the motifs that will later be elaborated.[13]

Deuteronomy 12:2–7 also has the important function of drawing up the contrast between the religions of the nations, which must be destroyed, and the religion of the Israelites, which should not be like the religion of the nations. As we shall see, Deut 12 also ends with the theme of warning against the religion of the nations (Deut 12:29–32). Deuteronomy 12 opens and closes with this very important theme, which appears to make

---

12. The command to rejoice appears in Deut 12:7, 12, 18; 14:26; 16:11, 14, 15; 26:11; 27:7; 33:18. A command to rejoice for seven days accompanies the legislation on the festival of booths in Lev 23:40.
13. I am in agreement with Lohfink here, in "Zur deuteronomischen Zentralisationsformel."

up something like the rationale for the whole legislation. The same structure can be found in Deut 7.[14]

Deuteronomy 12:8–12

The next section begins by bringing the reader/audience back to the narrative reality of the plains of Moab:

> You shall not act as we are acting here today, all of us according to our own desires; for you have not yet come into the rest and the possession that YHWH your God is giving you. (Deut 12:8–9)

The Israelites have heard the first command to dispossess the nations and fulfill YHWH's command of worship at *the place*. They have had the first taste, as has any reader who identifies with them, albeit imaginary, of the good times to come, when they will eat and rejoice with their households before YHWH. Then the Israelites are reminded of their present situation: they are wandering in the wilderness; they have not yet crossed the Jordan and entered the land that has been promised to them as their inheritance. With Deut 12:8 the implied audience on the other side of the Jordan is quickly brought back to their present reality, to the vulnerable, marginal experience that later generations of readers/hearers in multiple situations no doubt could identify with:

לא יעשון ככל
אשר אנחנו עשים פה היום
איש כל־הישר בעיניו
כי לא־באתם
עד־עתה אל־המנוחה ואל־הנחלה
אשר־יהוה אלהיך נתן לך

Deuteronomy 12:8 begins, as Deut 12:4 did, with a negation (12:4 read, "You shall not do this to YHWH your God"). After the positive formulation in 12:5–7 of how they *are* to worship, 12:8 reads, "You shall not do (לא יעשון) according to all that we are doing here this day, every man doing whatever is right in his own eyes."

After having contrasted the laws of correct worship for Israel with the "nations" in Deut 12:2–7, the religious legislation is now set in contrast to the ways of Israel before they enter the land. Now, in their present state, the Israelites have not yet entered the land, thus they have no law, and are acting according to their own judgment. The phrase איש כל־הישר בעיניו is best known from the book of Judges, where the explanation for the state of chaos is that there is no king in the land. In Deuteronomy this

---

14. For more on the role of Deut 7, see Chapter 7, on divine election as a principle of authority.

motif of chaos is used in a subtly different way. The implication from the context of Deuteronomy is that when they enter the land, the worship at the chosen place will provide the safeguard from the present chaos. With this reference in Deuteronomy in mind, the whole concept of the king as someone who could be a safeguard from chaos could be interpreted ironically. The kings of Israel and Judah, even the best kings, were not able to protect Israel from YHWH's punishment. The story of the kings of Israel and Judah is one of continuous, and ultimate, failure. It could be that the writer(s) of Deuteronomy are playing on this, and setting the experience of failure in contrast to their projection of a utopian new existence in the land, with the law as the new guarantee against chaos.[15]

Whatever the case may be, it comes across clearly that the only true religious practice can be in the land that the Israelites have been given by YHWH. Deuteronomy 12:8–9 implies that they have not yet come to their inheritance, but later they will, and then they shall not do as they are doing now, before the time of the crossing. This aspect, which is brought into clarity through the explicit contrasting of the present ways of the Israelites and future cultic practice, makes it very clear that the laws that are being given are tied closely to the promise of land and protection once they enter the land:

ועברתם את־הירדן
וישבתם בארץ
אשר־יהוה אלהיכם מנחיל אתכם
והניח לכם
מכל־איביכם מסביב
וישבתם־בטח

> When you cross over the Jordan and live in the land that YHWH your God is allotting to you, and when he gives you rest from your enemies all around so that you live in safety.

Deuteronomy 12:10 sets up four conditions that must be fulfilled before the law can have validity, and comes out clearly in four clauses in the perfect continuum mode. Deut 12:10 begins: "But when you cross (ועברתם)..." This recalls Deut 11:31, which can be seen as an introduction to Deut 12. It is after they cross the River Jordan that the commands are to be observed. This is one of the conditions that must be present before the law can take effect. The phrases in 12:10 are very important in defining the boundaries of Israel in its relationship to YHWH through the law. The validity of the law is bound to the time after they enter the land; it is separated from the era of the wilderness, and it is made clear that it

---

15. The idea of kingship is explored more fully in Chapter 8, below.

is separated from the religion of the "nations" who occupy the land and who must be destroyed (Deut 12:2–3).

The second precondition is that they must settle the land. The land is further qualified as the land that YHWH has passed on to them as inheritance. This way of qualifying ארץ in different variations is very typical in Deuteronomy, and there never seems to be a chance to forget this point.[16]

Another interesting point to note in Deut 12:10 is the clause mentioning "when he gives you rest from all your enemies round about, so that you live in safety." This is the third precondition listed in this verse. The previously announced preconditions have required that the Israelites cross the river and settle the land. Now, in addition, they are to wait until there is peace. This is another specification drawing the boundaries for the conditions under which the law can be practiced and have validity.

The motif of "peace from enemies" as a precondition is also found in 2 Samuel and 1 Kings. At the beginning of the temple building narrative the reader is reminded, through Solomon's message to Hiram, that David could not build the temple because YHWH did not give him rest from his wars. Now, however, Solomon is in a position to fulfill this promise to build a "house for YHWH" (1 Kgs 5:3–5).

The appearance of this motif in Kings is another example of the type of links that exist between Deuteronomy and the books of Samuel and Kings.[17] It is not simple to determine the nature of the relationship between the two appearances of the motif. It is part of a network of motifs that connect Deuteronomy and Kings, and especially the Solomon narrative. For now, let me just test one thought. The reference to "rest from the enemies" could perhaps be read as a warning about a future story of failure. If this is a necessary precondition for keeping the law, when can the law ever be valid? When is there ever really "rest"? The very deliberate reference to it in 1 Kgs 5:3 could be read ironically, since the reign of Solomon, in spite of being peaceful, ends with his apostasy, deferred punishment, and a series of enemy attacks.

16. E.g. Deut 3:20; 8:10; 9:23.
17. On the motif about "rest from the enemies" very curious argumentation is put forth by A. Rofé in "The Strata of the Law about the Centralization of Worship in Deuteronomy and the History of the Deuteronomic Movement," in *Congress Volume: Uppsala 1971* (VTSup 22; Leiden: Brill, 1972), 221–26 (223–24). He fails to convince that the reference in Kings must be the one that the author of Deuteronomy has in mind, whereas the motif in Joshua is merely a "mechanical addition of an ancient scribe who stood under the influence of the Dtr. Phraseology."

It seems that trying to read the one reference in light of the other leads to many problems. A simpler way out is to read Deut 12:10 in light of its own context, where "rest from enemies" most likely refers to its many commands to conquer and settle the land. Further, the motif of "rest from the enemies" is also found in a number of other texts of conquest, such as in the story of the tribes of Reuben, Gad, and the half-tribe of Manasseh and their role in helping their brothers to conquer the land in Num 32 (also referred to in Josh 1:15), and in Deut 25:19, in reference to the command to annihilate the Amalekites.

The final precondition in Deut 12:10 is a follow-up of the third: they must dwell in safety, securely, free from their enemies, and following the commands of YHWH. Finally, when they have crossed the Jordan, live in the land they have inherited, when they dwell in safety, *then* "there will be (והיה) the place which YHWH your God will choose to let his name dwell there,"

והיה המקום
אשר־יבחר יהוה אלהיכם בו לשכן שמו שם
שמה תביאו את כל־
אשר אנכי מצוה אתכם
עולתיכם וזבחיכם מעשרתיכם ותרמ ידכם
וכל מבחר נדריכם אשר תדרו ליהוה

> then you shall bring everything that I command to *the place which YHWH your God will choose as a dwelling for his name*: your burnt offerings and your sacrifices, your tithes and your donations, and all your choice votive gifts that you vow to YHWH.

This sentence, beginning with והיה המקום is perhaps the most explicit direct reference to the *place* in Deut 12. As we have pointed out, the clauses containing the "centralization" formulae are always a part of an attributive clause, remaining syntactically subordinate.[18] Even here in Deut 12:11, though at first sight it may seem as if the formula is part of a main clause, it is in fact a type of adverbial clause that remains subordinate to the following clause, defining the time at which the offerings can be brought. This is reflected in the NRSV translation.

When all the preconditions of Deut 12:10 are in place, then there shall be the place, and to it, they shall bring (יביאו) all that YHWH commands. The list of cultic acts does not add any more detail than the first list in Deut 12:6. It is wholly clear that the emphasis is on the place, and not on the cultic acts. One may assume that the content and procedure for the sacrifices and offerings are known. What is important at this point in the

---

18. Weippert, "Den Ort, den Jahwe erwählen wird," 80.

legislation is to make clear that these offerings and sacrifices shall take place at the chosen place, after the preconditions have been met.

Finally, as in Deut 12:7, which closes the previous section, this section also ends with an admonition to rejoice before YHWH, with the entire household. As in Deut 12:7 above, the reason given for the command is that they shall rejoice (שׂמח). This time, in 12:12, the members of the household are also listed:

ושמחתם לפני יהוה אלהיכם
אתם ובניכם ובנתיכם ועבדיכם ואמהתיכם והלוי
אשר בשעריכם כי אין לו חלק ונחלה אתכם

And you shall rejoice before YHWH your God,
you and your sons and your daughters, your menservants and your maidservants, and the Levite
that is within your towns, since he has no portion or inheritance with you.

If we look at Deut 12:8–12 as a whole, we can say that the rhetorical emphasis is: you shall not do as *now*, but *when*...you cross, and dwell, and have rest, *then* the cultic activity can take place at *the place*. Whereas Deut 12:4–7 drew the boundaries between the nations and Israel, Deut 12:8–12 draws the boundaries between the present and a time in the future when the conditions are right for practicing the law. At this future point in time, then there will be the *place*, to which they shall bring offerings, the tithe etc. Only the verb "bring" (יביאו) is explicit here, but all types of gifts, offerings, and sacrifices are listed. So whereas in Deut 12:4–7 all types of acts were specified, "do," "seek," "go," "bring," "offer offerings," "eat," here only the verb "bring" is specified. The promise of rejoicing with the whole household is given again, as in Deut 12:7, and this time the members of the household are specified.

Deuteronomy 12:13–28: Laws Governing Sacrifice, Gift Offerings, and Non-Sacrificial Slaughter
This next section begins with a warning, emphasizing not to offer the burnt sacrifice at any random place:

השמר לך פן־תעלה עלתיך
בכל־מקום אשר תראה
כי אם־המקום
אשר־יבחר יהוה באחד שבטיך
שם תעלה עלתיך
ושם תעשה כל אשר אנכי מצוך

> Take care that you do not offer your burnt offerings at any place you happen to see. But only at *the place which YHWH will choose* in one of your tribes—there you shall offer your burnt offerings and there you shall do everything I command you. (Deut 12:13–14)

No mistake can be made about *where* the religious duties should be performed. The duties should be performed, not anywhere, but at *the place*. Neither is there any question that the command about *the place* is extremely important. They are not to make burnt sacrifices (עלה) at any place (בכל־מקום) but at *the* place (המקום). The deliberate contrasting of כל־מקום and המקום echoes this contrast made in the opening of Deut 12, where the many places of the nations was contrasted with the one place of the Israelites.

Again, the text specifies in a summary way what they shall do at the place: they shall sacrifice the עלה and do (עשה) all that YHWH commands. The text contains some nice alliteration here. It is not entirely clear whether Deut 12:13–14 should be read as belonging to the preceding or the following. It can be read as transitional, picking up on the motif of burnt offerings, and providing a transition to the provision on non-sacrificial slaughter. As a contrast to the previous section, the second person singular is used, instead of the plural. Traditionally, it has been read as an independent unit that perhaps was the oldest part of Deut 12.[19]

---

19. There seems to be consensus on dating Deut 12:13–18 (19) to the earliest stage of development. See, e.g., Römer, *The So-Called Deuteronomistic History*, 57–61; Halpern, "The Centralization Formula in Deuteronomy," 27. Although many of the suggestions seem to make sense according to the various criteria posited, I find it difficult to be convinced that we have access to the text's growth process. The extent to which scholars connect the concept of "cult centralization" to Josiah is made clear when we discover that those who argue for an early date of Deuteronomy do so by saying that it was not concerned with centralization (e.g. A. Welch and others, see Chapter 1). More recently, a similar argument has been posed for a separation of Deut 12 into several layers. In arguing for a date to the time of Hezekiah for Deut 12:13–19, M. Rose proposes that the phrase "in one of your tribes" in v. 14 was added, with vv. 20–27, in the time of Josiah, and that these verses only then came to be concerned with centralization of the cult to Jerusalem; see the reference to and critique of Rose's argument in T. Veijola, "Deuteronomismusforschung zwischen Tradition und Innovation (I)," *ThR* 67 (2002): 273–327 (285–86). Rose's methodology has also been criticized earlier, with respect to Deut 12, in Lohfink, "Fortschreibung?," 131, in which Lohfink interrogates and very honestly debates the problems and merits of various methodologies for reconstructing the history of the text; this article also contains one of the best arguments in support for a probable earliest date for 12:13–19.

As the text stands, what does seem clear about this section is that there has been a movement in the implied audience, from standing outside the land on the plains of Moab, to the future time when they will be in the land. In Deut 12:13–19, the Israelites seem to have settled the land already, living in towns and villages with city gates and owning cattle and other animals. The formula of the chosen place focuses on where one is allowed to "do" the burnt sacrifice and where one is allowed to eat the sacrificial gifts and offerings. Although there is also legislation about what can be eaten and what should not be eaten, we notice again that it is the *place* of activity that is given primary emphasis.

Deuteronomy 12:15–16 appears in a way as a sort of parenthesis in the present shape of the text, and concerns non-sacrificial slaughter, for which it is not necessary to be clean or to do it at *the place*. The idea of non-sacrificial slaughter of domestic animals is introduced for the first time here, and is a natural consequence of the centralization command.[20] The detail of pouring out blood is introduced here. The appearance of legislation about non-sacrificial slaughter seems to become subordinated and in turn becomes part of the contrasting background for the reemphasis on what cannot be eaten in the towns (gates), of the tithe, firstlings, or other gift offerings. Regulations for non-sacrificial slaughter, including the law about pouring out the blood, are thus introduced in this context as something quite natural. It follows from the limitation of ritual slaughter that non-ritual slaughter must then be allowed, and commented on. See also Deut 15:21–23, where any animal that is supposed to be sacrificed as a firstling, that has a flaw, also may be eaten as non-sacrificial meat.

Deuteronomy 12:17–19 continues the motif of eating, and brings the focus back to the law pertaining to religious practices at the *place*. Once again, a negative command is followed by a positive one, as we have seen in several previous cases:

> Nor may you eat within your towns the tithe of your grain, your wine, and your oil, the firstlings of your herd and your flocks, any of your votive gifts that you vow, your freewill offerings, or your donations; these you shall eat in the presence of YHWH your God at *the place which YHWH your God will choose*, you together with your son and your daughter, your male and female slaves, and the Levites resident in your towns, rejoicing in the presence YHWH your God in all your undertakings. Take care that you do not neglect the Levite as long as you live in your land. (Deut 12:17–19)

---

20. For more details on this provision, see, e.g., J. Milgrom, "Profane Slaughter and a Formulaic Key to the Composition of Deuteronomy," *HUCA* 47 (1976): 1–17.

In Deut 12:17, following the law allowing non-sacrificial slaughter, legislation follows on what they may *not* eat (לא־תוכל לאכל) in their own cities: the tithe of the grain, wine and oil, the firstlings of the flock, the votive gifts, the freewill offerings, or the donations. Again, as in 12:4, 8, and 13, a new specification and contrast is begun with a negation.

They are not to eat these things at home, but they are to eat them before YHWH at the *place*, together with the whole household (as in Deut 12:12, the members of the household are listed, together with the Levite). The implications of these verses are that even though, as a consequence of centralization, provisions are made to allow slaughter and the eating of meat in the provincial towns, the tithe and other gifts are still to be brought to the central place.

It is usually observed by scholars that Deuteronomy is not interested in sacrificial religion. I think this point has been in danger of being exaggerated. The importance of cult and ritual is clear in that cultic legislation comes first in the legal body of Deuteronomy. It is true that there is not the preoccupation with exact methods and with detail, such as we find in Leviticus and Numbers. However, the explanation for this could be that it was not considered necessary to repeat these, since they were already described, or else, they were presupposed as well known. The sacrifices are mentioned by name, and other gifts and offerings as well as the tithe. One aspect that is not mentioned specifically in Deuteronomy is the incense offering.

Further legislation about the tithe and firstlings is found spread out in different parts of Deuteronomy, and the centralization formula is consistently a part of it each time.[21] The legislation is thoroughly consequential when it comes to applying the idea of the "chosen place" to all laws that have to do with cultic practice.

We can now summarize Deut 12:13–19. As we have observed for each section in Deut 12, Deut 12:13–14 again provides boundaries for the practice of the law. The rhetorical emphasis here is: they shall not make the burnt offerings at *every place*, but at *the place*. In the two preceding sections, boundaries were drawn between the nations and Israel and between the present and a future time. Now it is drawn between *every* place and *the* place. Summarizing the thrust of Deut 12:13–19, then, the command is: "Not at *every* place but at *the place*, they are to *offer* and *do* all that YHWH commands." The acts that YHWH demands are to *bring* all

---

21. For the tithe, this means a system of turning the tithed goods into money, and then turning it into goods again once at "the place" (Deut 14:22–26). For firstlings, see 15:19–20 and 26:1–2.

that he commands, *rejoice*, *offer* the burnt offering, and *do* all that he commands—all a repetition of previous verbs of action.

A new topic comes up in Deut 12:15–16, which deals with non-sacrificial slaughter. This is exempted from the mandate to slaughter at the "chosen place," and is a law that seems to become necessary as a consequence of the centralization of sacrifice. Otherwise the law would have had to advocate the practice of a type of vegetarianism, with only a few meats allowed, such as wild game. This law is neatly tucked into the law on cultic sacrifices at the chosen place.

Picking up on the motif of slaughter and eating, Deut 12:17–18 again brings the focus back to the *place*, closing off this section with an emphasis on where one should or should not eat specific things: the tithe, firstlings, and vowed offerings may *not* be eaten at home, but must be eaten at *the place*. So, whereas the reality of distance opened up for the legislation non-sacrificial slaughter and the eating of meat that is not sacrificial, this secularization does not extend to the tithe and first-fruits. The new aspect of distance from home that is implied by the centralization command instead signals the expectation of specific legislation on these topics, which are treated in later chapters in Deuteronomy. Deuteronomy 12 thus announces topics that will later be treated in more detail in the legislation of later chapters. Finally, v. 19 reminds the audience of the Levite, forming a kind of chorus that we found also closing off the sections of vv. 2–7 and vv. 8–12.

Deuteronomy 12:13–14 focused on bringing and offering. Deuteronomy 12:17–18 focuses on eating, and is set in a context of what can be eaten where. This is the difference in emphasis compared to Deut 12:13–14, which emphasized where the עלה should be sacrificed. The two parts frame the section on what they *may* eat in the cities. The promise that they shall rejoice is consistent with all the preceding sections.

Deuteronomy 12:20–28

Deuteronomy 12:20 contains yet another specification of the time when the validity of the law begins. Previously there were the conditions of when they cross the Jordan, when they possess the land and settle there, and when the enemies give them rest (Deut 11:31; 12:1, 9, 10). In Deut 12:20 the text adds, "when YHWH enlarges your territory, as he has promised you." Again it is concerned with the land, borders, and space that are promised to be given the Israelites. The land is a necessary precondition for the practicing of the laws.

Proceeding on to the next "centralization" formula, we find in Deut 12:21 an arrangement for slaughter in case the *place* is too far away:

When YHWH your God enlarges your territory, as he has promised you, and you say, "I am going to eat some meat," because you wish to eat meat, you may eat meat whenever you have the desire. If *the place where YHWH your God will choose to put his name* is too far from you, and you slaughter as I have commanded you any of your herd or flock that YHWH has given you, then you may eat within your towns whenever you desire. Indeed, just as gazelle or deer is eaten, so you may eat it; the unclean and the clean alike may eat it. Only be sure that you do not eat the blood; for the blood is the life, and you shall not eat the life with the meat. Do not eat it, so that all may go well with you and your children after you, because you do what is right in the sight of YHWH. But the sacred donations that are due from you, and your votive gifts, you shall bring to *the place which YHWH will choose*. You shall present your burnt offerings, both the meat and the blood, on the altar of YHWH your God; the blood of your other sacrifices shall be poured out beside the altar of YHWH your God, but the meat you may eat. Be careful to obey all these words that I command you today, so that it may go well with you and with your children after you forever, because you will be doing what is good and right in the sight of YHWH your God. (Deut 12:20–28)

Deuteronomy 12:21–25 contains much that is identical to Deut 12:15–16. It contains the law sanctioning the slaughtering and consumption of any animal, only not the blood, adding the ordinance to pour the blood out on the ground like water.[22] Deuteronomy 12:15–16 emphasizes what may be eaten where, whereas Deut 12:22–25 emphasizes the distance to the chosen place. After permitting non-sacrificial slaughter in Deut 12:21–25, the text goes on to specify the things that they *are* to do at the *place*. They are to take all the gifts that are due YHWH and bring them to the *place*. Verse 27 is the only verse in this chapter that mentions the altar of YHWH. In fact, it is the verse that is most detailed in cultic instruction, the only verse that actually specifies particular ritual acts.

Deuteronomy 12:21–25 is a repetition of the law on non-sacrificial slaughter in vv. 15–16. The difference here is that the condition for it, namely that it is too far to the *place*, is specified. Even though this is a repetition, it thus also serves as a further specification of how to practice the commands. If the place is too far away, they may slaughter animals to eat. However, as we read in Deut 12:26–27, the holy things (קדשים),

---

22. Baruch Halpern has argued that of these two versions concerning non-sacrificial slaughter, Deut 12:13–19 is the older version, thus arguing for two main strata in the centralization laws. One of his points is that Deut 12:15–16 do not contain the clause about the distance being too far as the criterion for profane slaughter, whereas this is the case for v. 21. The two versions are in tension with each other, reflecting different literary strata. This may very well be true, but the repetitions are set in different contexts, thus adding different emphases.

they must take, and go (תשא ובאת) to the place, and do the burnt offering, the meat and the blood; for the other sacrifices, they shall pour out the blood and eat the meat. The motif of blood in the offering is new here, and the word שפכ, "pour out," or "shed," is new and has not been mentioned before. It picks up on the specification about pouring out the blood in the legislation of non-sacrificial slaughter.

To sum up this section, then, Deut 12:21 brings in a new type of quite specific condition for the implementation of the laws: if the place is too far, then you may practice non-sacrificial slaughter. Deuteronomy 12:22–25 is concerned with the particulars of non-sacrificial slaughter. Verse 26 picks up the conditional in v. 21, with the specification of what is still, even though it is far, necessary to take to *the place*. "These things" are the holy things, the votive gifts, which they are required to *take*, and *go* to the place, and there *make offerings*, *pour out* (השפכ), and *eat*. The motif of pouring out blood appears again, as in Deut 12:23–24. In this last section there is no promise of rejoicing.

Deuteronomy 12:28 closes the giving of laws with a hortatory call to observe and hear (שמר ושמעת) all these words (כל־הדברים האלה), that it may go well. Deuteronomy 12:8 drew the border at the River Jordan, with the explicit command ordering the Israelites not to do as they are now, "every man doing whatever is right in his own eyes." Deuteronomy 12:28 closes with the promise of blessing when they do what is good and right in the eyes of YHWH their God (תעשה הטוב והישר בעיני יהוה אלהיך). This verse forms a transition to the closing verses of Deut 12.

Deuteronomy 12:29–31: Warning Against Idolatry
Deuteronomy 12 opened with the command to destroy the religious sites and objects of the "nations," and set the Israelite laws of worship in contrast to this. The chapter closes with a warning not to follow the ways of the "nations":

> When YHWH your God has cut off before you the nations whom you are about to enter to dispossess them, when you have dispossessed them and live in their land, take care that you are not snared into imitating them, after they have been destroyed before you: do not inquire concerning their gods, saying "How did these nations worship their gods? I also want to do the same." You must not do the same for YHWH your God, because every abhorrent thing that YHWH hates they have done for their gods. They would even burn their sons and their daughters in the fire to their gods. (Deut 12:29–31)

Deuteronomy 12:29 introduces this section yet again with a description of the time at which the Israelites will master the land, this time is described as "When YHWH your God has cut off before you the nations whom you are about to enter to dispossess them, when you have dispossessed them and live in their land." The verbs of destruction and violence that we found in Deut 12:2–3 appear again, and the description of the "nations" in terms of dispossession and the Israelites' possession (with the verbal root ירש) and dwelling in their land, again capture the relationship between them in terms of power.

As religious law the "statutes and ordinances" are given a context that places the Israelites in a position of privilege. This is a gift from YHWH. They are given the land as an inheritance; they are given protection to destroy the nations, and are commanded to obey YHWH's laws. The protection and blessings of YHWH are intrinsically bound to the observation of the law.[23]

Centralization Affirmed

Through this reading of the text, we have been able to see that the election phrase in Deut 12 is used in a way that brings the focus on the command to perform cultic activities at the "place." The various repetitions support the centralization command and formulate it from different angles. Different aspects of the religious duties are emphasized, such as going to the place, bringing gifts, doing what YHWH commands, offering sacrifices, eating the meat, rejoicing.

Each formulation of the command to perform religious duties at the "place that YHWH chooses" has a different rhetorical emphasis that contributes to focusing the space within which the laws have validity. This is attained by contrasting the correct way with something undesirable. As such, Deut 12:4–7 emphasizes the contrast with the nations, and also contains a summary of the acts that the Israelites are to perform at the *place*. Deuteronomy 12:8–12 contrasts the time now with the time in the future, when they shall do the duties. Deuteronomy 12:13–19 emphasizes the place itself. They shall not worship at *every* place, but only at *the* place. It also provides provisions for non-sacrificial slaughter, in order to accommodate the Israelites' future "places" in the land. Deuteronomy 12:20–27 emphasizes which things can be done at home, in their places, and which things must be done at *the* place. We see that each section brings something new, and that the repetitions are crucial in gradually formulating the exact preconditions for the proper practice of the law.

---

23. For further discussion of the close interdependence between the relationships of Israel to the nations, Israel to YHWH, YHWH's gifts to Israel, and Israel's duty to be obedient to YHWH, see Chapter 7.

The different introductions to each section serve to draw up the space within which the law has validity. Simultaneously, each section serves to define the relationship between the Israelites and their various counterparts. In the course of ch. 12, relationships are organized between Israel and the nations, the Israelites' existence now in the wilderness and in the future in the land, between every place and *the* place and ultimately between the people of Yhwh and Yhwh. All of this happens and is put into effect within the framework of cultic regulations. It also becomes clear that the power of centralization is achieved through the emphasis on divine election of the place. It is this act of divine sanction and authority that underpins the whole scheme. The effect of this is to create a new world, a new order of meaning, one in which Israel is commanded to rejoice.

Chapter 4

"JERUSALEM" IN THE FORMER PROPHETS

As we saw in Chapter 2, Jerusalem as YHWH's "chosen city" becomes constructed in the book of Kings as a place of privilege and divine protection. This status is not enough to protect it from destruction, however, and the privileged status ends up being ironically turned around against the city. The present chapter will investigate the construction of "Jerusalem" in the Former Prophets, book by book. Joshua and Judges are not concerned with Jerusalem to any real extent, as we shall see. This investigation will highlight the distinctive ways in which Samuel and Kings each perceives Jerusalem, by mapping out how "Jerusalem," "city of David," and "Zion" are portrayed in these books. Among the reasons for doing this is the need for clarification when scholars claim that the deuteronomistic historians were interested in centralization of the cult to Jerusalem. The eagerness to identify this intent in the so-called Deuteronomistic History has perhaps colored scholars' view of Jerusalem and its role in these books. Jerusalem as a specific location in time and place is somehow assumed by scholars, though not always clearly based on the texts. What has perhaps been overlooked is how "Jerusalem" is actually portrayed and what role it plays in the books of the Former Prophets. This inquiry will also help to demonstrate the distinctive character of "Jerusalem" in the book of Kings, and thus help us to further our understanding of the meaning of the "chosen city" in Kings.

But also, the simple investigation of "Jerusalem" in the books of the Former Prophets is yet another avenue into the distinctive character of each of these books, and of some of the ways in which they relate to each other and to other books. Following this one motif may yield pertinent insight into the story that unfolds across these books. As the investigation of cultic and ritual activity in the next chapter will also show, the narrative that unfolds over these books is not characterized by a high degree of consistency. The investigation of "Jerusalem" will add to the total picture that is emerging.

Jerusalem in Joshua, Judges, and 1 Samuel

The six references to Jerusalem in Joshua and Judges probably all qualify as anachronistic (Judg 1:7, 8) or explanatory. In Josh 15:8; 18:28, and Judg 19:10 the former town of Jebus is identified as Jerusalem to a present narrative audience. Joshua 15:63 and Judg 1:21 are both references to how the Israelites did not drive out the Jebusites, but that they live together in Jerusalem "to this day." In Joshua and Judges, therefore, Jerusalem is identified as the town that was formerly Jebus, and as one of the towns of Benjamin. In the books, it is clear that the narrative present is a time in which the town exists or is known as Jerusalem. Because the story is set in the past, however, the place known today as Jerusalem is identified as a town formerly known as Jebus.

The one reference to Jerusalem in 1 Samuel (17:54) appears in the story about the young David's slaying of the Philistine giant. At the end of the battle, David is said to have brought Goliath's head to Jerusalem, a clear anachronism. Perhaps this note now serves as an early pointer in the narrative about the close connections that eventually will be developed between David and Jerusalem?

We observe at this point that in the first half of the Former Prophets there is little or no concern with Jerusalem. Jerusalem is mentioned in order to identify the city that used to belong to the Jebusites in the past, and is not connected in these narratives to any idea of a place chosen by YHWH, either for cultic activity or as a place of his protection. To the extent that there is a concern in these books with a place that YHWH will choose (barely), or a central sanctuary, there does not seem to be a concern to limit cultic activity to that one place.[1]

Jerusalem in 2 Samuel

"Jerusalem" appears over thirty times in 2 Samuel following the narrative of its conquest in 2 Sam 5. Before we examine 2 Sam 8–24, however, we will take a look at chs. 6 and 7, which are of special interest to us even though they do not mention Jerusalem.

---

1. As examples, we may mention the command to build an altar in Deut 27:5–8, which is followed up in Josh 4 and also in Josh 8:30–35. We also observed in Chapter 2 that Josh 9:27 refers to "the place which YHWH will choose." Further, Joshua contains a commandment to build a sanctuary in Shiloh. See further on these texts in the following chapter, Chapter 5.

The "City of David" in 2 Samuel and Kings

The expression "city of David" appears in 2 Sam 5 and 6. Second Samuel 5:6–10 relates the actual conquest of city. This text, though it has some relatively incomprehensible sections,² clearly narrates that David takes (לקד, 5:7) and settles (יש׳, 5:9) the "stronghold of Zion," and names it "the city of David." Both before and after these verses, "Jerusalem" is mentioned; as the place from which David reigns over Israel (5:5), as the town of the Jebusites that David is attacking (5:6), and as the place that he settles after coming from Hebron (5:13). This narrative also clearly associates Jerusalem as the city that David captures and reigns from, with the names "Zion" and "City of David."

Second Samuel 6 does not mention Jerusalem by that name. This chapter describes how David and his men and "all the people with him" move the ark to the "city of David" from its sojourn at Baale-judah (Kiryat Shearim).³ At this point in the narrative, the ark has not been mentioned since 1 Sam 7:2, when it was deposited in Kiryat Shearim after being retrieved from the Philistines. One of the effects of 2 Sam 6 is to tie together the narrative of the capture of Jerusalem and its consolidation as David's powerbase in 2 Sam 5 with the story of the fate of the ark and its movement to a "home."

Second Samuel 6 then relates how, in spite of an initial set-back due to the harm caused to Uzzah when he touches it, the ark is finally brought to the city of David amidst much rejoicing. It is placed in a tent pitched for it, after which David officiates in cultic acts of sacrifice. The term "city of David" thus becomes closely associated with the ark and the capture of the city.

Surprisingly, perhaps, the designation "city of David" does not appear very often in the narratives covering the reign of David. Besides the places mentioned already, it is only found otherwise in 1 Kgs 2:10, in the note recounting the burial of David. The preferred term for the city in 2 Samuel is "Jerusalem." We shall return to the investigation of "Jerusalem" after a few more remarks about the "city of David."

---

2. The textual problems of 2 Sam 5:8 concern the rendering of the Qere את־שהעורים שנאו נפש דוד, "those whom David hates," and the Kethib את־שהעורים שנאה נפש דוד, "those who hate David." Both expressions seem difficult to understand; for comment on these, see, e.g., P. K. McCarter, Jr., *II Samuel: A New Translation with Introduction, Notes and Commentary* (AB 9; New York: Doubleday, 1984), 135–41; A. F. Campbell, *2 Samuel* (FOTL 8; Grand Rapids: Eerdmans, 2005), 54.

3. See Chapter 5, below, on the "ark narrative."

The name "city of David" is also associated with the theme of the transition of the throne, or of the establishment of a new monarch. Shortly after the burial notice in 1 Kgs 2:10, the "city of David" is mentioned as the place that Solomon sets up for his wife, the daughter of Pharaoh, to live until he has built his own house and the walls of Jerusalem. As a fortified place, it serves as a transitional house for Solomon's family until Jerusalem has been properly fortified and a house built for the king there. Of interest to us is that, just as we found it embedded in the account of the establishment of David's throne in Jerusalem, we find the "city of David" at the transition to Solomon's reign as monarch. Further, we note that Solomon's Jerusalem replaces the "city of David" as the *locus* for his seat of power, his "house."

When this has all been done, and the temple has been built, Solomon brings the ark from "the city of David, which is Zion," to Jerusalem (1 Kgs 8:1), and brings the daughter of Pharaoh from the city of David to "her own house that Solomon had built for her" (1 Kgs 9:24). Somehow, with these acts, "Jerusalem" in Kings seems to be reconstituted as a place. It is now Solomon's Jerusalem, with palace and temple and walls. The moving of the ark into the temple from the "tent of David" marks a transition from David's time. This transition is associated with Solomon's building activities.

It is not so clear what it means, but I will add one more observation. In the opening of the Jeroboam narrative in 1 Kgs 11:27, Jeroboam is described as Solomon's foreman in the king's building activities involving forced labor. Specifically, the building of the Millo is mentioned. Curiously, the Millo is also mentioned in 9:24, where Pharaoh's daughter is described as moving from the city of David. In these two verses, the Millo could almost be seen as a sort of signal for Solomon's (eventually disastrous) building activities. At the same time, since the Millo is introduced in 2 Sam 5:9 describing David's conquest of city of David, these texts also tie in with the "city of David" and the transition from David's Jerusalem to Solomon's.

Following the Solomon narrative, references to the "city of David" in the rest of 1 and 2 Kings occur almost exclusively in the regnal summaries of the kings of Judah, saying that the king was buried in the "city of David." In the book of Kings, therefore, with the exception of the mentions in 1 Kgs 3–11 that tie in with the transition from the reign of David to Solomon, the "city of David" is associated with a royal burial place.

To summarize, the "city of David" in 2 Samuel and Kings is associated with three different but interrelated *themes*. First, it seems to be associated with the ark and the capture of the city. Second, it is associated with the theme of transition of the throne, or of establishment of a new monarch. This association is achieved through the way that the "city of David" figures in the establishment of David's new seat of power in Jerusalem, in recounting the transition from David to Solomon, and in the transition of the ark and the moving of Pharaoh's daughter from the "city of David" to the new buildings of Solomon. Third, and exclusively in Kings, the "city of David" is associated with a royal burial place. It is particularly interesting that the place that David names as his new center of power and the seat of his throne becomes the name used of the burial places of the future kings of Judah.

Sense of Place in 2 Samuel 7

Second Samuel 7 is an odd one out within the book. However, it has important motif connections with Kings and also some links with Deuteronomy.[4] For example, the chapter opens by observing that YHWH has given the king "rest from all his enemies around him" (cf. Deut 12:10).[5] David now sees it fit to build a permanent building for the ark of God, a "house for YHWH."

In Nathan's oracle (2 Sam 7:4–16), God promises an unnamed "place" for Israel, "I will appoint/set a place (שמתי מקום) for my people Israel and I will plant them, so that they may live in their own place..." (7:10). The word מקום might signal the sense of "chosen place" to some readers. If it does, however, this verse seems to convey more of a sense of a place among the nations or enemies, a space that is secure, rather than a chosen place for cultic practice such as that which Deuteronomy advocates. We note further that even the verse that most directly speaks of the future temple does not focus on the idea of limiting cultic practice at a chosen place, "He (David's offspring) shall build a house for my name, and I will establish the throne of his kingdom forever." It is the mutuality of

---

4. 2 Sam 7 was seen by literary critics as a late insertion because it did not fit in with the sources thought to be behind the book of Samuel. In the latter half of the twentieth century it was seen as a key chapter for redaction critics who saw it as a deuteronomistic text. See, for textual comment and a brief but thorough review of scholarly positions on this text, McCarter, *II Samuel*, 195–210, for comment on the text, and 210–31 for notes on scholarship.

5. As discussed in Chapter 3, above, this is one of the preconditions that Deut 12 demands must be fulfilled for worship to be practiced at "the chosen place." In 2 Samuel, this piece of information is contradicted by the next fifteen chapters, and by 1 Kgs 5:3–4, where it is explicitly stated that "rest from the enemies" was not achieved during the time of David. Chronicles does not give this detail in its parallel to 2 Sam 7, thereby avoiding this contradiction with the literary context (1 Chr 17:1).

the future house of God and the "house" of David that is in focus.⁶ In 2 Sam 7, the temple of Solomon and the chosen city of the book of Kings are close within the range of its conceptual world, but the "chosen place" of Deuteronomy, however, seems much more distant. Yet, even though Jerusalem is by now, in narrative time, the seat of David's throne, this chapter about the future "place" of Israel and house of God does not mention the city by any name. Somehow, the chapter that deals most explicitly with the promised "place" and "house" does not name it, whereas the chapters preceding and following abound in place names accounting for David's every move.

In 2 Sam 7 God also promises to make David a "house," that is, a dynasty. Importantly, however, the task of building a "house," as in "temple for YHWH," is relegated to his son, and thus postponed into the future. This chapter is ideologically important in the book of Samuel, and is the only time in the whole book that the idea of a future temple is elaborated on. David, in his response to Nathan's oracle, speaks to YHWH (7:18–29). This text has its difficulties.⁷ The main impression is, however, that David has forgotten about his original intent to build a house for YHWH, and Nathan's response in 2 Sam 7:3 has been completely negated by the lengthy oracle of 7:5–16. Instead, David in his response focuses on the honor bestowed on him by YHWH through the promise about *his* house, the future Davidic dynasty. This could be understood as a natural response to the fact that the building of a temple for YHWH has been postponed and will not be carried out by David. It also provides a transition to the rest of 2 Samuel, which is not concerned with the idea of building a temple at all.

In fact, the whole of ch. 7 is in many ways an intrusion into the flow of the story from ch. 6, and has of course been considered by source and redaction critics as belonging to a different source or a later addition. It is clear, in any way one reads the present text, that the idea of a future temple is fully announced here. This helps to connect the establishment of Jerusalem as the royal seat in 2 Sam 5:5 with the building of the temple in 1 Kings. The story of 2 Sam 7 also helps to explain why David goes on to fight wars for another fifteen chapters after 2 Sam 7:1 prematurely, readers now know, announced that he was settled and had been given rest.

---

6. See further on the "houses," R. Polzin, *David and the Deuteronomist: A Literary Study of the Deuteronomic History: Part III, 2 Samuel* (ISBL; Bloomington: Indiana University Press, 1993), 54–87. See also L. M. Eslinger, *House of God or House of David: The Rhetoric of 2 Samuel 7* (JSOTSup 164; Sheffield: JSOT, 1994).

7. See, e.g., McCarter, *II Samuel*, 232–41.

Jerusalem in 2 Samuel

Returning now to the survey of "Jerusalem," we will go back again to 2 Sam 5. In 1 Sam 5:5 Jerusalem appears for the first time in a summary of David's reign. This occurrence appears before the account of the actual capture of Jerusalem.

The verses recounting the capture of the city are confusing, but v. 6 makes it clear that it is "Jerusalem" that is being attacked. As we saw above, the next few lines refer to the city David captures as "Zion," "City of David," and "the city." In 2 Sam 5, Jerusalem is also established as the place of David's throne (5:5) after he captures it and moves there from Hebron. King Hiram even sends him cedar trees, carpenters, and masons, to build him a house (5:11), which becomes the cue for David to "know" (ידע) that YHWH has established him as king. The next verse tells of the concubines and wives that he took in Jerusalem, and the names of his children who were born to him in Jerusalem, reinforcing the idea of his "house" in Jerusalem in a way we will recognize in the Solomon narrative. The perception of David as king over all Israel leads to another war with the Philistines, in which David is successful, which serves to set up Jerusalem as the home base of his wars.

The theme of David's wars is picked up in 2 Sam 8 onward. From this point on, Jerusalem is referred to consistently over thirty times as a city from which David or other characters go out, to which they return and in which they stay.[8] In this sense, "Jerusalem" is the center point for action in 2 Samuel. It is contested ground. The place of David's throne is grappled over in complex ways with many characters involved, including YHWH.[9] Jerusalem is for a while in the hands of Absalom, son and usurper, but David regains it.

This complex story is not the focus of our attention here, but we observe that throughout, Jerusalem is not a place of explicit cultic activity. When the ark is first brought to the city of David, there is a ritual celebration, officiated by David (6:17). In the rest of the book, however, there is no preoccupation with ideas of how to worship, how not to worship, or of cultic infidelity to YHWH. This is in contrast to 1 Samuel, where Saul's disfavor with YHWH is cast in terms of cultic sin and in which ritual in warfare plays a more dominant role than in 2 Samuel.[10]

---

8. 2 Sam 8:7; 9:13; 10:14; 11:1, 12; 12:31; 14:23, 28; 15:8, 11, 14, 29, 37; 16:3, 15; 17:20; 19:20, 26, 34, 35; 20:2, 3, 7, 22; 24:8, 16.

9. Many fine literary studies on the David story are available; see, e.g., D. M. Gunn, *The Story of King David: Genre and Interpretation* (JSOTSup 8; Sheffield: JSOT, 1978); Polzin, *David and the Deuteronomist*.

10. E.g. 1 Sam 13:8–15 (Saul); 14:3 (ephod); 14:18 (the ark/some mss, ephod); 14:37 (divine inquiry); 14:51 (thummim); the taking of the booty in 1 Sam 15; the

Perhaps, with the idea of a house of YHWH postponed into the future by 2 Sam 7, the narrative can comfortably concentrate on other points of interest in the King David story. At the end of the book however, a concern for a place of cultic activity returns, with the episode of Araunah's threshing floor.[11] David buys this plot of land in order to offer sacrifices there to avert the plague. In 2 Samuel, this story is not explicitly connected to the future place of Solomon's temple. No reference is made to it in 1 Kings, as opposed to Chronicles, which explicitly ties these events together, as we will see below.

We can conclude that, as a whole, 2 Samuel is concerned neither with Jerusalem as a place of YHWH-worship, nor with cult and worship beyond a couple of significant episodes. Jerusalem is the seat of David's throne and a home base for his wars; it is a place that the characters stay in, go out from, or come back to. As such, in 2 Samuel the name "Jerusalem" does not explicitly imply a privileged place beyond being David's capital, the central fortified city of his expansive wars. In 2 Sam 6, which is concerned with the movement of the ark to Jerusalem, the preferred term is "city of David." And 2 Sam 7, deeply concerned with a future house of YHWH, does not name the "place."

Ornan's Threshing Floor in 1 Chronicles 21

The Chronicles account of the census and the plague differs from Samuel on significant details, focus, and information. Most importantly, Chronicles makes an explicit connection between the location of the altar David erected on Ornan's threshing floor with the location of the altar of burnt offering in the future Solomonic temple (1 Chr 22:1; 2 Chr 3:1). This identification is a part of the Chronicler's tendency to credit David with the idea of building the temple and preparing for it more than Samuel/Kings does.

Commentaries and other secondary literature, however, have a tendency to import from the reading of Chronicles into the reading of Samuel, not making clear that this connection is not made in Samuel/Kings.[12] This is an important example of how Chronicles has helped to support ideas that scholars may have wished that the so-called Deuteronomistic History had contained.

killing of the priests at Nob in 1 Sam 22:17–19; the medium of En-dor in 1 Sam 28. Of course, Samuel was originally one book, so it would be more correct to say that the last part of the book contrasts with the first.

    11. Araunah, known as Ornan in 1 Chr 21.

    12. E.g. H. W. Hertzberg, *1 and 2 Samuel: A Commentary* (OTL; Philadelphia: Westminster, 1984), 415; *The New Oxford Annotated Bible* (3d ed.; Oxford: Oxford University Press, 2001), 485.

Jerusalem in the Book of Kings

Jerusalem is constructed in a different way in Kings than in Samuel. In Kings Jerusalem becomes clearly identified as a city of privilege and special divine protection. As we saw in Chapter 2 in texts that repeatedly emphasize Jerusalem's status as chosen, such as Solomon's prayer at the inauguration of the temple (1 Kgs 8) and the emblematic narrative of the division of the kingdoms (1 Kgs 11), Jerusalem and the idea that YHWH has chosen a city becomes a crucial component of the ideological tapestry. This is done quite subtly, and what ends up coming across as a clear and strong identification of Jerusalem as the place of special status and divine protection, with temple and palace, is built up through a series of associations that is quite complex and not at all straightforward.

The Kings text that makes the clearest reference to the promise in 2 Sam 7 is 1 Kgs 8:15–21, with two references to a "chosen city." Perhaps surprisingly, this text does not name the city Jerusalem. Rather, it speaks of YHWH choosing a "place" or a "city." To be absolutely correct, it speaks of YHWH *not* having chosen a city, but having chosen David. In 1 Kgs 8:16, Solomon is quoting YHWH as announcing his promise in the past. This may be why unspecific language is used, but it is still quite striking that in this text, when the ark is finally brought into the finished sanctuary and the king speaks, tying this event back to the promise made to David, the name "Jerusalem" is not introduced. One is tempted to think that if it were crucial to a biblical editor to make that identification, this is where it needed to be made. But this is to speculate from silence. In this case, it is, however, interesting to note that 2 Chronicles *does* reference Jerusalem in its account of this event, 2 Chr 6:6.

In the narrative setting of 1 Kgs 8, Jerusalem is, nonetheless, explicitly mentioned at the beginning of the chapter, setting the scene for a gathering in Jerusalem to bring the ark of the covenant into the sanctuary. Both Solomon's audience and any reader/audience of the text will know that the temple is a *fait accompli*, and that it has been built in Solomon's city, Jerusalem. It is interesting to note yet again however, that Chronicles is more careful to identify the place of the temple as Jerusalem. For example, at the beginning of the account of the actual building of the temple, Chronicles identifies the place that Solomon began to build as Jerusalem, as Mount Moriah, where Abraham attempted to sacrifice Isaac, and as the threshing floor of Ornan, that David had bought (2 Chr 3:1). None of these identifications is made in Kings. In fact, the name "Jerusalem" is missing from the entire temple building account (1 Kgs 5:1–6:37). I am certain that the details from Chronicles have colored the reading of the

Kings account by all types of readers, including scholars eager to see "deuteronomistic" tendencies in the Former Prophets. This is an example of where it might be correct to say that Chronicles is more "deuteronomistic" than the "Deuteronomistic History."

As mentioned, among the texts that identify the city as chosen by YHWH the texts from 1 Kgs 8 tie back to 2 Sam 7 in particular. Even though the Samuel text does not use the language of election, or speak of a city as chosen, let alone identify this city as Jerusalem, the interplay of these texts leads to this identification. By referring back to the promise of a house for YHWH, in what could be called the "non-telling" of 1 Kgs 8:15–21, the Kings narratives make this connection. In fact, six of nine texts referring to Jerusalem or the city as "chosen by YHWH" in Kings, also mention the "house built for your/my name," thus associating the concept of "chosen city" with the temple. Furthermore, a parallel is consistently drawn between the election of the city and the election of David and his house.

The first specific reference to Jerusalem as chosen occurs 1 Kgs 11, in the expression "for the sake of Jerusalem, which I have chosen," 1 Kgs 11:13, 32, 36 (the last two add "the city"). Occurring both in a speech of divine judgment to Solomon, and in a prophecy to Jeroboam, this phrase introduces the idea of Jerusalem, the chosen city, as an entity that will mitigate the punishment that YHWH intends. Jerusalem as a city chosen by YHWH means that its status as elected grants protection to the royal house. David, YHWH's servant, and Jerusalem, his chosen city, serve as protection for Solomon. For the sake of David, Solomon will be spared and the punishment deferred to his son. And for the sake of David and Jerusalem, YHWH will keep one tribe, let one tribe survive. The status of David and the status of Jerusalem curb the harshness that the punishment potentially could have had. This rationale had all been developed through the associations spun between the election of David, the dual promise of the two "houses," and the realization of their building and inauguration.

In 1 Kgs 14:21 and 2 Kgs 21:7–8, the phrase "Jerusalem (the city) which I have chosen" serves to identify Jerusalem in the context of the presentation of the reigns of two kings of Judah. It functions, in a way, as a kind of tag or slogan associated with the city. The first one is found in the formulaic summary of the reign of King Rehoboam, son of Solomon, and the second one is associated with the reign of Manasseh.[13]

Solomon was protected from punishment even though he worshipped other gods, "for the sake of David" and for the sake of Jerusalem. His son Rehoboam, who received the punishment due Solomon, was also not

---

13. These texts are discussed in more detail in Chapter 2, above.

fully punished but received one tribe, "for the sake of David" and Jerusalem. However, by the time of Manasseh, his sins seem only to increase in depravity when contrasted with the promise of YHWH to David and Solomon about the "house for his name." Manasseh has desecrated this house, and the promise to David and Solomon will no longer protect it, and YHWH will wipe Jerusalem as one wipes a dish.

Second Kings 23 contains the final occurrence of an instance, as in the Manasseh narrative, where the understanding of the chosen city as *protected* is turned around and instead becomes the grounds for punishment. This is also the final occurrence of the reference to the chosen city in Kings. Whereas we can classify the utterances in 1 Kgs 8 and 11 as promises or reassurances of protection, the judgment speech in 2 Kgs 23:27 plays on this promise and turns it around, turning it into a threat of destruction. As we will see in the following two chapters, this judgment is carried out, in spite of all the good actions of King Josiah. In fact, even the prophecy about him avoiding a violent death is contradicted by action.

The idea of the "chosen city" as a place granted special privilege and divine protection is not the only way in which "Jerusalem" is constructed and developed further in Kings. In fact, the unnamed place of 2 Sam 7 is unequivocally established as "Jerusalem," through the consistent identification of that name with the place of the reign of each king. This practice begins with the initial summary of David's reign (2 Sam 5:5) and also closes the story of David (1 Kgs 2:11). "Jerusalem" also appears in the regnal summary of Solomon in 1 Kgs 11:42. After this, each subsequent Judean king is introduced with the same type of regnal summary, beginning with Rehoboam in 1 Kgs 14:21 and ending with Zedekiah in 2 Kgs 24:18, for a total of nineteen Judean kings.[14] With Jerusalem always explicitly identified as the seat of the throne, and often also specifically mentioned as the place of origin of the king's mother, Jerusalem becomes clearly established as the center of royal power, of the "house of David."[15]

Another thread from 2 Samuel that is quite neatly tied up in Kings is the story of the ark. As we saw in the above section on the "city of David," Solomon brings the ark from "the city of David, which is Zion,"

---

14. 1 Kgs 14:21; 15:2, 10; 22:42; 2 Kgs 8:17, 26; 12:2; 14:2; 15:2, 33; 16:2; 18:2; 21:1, 19; 22:1; 23:31, 36; 24:8, 18.
15. This aspect of the "chosen city" contrasts greatly not only with the way that Deuteronomy envisions the "chosen place," but also with Deuteronomy's concept of the role of the king. The tension between the place of kingship in Kings and in Deuteronomy will be discussed further in Chapter 8, below.

to Jerusalem (1 Kgs 8:1). We observed that "Jerusalem" is reconstituted as Solomon's Jerusalem, marking a transition from David.

The function of Jerusalem as the home base for the king's wars, as we saw so clearly in 2 Samuel, is also carried into Kings, but does not dominate the usage in the way that we saw in 2 Samuel. More than being a home base for the kings' offensive wars as in 2 Samuel,[16] in Kings, Jerusalem is a city that enemies attempt to attack. Shishak attacks from Egypt (1 Kgs 14:25), the Aramean king Hazael goes up against Jerusalem in 2 Kgs 12:18–19, Jehoash of Israel captures King Amaziah and raids the temple and the king's treasuries in 2 Kgs 14:13, King Rezin of Aram and King Pekah of Israel align against Jerusalem, and fail, in 2 Kgs 16:5. Finally there is the protracted siege of Assyria in 2 Kgs 18:17, in which Hezekiah prevails, and finally the series of attacks and sieges of Babylon (2 Kgs 24:10, 14, 15; 25:1, 8, 9). The great powers, in turn, threaten Jerusalem and finally, of course, Babylon prevails. This "reality" makes for an interesting foil to the idea of Jerusalem as the place which YHWH has chosen and will protect "for the sake of David."

A cluster of occurrences of "Jerusalem" is found in 2 Kgs 23:4–20. This text, usually referred to as the "reform report," will be studied carefully in Chapter 6. The way in which "Jerusalem" is used here is completely uniform, however. All of the acts of the king are recorded as movements in relation to Jerusalem. In many ways, this type of usage is similar to the way it is used in 2 Samuel, as a constant point from or toward which movement occurs. In the sense that "Jerusalem" is referred to as a place at which cultic actions are carried out, such as here, we find some similar mentions of "Jerusalem" in 2 Kgs 18 and 19, in the story of Hezekiah's reign. Also, as we saw above, descriptions of Solomon's building activities and cultic activities include references to "Jerusalem," in, for example, 1 Kgs 3:1, 15; 8:1; 9:15, 19. Jerusalem is specified three times in the account of the visit of the Queen of Sheba (1 Kgs 10:2, 26, 27).

Another point to be mentioned is the assessment of each king in terms of cultic fidelity as a standard part of the regnal summaries, so closely associated with Jerusalem. The regnal summaries comment on cultic behavior. This tells us, among other things, that the kings' faithfulness to

---

16. Other wars that involve Judah in Kings include a state of war between Rehoboam and Jeroboam (1 Kgs 14:30), continued in the days of Abijam (1 Kgs 15:6, 7), and the war between Asa and Baasha of Israel, initiated by Baasha (15:16–17). Amaziah attacked Edom (2 Kgs 14:7), which led to his challenging Israel and King Joash (2 Kgs 13:12; 14:8–14, Judah was defeated). Israel attacked Judah (2 Kgs 16:5), leading King Ahaz to seek an alliance with Assyria.

YHWH was important to those who wrote Kings. As a small thought experiment, one might think that if Kings was written by an author truly vested in applying the principles of Deuteronomy's legal thinking, one might have found a judgment on the kings in which the yardstick was adherence to the law. Something like: "King X did what was right in the eyes of YHWH. He read from the law night and day and never departed from it."

As it is, each king is consistently assessed as to whether or not he "did what was good or bad in the eyes of YHWH," but the only consistently mentioned specific point is whether or not he built, tore down, or did not tear down the *bamot* (במות), the high places. Although scholars have concluded from this that tearing down the *bamot* meant limiting cultic activity to Jerusalem in the sense of Deut 12, this conclusion is not without its problems, as I argue in detail in the next two chapters.[17]

Summary and Conclusions

To sum up, in Joshua, Judges, and 1 Samuel, Jerusalem does not play a role except to identify the former city of Jebus. The anachronistic mention of David bringing Goliath's head to Jerusalem might function as an early signal of the conquest of Jerusalem. Neither do these books express any particular concern for a specific place for cultic worship or a future chosen place. Joshua operates with several cultic centers: Gilgal, Shiloh, and Shechem. Judges seems to reveal a different perspective and concentrates more on individuals and families and their religious activity than on collective religion. The concept of a central sanctuary is expressed in the centrality of Shiloh in 1 Samuel, for example, but there is also Ramah, Gibeah, Nob, and others.

In 2 Samuel three things happen. (1) Jerusalem is established as David's monarchic power base, through the narrative of the capture, and through the constant reference to Jerusalem as David's home base in chs. 8–20. (2) Jerusalem is established as the place of the ark through the tangential identification of Jerusalem with "city of David" and "Zion." (3) Without naming Jerusalem, the idea of a future promise of a "house of God," bound up with a promise to the "house of David," is announced and allowed to float and hover.

In Kings, these ideas develop further. I do not know if this is the result of conscious editing or the effect of a cumulative reading, or perhaps

---

17. The identification of the agenda of getting rid of the *bamot* with Deuteronomy's agenda of cultic centralization has been assumed, most often without comment, in the DH hypothesis in its various forms.

both, but Jerusalem becomes further established as the seat of royal power and the place of the temple, through the accounts of transition from David to Solomon, with the completion of the buildings and the moving of the ark into the temple. This status of the city of the "two houses" is maintained in part through the consistent reference to Jerusalem in the regnal summaries, in spite of the threats to it almost from the beginning. Jerusalem is now not so much the city from which wars are waged (as in Samuel), but a city that is attacked by successive enemy powers, and to which it finally succumbs. Further, Jerusalem is a place that is violated and purged.

Of the several ways that Jerusalem is constituted in Kings, the most significant is the elaboration of the idea of Jerusalem as chosen and the promises about the Davidic dynasty, ideas that are introduced in Samuel and brought together in 1 Kings. This is done quite subtly, and there is evidence to allege that the Chronicler wanted to make it clearer. What emerges in Kings is the idea that Jerusalem, as chosen, supports a rationale for the protection of the royal house, in spite of its failure to uphold loyalty toward YHWH. Jerusalem, the city that YHWH chose for the "house for his name," together with David, whom he chose, serve to protect that city, until the day that YHWH decides to destroy it.

Although not the most dominant in terms of how often it is iterated, the idea of Jerusalem as the city YHWH has chosen and promises to protect comes across quite forcefully in the book of Kings. With the opening of Kings, chs. 5–8 in particular, Jerusalem is established as the seat of the throne, the center of royal power (house of David) and as the place of YHWH's temple, the place of worship and cultic activity. Already at the outset, however, this chosen city is under threat.

A potentially interesting strand in the shuttle that weaves the fabric of Samuel–Kings is the "remaking" of David, the divinely inspired warrior of 1 and 2 Samuel, into the king that all other subsequent kings are measured up against. Unfortunately, this subject is too large to do justice to at present. For the present study, the most significant is the elaboration in Kings of the idea of Jerusalem as chosen and the promises about the Davidic dynasty, ideas that are introduced in Samuel and brought together in 1 Kings.

Now that we have introduced and presented the idea of Jerusalem as "chosen city" in Kings and other books of the Former Prophets, the next chapter will follow up more closely the cult site, sanctuary, ritual cult, and the idea of a "house built for YHWH," before turning to a focus on cultic reform in the book of Kings, in Chapter 6.

Chapter 5

THE CULTIC CONTEXT OF THE "CHOSEN PLACE"

Chapters 2 and 3 showed that the idea of cultic centralization is forcefully present in Deuteronomy. At the same time, we have noticed that Deuteronomy has no directive for the sanctuary and no mandate to build a cult site or even an altar within the core of the legal material (chs. 12–26). There are references to acts of sacrifice, gifts and the tithe, and to festivals, and a place for cultic activity is definitely presupposed. Yet there is little or no description of what the cult site should look like, what kind of equipment it would need or how it should be staffed. In this respect, Deuteronomy differs greatly from most other Pentateuchal legislation, which contains detailed specifications for the sanctuary, its furnishings, the cultic personnel, and the sacrificial cult.

This lack of attention to the specifics of ritual cult and the sanctuary has been one reason for the prevalent understanding among scholars that Deuteronomy is "secularizing," demythologizing, and abstract in its conception of religion.[1] The centralization of the cult, it is argued, led to a de-sacralization of the periphery that required a new form of religion. As a part of this paradigm, it has been thought that Deuteronomy is not really interested in the cult. Or, Deuteronomy has been read as a book that does not see the cult as really necessary, and that the attitude of the worshipers was what counted, not so much the acts that were performed. This reading of Deuteronomy's understanding of cult may also tie in with the view that there is a major difference between Deuteronomy and the priestly legislation in how holiness is perceived.

While it is helpful to contrast texts in order to gain a sense of their distinctiveness, their present context and the relationship between them should also be considered. As a part of the Pentateuch, Torah, or law of Moses, Deuteronomy has a literary context that includes Genesis–Numbers. When read in this context, one will read Deuteronomy as presupposing the sanctuary of Exodus, Leviticus, and Numbers. Even in a

1. See the literature cited in n. 18 of Chapter 2, above.

diachronic perspective, assuming that the cultic legislation usually subsumed under the P and H material was composed later than Deuteronomy, it is natural to suppose that the writers of Deuteronomy knew of specific cultic practices that they considered to be commonly known, and therefore saw no need to describe them. There is at least one reference to "the priest who is in office at the time," in Deut 26:3, in connection with legislation about the presentation of the first fruits of the harvest, so we can assume that knowledge of a priesthood is taken for granted.

Whatever the strategy of the interpreter may be, it is useful to map out the information on ritual cult and the cult site in Deuteronomy's literary contexts when seeking to understand the idea of the "chosen place." Therefore, this chapter will focus on the sanctuary, the cult site, and ritual cult in Deuteronomy and its contexts. First, an overview of the sanctuary and ritual cult in Deuteronomy's Pentateuchal context will refresh our understanding of the distinctiveness of Deuteronomy, but also remind us of its links with the legislation of Exodus–Numbers and its literary connections with Genesis. After this we will examine each of the books of the Former Prophets, book by book, in a similar way as we did with "Jerusalem" in the previous chapter. Keeping in mind scholars' preoccupation with the idea of cult centralization as a central tenet of Deuteronomy (that also influenced the composition of other biblical books), it seems warranted to set "cult centralization" within a larger context of cult and ritual as it is actually portrayed in these books. By seeing how each book portrays ritual and sacrificial cult and what each says about where cultic activity takes place or should take place, we might better be able to assess the ways in which cult centralization plays a role in these books, if it does at all.[2]

2. Until the 1970s there had been little concern with the relationship between Deuteronomy and the other books of the Pentateuch. Even in the source-critical models, the general view was that there were few traces of the D source in the other Pentateuchal books. In a classic expression of this understanding, S. R. Driver set up a chart comparing the legal material between the sources JE, D, and P (including H), in order to establish that D is an expansion of JE (and dependent on it), is parallel to H (though it may be dealing with similar law), and is essentially independent of P; see Driver, *Deuteronomy*, iii–xix.

M. Noth had claimed that the compilers of Genesis through Numbers were completely different from the Deuteronomist, and that there were few signs of deuteronomistic redaction in the Tetrateuch. In much the same way that the DH hypothesis has become unmanageable and not well suited to explain many features of Deuteronomy and the Former Prophets, recent research on the Pentateuch has presented completely contradictory models for understanding the relationship between Deuteronomy and the Tetrateuch, or between Genesis–Numbers and

5. The Cultic Context of the "Chosen Place"

The Pentateuch

The Sanctuary

In the Pentateuch, no other element receives as much attention, in terms of the number of verses dealing with it, as the sanctuary or tabernacle (משכן). משכן is usually translated "sanctuary" or "tabernacle." According to many scholars, it may connote a temporary abode associated with a nomadic lifestyle and tents.[3] The main legislation concerning the tabernacle is found in the composition of Exod 25–40, in chs. 25–27 and 36–38 in particular. YHWH tells Moses to have the Israelites donate items and "have them make me a sanctuary/holy place (מקדש), so that I may dwell among them (ושכנתי בתוכם). In accordance with all that I show you concerning the pattern (תבנית) of the tabernacle (משכן) and of all its furniture, so you shall make it" (Exod 25:8–9). מקדש, although often translated "sanctuary," is a word whose meaning is not necessarily that specific. It refers to the "holy area," and does not denote a specific cultic installation in the same way that משכן seems to do.

The word מקדש is also used much more sparingly than משכן. It appears in the first commissioning of the sanctuary in Exod 25:8, mentioned above, and has an interesting distribution in the MT. Occurring only once in Exodus besides 25:8, in the poetic text of 15:17, it there expresses the idea of YHWH's mountain and the building of a sanctuary there, an abode, in a way similar to Josh 24:26, where it refers to the sanctuary at Shechem (see also Josh 22:19; Pss 78:54–55, 59–60, 67–72). There are a handful of occurrences of מקדש in Numbers and a few more in Leviticus, where it refers to the sanctuary. But it is most prevalent in Ezekiel (30 times) and Isaiah (where it is also used of the sacred places of other nations), and occurs in Chronicles[4] but not in Samuel or Kings. In

---

Deuteronomy–Kings. See the literature cited in Chapter 1, n. 34. The purpose of the present survey is to offer a survey of the literature in a synchronic reading, so as to gain a full picture, albeit cursory, of the content of these books, with a focus on the cult site and ritual activity. A comprehensive picture of the textual material is difficult to obtain from the highly stratified presentation of the material in most redaction-critical presentations.

3. E.g. W. H. C. Propp, *Exodus 19–40: A New Translation with Introduction and Commentary* (AB 2A; New York: Doubleday, 2006), 377.

4. מקדש in Chronicles is used of the temple and temple area. For example, 1 Chr 22:19; 28:10: David instructs Solomon about the building of the temple; 2 Chr 20:6: Jehoshaphat is portrayed almost as a new Solomon; 26:18: King Uzzia tries to make sacrifices at the altar of incense, a job of the priests, and is told by the priest to go out of the sanctuary and is struck with a skin disease; 29:21: portrays a sin offering for the sanctuary and restoration of temple service; 30:8: a letter of Hezekiah, asking the

general, it is not common in the Pentateuch, and does not occur at all in Deuteronomy.

Following the details for the building of the sanctuary is the instruction for the priestly vestments and their consecration. The subsequent carrying out of this instruction is related in Exod 28–29 and 39:1–31. The final summary of the finished work is found in 39:32–43 and the pitching of the tent for the tabernacle and setting up of all its furnishings, including the various altars (altar for the burnt sacrifice, altar for the incense offering), close the book of Exodus, in ch. 40, with Moses actually setting up the tabernacle himself (40:18–19).[5]

In addition to the משכן, the term אהל מועד, "tent of meeting," also refers to the tabernacle in Exodus–Numbers. The tent of meeting is envisioned in two distinct ways in the Pentateuch, one in which it is used interchangeably with משכן, as we find most commonly in the legislation of Exod 25–31 and 35–40, or together with it, as in Exod 40:2, 6. It is also used as distinct from the משכן, but referring to the outer tent of goat hair surrounding it, as in Exod 26:1–14; 36:8–19; 40:19, and Num 3:25. Numbers 2 draws up a map of the camp in which the sanctuary is at the center and the various tribes are encamped around it, corresponding to this understanding. But in another distinct usage it refers to a tent pitched outside the camp, in which Moses speaks to YHWH. No priests are involved, but Moses' helper Joshua stays there (Exod 33:7–11). Matching this view, Lev 11:26 visualizes the tent as being outside the camp, there envisioned more as a place to prophesy. This highlights the two main understandings within the legislation about the "tent of meeting."[6]

Leviticus 1–7 forms a sort of pause concerning the sanctuary itself. These chapters lay out the sacrificial cult in detail, so that when the

---

people to return to YHWH to celebrate the passover, and come to his sanctuary in order to avert his anger; 36:17: the king of Chaldeans kills the youth in the sanctuary and destroys the house of God, house of YHWH.

5. For a reading that emphasizes narrative structures in the "Sinai" composition, see, M. R. Hauge, *Descent from the Mountain: Narrative Patterns in Exodus 19–40* (JSOTSup 323; Sheffield: Sheffield Academic, 2001).

6. See also Num 11:16–17, 24–26; 12:1–8. V. Fritz explains the difference in terms of texts originating from different traditions, with Num 11 and 12 testifying to a background in ecstatic prophecy, and the use in, e.g., Exod 33 seeing the tent of meeting as a place of revelation; see Fritz, *Tempel und Zelt: Studien zum Tempelbau in Israel und zu dem Zeltheiligtum der Priesterschrift* (WMANT 47; Neukirchen–Vluyn: Neukirchener, 1977), 103–6. In general, Fritz's view of the history of Israel and his identification of texts with religious institutions is outdated. Nevertheless, his study represents a valuable description of the textual material about the sanctuary in Exodus and other texts.

priests and sanctuary are commissioned in ch. 8, and begin practicing the cult in ch. 9, the rules have been specified. As a new element in relation to Exodus, the purity of the sanctuary and the rites that the priests must perform to ensure that purity come up in Leviticus (e.g. Lev 4; 21:1–12; see also Num 19:13, 20, which also uses the term מקדש). The Day of Atonement, for which legislation is found in Lev 16, is also concerned with the purification of the sanctuary. Leviticus 24:1–9 contains further rules for the sanctuary lamp and for the bread to be put out for the priests.

Numbers 7:1 picks up the narrative thread from Lev 8–9, on the consecration of the sanctuary. Here we find the details of the offerings that the heads of each tribe offer on the day of the dedication of the sanctuary. Interspersed within this account is also information about how the Levitical clans obtained the wagons and oxen for the transport of the sanctuary (Num 7:6–8). Next, the Levites are dedicated to sanctuary service (Num 8). Numbers 9:15 again mentions "the day the tabernacle was set up," tying together the narrative with Num 7:1; Lev 8–9, and back to Exod 40 in particular, in this case, with the deliberation on the cloud covering the tabernacle.

Next, we find further instruction about how the sanctuary is to be assembled and moved during the desert march (Num 10:17, 21). Numbers also contains additional details about the responsibilities of the various clans of the priests pertaining to the sanctuary: on the duties of the Levites as "workers" (Num 3:5–10); on the dedication of the firstborn to temple service and the Levites are substitutes (3:11–13, 44–50); on the duties of the Gershonites, the Kohathites, and the Merarites (3:14–39; 4:1–49); further on the duties of the priesthood and Levites, following the account of Korah's rebellion in ch. 16 and Aaron's reaffirmation in ch. 17 (Num 18). Reference is made to the Levites' responsibility for the tabernacle/sanctuary (משכן) in Num 31:30, 47 in connection with the portions due to them from the booty taken from the Midianites.

This sweep through Exodus, Leviticus, and Numbers helps to highlight the central importance of the sanctuary in Pentateuchal legislation. In regard to the subject of the sanctuary, Genesis and Deuteronomy both differ from these three books in that the concern for the sanctuary reflected in Exodus–Numbers is not found. Genesis is different in another regard, not having any legal collections. It does, however, contain descriptions of sacrificial activity, the setting up of altars and acts of worship. For example, the Bible's first murder takes place after a sacrifice of first fruits (Gen 4) and Noah's first act after the flood has subsided is to offer a burnt sacrifice (Gen 8:20). Abraham builds altars as he travels into Canaan (Gen 12:7, 8; 13:4) and also prepares to sacrifice his son as a burnt offering in Gen 22, but sacrifices a ram instead. Jacob is described as building an altar at Bethel and offering libations in Gen 28:18–22, he also offers a sacrifice to seal the border deal between Laban and himself, in 31:44–54. These sacrificial acts in Genesis are *ad hoc* and, as narratives, many of them can be classified as etiological stories of theophanies and acts of God that sometimes lead to the naming of a place. In Genesis, ritual and sacrificial acts are presupposed as a part of life, but there are no indications of pushing any agenda of specific requirements for worship, such as Leviticus and Numbers do, any specific type of sanctuary, like Exodus does, or any ideas of cultic centralization. There is no concept of a professional priesthood. On the contrary, the ritual activity in Genesis is led by the head of the household.

The tent of meeting (אהל מועד), so prominent in Exodus, Leviticus, and Numbers, is mentioned only once in Deuteronomy. In Deut 31:14–15, Moses and Joshua are summoned to the tent of meeting by YHWH so that Joshua may be commissioned (צוה). It is not clear which of the two views of the tent of meeting this reflects, but the presence of Joshua as Moses' helper in Exod 33 leads us in the direction of the "non-sacrificial," tent of meeting involving prophecy and revelation. Other texts that speak of Joshua's commissioning include Num 27:18–23 and Deut 3:28.

Yet another expression of the lack of interest in the sanctuary in Deuteronomy is the fact that the משכן is never mentioned in Deuteronomy. For a book that is supposedly mainly interested in a central place of cultic practice, it is very uninterested in the actual sanctuary or place of cultic activity itself. Again, as suggested above, it may presuppose this knowledge and information about other legal material. It remains striking, however, that the sanctuary is passed over to the extent that it is.

The Altar

The altar of YHWH is mentioned only seven times in Deuteronomy, as opposed to around fifty mentions of various altars in Exodus, over eighty in Leviticus and almost thirty in Numbers. In Deut 12:27 we find provisions that the burnt offerings should be presented "on the altar of YHWH." Further, it occurs in the section that further specifies the law on secular slaughter in Deut 12:13–18, which specifies that the blood of other sacrifices should be poured out "on/beside the altar of YHWH" (cf. Exod 29 and Lev 1; 3–5; 7–9).

The most specific ordinance concerning the altar in Deuteronomy is in a sentence specifying what the cult site should *not* have. Deuteronomy 16:21–22 specifies that the altar should have no *asherah* next to it, nor

5. The Cultic Context of the "Chosen Place" 101

should they erect any *matzevah* (מצבה), "which YHWH hates." These cultic objects are only mentioned once in Genesis–Numbers. In Exod 34:13, in a divine speech warning the Israelites about what they must not do in order to keep the covenant, YHWH speaks to Moses on Mount Sinai and is told that he must destroy the *asherim* and *matzevot* of the nations listed in v. 11. The comments made about the altar in Deut 16:21–22 are therefore modeled in opposition to the altars of the "nations," with Exod 34:13; Deut 7:5, and 12:3 as the previous descriptions of altars of the "nations" that they are to destroy. In that respect, Deut 16:21–22 is consistent with other legislation concerning worship, in which a contrast with what other nations do with other gods serves to highlight what the Israelites are to do (cf. 12:2–3).

We note another interesting detail with regard to the *asherah*. While the places that mention *asherah* in the Former Prophets (Judges and Kings) almost always also contain a message about the *bamot* ("high places"), the Deuteronomy text does not. In fact, Deuteronomy never mentions the *bamot*. This point will be investigated in more detail below.

In spite of the lack of interest in the specificities of the cultic site or altar in the legislation of Deuteronomy, considerable attention is devoted to the narrative about the building of one specific altar. This is the altar they are to build on Mount Ebal, commissioned in Deut 27. Although the name Shechem is never mentioned in the book of Deuteronomy, associations to the area near Shechem (with nearby Mount Ebal and Mount Gerizim) play a role in framing the legal corpus of Deut 12–26, as will be discussed below, in the section on "place and places in Deuteronomy." The building of an altar on Mount Ebal, near Shechem, is narrated in Josh 8, with the implementation of a ritual of blessings and curses also mandated by Deuteronomy (11:29–30; 27:11–26).

In Deut 27, the Israelites are told by Moses and the elders in a complex and seemingly contradictory text to erect plaster-covered stones on which they are to write the law (vv. 2–3), and a sacrificial altar of unhewn stones (vv. 5–7). The stones of vv. 2–4 are to be erected as soon as they cross over the Jordan (connecting it to Gilgal in Josh 4, and back to Exod 24), but the text then indicates that the place is Mount Ebal, connecting it to Josh 8:30–35. It is unclear to which construction v. 8 is referring, but it seems to be going back to the stones of vv. 2–4. The motif of writing the law on stones is also reflected in Exod 24:4 (and erecting twelve stones) and Josh 24:26.

Since the "chosen place" is never identified in Deuteronomy, and no other place name is mentioned for the building of a cult site, a straightforward reading of Deuteronomy quite simply identifies the "chosen place" as Ebal. The Samaritan Pentateuch reads Gerizim, instead of Ebal,[7] making this text a crucial one for its advocacy of Gerizim as the legitimate cult site over against those who advocated Jerusalem. Yet, most scholars do not give the text of Deut 27 much credit, and blame its complicated compositional history for the problems.[8]

Early readers also obviously struggled to make sense of this text. For example, Josephus probably understands the ritual acts on Mount Ebal and Mount Gerizim and the building of an altar near Shechem to be a one-time event.[9] This understanding is also chosen by many commentators. In spite of being the only place in Deuteronomy that specifies *where* a cult site should be, advocates of a DH have not taken this text seriously, but have instead tried to find excuses for it and why it contradicts the idea that the writers of Deuteronomy had Jerusalem in mind for the centralization of the cult. It is not surprising to find that MT traditions,

---

7. This choice is reflected also in the Samaritan version of the tenth commandment in Exod 20, where the Samaritan Pentateuch reflects material found in both Deut 11 and 27 of the MT. For a thorough discussion of the textual character of the Samaritan Pentateuch, see the chapter entitled "The Pentateuch that the Samaritans Chose," in M. Kartveit, *The Origin of the Samaritans* (VTSup 128; Leiden: Brill, 2009), 259–312, and especially the excursus on Deut 27:4 (pp. 300–9).

8. G. von Rad saw in Deut 27:1–8 an originally pre-deuteronomistic, Shechemite tradition, but does not really explain why it is now inserted here; see von Rad, *Deuteronomy*, 165. Scholars have argued that this text was an early tradition attesting to early Israelite Shechem traditions, and that it was included for this reason. This fits in with the model that has understood Deuteronomy as having a "Northern" provenance, and that refugees from Samaria brought this literature with them after the fall of Israel in 722. The argument for scholars such as Weinfeld has been that the "Northern" traditions, in which Shechem was central, were so authoritative that they left their mark on the text of Deuteronomy, and later deuteronomistic editing did not remove these, even though they conflicted with the idea of Jerusalem as the "chosen place." In a contribution challenging this point of view, N. Na'aman argues that this does not make sense, and offers his own explanation, which is that Deut 27:1–8 was added late, by a scribe who wanted to emphasize the antiquity of the Shechem tradition and legitimize it as a cult site. See the summary of these positions in Na'aman, "The Law of the Altar in Deuteronomy," 141–47. Another convenient summary of positions in research is found in P. A. Barker, "The Theology of Deuteronomy 27," *TynBul* 49 (1998): 277–303 (277–79). See also C. Nihan, "The Torah Between Samaria and Judah: Shechem and Gerizim in Deuteronomy and Joshua," in Knoppers and Levinson, eds., *The Pentateuch as Torah*, 187–223 (200–212).

9. Textual critics think that the word ἐμπεριάγειν may be a gloss, or a correction, of ἀναστῆσαι. This would allow the interpretation that the altar was carried there and set up, but then taken down again, so that it would not be understood as the erection of a permanent altar; see Josephus, *Ant.* 4.305.

5. The Cultic Context of the "Chosen Place" 103

LXX traditions, Qumran manuscripts, and early retellings of these texts (Deut 27 and related texts in Joshua) have many variants regarding place names and order of events. It has been a contested tradition.[10] But this does not change the fact that the Masoretic tradition remains clear about this altar being built on Mount Ebal, and that it otherwise never names the "chosen place."

The legal corpus of Deut 12–26 is framed by references to some type of concluding ceremony of blessing and curse associated with Shechem. In Deut 11:29, Shechem is not mentioned specifically, but the mountains of Gerizim and Ebal are mentioned, and their location is specified in the next verse, which connects it to the geographical indicator "the oaks of Moreh." In Gen 12:6, the oaks of Moreh are connected to Shechem, and Abraham, or Abram, is reported to have built an altar there, because YHWH appeared to him there.

The association to Shechem, more specifically Ebal and Gerizim, also complicates the otherwise fairly straightforward setting in Deuteronomy of a covenant concluded on the plains of Moab. The narrative present of Deuteronomy is located on the plains of Moab. The "here today" of ch. 26 is in Moab, and the conclusion of the covenant in Deut 26:17–19 takes place there, in narrative time. Deuteronomy 28:69 is also in Moab, and specifies "this" covenant as being in addition to the one made at Horeb. This is not the case in the introductions of 4:44–45; 5:1, and 12:1.

In contrast to the Deut 28:69 covenant closing in the narrative present, the reference to the ritual on Ebal and Gerizim is spoken about as something that will take place in the narrative future. The Moab setting is the narrative present. Further, the ritual of curses and blessings is concrete and participatory, a ritual with specific roles and the erection of a stone and an altar. The Moab covenant seems more abstract, but it is clear that it is to be sealed with an oath (29:13, 18), and refers to curses written "in this book." So, although the Moab covenant seems to lack a ritual, cultic setting, it is nevertheless conceived of as a binding ritual. At the same time, the ritual on Ebal and Gerizim ties both back to Genesis and the story of the fathers (with the association with Shechem) and points forward to the future existence in the land. See more on Shechem in the Former Prophets, below.

---

10. For a discussion, see R. Pummer, "The Samaritans and Their Pentateuch," in Knoppers and Levinson, ed., *The Pentateuch as Torah*, 237–69 (241–47). See also Hjelm, *Jerusalem's Rise to Sovereignty*, 197–203; and Nihan, "The Torah Between Samaria and Judah," 213–22.

Apart from the altar of Deut 27, the two other mentions of an altar in Deuteronomy concern altars of the Canaanites. Deuteronomy 7:5 concerns what to do with Canaanites' altars once the Israelites enter the land and YHWH drives out the population. They are to "break down their altars, smash their pillars, hew down their sacred poles, and burn their idols with fire." This is very similar to Deut 12:3, which opens the legal core of Deuteronomy, and was discussed above in Chapter 3. A similar text is found also in Exod 34:11–16.

Exodus 20:22–23:19, usually referred to as the Covenant Code, opens with provisions for an altar and ritual acts (20:23–26) and closes with its Festival calendar (23:14–19). The collection is followed by a description of a ceremony involving ritual acts and a covenant ceremony in Exod 24:1–11. The opening of the Covenant Code contains what has been referred to as the "Altar Law" of 20:24–26. According to these verses, in a law given by YHWH to tell the Israelites, in the second person form as in the Decalogue, they are not to make cult statues of silver or gold, only an altar on which to sacrifice. They are to sacrifice burnt offerings and sacrifices of well being. The law then adds, "In every place where I cause my name to be remembered I will come to you and bless you." This text is usually seen as the text that Deuteronomy is in opposition to when it mandates sacrifices to take place "at the place which YHWH will choose."[11]

---

11. B. M. Levinson presents a thorough argument for how the authors of Deuteronomy have reworked the text of Exodus to subvert that text using a method of legal innovation, in his *Deuteronomy and the Legal Hermeneutics*, especially 31–38. For other points of view, see the literature cited by Levinson on p. 7 n. 10, and on literature discussing this issue and summarizing it, p. 11 n. 27. See also B. M. Levinson, "Is the Covenant Code an Exilic Composition? A Response to John Van Seters," in *In Search of Pre-exilic Israel: Proceedings of the Oxford Old Testament Seminar* (ed. J. Day; London: T&T Clark International, 2004), 272–325.

There are also those who argue that this text post-dates both P and D; see, e.g., J. Van Seters, *A Law Book for the Diaspora* (Oxford: Oxford University Press, 2003). For the argument that the altar law of Exodus was inserted in the exilic period as a polemic against the deuteronomistic idea of cult centralization, and was placed first in the covenant code in a way to match the position of the centralization law in Deuteronomy's law collection, see C. Levin, "Das Deuteronomium und der Jahwist," in *Liebe und Gebot: Studien zum Deuteronomium. Festschrift zum 70: Geburtstag von Lothar Perlitt* (ed. R. G. Kratz and H. Spieckermann; FRLANT 190; Göttingen: Vandenhoeck & Ruprecht, 2000), 121–36. See also Van Seters' criticism of H.-C. Schmitt's views, similar to Levin's, and the summary of his own view of the issue, in J. Van Seters, "The Altar Law of Ex 20,24–26 in Critical Debate," in Beck and Schorn, eds., *Auf dem Weg zur Endgestalt*, 157–74.

The instructions in Exod 20:24–26 about the altar itself do not necessarily conflict with anything in Deuteronomy, because Deuteronomy does not specify anything about the altar. On this point, the instructions about it only being necessary to make an altar of earth (מזבח אדמה), seems more to be in tension with later (later, in terms of narrative time) provisions in Exodus (such as 27:1–8 and 38:1–7, usually considered P). It is the next sentence that has been understood as being fundamentally in tension with Deuteronomy's legislation about "the place which YHWH will choose." Several aspects of the verse contrast with Deuteronomy's conception of what takes place at the "chosen place." For one, there is the contrast between "every place" and "the place."[12] Also, Deuteronomy envisions a place that YHWH will "put/set his name" or "make his name dwell," whereas Exod 20:24 talks about places that YHWH will cause his "name to be remembered."[13] Further, in Deuteronomy, the people are to go to the place, and bring their sacrifices, whereas in Exodus it is YHWH who says he will come to them.

The Exodus text seems to be holding up a promise that when an altar is built, and sacrifices offered on it, YHWH will still bring his presence and blessing to any place where his name is remembered or invoked. The versions differ on whether or not the invocation is caused by him or by a human, and the Targumim leave out any reference to YHWH "coming to" the worshiper.

According to M. Weinfeld, the revolution of Deuteronomy comes as a consequence of centralization of the cult and the elimination of local sanctuaries.[14] At the same time, it seems that his profiling of the Deuteronomist depends fundamentally on the contrast he draws up between it and a priestly view of religion, not between the Deuteronomist and an earlier understanding of religion, in the way that was important to Wellhausen. This contrast is based on what Weinfeld describes as fundamentally different theological positions regarding the understanding of God and the sanctuary. For example, whereas the priestly writings presuppose God's dwelling in the sanctuary as the rationale for all cultic activity, Deuteronomy redefines the understanding of God to mean that

---

12. The Samaritan Pentateuch of Exod 20:24 has "in the place"; the Tiberian, Syriac, and LXX versions seem to omit the definite article, "the place."

13. There is a considerable text-critical discussion of the word אזכיר. See the literature cited by Levinson, "Is the Covenant Code an Exilic Composition?," 302–3, and his useful tabulation of the early textual witnesses (p. 307), and the discussion following. See also, e.g., Propp, *Exodus 19–40*, 184.

14. See, in particular, Weinfeld, *Deuteronomy and the Deuteronomic School*, 190–209.

he is not immanent, but only his name is present. Weinfeld's argument becomes confusing because although he posits the Deuteronomist as revolutionary, the main way that he profiles deuteronomic/istic theology is by contrasting it with the priestly writings, which he understands as later.

We might ask: Is there really anything in the priestly writings that negates a central cult site? Is not the contrast really between the views of Exod 20:24 and the views of both the Priests and the Deuteronomy? With regard to a central cult site, we find affinities between Deuteronomy's understanding of cult centralization and the implicit expression of this idea in the legislation of Exod 25–40, Leviticus, and Numbers. It is actually Exod 20 that stands out as different from the rest in this regard, if one chooses the reading preserved by the MT. In my opinion, while Weinfeld's description of a contrast between P and D in terms of their respective understanding of the immanence or transcendence of the deity might be consistent,[15] his explanation that Deuteronomy's view is dependent on the idea of cultic centralization is confusing and misleading. The so-called P writings also contain a distinct perspective of a centralized cult, as we have seen in the rough survey, above, and do not differ significantly from Deuteronomy in that regard.

The Ark
The ark, or ark of the covenant, can be traced as a specific thread in the tapestry of legislative material of the Pentateuch that may be followed on into the narrative material of the Former Prophets. The ark of the covenant figures as one of the components of the sanctuary and all that goes with it in Exod 25–40, where it clearly suggests YHWH's presence among his people. It serves as the chest into which the covenant (העדת) that YHWH will give them shall be put (25:16; 40:20).

In Numbers the role of the ark is more clearly as the "head" of the march (e.g. Num 10:33–36). It functions both as a guide and as a sign of the presence of the deity.[16] For example, in 14:44, the people are so eager to go to the "land" that they go without the ark of the covenant of YHWH, and they lose the battle. In the battle against Midian in Num 31, the ark participates, and this is a successful battle.

---

15. M. Weinfeld, "Pentateuch," in *Encyclopaedia Judaica*, vol. 13 (New York: Macmillan, 1971–1972), cols. 232–63. This contrast is also open to critique, of course, and has been the subject of debate. See Chapter 7.

16. J. Milgrom, *The JPS Torah Commentary: Numbers* (Philadelphia: Jewish Publication Society, 1990), 373.

The ark is mentioned twice in Deuteronomy. Deuteronomy 10, following the retrospective telling of the making of the golden calf, details how Moses was told to make the ark of the covenant into which the new tablets of the law are to be placed. In Deut 10:8, in a kind of parenthetical note, information about part of the itinerary is given. Aaron's death is mentioned, along with information about the consecration of the Levites to their duties to carry the ark of the covenant, to minister before YHWH and to bless his name.[17] Deuteronomy 31:9 also refers to the Levites and their task of carrying the ark of the covenant. The reference occurs in the context of the narration of Moses writing down the law, after giving his departing speech, and before the commissioning of Joshua.

These references indicate that Deuteronomy is in agreement with Exodus and Numbers about the role of the Levites in carrying the ark, but it incorporates this into its own narration of Moses' role in writing the law. The ark of the covenant becomes associated with the requirement to read the law every seven years "at the place which YHWH your God chooses."

In the Former Prophets, the ark has a particular narrative that we can follow through 1 Sam 4–6 and 2 Sam 6; 15; and to 1 Kgs 8:1. These texts were discussed in Chapter 4, above, and form an important element in the story of David's involvement in capturing Jerusalem and preparing for the eventual building of the temple.[18]

The ark of the covenant is one of the features that connects Deuteronomy with Samuel and Kings, but in a less explicit way than it connects Exodus and Numbers with these books. The role of the ark in warfare and as a ritual object is less pronounced in Deuteronomy than in Exodus, Numbers, and Samuel and Kings, though it is not absent. In Deuteronomy, more important is its role as the keeping-place of the law. Joshua combines both of these aspects (Josh 3–4; 6; and 8). In Kings, the significance of the ark relates to the place of the sanctuary and the initiation of the ritual cult at the temple. In this way Kings connects much more closely to Exodus than to Deuteronomy on the topic of the ark. Chronicles expands these connections and makes them more explicit. Ezra–Nehemiah does not mention the ark of the covenant in connection with reading the law, and neither does 2 Kings. So, it is not used by those books "in the way of Deuteronomy" so to speak. This should be surprising to the adherents of the concept of a DH.

---

17. Deut 10:6–9 is usually considered to be an editorial insertion, and considered to be part of the redaction that is concerned with the law.

18. The ark has an expanded role in Chronicles; see 1 Chr 13; 15–16; 2 Chr 5–6.

Sacrificial Cult

The most detailed legislation on the sacrificial cult is found in Lev 1–7, with details on all of the sacrifices and the role of priests. Leviticus 11–15 fills in on sacrifices mandated by impurity, and is supplemented by Num 5:5–10 on the guilt offering. After the legislation of Lev 1–7, Lev 8:6 continues with the story from the end of Exodus, with Moses consecrating Aaron and the priesthood. After the priests have been consecrated, the cult is initiated. Aaron offers sacrifices and blesses the people, much like Solomon does in 1 Kgs 8. The tent of meeting is also mentioned (Lev 9:23) again here, bringing the story from Exod 40 forward. YHWH's כבוד appears to all the people, and fire comes out from YHWH and consumes the sacrifices. This detail is also present in the Chronicler's version of the initiation of the temple cult by Solomon, 2 Chr 7:1. We note, in passing, that the first thing that happens when the cult is initiated is that the priests make deadly mistakes (Num 10).[19]

Leviticus 17 concerns slaughter at the sanctuary. On this topic, Leviticus is more radical than Deuteronomy, and does not allow secular slaughter at all, as we saw that Deuteronomy does (see Chapter 3, above). In other words, for Leviticus, all slaughter of animals is a sacrifice, and should take place at the sanctuary. Other texts dealing with sacrifices include Lev 19:5–8, which is followed by Decalogue laws (19:11–13), and Lev 20:2–8, which juxtaposes a prohibition against Moloch-worship/child sacrifice and types of divination in a way similar to Deut 18:10. Leviticus 21–22 contains laws on priests and how they must stay pure and perform sacrifices and Lev 25 the laws of the Jubilee year and sabbatical year.

Numbers 15:1–31 comments on various types of offerings, mostly described in Lev 1–7. An interesting detail is that this text is prefaced by a reference of a time when Israel will "come into the land [they] are to inhabit," much like Deuteronomy often does. Numbers 19 contains various types of purification rituals, including purification of the sanctuary. Finally, we find extensive sacrificial legislation in Num 28–29.

Deuteronomy is concerned with sacrifices and comments on various aspects. First of all, it enumerates a number of sacrifices and sacrificial gifts: the burnt offering (עלה), the sacrifice (זבח), the tithe (מעשר), donations (תרומה), votive gifts (נדר), freewill offerings (נדבה), and firstlings (בכור). Further, it comments on details of the sacrificial animal in 15:21–23 and 17:1. In 26:3–4 it comments on the role of the priest in receiving the offering of first fruits and in 26:1–15 on the very first fruits of the land to be presented. Here, Deuteronomy assumes a "priest who is in

---

19. On priestly controversy and insurrection, see also Num 16.

office at that time." This legislation on first fruits may contradict Lev 19:23-25, but that might just pertain to fruit trees that they plant. That firstlings can be "turned into money" (Deut 14:24-25), however, contradicts Lev 27:32.

Deuteronomy also comments specifically on the tribe of Levi in 33:10. This tribe has a prominent role in Deuteronomy, and the Levite is consistently included, along with the household, as a participant in the cultic celebrations.

Festivals

The very first festival legislation in the Pentateuch is found in Exod 12, describing how the passover should be celebrated, while simultaneously telling the story of the Israelites leaving Egypt. Festival legislation is found in several other texts, including Exod 23:14-17 (closing of the Covenant Code), Exod 34:11-26 (the "new covenant" contains various types of festival and sacrificial legislation), the extensive festival legislation of Lev 23, and Num 28:16-25 (passover) and 29 (seventh month, day of atonement, booths).[20]

In Num 9:1-14 a celebration of passover, the second one in narrative time, is described. The description is focused on the part of the ritual celebrated in the *sanctuary*, and gives special provisions for problems that arise because of impurity from touching a corpse (cf. Hezekiah's passover). Deuteronomy also has its version of the festival calendar, in Deut 16:1-17, which differs from the description of the ritual in Exod 12. This text is discussed in more detail in Chapter 6, below.

From the biblical material, it seems that passover was always centralized, that is, centered on the sanctuary or the center of the camp, except the very first one. The story of the exodus out of Egypt is set, in narrative time, at a time before there was a sanctuary. On the passover in the book of Joshua, see below.

Ritual Purity

The concept of ritual purity is mostly concentrated in Lev 11-15, and in Num 19. Leviticus 4, which gives rules for the purification offering, should also be mentioned. Ritual purity is not given much consideration in Deuteronomy, but the presence of the dietary laws in Deut 14, for example, shows that Deuteronomy is also concerned with the phenomenon.

---

20. A proper discussion of these texts cannot be undertaken here, but see, e.g., K. W. Weyde, *The Appointed Festivals of YHWH* (FAT 2/4; Tübingen: Mohr Siebeck, 2004).

Vows and Gifts

A feature of the legislation of Lev 27 and parts of Numbers (the חרם vow in Num 21:2 and women's vows in Num 30), the regulation of vows is not found in Deuteronomy. Interestingly, the Nazirite vow and its sacrifices, regulated in Num 6, plays a role in two so-called deuteronomistic books, Judges and Samuel. In Judg 13:4–7, the Nazirite vow regarding Samson is given because his mother was barren, and is mentioned again in Judg 16:17. In a similar story of the beginnings of a hero's life, Hannah vows to offer her son to YHWH if he honors her prayer for a male offspring (1 Sam 1:11).[21] There is no Nazirite law in Deuteronomy, which, however, does not mean that such a law was not known by those who were responsible for developing the legal corpus of Deut 12–26.

The Sabbath in Deuteronomy

In Deut 5:12–15 the rationale given for the Sabbath law is different than in Exod 20:8–11; 31:12–17 and 35:2–3, but similar to Exod 23:12 and 34:21. In Lev 23:3 a reference to the Sabbath opens the ritual calendar. This seems to be a harmonization of two types, but very "generic" and unspecific (see also Lev 19:3). The Sabbath explanation is the longest of the laws in the Decalogue. It is also structurally important in Exod 25–40, marking the climax of chs. 25–31, and the very first law to be presented in Exod 35.

The two main rationales for the Sabbath found in the Pentateuch may represent two different ways of arguing its importance. Interesting to our purpose is that the contrast between Deuteronomy's rationale for the Sabbath and the majority of the Exodus references does not seem to have anything to do with Deuteronomy's argument of centralization. Sabbath is not really something that is tightly bound to the idea of cult centralization. The regulation of the Sabbath does involve specific sacrifices (Num 28:9–10, 11–15). However, Deuteronomy does not see the need to tie Sabbath legislation explicitly to the idea of the "chosen place." There is no command saying something like, "When you observe the Sabbath, you must bring your gifts and sacrifices to the place which YHWH your God will choose."

---

21. There is no mention of the word "Nazirite" in the MT text of 1 Sam 1:11 or 22, but there is mention of the vow associated with the Nazirite, "no razor shall touch his head." The Codex Vaticanus is longer and does contain reference to "one who is devoted" (ἐνώπιόν) in v. 11. 4QSam[a] contains the word *nzyr* in v. 22, which points towards efforts to expand the MT or that the MT has been shortened, purposely or by haplography. The Samuel text has normally been interpreted to denote that Samuel was offered as a Nazirite.

Traditional source criticism would probably point out that Deuteronomy's idea of Sabbath is different than the priestly one, and that perhaps Deuteronomy's Sabbath is more in line with an earlier Pentateuchal source E or J which did not emphasize the sacrificial requirements associated with the Sabbath, but emphasized it as a day of rest for the animals and workers.[22] Therefore, there was no need for Deuteronomy to write the Sabbath laws so as to fit with the idea of centralization, as had presumably been done with the sacrificial cult in general.

Further Comments on Cult, Ritual and the Cult Site in Deuteronomy
Deuteronomy's interest regarding cult and worship seems more focused on the prohibition against worshiping other gods and the prohibition against making any idol to worship, than on details concerning the sacrificial cult (Deut 5:6–10; also Deut 4:15–28; 9). This aspect, also found in the other legal bodies of the Pentateuch (cf. Exod 20 and 32; Lev 19:4; Num 25), is relatively much more pronounced in Deuteronomy.

Related to the focus on the prohibitions against illicit Yahwistic and non-Yahwistic worship are the commands to destroy the cults of the nations. In Deuteronomy, the focus of this concern is found in Deut 7, the opening and closing of ch. 12, and in the חרם laws of ch. 20. The command to destroy the nations in order to eliminate their cult is in a prominent position in these texts. Parallels to this concern elsewhere in the Pentateuch are Exod 23:23–24, which contrast with 23:25 much like Deut 12:2–3 with 12:4 (see Chapter 3, above); Exod 34:12–16; and Num 33:50–56. The idea of destroying the cults of the nations is not limited to Deuteronomy, but is a common cause of the Pentateuch. However, in the way that Deuteronomy is arranged, this concern is much more sharply focused than in the other books, and harsher, because only Deuteronomy demands extermination (חרם) of the "nations."

A related text that is interesting is the warning against following the practices of the "nations" in Lev 20:22–26. This is actually also a kind of "election" text. YHWH has separated the Israelites from "the nations."[23]

---

22. Levinson, *Deuteronomy and the Hermeneutics*, 20 n. 55, points out the "inner-biblical tendency toward the programmatic incorporation of the Sabbath in the ritual calendar" (in talking about Lev 23), citing, among others, Israel Knohl. The point being argued is that the significance of Sabbath is a late development.
23. More on the election of Israel in Chapter 7, below.

Summary
The above survey, however superficial, supports the claim that the writers of Deuteronomy probably knew of the sacrifices, presupposed them and probably saw no need to describe the rituals in detail. Whether they were known in the form specified in Lev 1–7, in Exodus, or in Numbers, or perhaps in some other form, we cannot be certain. In a synchronic approach, the reader/hearer will assume the details that have been laid out in Exodus–Numbers, when they read/hear Deuteronomy. One detail we might mention is that Deuteronomy does not mention the incense offering anywhere in the legislative portion of the text. It is only mentioned in the poetic blessing of Moses in 33:10. In contrast to the sacrifices, festival legislation is given in more detail in a way sacrifices are not, especially passover, in Deut 16:1–17 (Exod 23:14–17; Lev 23). On the Sabbath, as specified in Deut 5:12–15, the rationale is different than in Exod 20:8–11; 31:12–17; 35:2–3, but see Exod 23:12; 34:21. Finally, one point that could be mentioned is the presence of the blessings and curses of Deut 28 (cf. Lev 26). In the same way that Deut 28 formally closes the Moab covenant, the blessings and curses close the Sinai covenant in Lev 26:46.

Sinai, Horeb, and Moab
It is appropriate to make just a few comments about the "places" of the narrative that frames the legal material of the Pentateuch. The legal material of the Pentateuch has two main locations. One is Sinai, where the legal material of Exod 20–Num 9 is "situated." Some scattered material in Numbers is set into different locations along the route after breaking camp at Sinai. The other main location is Moab. Deuteronomy 1:1–5 takes great care to specify the exact location of Moses' subsequent speech "expounding this law/teaching," and also identifies the location in relation to Horeb, Deuteronomy's name for Sinai. In the received shape of the text, the location, "beyond the Jordan, in the wilderness…in the land of Moab," is the location for the whole of the book of Deuteronomy. From the place in the wilderness, Sinai/Horeb, and Moab, legislation is given for Israel's future in "the land," with reference to its past, in Egypt.[24]

---

24. Egypt plays a crucial and significant role in the book of Deuteronomy. The function of Egypt within the book will be commented on in Chapter 7, below. For a detailed analysis of space and place in Deuteronomy, see the study of M. Geiger, *Gottesräume: Die literarische und theologische Konzeption von Raum im Deuteronomium* (BWANT 183; Stuttgart: Kohlhammer, 2010) (the manuscript of which

Much more can be said about the spatial structure of Deuteronomy and of the Pentateuch as a whole. For now, we will make a couple of observations about the ceremonial aspects of the law in Deuteronomy. The Moab covenant is sealed with two "witnesses." The command to Moses that he write down "this song…in order that it may be a witness against the Israelites" (31:19, 21) intimates something like a stone or other sign that stands as a witness to the covenant. Further, Moses then writes down the law (31:24), and commands that it be a witness against the people, and that it be placed next to the ark of the covenant. He puts it in the care of the Levites who carry the ark. With this comes the command to assemble the people and read the law to them every seven years (31:9–13). The Moab covenant is thus tied intimately to the idea of a written law as something that is binding on the Israelites. The written law actually becomes the witness against the people.

Cult and Ritual in the Former Prophets

In the biblical narrative chronology, the laws of Deuteronomy are given through a speech that Moses delivers on the east side of the River Jordan, on "the plains of Moab," before the Israelites cross over and possess the land that has been promised to their forefathers. Presented as a set of speeches Moses makes before he dies, Deuteronomy contains the last recorded acts of Moses, forming the end of the story that began in Exod 2. As such, the content of Deuteronomy forms a natural part of the content of Exodus–Numbers, although some may say it is an unnecessary addition to Numbers.

The story also clearly continues from Deuteronomy on into the book of Joshua, which narrates the actual conquest of the land after authority has been handed over to Joshua at the end of both Numbers and Deuteronomy. The book of Joshua is careful to record that Joshua carries out everything "as YHWH had commanded by Moses." In many ways, the book of Joshua is a success story. The land is conquered, the "nations" are dispossessed and the Israelites settle their allotted shares of the land. The people come together to pledge their allegiance to YHWH and enter into a covenant through a ceremony. By the end of the book of Joshua, the allotment and capturing of the land have been accomplished, which are the major criteria for the validity of the law, according to Deuteronomy. But what about the concern for cultic activity at the

---

Michaela Geiger graciously provided me with prior to its publication); see also McConville and Millar, *Time and Place in Deuteronomy*.

"chosen place," what we might call the "second commandment" of Deut 12? Or what about the commandment to destroy the cult sites of the "nations"? These are not in focus in the conquest accounts in Joshua.

If, as some have claimed, the Former Prophets have been written or edited by writers with an interest in the ideology of cultic centralization, would we not expect to find references to this concern in the books themselves? As mentioned above, the narratives most often claimed to support the idea of centralization are first and foremost 2 Kgs 22–23 (discussed in Chapter 6) and 2 Kgs 18:1–12. While these accounts have stood at the center of scholarly scrutiny of the idea of cultic centralization, I think it is appropriate to investigate what each of the books of the Former Prophets contains that pertains to cultic activity. Only by taking into account the entire material can we be in a position to discuss what kind of ideology of the cult might be reflected in these books as a whole, if one can be found.

Joshua

The book of Joshua in general seems to reflect "cultic" material that provides continuity from both Numbers and Deuteronomy. This would be consistent with the source-critical observations that led to the hypothesis of the Hexateuch. Beginning with the crossing of the Jordan and the first conquests we find an account that is highly ritualized, with connections to Numbers. Some of the main features include the carrying of the ark, and the Reubenites and Gadites as vanguard storm troops (cf. Num 32:6–27).

Three towns are significant in a cultic sense in the book of Joshua. These are Gilgal, Shiloh, and Shechem (see on Shiloh and Shechem, below). Gilgal is the place of the first ritual acts in Josh 4. These consist of a circumcision ceremony and a passover celebration.

Passover marks a second crossing in Joshua, the crossing of the Jordan into the land that has been given as a heritage, recalling the crossing of the Reed/Red Sea in Egypt, out of the land of bondage. Passover is instituted and celebrated as the last thing before leaving Egypt and crossing the Red Sea in Exod 12–15. Passover is also the first celebration when the Israelites enter the land of Canaan, after crossing the River Jordan and going through the ritual of circumcision, the sign of the covenant. There is no description of how they celebrated the passover in Joshua, and there is no comment about it being celebrated according to any specific command or law or even according the way in which "YHWH had commanded by Moses," often found elsewhere in Joshua. As we shall see, this is the only account of passover in Joshua, so the book does not really give us any clues as to which ritual it follows, and there is no account of any passover celebration in Judges or Samuel either.

After the description of these first rituals the chapters that focus on the חרם follow, in Josh 6–8. These accounts tie in with the חרם laws in Deut 20, but they also continue the ritualized conception of the military camp and the conquest narratives of Numbers, as in Josh 1–3. Joshua 7, the account of the loss in battle because of Achan's sin, and the account of the conquest of Ai in Josh 8 also belong under this paradigm, as do the conquest accounts of Josh 9–12. There is no place that constitutes a ritual center in these narratives, but we may assume the layout of the camp as we know it from Numbers as a kind of "base."[25]

Joshua 8:30–35 has been mentioned above. This text recounts the enactment of the ritual commanded in Deut 28:11–26. In Joshua, as in Deuteronomy, Ebal and Gerizim are specified as the locations of the ritual. The altar or house of God in Josh 9:23, 27 was discussed above in Chapter 2, and it is in these verses that the election phrase "the place that he will choose" appears. We observed that it seems to be anachronistic in its present context, much like the mentions of Jerusalem in Joshua (see Chapter 4).

Shiloh[26] is the cultic center from Josh 18:1 and in the rest of Joshua. The tent of meeting is set up in Shiloh and becomes the center of Israel, the center of the camp. From there, the orders to possess the land go out. Shiloh is not mentioned in the Pentateuch at all. Shiloh is also of significance in Judg 18–21 and 1 Sam 1–14 (see below) and figures as the home town of the prophet Ahijah in 1 Kgs 11–14. Psalm 78 and Jer 7, 26 and 41 give testimony to a tradition that understands Shiloh as a predecessor to Jerusalem as a place that YHWH has "put his name."

In addition to Gilgal and Shiloh, Shechem is a third cult site that figures in Joshua. Unlike Gilgal and Shiloh, Shechem is important also in Genesis, and is associated with Abraham's wanderings into the land (Gen 12:6), as well as with Jacob, who buys land there after his stay in Haran and settles there (Gen 33:18–20). Shechem is a personal name in

---

25. A thorough examination of Josh 6–12 as an example of the genre of "conquest account" in the ancient world is K. L. Younger, *Ancient Conquest Accounts: A Study in Ancient Near Eastern and Biblical History Writing* (JSOTSup 98; Sheffield: JSOT, 1990).
26. For more on Shiloh, see, e.g., D. G. Schley, *Shiloh: A Biblical City and Tradition and History* (JSOTSup 63; Sheffield: JSOT, 1989). This book is useful for the surveys of the biblical material and the secondary literature, although I do not have the confidence of the author as to what we can know of "historical" Shiloh.

the following story of the rape of Dinah. The second census of Numbers enumerates the Shechemites as one of the clans of Joseph (26:31–32). As we saw above, allusions to Shechem frame the opening of the law of Deut 12–26, and immediately following it is commanded that an altar be built at on Mount Ebal as the only explicitly named future place for an altar. In this way, Shechem is alluded to as a cult center in Deuteronomy, and most likely, as seen in the discussion above, this has represented a contested tradition.

In the book of Joshua, Shechem is mentioned specifically in the description of land allotment in Josh 17:7 and is appointed as a city of refuge Josh 20:7 and 21:21. In the final gathering of Josh 24, Joshua assembles the leaders and all the tribes to Shechem. This text is a climax of the book, and together with 23:1–16, a speech directed at the leaders of Israel, summarizes both the past history and the future challenge. The people swear to obey YHWH, and enter into a covenant with Joshua. In this scene, Joshua behaves like Moses.

Finally, as a way of tying up the whole sweep of the story from the migration to Egypt in the Joseph story, to the final return to the land, Josh 24:32 recounts how Joseph's bones, which had been brought from Egypt (Gen 50:25; Exod 13:19) were buried on Jacob's plot of land that he had bought from Hamor, the father of Shechem (Gen 33:18).[27]

A challenging little story is the narrative of Josh 22. The tribes on the east side of the Jordan build a sanctuary. This text takes for granted that there is an altar in the "land" which is the legitimate one, even though not much emphasis has been placed on the building of this site. Within the context of Joshua, there has just been the one verse in 18:1. The only significant activity that has been reported from this location is the casting of lots for the allotment of land. It is clear from ch. 22, however, that the pressing issue was to avoid having a competing sacrificial altar. This is a cause for war, though there are no laws anywhere in the legal corpus to suggest what the penalty for sacrificing at a competing altar would be. Do the Israelites misunderstand the motive of Reuben, Gad and the half-tribe of Manasseh when they charge them with rebellion? The Israelites even offer them a share in the land on the west side of the Jordan, "if your land is unclean, cross over into YHWH's land where YHWH's tabernacle now stands, and take for yourselves a possession among us"

---

27. In Judges and Kings, Shechem is associated with kingship; see Chapter 8, below. The story of Abimelech in Judg 9 takes place there and Rehoboam is crowned there in 1 Kgs 12. In Ps 60:6 (= Ps 108:7), Shechem is mentioned in an oracle of victory.

(Josh 22:19). An understanding is reached when the Transjordanian tribes explain that it is not a sacrificial altar, but simply a copy of the altar, a reminder of it, that will be a witness.[28]

This rough overview of Joshua gives us a picture that is not straightforward. Even though many aspects of the narrative voice lead us to think that Joshua is acting according to what "YHWH had commanded by Moses," there are many parts of Deuteronomy that are not clearly carried out or even mentioned. When it comes to concern with cultic activity, aspects from both Numbers and Deuteronomy are clearly being "followed up." The overall impression is that the concern for a "chosen place" is fudged. It is not forgotten, but it is not anchored or shored up in any way either. Three cult sites are named and are each significant—Gilgal, Shiloh, and Shechem, in addition to the "altar" in Josh 9:27 where the Gibeonites will do service.

Judges

The book of Judges offers rich textual material. As narrative, though it is different, it gives a feel that is more in tune with Genesis than with any of the other books of the Pentateuch or even Joshua. As in Genesis, we find angels, men of God, and multiple places of theophanies.

In Judg 2:1–5, the angel of YHWH goes from Gilgal to Bochim.[29] The angel accuses the people of not keeping the covenant and not tearing down the altars of the inhabitants of the land. The angel speaks to "all the Israelites." They weep and name the place Bochim, and the sacrifice there to YHWH. This text immediately follows the lengthy introductory section of Judges, which first relates in summary fashion the wars that the Israelites fight against the Canaanite inhabitants, as they settle and claim their allotments, and then relates in equally summary fashion that they did not drive out the inhabitants.

This first reference to a "cultic" concern is therefore one that is directly related to Deuteronomy and its command to wipe out the cult of the "nations," but also to Exod 34 and Num 33:50–56. The first chapters of Judges thus fit well into a "deuteronomistic" mind set, following up concerns from Deuteronomy and recapitulating much of Joshua and then picking up the story from the ending of Joshua, even retelling the event of his death. But it is important to remind ourselves that this ideology is

---

28. For references to literature, and a literary analysis of Josh 22, see E. Assis, "The Position and Function of Jos 22 in the Book of Joshua," *ZAW* 116 (2004): 528–41.

29. The place name Bochim ("those who weep") is attested nowhere else; in the LXX it is Bethel.

not restricted to the book of Deuteronomy, and it may not even be totally correct to call it a "deuteronomistic" concern. Perhaps it is fairer to the material to acknowledge that the command to tear down the altars of the nations and wipe out their cult sites is represented by the narratives of Exodus, Numbers, and Deuteronomy.

Judges 2:6 seems to begin the story over again. In addition to giving redaction critics material, this "retelling" of Joshua's death allows for another important motif from Numbers and Deuteronomy to be picked up again, namely the idea that only the actual conquest generation was righteous, because of the "sin of Baal-Peor." In Judges, the motif of the wilderness is reversed; after the conquest, a new generation is born that does not know YHWH, and they begin to worship "the baals."

It is this motif of the Israelites' worship of the *baalim* and the *asherim* that is the subject in Judg 3:7, which begins the first "cycle" of narratives about the judges. The motif of the Israelites' worship of "other" gods is one of the fundamental tenets of the wilderness narrative, of the prophetic literature, and of Judges and Kings (see below) and Chronicles. This comprehensive subject cannot rightly be characterized as "deuteronomistic," because it is not limited to Deuteronomy, but is a shared concern of large portions of the biblical literature. If it should be called anything, maybe "Sinaiitic" is more correct, representing the revelation of law at Sinai, and would include the version in Deuteronomy. Or "prophetic," since the concern not to worship other gods is one of the main topics of prophetic preaching.

As we continue into Judges, we will make note of the richness of the material pertaining to ritual activity and the cult site. This material cannot easily be subsumed under a general ideology. In Judg 4:5, we note that two places of cultic importance are mentioned as Deborah's place of judgment: between Ramah and Bethel in Ephraim. The book of Judges operates with multiple sites of cultic importance, and never addresses the concern of a "chosen place."

The Gideon cycle begins in ch. 6. In Judg 6:11–24, the angel of YHWH comes to the oak at Ophrah and speaks to Gideon. He brings it food and it is consumed by fire. Gideon recognizes the angel, is afraid but is comforted by YHWH, and responds by building an altar, calling it "YHWH is peace." Readers are told that it stands "to this day" at Ophrah, which belongs to the Abiezrites. This story brings to mind some Genesis stories that relate a theophanic event and the subsequent construction of an altar (e.g. Gen 28:18–22).

In Judg 6:25–32 Gideon becomes "Jerubbaal." Gideon is told by YHWH to tear down the altar of Baal that belongs to his father. He does so, secretly at night, and sacrifices a bull on the altar using *asherah* he has torn down as firewood, in effect sacrificing that too. The townspeople are at first upset and want to put him to death, but Joash, Gideon's father, intervenes. Gideon is possessed by the spirit of YHWH (Judg 6:34). They prevail against Midian. In this story, there is no narratorial comment about the way in which he worships or about Gideon fulfilling the command to tear down altars of Baal. It is ironic, however, that in tearing down the Baal altar, Gideon receives a Baal name (meaning "let Baal indict").

In 7:15, after several rounds of demanding signs that God is with him and he finally feels convinced, Gideon worships (וישתחו; LXX specifies, κυρίου). There are no details on how he worships. In the battle against the Midianites (7:19–23), we find characteristics of ritual battle, recalling Numbers, with much blowing of trumpets.

In a story that recalls the golden calf episode, we find the episode of Gideon's ephod (8:24–27). Gideon refuses to be made king (8:22–23), but, in return, it seems, he asks the people to collect earrings, and he makes what is referred to as an ephod, which seems to be a statue. In a comment that ties back to 2:3, the eager worship of the people ("and all Israel prostituted itself") is presented as forming a trap (מוקש) for Gideon and his house.

Gideon lives in Ophrah, has seventy sons, and is buried there. He also has a son with a Shechemite concubine. This son, Abimelech (8:29–32), is the next protagonist. As throughout Judges, there are connections to multiple towns and places, and no one particular cult site seems to be favored. The Gideon cycle seems to contain elements from various traditions, but there is no obvious connection to Deuteronomy, and it stands on its own.

The transitional 8:33–35 is quite interesting. After Gideon's death, the Israelites fall away, and begin "prostituting themselves with the Baals, making Baal-berith their god" (8:33).[30] In 8:34–35, remarks follow on the behavior of the Israelites. According to the narrator, they do not remember YHWH their God, and did not show loyalty to the house of Jerubbaal (Gideon). They are chastised for not following YHWH and not being loyal to their leader's house, for all the good that he did. In the book of Kings, it is the rulers who receive a comment of judgment on their reign.

---

30. This is the recurring pattern in the Judges cycles, occurring also in 10:6–16. In 3:7, which introduces this theme, the people are accused of worshiping Baals and Asherahs, but the accusation of worshiping Asherahs is not made again in the book of Judges after the Gideon story.

Here, in Judges, it is the people who are judged for their lack of faithfulness.

The story of Abimelech in Judg 9 will be brought up again in Chapter 8, below, which discusses kingship. We observe for now that it is centered on Shechem. I will also briefly mention the "temple of their god," in 9:27. The people of Shechem eat and drink there, ridiculing and plotting against Abimelech. What kind of temple and which deity is this? It is not clear, but it could be El-berith. A "stronghold of the temple of El-berith" is mentioned in v. 46 (cf. Baal-berith in 8:33). The moral of the story is given in v. 56: Abimelech is punished for having killed off the seventy heirs to the throne.

Although interesting in their own right, the stories of Jephthah in Judg 11:1–12:7 and Samson in Judg 13–16 will only be mentioned in passing here for their connection to cultic practice. The Jephthah story involves no particular cult site, but involves the vow of burnt sacrifice. Samson is a Nazirite. The law of the Nazirite vow is given in Numbers, but not mentioned in Deuteronomy. Samson's parents sacrifice a kid as a burnt offering to YHWH, together with a grain offering. The angel ascends with the flame of the altar (13:15–23).

The next story to mention is that of Micah and the Danites in Judg 17–18. Micah sets up his own private temple (house of God). The silver for the sanctuary is originally stolen from his mother, but he returns it to her and she consecrates it to YHWH and makes an image, which she sets in Micah's private "house of God." He also installs an ephod, teraphim, and his own son as a priest. Then, a Levite from Bethlehem comes and takes a job there (17:7–13).

This whole shrine, including the priest, is then seized and taken away by the Danites on their migration to find land. They settle in Laish, which they conquer. They set up the idol there, and maintain it "as long as the house of God was at Shiloh" (18:31). The ephod in question here, as in the Gideon cycle, is a cultic object, not a priestly garment associated with divination, as in Samuel or the Pentateuch.

The reference to the "house of God at Shiloh" gives some support to the idea that this was recognized as a central shrine. It is, however, the first time that Shiloh is mentioned in the book of Judges, and there has been no indication so far that there has been a concern for a central cult location. It comes almost as a kind of excuse or explanation in the Micah story, one that is not really needed within the context of the book of Judges. However, in the last part of Judges, Shiloh plays a role, as it also does in the opening of 1 Samuel.

5. *The Cultic Context of the "Chosen Place"*

The details of the story of Judg 19 will not be commented on in this context, although it is the pretext for the next two chapters, which I will comment on.[31] In a detail that ties Judg 17–18 together with ch. 19, a Levite from Bethlehem becomes a priest in Ephraim, whereas in ch. 19, a Levite from Ephraim takes a wife/concubine from Bethlehem.

In Judg 20:1, all of Israel gathers for the first time since 1:1. They assemble before YHWH at Mizpah (in Benjamin?). It is decided to avenge the rape of the Levite's concubine and put the perpetrators to justice. The Benjaminites do not cooperate, but instead assemble in Gibeah, to fight against all the other tribes. The Israelites proceed to move to Bethel to consult YHWH (actually, the text says Elohim, 20:18), three days in a row. This type of gathering for divine consultation also happens in 1:1, where the Israelites ask how to proceed in the conquest against the Canaanites. In Judg 20, they fast and offer sacrifices. In 20:27, there is a piece of information detailing that the ark of the covenant was at Bethel in those days, and that Phinehas, son of Eleazar, son of Aaron, was ministering there. This information seems to provide a rationale for the ritual consultation of YHWH at Bethel, but it is also odd in the context of Judges. Gideon, for example, did not need the ark of the covenant in order to consult YHWH for advice. It is the only point at which the ark of the covenant is mentioned in Judges.

The ritual preparation for battle that is described reminds us more of Joshua than Judges. The city of Gibeah is destroyed and all the area of the city is *heremized* (20:37, 48). Six hundred flee to the rock of Rimmon (20:47). In Judg 21:2–4, in the post-massacre gathering at Bethel, the Israelites carry out a ceremony of lament, lamenting the lack of a tribe in Israel. The next day, the people get up and build an altar, and sacrifice the burnt sacrifice and the sacrifice of well-being (שלמים). In the following, two issues are solved with one action. First (21:5–12), the Israelites recall their vow to kill anyone who had not come to Mizpah. This comes up in order to find someone who had not promised not to marry Benjaminites, because they regret having a tribe be cut off. They remember that the people of Jabesh-gilead had not been there. They send off soldiers to kill them all, including children, but take 400 virgins, who they bring back to "the camp at Shiloh, which is in the land of Canaan."

As a final follow up, in 21:13–14 the Benjaminites return to Gibeah, presumably from the rock of Rimmon, and get the women from Jabesh-gilead, but they are not enough for them. The problem of there not being enough women is discussed, and the solution to abduct dancers from the

---

31. For an insightful study of Judg 19, see S. Lasine, "Guest and Host in Judges 19: Lot's Hospitality in an Inverted World," *JSOT* 29 (1984): 37–59.

yearly festival in Shiloh is arrived at. It is not clear at all how, if in any way, Shiloh is affected by these events, which are associated with it from now on. It is quite clear, however, that the narrator wishes to highlight the outrageous nature of both the initial crime in ch. 19, the revenge of the Israelites, and the manner in which they solve the problem of the continuity of the tribe of Benjamin.

In sum, the book of Judges begins with what can be seen as close reference to the agenda of Deuteronomy, but also of Exodus–Numbers. The main portion of the book, however, does not follow through on this agenda, although the opening of the book may have helped provide a reason for why there is no concern with a central cult site or the elimination of the cult of the "nations." Toward the end of the book, in spite of references to motifs such as the cult site of Shiloh or the place of the ark of the covenant (when did it ever get to Bethel anyway?), the main theme is the internal meltdown of Israelite social structures and a descent into chaos. The refrain that "at that time there was no king in Israel" does not even begin to explain this situation.[32]

Samuel
The book of Samuel begins with Shiloh as the central shrine. We are told that Elkanah went up "year by year" from his town to worship and sacrifice at Shiloh, to the "house of YHWH" (1:7) and that the sons of Eli were priests of YHWH there. Elkanah goes up to offer the "yearly sacrifice" (1:21, also 2:19). Hannah goes later, when Samuel is weaned, to give him as a Nazirite, and to offer a (three year?) bull, an ephah of flour and a skin of wine.

There is an intertwining of the story of the young Samuel and his dedication and the story of the downfall of Eli's sons. In this context the oracle of man of God in 2:27–36 is significant.[33] YHWH refers to having chosen a priest "out of all tribes of Israel" (see above, Chapter 2, on this expression). Now he passes judgment on this "house," even after making an eternal promise (2:30). In the future, there will be a new priest who is faithful, and a promise of a "sure house" is made (2:35). In reference to this text (and ch. 15), themes of "sacrifice, obedience/hearing, disobedience/sin, life, and death…are interspersed throughout the text."[34]

32. See the summary on "cultic order" in Joshua and Judges in P. D. Miscall, *1 Samuel: A Literary Reading* (ISBL; Bloomington: Indiana University Press, 1986), 4–8. In general, this study offers valuable perspectives on the place of "cult" in 1 Samuel.

33. On this oracle, its connections to other biblical texts, and on the topic of a priestly "house" and its fate, see ibid., 16–24.

34. Ibid., 18.

The "ark narrative," mentioned above, figures prominently in 1 Sam 4–7. Eli falls backwards and dies when he hears the news that the ark has been captured (4:18). When the ark is returned to Beth-shemesh after causing the Philistines much suffering, the people offer the milch cows that had towed them as a burnt offering to YHWH. The Levites take down the ark and set it on a stone, offer burnt offerings and present sacrifices to YHWH (6:14–15). After the punishment of the family of Jeconiah, the village asks for Kiriath-jearim to come and get the ark. Abinadab's son Eleazar is consecrated to be in charge of it (7:1).

Chapter 7 paints a portrait of Samuel as a prophet calling for return to YHWH (7:3–4), as intercessor (7:5–6, 8), judge (7:6), leading a cultic, apotropaic ritual (7:8–10), and setting up a memorial stone (7:12). Ramah is the home base for Samuel. He builds an altar to YHWH there (7:17), travels to other towns, judging Israel there: Bethel, Gilgal, and Mizpah. We note that there is neither one place that is central, nor one type of cult, but this portion of the narrative is centered on Samuel as a person and on the threat from the Philistines.

In the complex narrative of 1 Sam 8–12 (discussed further in Chapter 8), several place names are associated with cultic activity. The gathering where the people demand a king takes place at Ramah (8:4–6). Chapter 9 mentions the land of Zuph, a sacrifice at the shrine (*bamah*), in Ramah, and the seer Samuel coming. First Samuel 10:8 mentions Gibeah, or hill of God (10:5, 9). Gilgal, previously also figured in Josh 4, is mentioned as the place that Saul will go to wait for Samuel to sacrifice burnt offering and well-being. Mizpah (10:17–27) is the location for the lot-casting ceremony convened by Samuel, in which Saul is chosen as king.

In a similar way, the rest of the book of Samuel operates with numerous place names and it will not be helpful to go into minute detail. What is clear is that in the relationship between Saul, Samuel, and YHWH portrayed in 1 Sam 13–15, Saul's transgressions are overwhelmingly cast as cultic sin. Thus, Saul sacrifices without waiting for Samuel, whereupon Samuel chastises him, predicting that Saul will lose his kingdom (13:8–14); Saul's men eat of the booty, eating blood, following which Saul builds his first altar to YHWH (14:31–34); Saul's troops spare part of the booty from the battle against the Amalekites, in order to sacrifice it to YHWH, an action which leads to Samuel chastising Saul, again emphasizing that Saul will have the kingdom taken from him (15:15–30). In general, Saul is portrayed as performing cultic and ritual acts regularly, but his efforts are often frustrated. This type of concern with ritual sin does not seem to be of central concern to Deuteronomy. Samuel's ritual hacking up of King Agag "before YHWH" has no corresponding law or information in any part of the Pentateuch or any other text.

Access to the divine will is a theme in the struggle between Saul and David (chs. 16–31). First Samuel portrays the king and king-to-be as both having legitimate ways to access God, but Saul is consistently disfavored. The most telling example of this is the story of Saul seeking out the medium at En-dor. This story is unique in its specific details, but at the same time it illustrates perfectly the workings of divine consultation.[35] This text also clearly illustrates a concern about legitimate methods of divination, something that Deuteronomy is concerned with (i.e. Deut 18:10–11). The characterization of Saul as someone who broke these laws is seen by the Chronicler as the single most important aspect to mention about him, and is presented as the cause of his death and of why the kingdom was given to David (1 Chr 10:13–14).

Second Samuel is dominated by the story of David's monarchy and his many wars, and there is very little material in it that relates to cultic interests. Some portions relevant for this survey were mentioned in the previous chapter, such as the "ark narrative" and 2 Sam 7. In 6:12–19 David plays the role of priest when he brings the ark to the "city of David." We noted there that "Jerusalem" in 2 Sam 8–20 basically connotes a strategic location. Its association with the place of the ark demonstrates the role of the ark in warfare (e.g. 15:24–29). Hebron is mentioned a couple of times as a cultic location in 2 Samuel, and is also a place associated with the anointing of kings (2:4; 15:7–10, 12). At the end of the book, David again plays a priestly role, when he is told by the prophet Gad to erect and altar to YHWH on Araunah's threshing ground. This is the spot where an angel of YHWH was standing (21:16–17), a figure who had been bringing destruction as punishment for David's census, when David spots him and confesses his guilt. David buys this land from Araunah and offers the עלה and the שלמים. As I have pointed out (Chapter 4), Chronicles makes an explicit connection between this spot of land and the place of the future temple, whereas Kings does not refer back to this story in Samuel explicitly.

Kings
Throughout this study, I have been dealing with multiple texts from the books of Kings. It is probably correct to say that on the topic of cult site and cultic activity, Deuteronomy has most connections with Kings out of all the books of the Former Prophets. The following section will fill in on some areas we have not touched on, and briefly mention others that will be discussed further in following chapters. For example, we have already

---

35. On this aspect of 1 Sam 28, see my *Ask God: Divine Consultation in the Literature of the Hebrew Bible* (Frankfurt a.M.: Lang, 2002), 86–91.

brought into the discussion the texts that account for the bringing of the ark to the City of David and then into the temple. First Kings 8 has also been discussed in previous chapters (Chapters 2 and 4). Further, we have looked into the texts that talk about Jerusalem as a "chosen city" (Chapter 2).

The account of the building of the temple itself (1 Kgs 6–7) is closely related to Exod 25–31 and 35–40, and follows a "temple-building" genre.[36] Although there is not space for a full exploration of the texts involved, I would like to pose that there is something of a parallel between the juxtapositioning of the legislation for the temple and the episode of the golden calf in Exodus, and the juxtapositioning of the account of Solomon's temple-building activity and the establishment of a competing cult by his rival, in 1 Kgs 12–13. Each figures the other.[37]

In Kings, the cultic and ritual activity of Israel and Judah is narrated mostly through the accounts of the kings and through the activity of the prophets (mainly Elijah and Elisha). The most significant story from the Elijah cycle is the contest between YHWH and the baals on Mount Carmel, in 1 Kgs 18. This text, a great illustration of the struggle between Baal and YHWH, does not concern itself whatsoever with any idea that sacrifice should only take place at one central location. What matters is to whom Ahab should have allegiance, and which deity it is that can made it rain.

The cultic activity initiated or practiced by the biblical kings is surveyed more fully in Chapter 8. What is important to mention at this point is that, contrary to what Deuteronomy stipulates for the king in Deut 17, kings are portrayed as cult leaders in Kings. They take an active part in leading cult reforms and are judged according to their merits in terms of cultic fidelity to YHWH. Only once is a king said to have read the law, actually "words of the book of the covenant" (2 Kgs 23:3). The king gets his guidance through prophets, even when a law book is found and read to him (2 Kgs 22).

---

36. Also found in Ezek 40–48. The dependence of the temple building account on ancient Near Eastern genres of temple-building was explored by A. S. Kapelrud, "Temple Building: A Task for Gods and Kings," *Or* 32 (1963): 56–62; see also V. Hurowitz, *I Have Built You an Exalted House: Temple Building in the Bible in Light of Mesopotamian and North-West Semitic Writings* (JSOTSup 115; JSOT/ASOR Monograph Series 5; Sheffield: JSOT, 1992).

37. This relationship is complicated and would involve careful analysis in order to say more at this point. For an idea of the types of links I have in mind, see, e.g., Hauge, *The Descent from the Mountain*, 174–89.

Deuteronomy and Exodus both have commands to destroy the *asherim* of the nations. In the Former Prophets, mention of *asherah* is found in Judges (five times) and in Kings (sixteen times). In Judges, four of the occurrences are found in the Gideon cycle, when he is commissioned to tear down his father's altar and told to erect a new one (Judg 6:25–30, see above).

In 1 Kgs 14:7–16, the prophet Ahijah speaks to Jeroboam's wife when she comes to him in disguise to inquire about her sick son. In the context of an oracle of judgment on the kingdom of Israel, Ahijah accuses Israel of having erected *asherim* (1 Kgs 14:15), among other offenses. Immediately following this story, which announces judgment on Israel in the future because of the "sins of Jeroboam," we find the summary of Rehoboam's reign. As a part of this, Judah[38] is accused of various misdeeds, among them of building *matzevot* and *asherim* "on every *bamot* and under every green tree" (1 Kgs 14:21–24). This is the most common context for the mention of *asherim* in the books of Kings. Similarly, in 2 Kings, *asherim* are mentioned in 17:10, 16, when Israel was destroyed because the people set up *asherim*, among other things; in 18:4, as part of Hezekiah's reform; in 21:3, 7, when Manasseh reverts the reform of Hezekiah, and five times in the reform report in 2 Kgs 23, see Chapter 6.[39]

Conclusions

On the subject of the sanctuary, sacrificial activity, and cultic ritual in the Pentateuch, not only Deuteronomy distinguishes itself from the others, but so does Genesis. Genesis, in many ways, reflects a different world, although we have pointed out many links between it and later biblical books.[40] The above survey showed that while Deuteronomy has some features that distinguishes it from the rest of the Pentateuch—for example, it is not concerned with a sanctuary, does not speak much of an altar, and does not describe the sacrifices—it nevertheless has multiple links to other cultic legislation. When read in context, the details of Exodus–Numbers are carried over into Deuteronomy. On specific ordinances,

---

38. The LXX manuscripts either do not contain the reference to Judah or have "Rehoboam" instead.

39. Asa, a good king, removes the *asherim* that his mother had set up (1 Kgs 15:13). *Asherah* figures also in the Elijah stories, as the goddess that Ahab's wife Jezebel followed, and her prophets are mentioned in 1 Kgs 18:19.

40. For a survey of the concept of holiness in Genesis as contrasted with Exodus, see S. Lasine, "'Everything Belongs to Me': Holiness, Danger, and Divine Kingship in the Post-Genesis World," *JSOT* 35 (2010): 31–62.

such as the Sabbath and festivals, Deuteronomy is more specific, and makes interpretations that distinguish it from the rest (however, Exodus contains multiple rationales for the Sabbath).

Joshua gives a mixed picture. On one hand, it is intent on following up ideas and themes from Deuteronomy as well as Numbers, and reports on how Joshua carries out activities "as YHWH had commanded by Moses." The idea of a central cult site is followed up by the reporting of the setting up of the sanctuary in Shiloh and the controversy over the sanctuary built by the two and a half tribes in Josh 22. However, there are multiple cult sites that are considered significant.

Judges gives a rich and unclear picture. Cult sites abound and there appears to be no idea of a single cult site. Although the book begins with the concern that the "nations" have not been wiped out or dispossessed, as Deuteronomy commands, this concern is not sustained actively in the rest of the book. The narrative is focused on individual leader figures and their actions. At the most, we can say that the picture painted in Judg 1 serves to provide an explanation for why the "nations" continued to inhabit the land, why Israel worshiped other gods, and why YHWH punishes Israel (2:20–3:6).

As we saw in Chapter 4, the interest in a "house for YHWH" in 2 Samuel and 1 Kings is connected to the "chosen city" rhetoric. Whereas Deuteronomy is not interested in the sanctuary at all, but is focused on the one place for cultic activity, Samuel and Kings are interested in the idea of a "house for YHWH," and relate the process toward the end result of building the temple in Jerusalem. Even though Samuel and especially Kings make connections between the idea of building a temple and the idea of "chosen city" and Jerusalem as chosen, there is not really an explicit connection between Deuteronomy's concept of "place that YHWH will choose" and the fact that the temple is built in Jerusalem. The survey in the present chapter has provided more reason to point to a tension between Deuteronomy and Samuel–Kings in the understanding of cult and the cult site.

One conclusion from this survey is that points of contact between Deuteronomy and Samuel–Kings *are only tangential* when it comes to the theme of cult and ritual, or of the cult site. In fact, on the topics of "chosen city," David and Jerusalem/Zion, Kings has much stronger links to other biblical textual traditions, for example Psalms and Prophets. And when Kings tells the story of the building of the "house for YHWH," it turns to a genre we otherwise find in several other biblical texts, but not in Deuteronomy: in Exod 25–40, in Ezek 40–48, and also in Chronicles.

As a general conclusion, I think the material surveyed in this chapter provides a basis for the conclusion that scholarship has overemphasized the points of contact between Deuteronomy and the books of the Former Prophets, and has overemphasized the distinction of Deuteronomy from the rest of the Pentateuch. In Chapter 6, I will explore what this finding has to say for the understanding of 2 Kgs 22–23.

Chapter 6

"CENTRALIZATION" AND THE STORY OF JOSIAH'S REFORM: IS DEUTERONOMY 12 CENTRAL TO JOSIAH?

Up to this point in this book there have been several findings that will impact the reading of 2 Kgs 22–23. Chapter 2 demonstrated the distinction between the "chosen place" in Deuteronomy and the "chosen city" in Kings. Deuteronomy's dynamic of centralization was explored further in Chapter 3. In Kings, rather than a concept of centralization, the phrases "the city that I have chosen" or "Jerusalem, the city that I have chosen" express an ideology of YHWH's protection that is closely associated with the privileged position of David and his dynasty. In 1 Kgs 8, this phrase was associated with the building of a "house for YHWH's name," the temple, but in most cases the concept is associated with the protection and eventual destruction of Jerusalem. Even though scholarship has identified the election phrases in Kings with the idea of the "chosen place" in Deuteronomy, and seen the "chosen city" concept as an application of the concept from Deuteronomy, it is, oddly enough, not really these "chosen place" texts that have been the crucial ones in arguing for the presence of cult centralization in the DH. Instead, the reform accounts of specific Judean kings, Josiah in particular, but also Hezekiah, have constituted the cornerstones for the idea of "centralization" in the DH. As the present chapter will illustrate, in the case of the idea of a "deuteronomistic program of centralization" and the closely interrelated construct of "deuteronomistic cult reform," the identification of the book found in 2 Kgs 22 has been fundamental.

Second Kings 22–23 is most commonly understood as a narrative counterpart to the legal text of Deut 12 with respect to the concept of centralization. In investigating 2 Kgs 22–23, this chapter will interrogate the commonly held scholarly opinion that 2 Kgs 23 narrates how King Josiah carried out a set of reforms that implemented a "deuteronomistic" demand for cultic reform, including what is referred to as centralization, and ended his reform with the celebration of the passover following the deuteronomistic ritual. Keeping in mind the analysis of Deut 12 from Chapter 3 and the surveys of Chapters 4 and 5, I will attempt to unravel some of the constructions of scholarship as we make a probe into this text that has so often been put to the task of demonstrating "in practice" the implementation of the laws of Deuteronomy.

Scholarship on Josiah's Reform: Some Remarks

The idea of a deuteronomistic reform program as understood in biblical research is readily observable in a wealth of scholarship, and is well summarized in R. Albertz, *A History of Israelite Religion*.[1] Josiah's reform as narrated in 2 Kgs 23 has been understood by many scholars, certainly by M. Noth, as the report of an actual deuteronomistic program of reform that was carried out in the late seventh century B.C.E. Others might see the story of Josiah's reform as an expression of the activity of a deuteronomistic school of thought that either stood behind the reform or was inspired by it and that had a far-reaching impact on the composition of biblical texts. As pointed out in the introductory chapter, 2 Kgs 22–23 has been pivotal for the dating the book of Deuteronomy, and has constituted a crucial component of the many variants of the DH hypothesis.

In spite of its crucial place in the enterprise of reconstructing the history of the religious and political development of ancient Israel, scholars have not reached any agreement on the literary history of 2 Kgs 22–23. There are multiple explanations of its literary growth and dating of discreet textual "layers."[2] This, in turn, deeply affects any attempt to explain the composition of the DH, since the Kings text is so central to it. To complicate things further, although one might hear the statement that the book found in 2 Kgs 22 is Deuteronomy, on closer inspection, an early version of chs. 12–26 is usually meant, not Deuteronomy in its present shape. Further, there is no agreement on the degree to which 2 Kgs 22–23 reflects "historical reality" or in what way it can be used as

---

1. R. Albertz, *A History of Israelite Religion in the Old Testament Period*. Vol. 1, *From the Beginnings to the End of the Monarchy* (trans. J. Bowden; OTL; Louisville, Ky.: Westminster John Knox, 1994), 195–231.

2. For one summary and discussion of this situation, see C. Conroy, "Reflections on the Exegetical Task: Apropos of Recent Studies on 2 Kg 22–23," in *Pentateuchal and Deuteronomistic Studies: Papers Read at the 13th IOSOT Congress Leuven 1989* (ed. C. Brekelmans and J. Lust; BETL 94; Leuven: Leuven University Press, 1990), 255–68. This situation has not changed notably in the years since this publication came out.

a source for historical reconstruction.³ This situation reminds us of how difficult some of these historical questions are, and how much it should caution us about the fragility of any reconstruction.

The idea of Josiah's reform as implementing centralization and the understanding of his passover as deuteronomistic bases itself to a large extent on the identification of the book found in 2 Kgs 22:8 with some form of Deuteronomy. The following will show how crucial this identification is to the reading of the text.

When de Wette suggested tentatively the identification of Josiah's law book with Deuteronomy as a "not-improbable deduction,"⁴ his main interest was to argue the distinction of Deuteronomy from the other books of the Pentateuch, especially with its emphasis on the centralization of the cult, and thus also to argue a date for Deuteronomy that was later than the Tetrateuch, and to put forward an argument against a Mosaic authorship for Deuteronomy. It was, however, the identification of Josiah's law book that he has become most famous for, and the link between Josiah and the book of Deuteronomy, or some form of it, has since been axiomatic in biblical research.⁵

---

3. The debate between the so-called maximalists and minimalists has made its mark also on the question of the "historicity" of Josiah's reform. The debate about the nature of the biblical texts as sources for historical knowledge has thus had an impact also on this question. If one takes the challenges seriously, historians are left with very little with which to reconstruct any reform in the seventh century B.C.E. For a discussion of the methodological difficulties, see Chr. Hardmeier, "King Josiah in the Climax of the Deuteronomic History (2 Kings 22–23) and the Pre-Deuteronomic Document of a Cult Reform at the Place of Residence (23.4–15*): Criticism of Sources, Reconstruction of Literary Pre-Stages and the Theology of History in 2 Kings 22–23*," in Grabbe, ed., *Good Kings and Bad Kings*, 123–63. See further, e.g., C. Levin, "Joschija im deuteronomistischen Geschichtswerk," *ZAW* 96 (1984): 351–71; H. Niehr, "Die Reform des Joschija: Methodische, historische und religionsgeschichtliche Aspekte," in Gross, ed., *Jeremia und die "deuteronomistische Bewegung"*, 33–55; Handy, "Historical Probability," 252–75; L. E. Fried, "The High Places (*BĀMÔT*) and the Reforms of Hezekiah and Josiah: An Archaeological Investigation," *JAOS* 122 (2002): 437–65. For a more optimistic, yet critically sophisticated approach, see B. Barrick, *The King and the Cemeteries: Toward a New Understanding of Josiah's Reform* (VTSup 88; Leiden: Brill, 2002).

4. According to Rogerson, *W. M. L. de Wette*, 40.

5. Modern commentators take various positions. M. Cogan and Ch. Tadmor, *II Kings: A New Translation with Introduction and Commentary* (AB 11; New York: Doubleday, 1988), 294, go for the general consensus regarding the identity of the book, though they do not disregard that Deuteronomy can be older than the seventh century (297–99); J. Gray, *I & II Kings: A Commentary* (2d fully rev. ed.; OTL; Philadelphia: Westminster, 1970), 715–20, claims that what was found was the legal nucleus of Deuteronomy, chs. 12–26 and 28, "which made such an impression on

Despite the general consensus regarding the identification of the book found in the temple with some form of Deuteronomy, there have been dissenting voices. Some have argued that it was the Covenant Code,[6] a document from the "Holiness school,"[7] or simply deny that it can be Deuteronomy.[8] Note, however, that all of these scholars do think that some type of religious reform did occur in seventh-century Jerusalem and that Deuteronomy or the Deuteronomists have some connection to it. The question is thus not about the historicity of Josiah's reform, it is more about the identification of the document he is said to have found, and about the literary history of the text chronicling his reform. The fact that there are good arguments in support of or in favor of different books as having been found in 2 Kgs 22 is an indication that the text is slippery, and that any reconstruction is fraught with difficulty.

The difference between the ancient understanding of the "book of the law" as Deuteronomy, or as the Torah, and the modern, scholarly application of this reading, is the implication that a historical reconstruction that is distinctly different from the biblical story can be reached. The church fathers and the rabbis thought that Moses had written the law and

Josiah" (716); G. H. Jones, *1 and 2 Kings*, vol. 2 (NCB; Grand Rapids: Eerdmans, 1984), 610–11, reviews several views on the law book, and argues by way of circular reasoning that he thinks it is Deuteronomy, because the account was written by a deuteronomistic writer. T. E. Fretheim, *First and Second Kings* (The Westminster Bible Companion; Louisville, Ky.: Westminster John Knox, 1999), 213, is not sure what is referred to by the book that is found, but nevertheless assumes that Josiah's passover was shaped by the ideas of Deuteronomy. T. R. Hobbs, *2 Kings* (WBC 13; Waco, Tex.: Word, 1985), 312, 325, cites literature on identification of book with Deuteronomy and refers the consensus but also challengers, such as J. R. Lundbom, "The Lawbook of the Josianic Reform," *CBQ* 38 (1976): 293–302, who thinks that it was not a part of the legal core that was found, but Deut 32. M. A. Sweeney, *I & II Kings: A Commentary* (OTL; Louisville, Ky.: Westminster John Knox, 2007), 444, 449–50, identifies the book as the "Torah...as a version of Deuteronomy." Even E. Würthwein simply refers to the consensus, *Die Bücher der Könige 1.Kön. 17–2.Kön. 25* (ATD 11/2; Göttingen: Vandenhoeck & Ruprecht, 1984), 447.

6. N. Lohfink, "Die Bundesurkunde des König Josias (Eine Frage an die Deuteronomiumsforschung)," *Bib* 44 (1963): 261–88, 461–98 (280–84); E. Reuter, *Kultzentralization*, 255–58, thinks the Covenant Code is the basis for Josiah's actions, and that Deuteronomy is a result of his reform rather than a cause of it.

7. G. R. Berry, "The Code Found in the Temple," *JBL* 59 (1920): 44–50; L. Shedletsky, "Josiah's Reform and the Dynamics of Defilement: A Phenomenological Approach to 2 Kings 23" (Ph.D. diss., New York University, 2004), has argued that a document originating in the Holiness School in the late seventh century was later modified by Deuteronomists in the postexilic period.

8. E.g. Wenham, "Deuteronomy and the Central Sanctuary," 114–16.

that the book had been lost and then was found again, but de Wette and his successors did not think that. They thought that "the book" had been composed recently, and began to dissect the biblical text in search of what plausibly and logically could have been the its contents. With varying methods and slightly different models, scholars have continued to do this for the last 200 years.

What we need to keep in mind for the present purposes is that whether or not interpreters view Josiah's reform as depicting a historical event,[9] as a piece of royal propaganda to give Josiah's reign legitimacy as a project of national assertion at a time of Assyrian drawback,[10] or as religious propaganda for an internal religious reform led by the Deuteronomists (whoever they were),[11] or see the account as written in a much later period, painting Josiah as an righteous king,[12] or as a composition that has a long and complicated literary history where the reform report itself might reflect an actual reform, but which in its present shape does not reflect an accurate historical event (and there are other possibilities), the fact remains that the association between the reform and Deuteronomy is made by most readers.[13] The details of individual reconstructions depend

---

9. E.g. N. Lohfink, "Die Gattung der 'Historischen Kurtzgeschichte' in den letzten Jahren von Juda und in der Zeit des Babylonischen Exils," *ZAW* 90 (1978): 319–47. Chr. Uehlinger, "Was There a Cult Reform Under Kings Josiah? The Case for a Well-Grounded Minimum," in Grabbe, ed., *Good Kings and Bad Kings*, 279–316 (a revised and translated version of his 1995 article in German, this study is mainly a response to H. Niehr's "minimalist" position; see n. 3, above).

10. For many scholars, the historical context of the Neo-Assyrian Empire in the seventh century constitutes an important matrix for understanding Josiah's actions, and his program is seen as a nationalistic endeavor to re-conquer areas of the Northern Kingdom and unify the land somewhat like a second Joshua or a second David.

11. Instead of seeing it as a response to Assyrian hegemony, Eynikel, *The Reform of King Josiah*, 8, argues that a pre-exilic DH was composed during the reign of Josiah to idealize him as "the monarch who reunited the people of Israel around the Temple in Jerusalem"; see also M. A. Sweeney, "The Critique of Solomon in the Josianic Edition of the Deuteronomistic History," *JBL* 114 (1995): 607–22; in 1976, E. Würthwein argued that 2 Kgs 22–23 did not reflect a historical reform, but that it was written to give support to the ideology of Deuteronomy in the exilic/post-exilic Jewish community; see Würthwein, "Die josianische Reform und das Deuteronomium," *ZAW* 73 (1976): 395–423.

12. E.g. Davies, "Josiah and the Law Book," 65–77.

13. Even scholars who might think that Deuteronomy's centralization laws are originally independent of 2 Kgs 22–23 recognize that, in their present shape, these texts do relate to each other; see, e.g., Kratz, *The Composition of the Narrative Books*, 131. In fact, even those scholars who argue that it was not Deuteronomy that was found, but a different document, will eventually associate the text of 2 Kgs 22–23 with the development of deuteronomistic texts.

upon the general assumptions made about the history of composition, the trouble being that these assumptions build on texts such as 2 Kgs 22–23, therefore creating a situation of circular argumentation.[14] No matter how one views the Josiah story, however, its connection to Deuteronomy remains an "Archimedean point" in scholarship.

In view of the role of 2 Kgs 22–23 in the various reconstructions of a DH, we should, in spite of the challenges, examine the indications in the narratives that have formed the basis from which for scholars argue for a "deuteronomistic" reform. In the following reading, I will attempt a reading that will seek to distinguish between the interpretations or conclusions that a reader might arrive at from the primary context of the book of Kings, and which ones are based on knowledge of other texts also, such as Deuteronomy. This approach might help "clear our heads," in a sense, so that we can make the distinction between what 2 Kgs 22–23 tells us, including how it may have responded or commented on other texts, and how it might be read (and how it has been understood by readers) in the context of the biblical corpus.

2 Kings 22: The Book-Finding Story

The king is introduced in the customary fashion, and is judged as a king who "did what was right in the eyes of YHWH." Josiah is one of only a few kings who is judged as measuring up to the standard set by David, according to the writers of Kings. In 2 Kgs 22:3–7, we hear of the first recorded act of King Josiah. In his eighteenth year, when he is 26 years old, he commands Shaphan son of Azaliah to go up to the temple (בית יהוה) and have the money that has been collected there counted and distributed to the workers. As readers, we wonder from the context whether the builders are working on an ongoing repair of the temple. We cannot know if these renovations are to be understood as routine, ordinary maintenance, or whether they have been especially commissioned.[15]

---

14. As pointed out by, e.g., B. O. Long, *2 Kings* (FOTL 10; Grand Rapids: Eerdmans, 1991), 252–53, and the literature he cites.

15. Of those who do comment on this detail, Sweeney, *I & II Kings*, 438, 443; (probably) Würthwein, *Die Bücher der Könige*, 447–48; and Cogan and Tadmor, *II Kings*, 293, think that the king is commissioning or initiating a refurbishing, whereas others think it is a continuing policy; see also Hobbs, *2 Kings*, 323. T. E. Fretheim thinks it is a continuing policy that had been forgotten for a while; see Fretheim, *First and Second Kings*, 213; so also I. W. Provan, *1 and 2 Kings* (New International Biblical Commentary; Peabody, Mass.: Hendrickson, 1995), 270, 275. Jones, *1 and 2 Kings*, 603, 609–10, thinks it had actually started earlier, in harmonization with Chronicles.

6. "Centralization" and the Story of Josiah's Reform

In any case, the king states that he knows that the workers are honest and that no accounting is needed from them, so we are meant to think that he has some experience with the workers, at least. This is reminiscent of 2 Kgs 12 and Joash's cultic renovation activities.

Rather than report on the issue of funds and workers, as we might expect, Hilkiah the priest, who is introduced in v. 8, announces to Shaphan that he has "found the book of the law" in the house of YHWH. This verse introduces the famous "book-finding narrative."[16] Shaphan is given the book and reads it. He then returns to the king and announces first that he has taken the money found in the temple and has given it to the workers, reporting on an act that was never recorded in the narrative. Next, after a new introduction, he informs the king that Hilkiah has given him a book. He reads it to the king.

In 2 Kgs 22:8–10, the story of the "finding of the book" intersects with the story of the distribution of funds to the workers. Shaphan is sent to take care of one issue, is confronted with the book-finding, and takes both issues back to the king. In the following, it is the book-finding that dominates completely the king's reaction, and the topic of temple renovations is not mentioned again.

The king reacts to the "words of the book of the law." He tears his clothes and dispatches a delegation to seek out YHWH on his and the people's behalf concerning the words of the book that was found, uttering that "great is the wrath of YHWH that is kindled against us, because our ancestors did not obey the words of this book, to do according to all that is written concerning us." It is confusing that the king understands his ancestors to be at fault, but that the wrath was to smite him and his people. We are not told what the book contained, except what we learn from Huldah's oracle, as we shall see below. But we know that it is referred to as "the book of the law/instruction" (ספר התורה)[17] in 22:8 and 11, and several times as "the book that was found," or simply "this book." And as readers we infer, from the subsequent narrative, that it

---

16. The book-finding has usually been interpreted historically in biblical research, though other interpretations have been offered. T. C. Römer points out the context of the "rediscovery" of foundation tablets in Mesopotamian sanctuaries, *The So-Called Deuteronomistic History*, 51–53, and Katherine Stott considers similar rhetorical techniques in classical literature, "Finding the Lost Book of the Law: Re-reading the Story of 'The Book of the Law' (Deuteronomy–2 Kings) in Light of Classical Literature," *JSOT* 30 (2005): 153–69.

17. The expression ספר התורה is found in Deut 17:18; 28:58, 61; 29:20, 21, 27; 30:10; 31:24, 26; Josh 1:8; 8:31, 34; 23:6; 24:26; 2 Kgs 14:6, and is also common in Ezra and Nehemiah. References in Kings to the law of Moses are to be found in 1 Kgs 2:3; 2 Kgs 10:31; 17:13, 34, 37; 18:6.

inspired the king to carry out a set of actions, as told in 2 Kgs 23, which will we examine in turn, below.

A reader who reads the narrative from beginning to end will have read the account of the discovery of the law book in the temple in ch. 22 before coming to the account of Huldah's oracle, the covenant renewal ceremony, the so-called reform report and the passover celebration. The book-finding therefore informs the reading of the following sequences. We know that it is called "the book of the law,"[18] that the king was upset by its contents (to the extent that he forgets about the renovations?), and that he seeks the advice of a prophetess, which is tantamount to declaring a national emergency.[19]

Huldah's Oracle: What Does It Say About the Contents of the Book?
Second Kings 22:14–20 contains the report of the consultation of Huldah the prophetess, who is very fully introduced. The prophetess, Huldah, brings an oracle of judgment on the people. The divine oracle brought by Huldah is the only place that we as readers catch a glimpse of what might have been the content of the book. In 22:17, we hear the reason why YHWH will bring disaster on Judah, "Because they have abandoned me and have burned incense for other gods,[20] so that they have provoked me to anger with all the work of their hands, therefore my wrath will be kindled against this place, and it will not be quenched."

The language of Huldah's speech contains two so-called deuteronomistic clichés, the accusation of abandoning YHWH and a reference to "provoking YHWH to anger."[21] The accusation of having abandoned

---

18. As to what was meant by this epithet, J. Ben Dov suggest that it might have been understood in various ways, and that an earlier, pre-deuteronomistic usage could reflect an understanding of an oracular document, a type of miraculous revelation of the divine will; see Ben Dov, "Writing as Oracle and as Law: New Contexts for the Book-Find of King Josiah," *JBL* 127 (2008): 223–39. Ben Dov presents valuable comparative material on divination. Although I am not sure about the details of dividing up the text into pre-deuteronomistic/non-deuteronomistic and deuteronomistic material, I think he points to an interesting dynamic concerning the secondary nature of the "deuteronomistic" reading of the narrative.

19. On the place of royal consultation of prophets in a time of national crisis, see my *Ask God*, 74–108.

20. Jer 1:16; 19:4; 44:5, 8, 15; 2 Chr 28:25. Deuteronomy does not mention anything about burning incense, but the warning against worshiping "other gods" is a prominent theme in both Deuteronomy and in the Decalogue.

21. Deut 28:20; 29:24; Josh 24:16, 20 (the covenant closing ceremony in Shechem, where the people swear that they will not abandon YHWH); Judg 2:12, 13; 10:6–16 (contains both the terms "abandon" and "provoke YHWH to anger"); 1 Kgs 9:6–9 (contains similar language as in Judg, in the form of a warning); 11:33 (in the

YHWH and the idea of YHWH being provoked to anger can be found in a variety of texts. The concept of something that has been "produced by your hands," idol production, which is the cause of YHWH's anger here, is found in Deuteronomy, but mainly prophetic texts such as Isaiah, in addition to Kings.[22]

The most striking link between the book of Deuteronomy and anything in 2 Kgs 22–23 is to be found between this portion of Huldah's speech and Deut 29. The links have to do with the logic of punishment. In Deut 29, where the formal closing of the Moab covenant occurs, Moses tells the people what will befall those who turn away from YHWH and follow other gods, "All the curses written in this book will descend on them, and YHWH will blot out their names from under heaven… YHWH will single them out from all the tribes of Israel for calamity, *in accordance with all the curses of the covenant written in this book of the law*" (Deut 29:20–21). After listing the disasters that will befall the descendants, the rationale is laid in the mouth of an imagined "foreigner," who sees what happened to Israel:

> They will conclude, "It is because they abandoned the covenant of YHWH, the God of their ancestors, which he made with them when he brought them out of the land of Egypt. They turned and served other gods, gods whom they had not known and whom he had not allotted to them; *so the anger of YHWH was kindled* against that land, bringing on it every curse *written in this book*." (29:25–27)

In this strong textual link, the rationale for divine punishment is identical in each text. The accusations are idolatry and the abandonment of YHWH. Committing this transgression equals breach of the covenant, and the result is the anger of YHWH which leads to the unleashing of the curses, "written in this book." The reference to a written document of curses also ties the two texts together. Also, the mysterious reference in Deut 29:29 to "the secret things" belonging to YHWH and the "revealed things" belonging to "us and our children," all of which are to be done according to all the words of "this law," resonates together with the phenomenon of the re-revealed book of the law in 2 Kgs 22.[23]

---

form of rationale for the division of the kingdom); 18:18 (where Elijah accuses Ahab); 19:10, 14 (where Elijah explains what he has been up to); 2 Kgs 17:16 (the rationale for the fall of the kingdom of Israel); 2 Kgs 21:19–26 (in the assessment of Amon, who is described as having "abandoned YHWH, the god of his fathers")).

22. Deut 4:28; 27:15; 2 Kgs 19:18 = Isa 37:19; Isa 2:8; Jer 1:16; Hos 14:4; Mic 5:12. Deut 31:29; 1 Kgs 16:7; Jer 25:6, 7; 32:30; 44:8 contain a combination of "work of your hands" and "provoking to anger."

23. E. Ben Zvi also points to the openness of 2 Kgs 22 regarding the contents of the book that was found; cf. his discussion of the similarities with Deuteronomy,

It is *idolatry* which is the basic accusation and reason for the punishment. Without neglecting the striking link with Deut 29, we need to remind ourselves that the concern with idolatry, as we have observed before, is not limited to Deuteronomy or even texts considered to be deuteronomistic.[24] Further, Huldah's accusation and oracle of doom is in line with many other oracles against kings in the book of Kings—for example, the divine warning to Solomon in 1 Kgs 9:6–9, the oracle against Jeroboam in 1 Kgs 14:7–16, especially vv. 9–10, the report of the oracle of Jehu son of Hanani against Baasha in 1 Kgs 16:7, and Elijah's accusation against Ahab in 1 Kgs 18:18.

Moreover, the accusation of having burned incense is closely associated with the concern in Kings to condemn cultic activity at the *bamot*, the "high places," which will be discussed more below. The accusation of having burned incense is interesting, since this ritual activity is one that is never mentioned in Deuteronomy.

The oracle of doom declares judgment on the people for idolatry, whereas the king is spared because his "heart was penitent" and he humbled himself. Though the book of Deuteronomy is deeply concerned with idolatry, this is not an exclusive trait of Deuteronomy. The language of Huldah's speech, usually characterized as deuteronomistic, could also be characterized as typically prophetic, or even as reflecting a common concern of the law and the prophets.

The accusation that Huldah brings against the people is general, and is followed by an oracle against the king. He is promised a burial in peace, and that he will not see "the disaster that I will bring on this place" (22:20), because he was penitent. The manner of the king's burial is described in language consistently used to describe the burials of the Patriarchs in Genesis. Because he was penitent, humbled himself, and performed acts of lament, Y<small>HWH</small> says in the message to Josiah that he "will gather you to your ancestors, and you shall be gathered (נאספת) to your grave in peace."[25]

"Imagining Josiah's Book and the Implications of Imagining It in early Persian Yehud," in *Berührungspunkte: Studien zur Sozial- und Religionsgeschichte Israels und seiner Umwelt: Festschrift für Rainer Albertz zu seinem 65. Geburtstag* (ed. I. Kottsieper et al.; AOAT 350; Münster: Ugarit Verlag, 2008), 193–212.

24. Huldah's oracle is widely understood as a prime example of deuteronomistic rhetorical speech. B. O. Long (*2 Kings*, 263) says, "Her prophecy appears to have been carefully integrated into its narrative context, crafted for rhetorical effect, and set like a jewel in the ring of the Dtr history."

25. Similarly, Abraham was "gathered (יסף) to his people" (Gen 25:8), and then buried; Isaac was also "gathered to his people" and buried (Gen 35:29); Jacob says to his twelve sons gathered around him on his death bed, "I am about to be gathered

The prophetess brings an oracle of disaster on the people, and an oracle of salvation for the king. Josiah is almost like an anti-Moses; he will be spared the disaster, whereas Moses would not see the Promised Land, as punishment. And Josiah is promised a burial like the Patriarchs, tying his life's work not just back to the time of Solomon, but pointing all the way back to the very origins of the story of the Fathers.

It is puzzling that this speech of divine judgment in a way precludes the possibility of averting the disaster pronounced on the people. All of the king's endeavors in the next chapter seem to be useless in the face of this pronouncement, since the people are given no chance anyway. Or perhaps we are to think that the king understands the oracle as conditional? The logic of the king's actions in light of this speech is somewhat unclear. Is he humbling himself and committing acts of penitence to further his own chances, or is there an underlying understanding that the disaster that is announced on the people can be averted, despite the seemingly unconditional oracle of judgment?

The Covenant Renewal Ceremony in 2 Kings 23:1–3

It is natural to read the opening of 2 Kgs 23 and onward as the king's response to Huldah's oracle. Immediately following the oracle, ch. 23 opens with the king calling for a gathering in the house of YHWH (בית יהוה). It is said that all the people of Judah, all the inhabitants, the priests, the prophets and all the people, gather with him. To this gathering, he reads the words of the "book of the covenant that had been found in the house of YHWH." The king then makes a covenant, in which the people join. They promise to follow YHWH, keep his commandments, his decrees, and his statutes, and to perform the "words of this covenant that were written in this book."

This portion of the text is the place where King Josiah exhibits what is, perhaps, the most "deuteronomistic" behavior in the whole account of his reign: he reads the law in front of a gathering of his people. In Deut 17:19 the king is commanded to read and study the law, though not publicly. In Deut 31:10–11 the Levitical priests are commanded to read the law in front of Israel when they gather at "the place which YHWH your God will choose" for the festival of booths at the "year of remission." Josiah's actions here do allow readers to make these connections.

---

to my people. Bury me with my ancestors" (Gen 49:29), and Joseph takes his embalmed body to Hebron and buries it; and, finally, Joseph (whose name is the same root יסף, "to increase, add to," "he increases") charges the Israelites to bring his body to "the land," which they do, and bury him in Shechem (Josh 24:32).

Further, the covenant closing of 2 Kgs 23:3 reminds us both of Moses in Exodus and in Deuteronomy, Joshua in Josh 24, and, to some extent, Solomon. Josiah's ceremony is a renewal of the covenant that he perceives as having been forgotten and rediscovered. This type of a renewed commitment is also reflected in the ceremonies performed by Ezra in Neh 8–9. In Nehemiah, the book that is read is described as "the book of the law of Moses, which YHWH had given to Israel" (Neh 8:2). However, in 2 Kings there is no reference in the text to help readers link his behavior to Deuteronomy directly. In other words, there is no comment such as, "And he read the words of the book of the law, according to the commands of YHWH through Moses," or any such editorial comment. Unfortunately, the content of the "words of this covenant" are not quoted or illustrated, so that we cannot know the exact nature of it, so as to identify it with any laws in Deuteronomy or any other canonical law book.

Some scholars have pointed out that it seems strange that Josiah should hold the covenant renewal ceremony at a time when the temple is in the middle of a major renovation, and before the acts of purging and cleansing described in 23:4–20. It is true that this might seem strange. On the other hand, the report of the cultic purging could also be seen as a reflex of the covenant renewal. In other words, it is the king's response to the renewed commitment and a demonstration that he is taking it seriously.

Josiah's Reform in 2 Kings 23:4–20

The Account of the Reform

The account of the covenant renewal ceremony is followed by what is commonly referred to as the "reform report" in 23:4–20. It is this report that contains the bulk of what is considered to be the actual cultic reform, and that is supposed to be a deuteronomistic reform, according to the general consensus. There are a number of difficulties with this consensus, as we shall see below.

A crucial point that any reader can observe is that the reform report does not refer to "the book" in any form, either as ספר התורה or as ספר הברית. The so-called reform report is sandwiched between the covenant renewal ceremony of 23:1–3 and the passover celebration recorded in 23:21–23, both of which do refer to ספר הברית. It is this compositional feature that allows the reader to read the reform report also as a response to the finding of "the book."

Let us now turn our attention to what King Josiah does actually do, according to the report. Scholars have noted that the whole narrative of

2 Kgs 22–23 is structured by a series of verbs that describe actions taken by the king: "sent" (שלח) in 22:3 and 23:1, and "commanded" (ויצו) in 22:12; 23:4, and 23:21.²⁶ The reform report, framed by the two last instances of ויצו, is characterized by a whole string of verbs of action describing what the king did.²⁷

First, the king commanded (ויצו) the High Priest Hilkiah and others to take out from the temple of YHWH (להוציא מהיכל יהוה) all the vessels made for Baal, Asherah, and "all the hosts of heaven." We note that the report uses the expression "temple of YHWH," not "house of YHWH," as in ch. 22. The first action he takes is to have the priests themselves clean out the temple of objects that were made for non-Yahwistic gods. If we compare this with the description of Hezekiah's acts of cultic cleansing in 2 Kgs 18:4, we note that Hezekiah's actions are recorded much more tersely, and that we do not get the same level of detail. It is, for example, not stated specifically whether or not Hezekiah got rid of cult vessels belonging to illicit cults from within the temple of Jerusalem.

Next, it is reported that the king burned (וישרפם) the vessels outside Jerusalem, in the fields of Kidron, and carried their ashes off to Bethel (not reported in Chronicles).²⁸ Wadi Kidron figures prominently in the reform report, being the scene also of the burning and pulverization of the *asherah* and the breaking of various altars (see below, on v. 6 and v. 12). In this first act of purging, the king has non-Yahwistic cultic vessels taken out from the temple of YHWH (X), he then burns them at Y and carries the ashes to Z. There is a movement that begins from the center of the temple, in Jerusalem, that moves outside Jerusalem and finally to a distant periphery outside Judah. As of yet, there is really nothing that could be called "centralization" going on. Rather, the movement is from the center to a periphery.²⁹ The role of Bethel in this account is of particular interest, and will be commented on further below.

---

26. Lohfink, "Die Bundesurkunde des König Josias," 270–71.
27. A straightforward computation of the royal acts from 2 Kgs 23:4–14 yields ten distinct acts of cultic purging and cleansing. In his detailed analysis of 2 Kgs 22–23, D.-H. Hoffmann similarly delineates ten acts within these verses, and a total of thirteen. See Hoffmann's *Reform und Reformen: Untersuchungen zu einem Grundthema der deuteronomistischen Geschichtsschreibung* (Zurich: Theologischer Verlag, 1980), especially pp. 226–27, and, on the whole of the text, pp. 208–51.
28. The Chronicles version of Josiah's reform is different in many ways from the Kings account. For one detailed comparative analysis, see Barrick, *The King and the Cemeteries*. On the account of the passover, see below.
29. F. Smyth, in his synchronic reading of the Josiah account, also makes note of this outward movement from the center, "When Josiah Has Done His Work or the

Next, the king deposed/put an end to (והשבית) the "idolatrous priests" (הכמרים)[30] of the high places (במות),[31] and those who offered sacrifices to other deities. There are two groups of priests mentioned here, those whom kings of Judah had consecrated for the high places, presumably priests of YHWH, and those priests who made offerings to non-Yahwistic deities, that is, Baal and various heavenly bodies. The priests of the high places in the areas surrounding Jerusalem are also "deposed," together with non-Yahwistic priests.

This is a place that one might begin to discuss whether or not an idea of centralization is the rationale for this move. One theme that permeates the book of Kings is the opposition to the *bamot*. In connection with the Josiah account we could ask about the reason for this opposition. Is it because cultic practice at these sites was not conducted correctly, or was it based on an understanding that no cultic activity should be carried out outside the Jerusalem temple? In other words, is the idea of limiting cultic worship to one place the reason for the struggle against the *bamot*, or is it simply that the practice conducted there was not correct?

The bamot

The *bamot* in Kings require some attention, simply because one of the assumptions underlying the idea of Josiah's reform as a deuteronomistic, centralizing reform is that the opposition to the *bamot* reflects Deuteronomy's concern for one central cult site. The *bamot* are crucial in the cultic polemics of Kings, but are never mentioned in Deuteronomy. In Kings, the *bamot* are a key component of the ideological exposition of the demises of the united kingdom of Solomon and the Northern Kingdom of Israel. Further, the building of *bamot*, or the failure to tear them down, is a consistent feature of the evaluation of the kings of Judah. The *bamot* are mentioned seven times in the reform report of 2 Kgs 23, and are thus central to that story. They are installations that Josiah breaks

---

King is Properly Buried: A Synchronic Reading of 2 Kings 22.1–23.28," in de Pury, Römer and Macchi, eds., *Israel Constructs Its History*, 343–58 (351–52).

30. This term appears otherwise only in Hos 10:5; Zeph 1:4. On this term, see Uehlinger, "Was There a Cult Reform under King Josiah?," 303–5.

31. The word *bamot* (במות) is usually translated "high places." This does not necessarily entail a physically high place. It is notoriously difficult to get a clear idea of what the *bamot* looked like, but they are clearly a cultic location in most cases, and in all cases in Kings. For a discussion, see Janice E. Caton, "Temple and *bāmāh*: Some Considerations," in Holloway and Handy, eds., *The Pitcher is Broken*, 150–65. For a tabulation of the usage of *bamot* in Kings, see Hoffmann, *Reform und Reformen*, 336–38. For more on the *bamot* in Kings, see below.

down (נתץ, 23:8, see also Deut 7:5, 12, 13), defiles (טמא, 23:13),[32] crushes (נתץ) the altars of, and burns (שרף, 23:15), and removes (הסיר, 23:19). The "priests of the high places" are put an end to (השבית, 23:5) and slaughtered (יזבח, 23:20) on the altars.

Although the word *bamah* (במה) occurs a couple of times in Deuteronomy, it is used in a completely different sense, and not as referring to a "high place." In this type of context, in poetry often celebrating feats of war, *bamah* seems to refer to the enemy's "back," usually in an expression implying total defeat of the enemy.[33]

Turning to Deut 12, we note that vv. 2–3 do require that the cultic installations of the Canaanites be destroyed by Israel, when they enter the land. The word *bamah*, however, is not used. We therefore note that a feature that is prominent in the report of Josiah's acts of reform is not a concern whatsoever, of the book of Deuteronomy, not even of Deut 12.

The absence of the *bamot* in Deuteronomy is one indicator that the most significant context for understanding Josiah's reform and the problem of the *bamot* is perhaps not to be sought in Deuteronomy, but within the context of Kings itself. A clear line runs through Kings, showing the significance of the *bamot* in this composition. The *bamot* are introduced in 1 Kgs 3, which describes how the people were sacrificing in high places "because the temple had not yet been built" (1 Kgs 3:2), followed by the sharply polemical observation that "Solomon sacrificed in high places."[34] The mention in 1 Kgs 11:7 that Solomon built high places for his foreign wives *after* he had built the temple is ideologically important and foreshadows the meaning of the *bamot* in the rest of Kings. Further, the reform report specifically makes a connection to Solomon's high places for Astarte, Chemosh, and Milcom, and describes their defilation by Josiah (2 Kgs 23:13–14).

First Kings 13 is also important. This text about the first Northern king, Jeroboam, the archetypal "bad" king, associates him with the future king Josiah through the prophecy uttered by the man of God. Jeroboam says about Josiah that he will sacrifice the priests of the high places on the altar at Bethel (13:2). King Jeroboam also builds houses on high places and appoints priests who were not Levites. In the reform report, the

---

32. This word appears only in this chapter in Kings (in 23:8, 10, 13, and 16), and is not "deuteronomistic," but is common in Leviticus.

33. In this type of understanding, we find the word mentioned twice in Deuteronomy, in the poem of chs. 32–33. Other occurrences of this type are in Num 21:28; 2 Sam 1:19, 25; 22:34, all examples of poetry.

34. Strangely enough, the following verse, which describes Solomon as going to Gibeon, does not seem polemical in the same way, but simply descriptive.

actions of Josiah are understood as a fulfillment of this prophecy (2 Kgs 23:15–20, see below).

After these texts associating the *bamot* with the last king of the whole land and the first king of Israel, we find the *bamot* in the summary evaluations of the reigns of several Judean kings. Most of these go something like: King X did what was right in the eyes of YHWH, *yet he did not take down the high places*... (1 Kgs 15:14, 44; 22:44; 2 Kgs 12:4; 14:4; 15:4, 35). Also, 2 Kgs 16:2–4 records that King Ahaz son of Jotham did *not* do what was right, and that he made sacrifices on the high places.[35] In the ideological chapter 2 Kgs 17, the downfall of Israel is explained as occurring because the people built high places and followed the ways of other nations (2 Kgs 17:9, 11, 29, 32). Finally, the anti-type of Hezekiah and Josiah, Manasseh, is described as actively rebuilding the *bamot* (2 Kgs 21:3).

The first king who is judged as doing right *and* described as removing high places is Hezekiah (2 Kgs 18:4). Later in the story, the Assyrian captain claims that Hezekiah told the people to worship in Jerusalem after he destroyed the high places. The Assyrians put forward this claim in order to demand that YHWH be on the side of the Assyrians, and seem to imply that YHWH should be upset that his high places have been removed.

This text is usually used to argue that Hezekiah instituted a cult reform of centralization, according to Deut 12. But any such use of the text is in trouble, first of all because it is only an allegation on the part of the Rabshaqeh, and we have to read his statements as propagandistic, even derisive, and serving the purpose of undermining faith in YHWH on the part of the Judeans. Secondly, we do not even know if Hezekiah ever said that Judah should worship in Jerusalem. This claim is made on his behalf by his enemy, so it is definitely unreliable.

The Chronicles version gives much more information about the cultic reforms of Hezekiah. As a part of his actions, a passover celebration in Jerusalem is also described, in the form of a gathering of the whole people. After celebrating and feasting for fourteen days, a collective destruction campaign is described, whereby "all Israel" goes out and pulls down the high places (נתץ), breaks down (שבר) the pillars (מטבת) and hews down (גדע) the sacred poles (*asherim*) throughout Judah,

---

35. Interestingly, the first Judean king, Rehoboam, is not personally accused of building or not dismantling *bamot* in the evaluation of his reign (1 Kgs 14:21). According to the MT, it is *Judah* who is accused of doing evil in the sight of YHWH here, and building is (1 Kgs 14:22–23). The LXX has "Rehoboam" where the MT has "Judah."

6. "Centralization" and the Story of Josiah's Reform

Benjamin, Ephraim, and Manasseh (2 Chr 31:1). Thus we might understand the Chronicler's version as describing a reform with intentions inspired by Deut 7, 12, and 16, the passover legislation (see more on this below). However, even this interpretation has its problems, and it is probably more correct to see this version of Hezekiah's reforms within the rationale of the Chronicler's view of the cult and cult reform.

In the Pentateuch, the *bamot* are mentioned in the sense of "high place" only twice, in Lev 26:30, and in Num 33:52. This indicates that these textual contexts might be important to Josiah, and argues against a privileging of Deuteronomy. However, there are also important connections between these texts and Deuteronomy. Leviticus 26:3–46 contains a series of promises/blessings and curses similar to Deut 28 in function. The chapter completes what is often referred to as the Holiness Code of Lev 17–26. As a part of these curses, we find in Lev 26:30–33 quite an odd statement. As a punishment for not obeying him, YHWH threatens to destroy (שמד, Hiphil) the high places, and "heap your carcasses on the carcasses of your idols." The same type of action that Josiah executes, namely the placing of carcasses on the altars (or idols) is described here in a divine threat. The oddness of this curse is that though YHWH threatens to break their high places, there seems to be no implication of polemic against having them. So the context here in Numbers is quite different from Kings. Yet, the same dynamic is present, of cult sites and *bamot* being destroyed as a punishment. The association of the destruction of high places and the act of defiling by carcasses is also present in both contexts. Is Josiah's reform really a "levitical" (meaning according to the book of Leviticus) reform rather than a deuteronomistic one?

The occurrence of *bamot* in Num 33:52 is noteworthy. Here, in a setting like Deuteronomy, YHWH speaks to Moses "on the plains of Moab," saying:

> Speak to the Israelites, and say to them: When you cross over the Jordan into the land of Canaan, you shall drive out all the inhabitants of the land from before you, destroy (אבד, Niphal) all their figured stones, destroy (אבד)[36] all their cast images, and demolish (שמד, Hiphil) all their high places. You shall take possession of the land and settle in it, for I have given you the land to possess. (Num 33:51–53)

We immediately associate Deut 7:1–5:

---

36. The only other occurrences of this verb in the Pentateuch are in Deut 11:4 and 12:2, so there is a subtle connection between this Numbers passage and Deut 12 when it comes to the idea of destroying the cult installations of the people in the land.

When YHWH your God brings you into the land that you are about to enter and occupy, and he clears away many nations before you...then you must utterly destroy them... But this is how you must deal with them: break down (נתץ) their altars, smash (שבר) their pillars, hew down (גדע) their *asherim*, and burn (שרף) their idols with fire.

We note, however, that none of the objects that are to be destroyed overlap in these two texts. The verbs of destruction are also different. The general ideology seems to overlap, however. Could Josiah just as well have been inspired by Num 33, as Deut 7 or 12?

In spite of the threads connecting the two instances in the Pentateuch which mention the *bamot* with texts in Deuteronomy, the overall impression we are left with after this survey is that Josiah's actions with the *bamot* are built on a logic that has been developed throughout the books of Kings, and is not necessarily dependent on Deut 12 or even any legal text. If it had not been for the book-finding narrative in ch. 22, would we have connected the rationale for the reform to the book of Deuteronomy? Idolatry, high places, and illicit cult are all themes of the books of Kings, as well as other books of the Pentateuch, and can be understood easily within its horizon.

Could it be that 2 Kgs 23:4–20, rather than implementing Deut 12 and the principle of centralization, in part serves the purpose of connecting Deuteronomy with the rest of the Pentateuch and integrating it into the discourse of demolishing the *bamot* and defiling illicit cult? In this sense, the Josiah account facilitates a reading of Deuteronomy that makes it relevant for the whole struggle against the *bamot*, even though this is not explicitly a part of Deuteronomy's program. This would help explain why scholars and other readers have understood the relationship between Deuteronomy and 2 Kgs 22–23 in the way that has been most common.

This review of the role of the *bamot* in the books of Kings leads us to the conclusion, among several, that they play a prominent role in Kings. In Deuteronomy, however, the *bamot* do not figure at all, and cannot be said to have any direct connection to Deuteronomy's idea of centralization as laid out in Deut 12–16. It was suggested that what does happen through 2 Kgs 23, however, is that the concern to limit and destroy the *bamot* in Kings is brought together with Deuteronomy's idea of centralization, through the tangential connection of Deuteronomy to the Kings narrative.

The Account of the Reform, Continued
Proceeding on from v. 6 of the reform report, the account relates that the king brought out (ויצא) the *asherah* from the house of YHWH, burned it (וישרף אתה), crushed it (וידק) to dust, and scattered (וישלך) the dust on

the common people's cemetery. After a move outside Jerusalem, the next action again takes us back into the temple, or house of YHWH, with the king bringing something out of it and burning it. This time, as in the first act, he brings it out to Kidron. In addition to burning, this time he also crushes it to dust and scatters it on the cemetery of the common people (בני העם).

This procedure reminds us of Moses' destruction of the golden calf. However, the terminology is not identical, except for the burning. In Exod 32:20, the word for grinding or crushing is טחן, and for scattering is זרה. In Deut 9:21, the word for scattering/sprinkling is אכת and טחן; dust/powder is דק (used as a verb in 2 Kgs 23:6) but the word for scattering is identical to 2 Kgs 23:6 (שלך). Another difference between Josiah's destruction of the *asherah* and Moses' destruction of the golden calf is that Josiah is targeting non-Yahwistic cult objects, whereas Moses in this case is targeting an illicit Yahwistic cult object. Phenomenologically, Josiah's act is similar to the destruction of the golden calf.[37] Of course, in neither version of the golden calf episode is the ground down calf scattered on graves, but in water. In Exodus, the people are made to drink the water.

Going back to 2 Kgs 23, we observe for now that the king's behavior is establishing a pattern of bringing objects out of the sanctuary, burning and pulverizing them, and scattering them on an unclean place.[38] Next, the king broke down (ויתץ) the houses of the קדשים (sacred prostitutes/temple prostitutes/cult prostitutes/sacred males) that were in the house of YHWH,[39] where women did weaving for Asherah. Installations used by illicit cult personnel *within* the temple are torn down. This fourth act

---

37. Both involve a ritual by which a dangerous object, one that is a threat to the deity, is destroyed and the threat removed, at least for the time being. Scholars have also compared these biblical texts to a Ugaritic text about the destruction of Mot, in a ritual that uses terminology associated with a grain offering. On this context, see F. C. Fensham, "The Burning of the Golden Calf and Ugarit," *IEJ* 16 (1966): 191–93.

38. See also Hoffman, *Reform und Reformen*, 222.

39. The concept of cult prostitution has occasioned a large amount of secondary literature. Much of this material is highly tendentious, and representative of an attitude that understood Canaanite religion to be degenerate. Because the biblical literature itself is highly ideological, information about "other" religions cannot be taken at face value. Cult prostitution is a phenomenon about which we know very little, but see E. A. Goodfriend, "Prostitution," *ABD* 5:505–10 (507–9); and K. van der Toorn, "Cult Prostitution," *ABD* 1:510–13. For a comparative perspective and a discussion of the biblical material, see H. M. Barstad, *The Religious Polemics of Amos: Studies in the Preaching of Am 2, 7B–8; 4,1–13; 5,1–27; 6,4–7; 8,14* (VTSup 34; Leiden: Brill, 1984), 22–33.

takes place within the house of YHWH. It is not detailed what he does with the debris.

Next, he brought out (ויבא) all the priests of the towns of Judah and defiled (ויטמא)⁴⁰ the *bamot* where the priests had sacrificed, from Gibeon to Beer-sheba. It does not say where the king brought these priests or that he did anything to them, in contrast to what he does with the priests of the high places in Samaria (23:20). Illicit Yahwistic (we presume) cult activity throughout Judah, from north south, is eradicated. The places of worship, the high places, are defiled so that they become unsuitable for cultic activity.

This act is similar to the second one mentioned above. As the priests (כהנים) are brought out (יבא) of the towns in v. 8, so also in v. 5, priests (כמרים) whom the Judean kings had appointed for the high places around Judah were deposed (השבית), along with priests of non-Yahwistic cults. In v. 8, the *bamot* are also defiled and destroyed. These had not been mentioned in v. 5.

We discover that even the local administration is exposed to the cult cleansing, when the king breaks down (ויתץ) the *bamot* of the gates of Joshua, the governor. This gate is located left of the gate of the city, representing the boundary between Jerusalem and what is outside the city. In the note about the "priests of the high places" in 23:9, it is not clear whether this is referring to the high places of the gates of Joshua, or to priests of high places in general. Yet it is made clear by this remark that the high places of the governor were considered to belong outside Jerusalem. These priests did not belong to the cult of Jerusalem.

Next, he (the king) defiled (וטמא) Topheth, the place of the cult of Molech. The location of the cult place is in the Valley of Ben-hinnom, and the reason given for defiling the cult is to prevent anyone from practicing the custom of letting a son or daughter "pass through fire," which was considered an abomination by the writer of the book of Kings (also Leviticus, Numbers, and Deuteronomy). Deuteronomy does not mention Molech in connection with child sacrifices, but Leviticus does. As with the first act and part of the second act, it is non-Yahwistic cult which is targeted here. The king renders a non-Yahwistic cult site unfit for cultic activity, in the Hinnom Valley, just south of the city.

---

40. As a verb, טמא appears only here in Kings, four times (23:8, 10, 13, 16). The usage here is different from the way it is used in Leviticus, as noted by Shedletsky, *Josiah's Reform*, 52–60, and more similar to the uses in Ezek 5:11 (an accusation of defiling the sanctuary); 6:3–5 (similar threat of defiling with corpses and destruction of cult objects and sites, but without the use of טמא), 8–9; 9:7 (Ezekiel is told by YHWH to defile the temple and fill it up with corpses); and Isa 30:22 (an instruction to defile the idols, and discard them, like unclean rags).

6. "Centralization" and the Story of Josiah's Reform 149

Next, the king removed/put an end to (וישבת) the horses which the kings of Judah had dedicated to the sun, and burned (שרף באש) the chariots of the sun. These horses and chariots are located at the "entrance to the house of YHWH, by the chamber of the eunuch Nathan-melech," another reference to a boundary between spheres surrounding the temple. The king rids the site of the horses and chariots which had been dedicated to be used in non-Yahwistic worship. An interesting detail here is that the name of the eunuch seems to play off the fact that the horses and chariots had been dedicated by the kings.

Moving, again, back into the area of the temple, we are told that the king tore down (נתץ המלך) and broke to pieces (וירץ משם) the altars that the kings of Judah had erected on the roof of Ahaz's "upper chamber" and the altars that Manasseh had erected inside the courts of the house of YHWH (2 Kgs 21:5, altars to all the hosts of heaven). King Josiah broke them apart and scattered (והשליך) their dust in the Kidron. Here, Josiah is following the pattern of Moses in scattering the dust of the destroyed abominable object in water. Again, the pattern repeats itself, whereby objects taken from within the confines of the house of YHWH and perhaps also from the royal premises and deposited in the Kidron, as were the Asherah (v. 6) and vessels for other gods (v. 4). In this case, illicit altars that had been erected by "bad" former kings are torn down and thrown into the Wadi Kidron.

Next we move to a circle that is outside the immediate zone surrounding Jerusalem. The king defiled (טמא) the *bamot* that Solomon had built for Astarte, the abomination (שקץ) of the Sidonians, for Kemosh, the abomination (שקץ) of Moab, and for Milcom, the abomination (תועבה) of the Ammonites. He broke (שבר) the pillars in pieces, cut down (כרת) the *asherim*, and covered (מלא) the site with human bones. East (facing) and south of Jerusalem, these sites of foreign cults were destroyed.

By mentioning Solomon in 23:13, this account has King Josiah clean up all the way back to Solomon. This also ties Josiah's acts in with the first acts of apostasy in the books of Kings. Solomon, as soon as he has built the temple and inaugurated the sacrificial cult, begins to build high places (1 Kgs 11:7). The reason he does this is for the sake of his wives, whom he clings to in love (11:2). The language of 2 Kgs 23:13 closely resembles 1 Kgs 11:7, and has Josiah reverse the actions of Solomon. The fact that Josiah removes and destroys these cult sites shows that we as readers are supposed to understand that they had existed from the time of Solomon and no one had rendered them completely unfit for use, as Josiah now does by covering them with human bones.

Second Kings 23:15–20 breaks the monotony of the previous verses, with more of an account of the king's doings in Samaria than the list of his actions in Judah in 23:4–14. Further, it ties in with the story of 1 Kgs 13, thus providing a connection between one of the last kings of Judah and the first king of Israel, as well as with Solomon, the last king of the "united monarchy," the king who built the temple and inaugurated the cult, but also the king with whom apostasy began.

In the final act of the previous section, the king defiles the *bamot* of the illicit cults that King Solomon had introduced. He breaks the cultic objects, cuts down the cult symbols, and piles bones on the place, rendering it unfit for cultic activity, and thereby defiling it. This act ties the report back to the first mention of *bamot* in the book of Kings, and also provides a bridge to the next section dealing with the defilation of the cult site at Bethel.

Second Kings 23:15 records the same actions.[41] The transitional v. 15 seems to seek to bind together the preceding reform report of vv. 4–14 with vv. 16–20. As a last effort in his actions, Josiah goes all the way to Bethel, he fulfills the prophecy of 1 Kgs 13 (without knowing it!), and later moves all around Samaria (in Chronicles, he moves even further beyond). The last act of Josiah, when he slaughters the priests of the *bamot* on the altars and defiles them with human bones, reminds us of 2 Kgs 10:18–27, when Jehu killed the priests and worshippers of Baal, and destroys the temple of Baal, making it into a latrine. See also 2 Kgs 11:17–19, when Jehoida tears down the altars of Baal, breaks the images, and kills the priest.

Is Deuteronomy 12 Central to Josiah?
The Josiah account ties back to the pairing of the stories of the building of Solomon's temple and the inauguration of the cult there contrasted with the establishment of Jeroboam's competing illicit cult, and to the stories of Moses receiving the instructions for the sanctuary contrasted with the event of the competing cult of the golden calf. Here, Josiah is cleaning up Solomon's temple to its original pristine state and cleaning up the surrounding areas, while also eliminating and stamping out Jeroboam's illicit and doomed cult in Bethel. He is, in a way, trying to go back and right the wrongs of Solomon and unite the kingdom once again. Like Moses, he burns and grinds up the illicit cult statues and vessels. Unlike Moses, who intercedes on Aaron's behalf, Josiah does not intercede for the priests or other cult personnel. Ultimately, however,

---

41. See the informative discussion on 2 Kgs 23:15 in Shedletsky, *Josiah's Reform*, 190–200. See also Barrick, *The King and the Cemeteries*, 46–50.

Josiah's acts are all in vain, and the judgment of destruction is pronounced on Jerusalem immediately after his passover feast.

From the context, the connection between the "words of this book" and Josiah's actions in 2 Kgs 23:4–14 seem fairly straightforward. His motivation for the acts of defiling cultic objects, places, and personnel are to avoid the disaster presumably spelled out in what we may assume are the curses of "this book." In 2 Kgs 23:15–20, however, another justification for the king's acts is brought into the mix, namely the "man of God who predicted these things" (23:16–17). This explicit reason the text gives for Josiah's actions offer the reader a wide-sweeping perspective on Josiah's role in the history of the kings of Israel and Judah. Although Josiah does not seem to know that he is fulfilling this prophecy, the dots are explicitly connected for the reader, inviting further reflection on the connection between these narratives.

First Kings 12:25–13:33 thematizes idolatry in a fundamental way with the narrative of Jeroboam and his cult at Beth El and Dan. Jeroboam is the archetypal opposite of Solomon, who performed the task of ultimate piety by building the temple and inaugurating the sacrificial cult. Jeroboam makes the two calves of gold for the people to worship, so that they will not revert to David's successor, Rehoboam, in Jerusalem. He set up a whole competing cult, complete with festivals, so that the people would have what they needed in terms of worship.[42] It is this competition that Josiah eradicates in the reform of 2 Kgs 23. But also, the cult of Jeroboam represents the consequences of Solomon's fall, so the history of Israel and its religious errors are deeply connected to Judah and its history. In the Josiah narrative, these come together in a last attempt to straighten the record.

In Deuteronomy, the law which mandates worship at one central cultic location is prefaced by a command about what to do with the cult sites of the land. It is therefore not wrong to say that Deuteronomy is concerned with idolatrous cultic installations (Deut 12:1–3; see the survey in Chapter 5). As such, the Josiah account is "deuteronomistic." However, perhaps the concern with centralized worship that we find in Deut 12 is then assumed automatically to have been a part of that cultic cleansing of idolatrous cults. In the case of 2 Kgs 22–23, Josiah's eradication of illicit Yahwistic and non-Yahwistic cult installations and personnel is perhaps equated with cult centralization *because of* Deut 12. On its own, however,

---

42. S. Lasine, "Reading Jeroboam's Intentions: Intertextuality, Rhetoric and History in 1 Kings 12," in *Reading Between Texts: Intertextuality and the Hebrew Bible* (ed. Dana Nolan Fewell; Louisville, Ky.: Westminster John Knox, 1992), 133–52.

the Josiah account is not really concerned with limiting worship to one location as a matter of principle, and does not even mention the idea of Jerusalem as chosen.

2 Kings 23:4–20 as "Centralizing" Reform?
What is there in 2 Kgs 23:4–20 that supports the conclusion that this is a centralizing reform? One point that I think will become clear to anyone who reads Deut 12 and 2 Kgs 23:4–20 carefully and compares them, is the contrast in the direction of movement in these two texts. This in itself should be a caution in positing *centralization* in Kings. In 2 Kgs 23 there is a consistent movement from the center out to the surrounding areas. In his acts of ritual destruction and defilation, the king consistently moves the objects and personnel to be destroyed *from* within the temple *out* to a periphery.

As we saw in Chapter 3, the text of Deut 12 forges a movement toward a center through language that emphasizes movement: bring, carry, there you shall do, and so on. It also establishes a center toward which everything moves. "The place which YHWH will choose" is constructed as the center around which all cultic acts takes place, and toward which all movement involving sacrifice and festivals moves. I do not think the significance of this contrast has been explored thoroughly.

We must point out, though, that the part of Deut 12 that seems most relevant to Josiah is the first segment that concerns the foreign and illicit cultic installations. This kind of command is not particular to Deuteronomy at all, but is common throughout the Pentateuch and also in the prophets. In fact, as pointed out earlier, much of the language of 2 Kgs 23:4–20 has much more affinity with typically priestly language, including Ezekiel, and is more easily comprehendible from within a paradigm of ritual defilation and cultic purity than from within a kind of deuteronomistic centralization ideology.

In support of this, we have noted that although there are some correspondences to language commonly used in the book of Deuteronomy, 2 Kgs 23:4–14 has far more in common with the language of Leviticus and the so-called Holiness Code of Lev 17–26.[43] These observations complicate the simple argument that 2 Kgs 23:4–20 contains the account

---

43. This point can also be seen from my above survey. As has also been mentioned, Shedletsky, *Josiah's Reform*, 49–52, demonstrates affinities between the language of 2 Kgs 23 and Lev 14 and Num 19, which contain rituals for purification from leprosy and contamination from having touched a corpse. See her useful table of language in 2 Kgs 23 and parallels in other biblical books (pp. 63–65), and the discussion following.

6. "Centralization" and the Story of Josiah's Reform

of Josiah's "deuteronomistic" cult reform, including centralization of the cult to Jerusalem.

Readers who choose a different interpretation often point out that this text appears to come from a different source than the opening three verses and the description of the passover in 23:21–23, on linguistic and stylistic grounds. While we certainly find a description of a cultic cleansing in 23:4–20, it is not so clear cut that Josiah's acts constitute centralization in the sense presented in Deuteronomy. A different view prefers to see Josiah's reform primarily as cultic cleansing and defiling as a prophylactic measure in order to avert the threats of the "book."[44]

These are directions that should be pursued more, instead of privileging the "deuteronomistic" interpretation. Together with the fact that the *bamot* are not mentioned in Deuteronomy, but are completely understandable within the books of Kings, and the fact that the reform report itself contains surprisingly little reference to anything exclusively deuteronomistic, the observation about the contrast in direction of movement should caution us in labeling the reform deuteronomistic or *centralizing* in a simplified way, especially when this tends to block the way for observations that do not fit into that picture.

More than being a reform of centralization, Josiah's reform is a reform of cultic cleansing, of "defiling." It is both presented as an apotropaic ritual and as the fulfillment of prophecy from 1 Kgs 13. Centralization in some measure is a *result* of the reform measures of Josiah, because he eliminates cultic places all over the country. Yet the narrative is not interested in this result. It is interested in making illicit cult sites, personnel, and paraphernalia unfit for use through defiling and "cleansing," in order to avoid the threats of "the book."

And last, there is nowhere any reference made to "the book" within the reform narrative of 23:4–20. There is, however, reference made to the "man of God" who prophesied against Jeroboam. This reference points to other literary connections, to 1 Kgs 13, first of all, and back to the beginning of the books of Kings. The story of Jeroboam and his golden calves, in turn, connect with the story of the golden calf in Deut 9 and in Exod 32. The ritual acts of Josiah, in burning, crushing, and scattering the *asherah* also connect directly with the golden calf episode.

In spite of how little explicitly "deuteronomistic" there is about Josiah's reform, however, we cannot get beyond the fact that this is how

---

44. See, e.g., already Oestreicher, *Das deuteronomische Grundgesetz*; and, later, Würthwein, "Die josianische Reform und das Deuteronomium"; H. Hollenstein, "Literarkritische Erwägungen zum Bericht über die Reformmaßnahmen Josias 2 Kön. xxiii 4ff," *VT* 27 (1977): 321–36; Shedletsky, *Josiah's Reform*, 200.

it has been read. An example from within the Bible itself, Chronicles, tells the Josiah account in a much more explicitly "deuteronomistic" way, as we will see below especially regarding the passover. Second Chronicles 35 might even be called the "true" deuteronomistic passover. Therefore, although I am arguing here that it is not as simple or straightforward as it has often been assumed to claim that the Kings account is advocating *centralization* the way it is laid out in Deut 12, 14, and 16, the simple fact that it has always been read this way forces us to reflect on the connections between this account and Deuteronomy.

Because of all the conflation and harmonizing readings, however, it is also necessary first to see each text free of the many constructs we have accumulated for ourselves, so that we can appreciate them on their own terms and in the context of their close literary context. Perhaps it will be more fruitful to understand the meaning of Josiah's reform within the paradigm of royal reform in the book of Kings before we proceed to see it in relation to Deuteronomy. This is definitely better than to continue to see it through the prism of "Deuteronomism" as the only key to its understanding.

In fact, in a historical interpretation, the problem of the Josiah account's connection to some type of contemporary law is compounded by the scholarly endeavor to distinguish between priestly and deuteronomistic law. It is perhaps de Wette's argument about the distinct character of Deuteronomy that has led to such obsession with all things deuteronomistic, when we perhaps should be looking for a more general idea of biblical law.

The reading presented here seems to be taking us in the direction of an argument as follows: it is not that it cannot be argued that Josiah's form is "deuteronomistic," but scholarship has been overly obsessed with the endeavor to identify Deuteronomy's demand for centralization in 2 Kgs 22–23. I think that instead of importing, somewhat uncritically, meaning found in Deuteronomy into Kings, it is more important to see Kings on its own terms as a work that has been, and can be, *read* in dialogue with Deuteronomy. It is important to distinguish between ways that Kings *can* be, and *has* been, read, and what we allege that the authors may have intended. If we want to make any statements about composition and literary development, we also need to consider that Kings may have preceded Deuteronomy and inspired its composition.

Another sense in which Josiah's reform can be considered "deuteronomistic" is the fact that the reading of a law book determined the king's behavior. R. Clements has suggested that the subordination of everything else to law is what should be considered truly "deuteronomistic." In his definition, it would not really matter what Josiah did, but the fact that he responds to a book of the law qualifies the story as "deuteronomistic."[45] In light of our observations of the links between Huldah's oracle and Deut 29, we see that it is the writtenness of the law that stands out as a clear link here.

Josiah's Passover

Josiah's passover is almost universally interpreted by biblical scholars as a deuteronomistic passover. Despite discussing some of the problematic issues, most commentators end up claiming that the passover celebrated by Josiah was "deuteronomistic."[46] Earlier commentators have emphasized what they see as a combination of Israelite and Judean features in Josiah's passover, which is also related to theories of the Northern provenance of Deuteronomy.[47] In a reading that takes various aspects of the text into closer consideration, T. R. Hobbs claims that the book that was found cannot, as such, be Deuteronomy, but that this is not inconsistent with the writers of the account having been inspired by laws that are the foundation for Deuteronomy; the passover is central, there had been no such passover since the time of the judges.[48] This might be as close as we can get.

Turning to the text describing the passover, we read,

> The king commanded all the people, "Keep the passover to YHWH your God as prescribed in this book of the covenant." No such passover had been kept since the days of the judges who judged Israel, even during all the days of the kings of Israel and of the kings of Judah; but in the eighteenth year of King Josiah this passover was kept to YHWH in Jerusalem. (2 Kgs 23:21–23)

---

45. Clements, "The Former Prophets and Deuteronomy," 93–95.

46. E.g. Cogan and Tadmor, *II Kings*, 290; Gray, *I & II Kings*, 740–45, on the passover; Fretheim, *First and Second Kings*, 216–17. Fretheim notes: "These reforms are shaped most fundamentally by the principles and precepts of the book of Deuteronomy," even though he does say that it is not sure what is referred to by the book that is found (p. 213). Sweeney, *I & II Kings*, 444, 449–50, sees the passover as a ritual of national independence, but associated with Deuteronomy.

47. Montgomery and Gehman, *Kings*, 535–36, completely assume Deut 16, even though the *matzot*, the supposedly "North Israelite element," is not even mentioned in the text. They also cite Hempel, who "finds here a statesmanlike combination of the festivals of the two regions…" Jones, *1 and 2 Kings*, 626–27, discusses the problem of *matzot* not being mentioned, and discusses the time of the festival, which is hard to reconcile with Kings' account. He sees the passover as a nomadic and nationalistic celebration.

48. Hobbs, *2 Kings*, 325, 337.

First of all, the three verses tell us very little. In 2 Kgs 23:21–22 we learn that the *king commanded* that the *people* keep the passover *as prescribed* in the book of the covenant, that no such passover had been kept *since the time of the judges*, that *no king* had ever kept such a passover, and that it was held in *the eighteenth year* of King Josiah's reign, in *Jerusalem*.

There seem to be three very clear pieces of information, and that is that Josiah kept the passover, not as the first king ever to do so, the text alludes, but as the first king to keep such a passover (כפסח הזה). It was held in Jerusalem, in the eighteenth year of his reign. The fact that no king had kept a passover like it is emphasized both in the Kings account and in Chronicles, but they differ in the reference to how long it had been since such a passover had been kept. Second Kings 23:22 claims that it had not been held since the "days of the judges who judged Israel, even during all the days of the kings of Israel and the kings of Judah," whereas 2 Chr 35:18 says that no passover like had been "kept in Israel since the days of the prophet Samuel;[49] none of the kings of Israel had kept such a passover as was kept by Josiah, by the priests and the Levites, by all Judah and Israel who were present, and by the inhabitants of Jerusalem."

The biggest riddle of 2 Kgs 23:21–23 remains the question of what is being referred to as "this book of the covenant," הספר הברית הזה. This is a very unusual term in the Hebrew Bible. It appears also in 2 Kgs 23:2, in the covenant ritual in the temple, described above. It appears otherwise only in Exod 24:7 and 2 Chr 35:30. What is immediately clear is that we cannot know what this book of the covenant is referring to from these verses alone, but need to consult the context. In the Chronicler's account of Josiah's reform, we find the term ספר הברית in the book-finding account (2 Chr 34:30), where the King's account has ספר התורה, and not in the account of the passover. It would therefore seem that for early readers of 2 Kings (assuming Chronicles used Kings as a source), the terms ספר הברית and ספר התורה (2 Chr 34:14, 15) were interchangeable. It could also be that another, common source of Kings and Chronicles differed from both traditions.

In the Chronicler's account of the passover, reference is made to the "written directions of King David of Israel and the written directions of his son Solomon" (בכתב דויד מלך ישראל ובכתב שלמה בנו, 2 Chr 35:4), and that preparations were made "according to the word of YHWH by

---

49. Samuel is mentioned in 1 Chr 9:22 as "Samuel the seer," and is reported as having acted together with David to organize the gatekeepers (9:17–32). However, he otherwise plays no role in Chronicles, so it is quite striking that he is singled out as a time-marker in the sense that he is.

Moses" (כדבר־יהוה ביד־משה, 2 Chr 35:6). Later, when the ritual is actually described, it is said to be performed "as it is written in the book of Moses" (ככתוב בספר משה, 2 Chr 35:12), and "according to the ordinance" (כמשפט), when describing the method in which the lamb is to be roasted (boiled with fire). Finally, in v. 17, it is summarized that the passover was kept "according to the command of King Josiah." Chronicles is therefore extremely careful to document that the ritual was carried out according to written precepts, far more careful than Kings. Chronicles also appeals to multiple authority figures, and lines up Josiah along with all of the "heroes," Moses, David, and Solomon.

The phrase ספר התורה is much more common in the Bible than the term ספר הברית. We read, for example, in Deut 29:21: ככל אלות הברית הכתובה בספר התורה הזה ("in accordance with all the curses of the covenant written in this book of the law").[50] The occurrence of this phrase in connection with the curses of Deuteronomy has led some scholars to equate the book that was found by Hilkiah with a collection that included curses, either like Deuteronomy, or like the so-called Holiness Code of Lev 17–26, with the curses in Lev 26.

We begin to appreciate how much it is the context that gives meaning to "Josiah's reform" and "Josiah's passover." It is the same type of readerly assumption that scholars rely on to know the content of the book that Josiah found. So, since 2 Kings tells us so little about what its Josiah's passover was like, where do readers get their assumptions from? Let us now review briefly some other contexts for this text, the passover legislation in biblical legal texts.[51]

Passover in Deuteronomy
The Bible contains several collections of festival legislation. Deuteronomy 16 contains one set of laws about the passover and the *matzot* and the *sukkot*. These three feasts can also be found described together in the summaries of festivals in Exod 23:14–17. Exodus 34:18–26 talks about the *matzot* and the *sukkot*, but not the passover. The passover feast and

---

50. This phrase is also close to the language of Huldah's oracle, as commented above.
51. For more background on the biblical festival legislations, see, e.g., A. Cooper and B. R. Goldstein, "The Festivals of Israel and Judah and the Literary History of the Pentateuch," *JAOS* 110 (1990): 19–31. See the further literature cited in B. M. Levinson, "Introduction," in *Theory and Method in Biblical and Cuneiform Law: Revision, Interpolation and Development* (ed. B. M. Levinson; JSOTSup 181; Sheffield: Sheffield Academic, 1994), 11 n. 3. See also Weyde, *The Appointed Festivals of YHWH*, 19–68; T. Veijola, "The History of the Passover in the Light of Deuteronomy 16,1–8," *ZABR* 2 (1996): 53–75.

the *matzot* festival are described in Exod 12–13. In Num 9:1–15 there is specific legislation regarding how to deal with the passover in the case of someone being unclean for having touched a dead body, or if someone is out traveling. We also find the passover, *matzot*, and *sukkot* listed in the festival calendars of Lev 23:4–8 and Num 28:16–25.

Deuteronomy 16:1–7 reads:

> Observe the month of Abib by keeping the passover to YHWH your God, for in the month of Abib YHWH your God brought you out of Egypt by night. You shall offer the passover sacrifice to YHWH you God, from the flock or the herd, at the place YHWH will choose as a dwelling for his name. You must not eat with it anything leavened (חמץ). For seven days you shall eat unleavened bread (מצות) with it—the bread of affliction—because you came out of the land of Egypt in great haste, so that all the days of your life you may remember the day of your departure from the land of Egypt.
>
> No leaven (שאר) shall be seen with you in all your territory for seven days; and none of the meat of what you slaughter on the evening of the first day shall remain until morning. You are not permitted to offer the passover sacrifice within any of your towns that YHWH your God is giving to you. But at the place which YHWH you God will choose as a dwelling for his name, only there shall you offer the passover sacrifice, in the evening at sunset, the time of the day when you departed from Egypt. You shall boil it with fire and eat it at the place which YHWH your God will choose; the morning you may go back to your tents. For six days you shall continue to eat unleavened bread (מצות), and on the seventh day there shall be a solemn assembly for YHWH your God, when you shall do no work.

The first point to comment on regarding the passover legislation in Deuteronomy is the calendar. The festival is to be held in the month of Abib, which is the first month of the year, in spring, to commemorate the departure out of Egypt. The time of sacrifice, which is evening (vv. 1, 4, 6), is also stressed, to commemorate the time that they left Egypt. The ban on leavened bread is also emphasized, and the festival of *matzot*, which is a pilgrimage feast separate from the passover in many of the references made to these festivals in biblical texts, is completely fused with the passover in Deuteronomy.⁵² The date, the time of the sacrifice,

---

52. The *matzot* festival is incorporated completely into the passover festival in Deuteronomy. These possibly originally distinct feasts are associated with one another in all of the biblical references. For a sustained discussion of the literary history of Deut 16 that highlights many exegetical and hermeneutical issues connected to it, see Levinson, *Deuteronomy and the Hermeneutics*, 53–97; J. G.

and the bread to go along with the sacrifice are all repeatedly connected to the flight from Egypt, which is specified four times in the legislation. Egypt is of crucial importance in Deuteronomy; in fact, the whole story of Israel begins with the recapitulation of the departure from Egypt.[53] Deuteronomy is in agreement with the Exodus passover legislation on the close connection between the passover feast and the event of leaving Egypt.

The second main emphasis is on the place of eating the sacrifice, which is to be at "the place which YHWH will choose." This way of using the phrase is typical of the book of Deuteronomy. This emphasis is unique to Deuteronomy, and is not found in Exodus.

Further points of contrast with the legislation of Exod 12–13 are several. First of all the passover legislation in Exod 12 describes the observation of a household feast, where each household celebrates at home. This is a direct antithesis to Deuteronomy's prohibition against celebration in the towns (Deut 16:5). The passover legislation in Deuteronomy is clearly directed at a collective "you." This is also the case for the cultic legislation of Deut 12. There, however, there is at the same time an emphasis on the family unit, with all its members enumerated, a feature we do not find here in Deut 16. The contrast with Exodus thus becomes even more pronounced.

In Exodus there is to be a solemn feast on the first and the seventh day. In Deuteronomy there is a feast only on the seventh day. There are very strict sanctions for failing to follow the law in Exodus; the person will be cut off from the house of Israel. We find no corresponding sanctions in Deuteronomy. The indication of the exact day of the month, and so forth, is also much more meticulous in Exodus, whereas Deuteronomy seems only to be interested in the total number of seven days. In Exodus the animal is to be roasted, in Deuteronomy cooked or boiled. The command to brush blood on the doorposts and lintels (Exod 12:7) is not found in Deuteronomy. In Deuteronomy, the feast is one of commemoration and cultic slaughter, and does not contain these apotropaic features. Evening is mentioned as the time of killing the sacrificial animal in Exod 12:6, the same is specified in Deut 16:1, 4, and 6.

McConville, "Deuteronomy's Unification of Passover and Massot: A Response to Bernard M. Levinson," *JBL* 119 (2000): 47–58; B. M. Levinson, "The Hermeneutics of Tradition in Deuteronomy: A Reply to J. G. McConville," *JBL* 199 (2000): 269–86.

53. See the discussion of the role of the reference to Egypt in Deuteronomy in Chapter 7, below.

The passover is also regulated in the cultic calendar of Lev 23. Here, the command not to do laborious work is very prominent in the passover legislation, a feature that has a very low profile in Deuteronomy, with only a brief mention of it in Deut 16:8. Another point that is emphasized in Leviticus is the time that they are to be observed. The concept of the "appointed time" is central, in a way similar to the centrality of the "place" in Deuteronomy.

Numbers 28:16–25 enumerates the offerings that are required for the passover feast. Numbers 9 contains a narrative description of a passover celebration in the desert, on the first anniversary of the departure from Egypt. The account contains an episode giving provisions for how those who are unclean on the day of the passover can keep it in the next month instead. This is similar to the situation affecting Hezekiah's passover.

What Is So Deuteronomistic about Josiah's Passover?
With the information about these various legislations of the passover festival in the Hebrew Bible in mind, we may now go back to the Kings account and ask, just as we asked about the reform: What is so deuteronomistic about Josiah's passover? We concluded regarding the reform that its main concern was the elimination of idolatry, a deeply deuteronomistic concern, but also equally a concern of the Tetrateuch or of the prophets.

If there is one thing that is said about Josiah's passover that one could argue is deuteronomistic, it is that it is held in Jerusalem, a centralized location, about which it is said that YHWH has chosen it (though not in this part of the narrative). There is nothing else specifically deuteronomistic, however. No mention is made of the *matzot* in Kings; there is no clue about the time of day, or calendar, or whether the animals sacrificed are roasted or boiled. There is no mention of remembering the Exodus. It is implied that it was a great feat to hold this passover, and this is underlined by the fact that it has not been held since the time of the judges. However, no active reason is given for why it was important or significant to hold a passover.

On the other hand, the fact that the king himself leads the celebration is perhaps enough to say that the passover is anti-deuteronomistic. The king, according to Deuteronomy, has no cultic function whatsoever. The law of Deut 16:1–8 is directed at individual Israelites, or at most, Israel as a collective "you." We are left with very little to go on, and begin to suspect that the only way that Josiah's passover can be said to be deuteronomistic is if one assumes that the "book of the covenant" is referring to Deuteronomy. And, strangely enough, we as readers must then accept that Josiah interprets this book in a way that the law itself does not seem to support!⁵⁴

It is thus clear that there is nothing in the description of Josiah's passover in 2 Kings that can tell us whether it is particularly deuteronomistic. It is on the basis of other clues in the larger narrative that this decision has been made by readers. The next question that seems appropriate to ask is how passover is described in other parts of the DH. One might have expected to find something as important as passover described as being celebrated during the course of Israel's history, in spite of the claims that no such passover had been celebrated by any king of Israel or Judah.

Passover in the Former Prophets

There is not much to find on the passover in the Former Prophets, as was also pointed out in the survey of Chapter 5. The passover is not mentioned anywhere else in 2 Kings, and not mentioned in Judges, 1 and 2 Samuel, or 1 Kings. The Former Prophets record only one passover celebration other than Josiah's, which is the one kept by Joshua when he had just entered the land, after the ceremony of circumcision, in Josh 5:11 (see Chapter 4). This passover was held in Gilgal on the fourteenth evening of the month. The next day they ate of the produce of the land, unleavened cakes, and the manna that had fed them on their long march through the desert ceased to be provided. In this respect, then, the remark of 2 Kgs 23:22 is correct. No such passover, in fact, no passover at all, had been held in Israel since the *before* time of the Judges, according to the so-called deuteronomistic historian. In that respect, the Israelites failed, which fits with the understanding of history claimed for the "Deuteronomists." In Chronicles, there is one other passover celebration, during the reign of Hezekiah, recorded in 2 Chr 30:1–26, but it is not judged to be as good as Josiah's.

Since there is no real help in the narratives of Joshua through Kings for understanding what might be the so-called deuteronomistic historian's view of passover, we conclude, in the end, that the labeling of the

---

54. In a clever analysis, this has been interpreted as typically deuteronomistic by Levinson, who sees the writers of Deuteronomy primarily as hermeneutical innovators and subjugators. By subjugating Deuteronomy, Josiah is acting according to the spirit of the Deuteronomists, he argues; see Levinson's *Deuteronomy and the Hermeneutics*, 95–97, and "The Reconceptualization of Kingship in Deuteronomy and the Deuteronomistic History's Transformation of Torah," *VT* 51 (2001): 512–34 (524–25). Although attractive, this kind of argument has the danger of quickly taking the discussion to a place with no textual controls.

passover as deuteronomistic is totally dependent on the association of the narrative of 2 Kgs 23:21–23 with the finding of the book in 22:8, and on interpretations of the reform report itself as setting in motion a "deuteronomistic" reform program.

Reform Narratives in Kings

In order to understand the narrative of 2 Kgs 22–23, perhaps it is more relevant to look at other reform narratives in Kings. For example, formal and structural parallels in Kings might be more helpful, and methodologically more sound to use in order to cast light on our narrative. In that regard, the reforms of Joash in 2 Kgs 12, Hezekiah in 2 Kgs 18, and Jehu in 2 Kgs 9–10 form important parallels. They were all preceded by particularly "bad" kings, who worshipped "Canaanite" deities.[55] The reforms are all specifically "anti-Canaanite,"[56] and they all introduce some type of reorganization or renovation of the temple. Finally, none of the reforms is successful and the story of each king ends badly. Perhaps the Josiah account, rather than being primarily "deuteronomistic," is simply typical of the book of Kings?[57]

The Chronicler's Passover: The "True" Deuteronomistic Passover?

The Chronicler's version of the passover celebration takes up nineteen verses, compared to the three verses of the Kings account. The king, Josiah, leads the celebration, and gives all the commands as to what is to be done to the Levites (2 Chr 35:2–6). These things are then done "according to the word of YHWH by Moses" (vv. 6, 12). Then the king gives all the animals to the people, and his officials also contribute

---

55. As Hobbs points out in his commentary, *2 Kings*, 320; the most thorough study of reform narratives in Kings remains Hoffmann, *Reform und Reformen*. In my opinion, his study is most valuable for the cataloguing cross-references of phrases (which he labels as "deuteronomistic"), appearing in different biblical texts, and for the detailed observations about royal reforms in Kings. These observations can be used without accepting his general theory of composition. His study has been controversial, and has received criticism on the level of individual details as well as for his conclusions (he argues for a single, independent author of the DH, dated to the exile). See, e.g., Lohfink, "Recent Discussion on 2 Kgs 22–23," 49–55; see also a consistent critique and engagement with Hoffman in Eynikel, *The Reform of King Josiah*.

56. Although Hobbs uses the conventional term "Canaanite," I prefer to use the terms "illicit Yahwistic" and "non-Yahwistic" to characterize the cults that Kings and other biblical texts polemicize against.

57. This is also Hoffmann's conclusion in his extensive study of royal reforms in the book of Kings, *Reform und Reformen*, 251–52. Hoffmann does specify 2 Kgs 16:10–18, Ahaz's reform, as an exception from this pattern.

(vv. 7–9). Everyone lines up, according to the king's command (v. 10). They slaughter the passover lamb (פסח).

The cultic role of the king is much more specifically emphasized in Chronicles than in Kings. As we know, the book of Deuteronomy does not prescribe a cultic role for the king at all. In that respect, Chronicles makes a more thorough, distinct role for the king than Kings does, even though Kings' view of the role of the king is closer to Chronicles than it is to Deuteronomy.[58]

There are several points of difference between Chronicles and Kings regarding the reign of Josiah. As we observed above, context is important for understanding the reform of Josiah as recorded in 2 Kgs 23, and the "book discovery" plays an important role as what readers identify as the motivation for the reform. Further, the content of 2 Kgs 23, with the covenant ceremony, cultic cleansing, and passover festival, contribute to the understanding of the book as Deuteronomy, or some form of it, in most reconstructions. In Chronicles, however, the cultic cleansing is dated to the twelfth year of Josiah, and is recorded before the "book finding." In fact, it is made explicit that Josiah first "purged the land," something that took six years until the eighteenth year, before he sends Shaphan, plus the governor and the recorder, to repair the house of YHWH. The cleansing of the land is therefore not understood to be a response to the book-finding in Chronicles, as it is usually read in Kings. The reform report itself is much shorter in Chronicles than in Kings, making up only four and a half verses compared to Kings' seventeen. In addition, Chronicles portrays the cleansing to have extended geographically to "as far as Naphtali," well beyond the areas of 2 Kings.

A reading of 2 Chr 35 reveals a description of a centralized passover. It is claimed to have been held according to the "written directions of David (בכתב דויד מלך ישראל) and the written directions of his son Solomon (ובמכתב שלמה בנו)" (35:4).[59] It is not totally clear whether these written instructions refer to the way in which the ancestral houses are to be divided, or if they pertain directly to the passover itself. The passover lamb is to be slaughtered according to YHWH's word through Moses (v. 6). It is clear is that there is great care taken here to appeal to the highest authorities in order to make absolutely clear that the celebration was carried out correctly.

---

58. More on the role of the cult in Chronicles in W. Riley, *King and Cultus in Chronicles: Worship and the Reinterpretation of History* (JSOTSup 160; Sheffield: JSOT, 1993).

59. The versions have usually read the particle כ instead of ב for MT בכתב and במכתב.

From the description itself, we see that the Levites have an important role, which is consistent with the Chronicler's understanding of the Levites. The celebration is described in some ways as consistent with Deut 16. It is held in a centralized location and the *matzot* is also celebrated. However, there is no mention of Egypt, which is so important in Deuteronomy. Further, there are also signs that the Chronicler seeks some harmonization with Exod 12, in that the *pesach*, the sacrificial animal, is described as being "boiled with fire" (ויבשלו הפסח באש). This seems like a conflation of the Exodus command not to boil the sacrificial animal, but rather to roast it (צלי־אש), and Deuteronomy's command to boil it (בשל). These are indications that the Chronicler has created an account using various possible sources, but most importantly, an account that serves the purposes of the books of Chronicles. Again, as with Kings, perhaps the fairest way to read it is to read more on its own terms, as a part its own, integral literary work.

As opposed to Kings, Chronicles records another passover celebration. Hezekiah is also described as holding a passover, but this was not considered as "good" as Josiah's. Hezekiah keeps it in the wrong month because the priests had not consecrated themselves. This narrative has possible parallels to Num 9, where a number of people are barred from keeping the passover because they have become unclean through touching a corpse, and are therefore instructed to celebrate it the next month. It is important for the Chronicler to show that Josiah's passover was unique and that it surpassed Hezekiah's. Second Chronicles 35:18 thus concludes that no passover like Josiah's had been kept since the days of the prophet Samuel, and none of the kings of Israel had kept such a passover as the one kept by Josiah. Incidentally, there is no account of a passover in the time of the prophet Samuel, but, as we know, Chronicles begins the fuller narrative portion of its history with King Saul. It is obvious that in order to understand more fully the account of Josiah's passover in Chronicles, it would be necessary to compare closely with the Hezekiah account, and other accounts of cultic celebrations in Chronicles, which really have an agenda of their own.[60]

As we have seen, the Chronicler's version of King Josiah's reign is different from the one in Kings, including an expansion of the time-period in which Josiah makes his reforms, a slightly different order, and an extended account of the passover celebration. The playful heading above, referring to the Chronicler's passover as the "true" deuteronomistic passover, is one way of suggesting that perhaps, as an early reader

---

60. Riley, *King and Cultus in Chronicles*, 19–22.

of the Kings' account, the Chronicler understood the passover in the same way that many other readers have understood it when read together with other ancient source material that has come down to us. The writers expanded the description and made it more specific to suit their needs. By reading the Chronicler's account, we are getting some hints as to how the Kings account was understood by some ancient readers, again, making the assumption that Kings was one of the Chronicler's sources.[61] Because the account of the passover that most scholars believe to be written by a deuteronomistic writer gives so little detail, 2 Chr 35 might qualify as containing a more deuteronomistic account, according to this line of reasoning. In this sense, 2 Chr 35 is the "true" deuteronomistic passover.

Josiah's Centralized Passover: Enough to Make it Deuteronomistic?
If a centralized passover is the main distinguishing characteristic of a deuteronomistic passover, both the Kings and the Chronicles accounts contain a deuteronomistic passover celebration. The question is whether or not it is correct to assume that centralization is an appropriate term in the narratives about royal cultic reform and celebrations of festivals. The activity described in Josiah's passover does not mention limiting cultic activity to one place, or to Jerusalem. Moreover, as we saw in Chapter 2 of this study, the meaning of the expressions "the place which YHWH your God will choose" in Deuteronomy, and "the city that YHWH your God has chosen" in Kings, are quite different. Whereas the phrase in Deuteronomy does entail the idea that cultic activity should be limited to one central location, in Kings the phrase is an expression entailing YHWH's promise of protection, and does not entail cultic acts at all. The fact that 2 Kgs 22–23 does not refer to Jerusalem as chosen in the account of the reform/cleansing gives further support to the findings about the distinct use of the idea of chosenness in Kings. If the idea of Jerusalem as chosen had a significant connection to the idea of cult centralization, we might have expected this idea to appear in the reform report or in the accounts of the covenant ceremony or the passover. In fact, it does not, and only appears later in the divine oracle of judgment on Josiah in 2 Kgs 23:27, fully in the understanding seen in Kings (see Chapter 2).

What we can say, however, is that both Kings and Chronicles quite clearly envision a passover more like the one prescribed in Deut 16 than

---

61. But see, e.g., Auld, *Kings without a Privilege*. For more on the methods of the writer of Chronicles, see, e.g., M. Graham et al., eds., *The Chronicler as Historian* (JSOTSup 238; Sheffield: Sheffield Academic, 1997).

the one described in Exod 12. If those are the choices, Josiah's passover may be called deuteronomistic, despite the conspicuous lack of reference to Egypt. But this is a concession with many conditions, and a far cry from the oversimplified assertion that Josiah implemented a deuteronomistic reform of cultic centralization.

Summary and Discussion

If we now try to draw together our discussion, we may summarize that concerning the law book found in Josiah's temple clean up, we do not know what it contained. We can deduce from Huldah's oracle that it contained a prohibition of idolatry and most likely a set of curses, and we know that the king was appalled by the content. Having embarked on a physical repair of the temple, he responds by holding a covenant renewal ceremony, and then carries out a set of acts of cleansing and defilement, purging the temple, Jerusalem and Judah, and parts of Benjamin and Samaria of illicit cultic activity, especially the idols of the cults of Asherah, Molech, and Kemosh, and the high places. He cleans up Jerusalem back to the time of the "early" Solomon, and Benjamin to the time before Jeroboam. Finally, he celebrates passover, a passover that is not described in the text.

Our exploration of 2 Kgs 22–23 shows that it is not as simple or straightforward as it has often been assumed, to claim that the Kings account is advocating centralization the way it is laid out in Deut 12, 14, and 16. Certainly, as the discussion above of the reform report shows, 2 Kgs 23:4–20 cannot be taken as an account of centralization, but is, rather, a report of cultic cleansing and defiling, beginning at the temple and moving in a centrifugal movement out into the whole land.

As for the passover, although the festival is held in Jerusalem, other features of the deuteronomistic passover are not specified in Kings, and it seems rash to read it as following the deuteronomistic legislation. In the end, we cannot know from Kings itself how those writers conceived the passover, only that it was in Jerusalem, led by the king, and that it restored a custom to Israel from its ancient past. As suggested, perhaps it is more fruitful to pursue the meaning of Josiah's reform within the paradigm of royal reform in the book of Kings, rather than continue to see it through the prism of "Deuteronomism."

In 2 Chr 35, however, it is much clearer that Josiah's passover is a centralized feast held at the Jerusalem temple, with the emphasis on all Israel participating. However, since this account also shows some harmonization with Exod 12, it seems likely that the writer of Chronicles has combined several available traditions about the passover and has embellished it according to his own agenda.[62]

Assuming that Chronicles is later than Kings, one might say that the writer of Chronicles has read Kings in the same way that others later read it, a reading that scholars have identified as "deuteronomistic." The writer of Chronicles interpreted it according to his own agenda, however. For example, the connection is not made in Chronicles between the finding of the book and either Josiah's cult cleansing or his passover. Therefore, in Chronicles the nature of the passover cannot be argued from the discovery of the "the book," which was the only clue in Kings. The passover itself, however, is described in detail. But even here we get a surprise. Chronicles' version of passover claims legitimacy from past kings, who, according to the account, do not themselves practice these instructions. That is, the Chronicler claims that he follows the instructions of David, Solomon, and Moses. It is not said of these figures, however, that they hold a passover, with the exception of Moses. So, in fact, Chronicles achieves the feat of cultic "rehabilitation" of both Solomon and David. Interpreting these texts continues to be a tricky business.

The reading of Deut 12 in Chapter 3 and the survey of Deut 16, above, in addition to the survey of the "election phrase" in Chapter 2, all demonstrate that the kind of centralization that is required in Deuteronomy is something quite distinct. We do not find this distinct phenomenon in 2 Kgs 22–23, nor do we find the election phrase in connection with the cult reform of Josiah. In fact, the appearance of the election phrase in 2 Kgs 23:27 is totally in line with the general usage in Kings, as we discovered also in Chapters 2 and 4, and has nothing to do with the concern for the limitation of cultic activity and worship to one location chosen by YHWH.[63] Yet, like other texts we have explored in Kings that

---

62. As such, we can say with Gary Knoppers that, "in this respect the Chronicler created a work that is more Deuteronomic than Kings is." But Knoppers does not draw the full consequence of his observation with respect to the Kings account, and insists that it, too, is deuteronomistic; see Knoppers "Rethinking the Relationship Between Deuteronomy and the Deuteronomistic History: The Case of Kings," *CBQ* 63 (2001): 393–415 (396).

63. L. J. Hoppe supports the understanding that the DH does not advocate centralization and the limitation of worship to Jerusalem, but that this, "Deuteronomic," understanding is post-exilic; see Hoppe, "Jerusalem in the Deuteronomistic History," in Lohfink, ed., *Das Deuteronomium*, 105–10 (107–8). Hoppe's historicist reading of the texts is different from my approach to the biblical texts, but his reading of the DH is more correct than many other scholars who do not see that 2 Kgs 22–23 does not unequivocally advocate centralization. He also correctly

bring together the ideas of the "chosen city" with the special privilege of David, 2 Kgs 22–23 also brings together multiple ideas in a way that gives the final text weight and allows it to stand out as ideologically crucial. With its appeal to the beginning of the monarchy, it invites readers to evaluate the whole of the story told in kings in light of the threat of YHWH's judgment, as revealed in the oracle or "book." In Chronicles, the perspective is explicitly drawn back to the time of Moses. Finally, one might point out the irony of the big cleansing of Josiah at a time when YHWH is going to destroy his chosen city anyway. The futility of the reform is a major point.

Conclusions

Some conclusions suggest themselves at this point. First of all, it has become clear that the significance of the narrative of 2 Kgs 22–23 for *centralization* has been exaggerated. Second, though it is possible to read the narrative as a story about discovering the book of Deuteronomy, or some form of it, and though it has been read this way by early readers, this is not the only possibility. Third, this narrative cannot carry the burden of being a proof text for the DH hypothesis. Although it does demonstrate some of the many connections between the books of Kings and Deuteronomy, it also shows connections to Leviticus, Joshua, Ezekiel, Jeremiah, and Chronicles. I suggest that rather than read it as a story that legitimizes the so-called deuteronomistic movement, or as the implementation of a historical reform carried out in the late monarchic period, or as a "founding myth" of the deuteronomistic school, this story is best read primarily within the context of the books of Kings. As such, it is a story about a royal attempt to reform the cult and cleanse it to an original, pristine state (*pre* the apostasy of Solomon), that ultimately failed to stave off the final disaster that befell the kingdom of Judah.

The essential issue in 2 Kgs 22–23 is the drive to eliminate non-Yahwistic worship and illicit Yahwistic cultic activity. The claim that Josiah (and Hezekiah) conducted reforms of cult centralization can only be made by reading these texts *in light of* "the law," whether one envisions Deuteronomy or the whole of the Torah. But it is a different step to say that this was the intent of the writers of Deuteronomy, or to say that

---

observes that for Deuteronomy, the most important message is "obedience to the Lord." Yet he does not draw the full consequence of his observations. He calls centralization a Deuteronomic innovation, but does not develop the way in which this innovation might or might not have influenced the way that Joshua–Kings has been read.

2 Kgs 22–23 was written with Deuteronomy in mind. When 2 Kgs 22–23 is read with critical questions in mind about where our reader's assumptions come from, we realize that 2 Kgs 22–23 in itself does not narrate a reform of centralization, a "deuteronomistic" reform, or a "deuteronomistic" passover.

Having said this, we are not finished with the exploration of the many links between the ideas of divinely chosen place, election, and authority. We need to take into consideration other biblical texts involving the supremacy of Jerusalem, the Davidic monarchy, and the special protection of YHWH. A further exploration of these motifs might help us to understand more clearly why a text such as 2 Kgs 22–23 has been read in the way that it has. The next chapter, therefore, will focus on election and authority.

Chapter 7

DIVINE ELECTION AS A PRINCIPLE OF AUTHORITY

We have observed repeatedly that the idea of "chosen place" in Deuteronomy is a distinct concept. This chapter will explore how divine election functions as a principle of authority in constructing this concept as a textual phenomenon in the book of Deuteronomy as a whole. In Deuteronomy, divine election is employed in a distinctive way that also includes underpinning the authority of the divinely elected place. Specific clusters of ideas and concepts which are associated with texts of divine election seem to be significant in forming this authority.

Election in the Pentateuch

The Hebrew root for "election" (בחר) is used extensively in Deuteronomy (31 times), but only appears three times elsewhere in the Pentateuch with YHWH or Elohim as the subject (Num 16:5, 7; 17:20). This seems to indicate that Deuteronomy uses the term יבחר יהו specifically to denote divine election, whereas this is not the case in Genesis through Numbers.

Divine election may not be expressed by the Hebrew root בחר in Genesis through Numbers, but this does not mean that the idea of divine election does not exist. In fact, the idea of YHWH's election of individuals that will become the ancestors of Israel is very much at the forefront of the narratives of Genesis, with the special chosenness of Abraham, the rivalry between wife Sarah and concubine Hagar and between sister wives Rachel and Leah, and the many sibling favorites such as Abel over Cain, Isaac over Ishmael, Jacob over Esau, and Joseph over his brothers, and the various degrees of favoritism between these brothers. These narratives weave complicated and challenging webs of relationships between humans, between the chosen and the ones not chosen, and between humans and God, with sets of fundamental interpretative and ethical implications.[1] Further, the election of Israel is a prominent idea in

---

1. Illustrated in J. S. Kaminsky's book, *Yet I Loved Jacob: Reclaiming the Biblical Concept of Election* (Nashville: Abingdon, 2007).

Exodus, for example when Israel is chartered with a special task; if they keep the commandments, they will be YHWH's prized possession (סגלה), a priestly kingdom and a holy people (Exod 19:4–5).

Divine election in Deuteronomy has four different objects of election, the election of Israel, the priests, the king, and the "place."[2] The majority of the occurrences in Deuteronomy deal with YHWH's chosen place, with 21 out of 29 occurrences. Five refer to Israel, one to the king and two to the priests. I will come back to these in turn.

So far, we observe two main differences between Deuteronomy and Genesis–Numbers: (1) Deuteronomy uses the Hebrew root בחר quite extensively, while Genesis–Numbers expresses divine election in other ways; (2) while Genesis–Numbers is deeply concerned with the chosenness of Israel, it is not overtly concerned with establishing any idea of one place for cultic activity that is chosen by the deity. The books of Exodus through Numbers are very much concerned with the sanctuary and the ritual cult, and clearly express the understanding that YHWH is present in the sanctuary in the midst of the people. However, the language of election is not used to express any idea about a specific location for this sanctuary. The idea of a central sanctuary is reflected through the description of how it should be built (Exodus) and the lay-out of the camp (especially in Numbers). Deuteronomy, on the other hand, is highly focused on a "chosen place," and employs the verb בחר extensively to develop this idea.

In the following we will explore in further detail how Deuteronomy expresses the idea of the chosenness of Israel in its own distinctive way, and also the way in which it is concerned with divine election applied to a completely different, though subtly related, concern, namely the chosenness of place of cultic activity. To assist us in the exploration of these interwoven strands in Deuteronomy, we will be charting the use of the verb בחר in the book.

The Election of Israel in Deuteronomy

The first four occurrences of בחר in Deuteronomy all refer to the election of Israel, and are found spread out in the first third of the book, which forms a set of introductions to the actual legal corpus of chs. 12–26. In Deut 4:37–38, we read that YHWH, "because he loved your ancestors, he

---

2. The two occurrences of בחר where YHWH is not the subject are Deut 23:17 and Deut 30:19. Deut 23:17 deals with fugitive slaves. He is to live in which ever town/place he chooses and is not to be oppressed. Deut 30:19 contains the options that Moses lays before the Israelites—life or death. Moses urges them to choose life.

chose their descendants after them. He brought you out of Egypt with his own presence, by his great power, driving out before you nations greater and mightier than yourselves, to bring you in, giving you their land for a possession."

This text refers to the unique character of YHWH, to his deeds, to his election of his people, and the promise to drive out the nations and give the people the land. That YHWH has chosen the descendants of the fathers is, among other things, a characteristic of YHWH in this text. That YHWH has chosen Israel is thus a trait of his person, and he has done it out of his love for the ancestors, a kind of mysterious election,[3] or perhaps out of his duty as the suzerain. The following verses bring a hortatory command to keep the laws and commands.

Deuteronomy 4:37–38, considered by many to be one of the latest parts of Deuteronomy and perhaps influenced by Isa 40–55, seems to summarize key thoughts in Deuteronomy; the idea of the election of Israel is connected closely to the duty to keep the law. The promise of land, in the fairly aggressive sense of Deuteronomy, is also tied together with these ideas here. This deity, who has elected Israel and given them the land, also drives out "the others" from that land.

The next reference to the election of Israel, in Deut 7, contains the text that perhaps most explicitly lays out an explanation and defense of Deuteronomy's idea of the chosenness of Israel. We read in vv. 6–7,

> For you are a holy people to YHWH your God; YHWH your God has chosen out of all the peoples on earth to be his people, his treasured possession (ובך בהר יהוה אלהיך להיות לו לעם סגלה מכל העמים). It was not because you were more numerous than any other people that YHWH set his heart on you and chose you—for you were the fewest of all peoples. It was because YHWH loved you and kept the oath that he swore to your ancestors…

The reasons given for YHWH's election of Israel are, again, his love for them, and in order that he may keep the promise to the ancestors. And again, an act on behalf of YHWH, that in turn, we observe, becomes a heavy burden on Israel.

This text follows commands forbidding intermarriage and following other gods, and directly follows a command to destroy the religious structures of the people of the land. The text is followed by descriptions of YHWH's saving deeds in Egypt, and hortatory command to keep the commandments, so that YHWH will keep the covenant and give blessings.

Deuteronomy 7 has a roughly chiastic structure with the following themes,

---

3. Kaminsky, *Yet I Loved Jacob*, 104.

A	vv. 1–5	Destroying the nations and their religion
	B vv. 6–16	The election of Israel and the terms of the covenant
A′	vv. 17–26	Destroying the nations and their religion

In fact, a similar structure is also present in Deut 12, the text that first introduces the idea of the "chosen place." Also there, the command to worship at the "place that YHWH chooses," is framed by the command to destroy the cult of the nations. We will be returning to this comparison; for now, we note how the elect status of Israel, with the duties it entails, is set in deliberate contrast to the ways of the nations of the land and the command not to mix with them.

Two main themes of Deuteronomy are the call to obey the law and the warning against the religion of the "nations." These are related to one another. The election of Israel as his holy possession is one of YHWH's acts that turn into a demand on Israel to keep his commandments. This clever dynamic, it seems to me, is one key to the rhetorical success of Deuteronomy. We see this dynamic at play clearly in the fourth reference to YHWH's election of Israel in Deut 10:15, "Yet YHWH set his heart in love on your ancestors alone and chose you, their descendants after them (ויבחר בזרעם אחריהם בכם), out of all the peoples, as it is today."

This text is framed by the call to serve, love, and obey YHWH, with descriptions of his uniqueness, his saving deeds in Egypt, and the call to keep his commandments. Again, the chosenness of Israel turns into a demand to serve YHWH. The nature of the love and affection of YHWH turns out to be quite demanding on Israel, the elected one.

Finally, the last reference to the election of Israel is found in Deut 14:2, after the main body of legislation has begun in ch. 12. In fact, it seems a bit out of place and odd. We read, "For you are a people holy to YHWH your God; it is you YHWH has chosen out of all the peoples on earth to be his people, his treasured possession."

This verse is identical to 7:6, but the context is completely different. It might be that the idea of a holy people to YHWH has become fixed together with the concept of election, in this specific wording, so that this expression could be used in various contexts. The context in this case is legislation forbidding the shaving of heads for the dead, with the justification that the Israelites are YHWH's children and a holy people. This short command is followed by the long and detailed legislation about clean and unclean food. In this verse, therefore, the reference to the people being a holy people, chosen by YHWH, functions as an explanation for why a command is supposed to be kept, and is thus a concrete application of the logic established in previous texts, of a direct connection between YHWH's election of Israel and the demand on Israel to obey

YHWH and follow his commands.⁴ The dietary laws are a concrete example of the type of law that Israel must keep, and serve to further draw together the idea of the obligations of being YHWH's holy people and his elected people, and thus separate from others, with specific laws concerning holiness/purity.

Scholars have noted that the understanding of Israel's holiness is quite distinct in Deuteronomy, and differs from the understanding of Israel's holiness in Leviticus and Numbers. There, holiness is a state that has to be attained by following specific rules of behavior and actions taken to remove impurity. In Deuteronomy, holiness is an attribute of Israel as a people that puts specific demands on them, including the necessity of keeping YHWH's laws.⁵ Deuteronomy does not seem consistent on this subject, however. In Deut 28:9, for example, the status of the people as holy is conditional, claiming "YHWH will establish you as a people holy to himself, as he has sworn to you, if you keep the commandments of YHWH your God, and walk in his ways."

As we have seen, the election of Israel is referred to in four places in Deuteronomy. The first three occur in the introductory section of Deuteronomy. These texts all include several motifs clustered together: the call to serve, love, and obey YHWH, with descriptions of his uniqueness, his saving deeds in Egypt and the call to keep his commandments, so that YHWH will keep the covenant and give blessings. The rare term סגלה (YHWH's treasured or prized possession) occurs in two of the texts, and the reference to Israel as a holy people is also found here. In these texts, the reference to the chosen people makes up part of the hortatory introduction to the legal material of Deuteronomy. The same motifs are found also in the last occurrence, in Deut 14:2, though the context here is different. In these first three occurrences, the reference to the election of Israel all recall a basic, what could be called "founding narrative," that implies many bonds of promise and the call for loyalty.

Even though the verb בחר is only used five times in connection with Israel, it is commonly thought in scholarship that a comprehensive theology of election is present in Deuteronomy.⁶ I think one of the

---

4. A. D. H. Mayes, "Deuteronomy 14 and the Deuteronomic World View," in Martínez et al., eds., *Studies in Deuteronomy*, 165–81.

5. Weinfeld, "Pentateuch." See, for a different view on the quality of holiness in Deuteronomy, N. Lohfink, "Opfer und Säkularisierung im Deuteronomium," in *Studien zu Opfer und Kult im Alten Testament mit einer Bibliographie 1969–1991 zum Opfer in der Bibel* (ed. A. Schenker; Tübingen: Mohr [Siebeck], 1992), 15–43.

6. R. E. Clements, "Deuteronomy and the Jerusalem Cult Tradition," *VT* 15 (1965): 300–12 (305); R. Rendtorff, "Die Erwählung Israels als Thema der deuteronomischen Theologie," in *Die Botschaft und die Boten: Festschrift für Hans*

reasons why the concept of the election of Israel comes across so forcefully in Deuteronomy is the consistent employment of another motif, which is the reference to YHWH's rescue of Israel from Egypt and the call to remember this deed. There are other motifs that also contribute to this comprehensiveness, such as the language of the YHWH's love for Israel.[7] However, for now we will take a step to the side and examine the motif of the rescue from Egypt and how it is employed in Deuteronomy.

Israel as Chosen, the Duty to Keep the Law, and YHWH's Rescue from Egypt

The book of Deuteronomy repeatedly makes references to YHWH's act of saving Israel from slavery in Egypt. This is a trope that serves as a reason for why the Israelites should keep the law. The Israelites are reminded of their situation as slaves, and the great acts of YHWH are used as part of a logic that serves to legitimize the law and persuade them to keep it.

Deuteronomy 4 is a key example. In this long speech, Egypt is referred to numerous times, beginning with the culmination of a passage warning against idolatry, "But YHWH has taken you, and brought you out of the iron-smelter, out of Egypt, to become a people of his very own possession (להיות לו לעם נחלה), as at this day" (4:15–24). In v. 20, נחלה ("possession") is used, which should not to be confused with סגלה. Further warnings about idolatry continue in vv. 25–31. After this begins a section about the nature of YHWH that dwells at length on his act of rescuing Israel from Egypt and the uniqueness of these acts, which is explicitly tied to the election of Israel in v. 37 (mentioned above). This text, as we observed above, neatly ties together and elaborates on the connection between key theological motifs in Deuteronomy: the chosenness of Israel, YHWH's uniqueness through his saving deeds, and the need for Israel to acknowledge these things and keep YHWH's commandments. Deuteronomy 4 in its present context functions as a comprehensive introduction to the key themes of the rest of the book.[8]

Walter Wolff zum 70. Geburtstag (ed. J. Jeremias and L. Perlitt; Neukirchen–Vluyn: Neukirchener, 1981), 75–86; P. D. Miller, *Deuteronomy* (Interpretation, A Bible Commentary for Teaching and Preaching; Louisville, Ky.: John Knox, 1990), 110–14; Kaminsky, *Yet I Loved Jacob*, 99–105.

7. The notion of "covenantal language" and the motif of the "love of God" in Deuteronomy have been studied in various ways; see, e.g., Moran, "The Ancient Near Eastern Background." The language of YHWH's love, expressed with אהב, is found mainly in Deuteronomy, Hosea, and Jeremiah, and is one of the traits that has supported the claim that Deuteronomy has "Northern" roots.

8. If this is a late chapter, as is often claimed, it builds on what can already be found spread out throughout the book of Deuteronomy.

For example, key texts are framed by the reference to the rescue from Egypt, such as Deut 5:6, which introduces the Decalogue, Deut 5:15, which introduces the Sabbath commandment, and Deut 6:12, in part of a closing speech following the *shema*. In Deut 6:20–25 (von Rad's "credo"), the deliverance from Egypt is part of the explanation for why the Israelites should keep the law. At important junctures in the text, the reference to the deliverance from Egypt inevitably appears, and serves to cement the connection between this event and the obligation to keep the law. The same appears in Deut 7, one of the election texts examined above. The reason why the Israelites should not have any dealings with the people of the land is that they are a holy people, chosen by YHWH even though they were the smallest of all people. He did this "because YHWH loves you, and is keeping the oath which he swore to your fathers, that YHWH has brought you out with a mighty hand, and redeemed you from the house of bondage, from the hand of Pharaoh king of Egypt."

Here the idea of the election of Israel is juxtaposed to the idea of YHWH's saving acts of deliverance from Egypt. The act of saving Israel underlines the election and the requirements it places on YHWH in terms of faithfulness. In return, the people will follow YHWH's commandments, and when they do, he will keep his covenant. All of these motifs come together to form a logic of the covenant, giving the terms and conditions.

Similar to Deut 6 above, Deut 8:11–20 is a hortatory speech spelling out the consequences of not following the commandments of YHWH. "Take heed lest…" The reference to Egypt is part of a listing up of the attributes of YHWH, all of the things that he did with Israel,

> …YHWH your God, who brought you out of the land of Egypt, out of the house of bondage, who led you through the great and terrible wilderness, with its fiery serpents and scorpions and thirsty ground where there was no water, who brought you water out of the flinty rock, who fed you in the wilderness with manna which your fathers did not know, that he might humble you and test you, to do you good in the end. (Deut 8:14–16)

If they forget YHWH, and begin to believe in their own power, or forget YHWH and follow other gods, they are warned by Moses that they will perish (Deut 8:19–20). Again, the context for the reference to Egypt is a passage warning against idolatry; however, it comes as a list of attributes with warnings of the punishment, rather than as a positive reason for keeping the command, as was the case in Deut 7. Moreover, the reference most likely carries with it the connotations of the logic that because YHWH rescued Israel out of Egypt, they should keep the commandments, even though it is not phrased this way in Deut 8:14–16. Finally, immediately preceding the legislation of chs. 12–26, ch. 11 contains highly forceful speech charging the Israelites to love YHWH, and keep his commandments, to remember his great deeds, especially in Egypt.

In the main legislative portion of Deuteronomy, there are at least a dozen references to being a slave in Egypt, or YHWH's rescue of Israel, as ways to raise support for keeping individual laws. In Deut 13:6, the reference to Egypt used to describe YHWH is in a text on false prophets committing treason and in Deut 13:11 it is again used to describe YHWH, this time in text on someone who tries to entice the Israelites to apostasy. In the law on manumission, support is mustered for the law by referring to the situation in Egypt, "Remember that you were a slave..." (Deut 15:15). As we saw in the previous chapter, the reference to Egypt is key in the passover law, where Deut 16:1 refers to YHWH bringing Israel out, vv. 3 and 6 refer simply to Israel going out, and 16:12 reminds them of their situation as slaves, as in 15:15.

The reference in Deut 17:16 is a little different than the rest. In the law of the king, he is warned not to "return the people to Egypt in order to acquire more horses, since YHWH has said to you, 'You must never return that way again.'" The warning against returning to Egypt seems to be referring to something known, but there is not much in the biblical literature to help us in understanding to what it is referring. Within the context of Deuteronomy, it might be best to interpret it as a warning to return to the state of bondage, from which YHWH has rescued Israel.

Deuteronomy 20:1 frames the law on warfare with a reassurance of YHWH's strength, as he who brought them out of the land of Egypt. Next, in the context of a warning against leprosy, and an urging to follow the instruction of the Levitical priests, Deut 24:9 contains a reminder of what YHWH did to Miriam on the way out from Egypt (Num 12). Again, this is a reminder of the punishment YHWH can bring, not the same as the usual reference to the rescue by YHWH or the Israelites' situation as slaves. Another reference similar to this is the reminder of what Amelek did on the way out from Egypt (Deut 25:17–19). Exodus 17:8–16 does not contain the details related here, however.

In Deut 24:18 Israel is urged not to pervert justice, with a reminder that he was a slave in Egypt and YHWH rescued him. Again, Deut 24:22 frames various civilian laws with "Remember that you were a slave in the land of Egypt, therefore I am commanding you to do this." Finally, as part of the liturgy of the first fruits, Deut 26:5–11 contains a recollection of past events, including Deut 26:8, "And YHWH brought us out of Egypt with a mighty hand and an outstretched arm, with great terror, with signs and wonders." This appeal to the past saving acts of YHWH forms a rationale for the bringing of the gift of first fruits (v. 10).

The way that the reference to Egypt appears as a way of mustering support for and building a rationale for the keeping of individual laws is also something that is found in Leviticus, and mostly in chs. 19–26, the Holiness Code.[9] The characteristic form of the reference here is something like, "I am YHWH your God, who brought you out of the land of Egypt." YHWH speaks in the first person here, as he does in the corresponding examples from Exodus and Numbers.[10] In Deuteronomy YHWH does not speak in the first person, with the exception of the Decalogue (Deut 5:6). The reference to Egypt very clearly becomes a part of YHWH's self-presentation, "I am YHWH," a part of his personality.[11] In some references it serves to describe the relationship between YHWH and Israel, such as when YHWH says, "for to me the people of Israel are servants; they are my servants whom I brought out from the land of Egypt: I am YHWH your God" (Lev 25:55; see also 26:11–13).

This foray shows that the rhetoric of Deuteronomy ties the concrete motif of YHWH's acts of rescuing Israel from Egypt into a whole complex involving the various attributes of YHWH, his love for and election of Israel, and the charge to Israel of obeying his laws. The appeal to YHWH's rescue from Egypt is intimately tied into individual laws and instructions for cultic rituals, and increases the obligation of Israel to keep these laws. The motif of rescue from Egypt serves to strengthen the special relationship between Israel and YHWH, weaving motifs that appear also in other biblical books, but in a way that is distinctive to Deuteronomy. In particular, the way in which the reference to YHWH's rescue of Israel from Egypt is tied together with the idea of Israel as chosen in Deut 4–11 serves to add weight to the duty of Israel to follow the laws and ordinances of YHWH.

Election of "Place" in Deuteronomy

We now move on to consider the divinely chosen place. As mentioned repeatedly, scholarship on Deuteronomy has been highly preoccupied with what is termed *centralization* of the cult. Our present investigation might be one more way to help explain why the dynamic scholars call centralization seems to come across as so crucial in Deuteronomy.

---

9. Lev 19:34, 36; 22:31–33; 23:43; 25:38, 55; 26:13, 45.
10. E.g. Exod 20:1; 29:46; Num 15:41.
11. In Joshua, Judges, and Samuel, the reference to YHWH's acts of rescuing Israel out of Egypt appears regularly as a way of identifying and describing YHWH and his greatness; see, e.g., Josh 2:10; 9:9; 24:16–18; Judg 2:1; 6:8, 13 (used ironically); 1 Sam 10:18.

So far we have seen that the use of the term בחר does not in itself denote any concept of centralization, which is a scholarly abstraction. However, through the course of this investigation it should be becoming clearer how the fact that the "place" is divinely elected might function as a way of giving authority to the idea of centralization.

As we observed above, the first third of Deuteronomy establishes authority and comprehensiveness for the idea of the chosenness of Israel. This idea is thematized and argued explicitly in Deut 4 and 7, and also 10. The text of Deuteronomy builds up the idea through the employment of the motif of Israel in Egypt and being rescued by YHWH, and how this incurs a debt on the part of Israel with the duty to serve, love, and obey YHWH.

For the idea of a chosen place at which all cultic and festival activity must be arranged, the authority associated with divine election *per se* intersects with the idea of the divine choice of a dwelling place on earth. The idea of YHWH choosing a dwelling place on earth is found also in other parts of the Bible, for example, the Psalms[12] and in Kings. The big difference between these references and the idea of the chosen place in Deuteronomy is that everywhere else it is a question of a specifically named place. It is thus contingent and specific. Only in Deuteronomy do we have the principle of a divinely elected place that is not specified, and thus remains somehow abstract.[13]

In Deuteronomy the chosenness of Israel becomes a reason why they must follow YHWH's commandments. In Deut 12, this is matched up with a further command: they must worship only at the chosen place. As we mentioned before, Deuteronomy 7 begins with the command to destroy the nations of the land and their religion, and warns against intermarriage. It then goes on to deal with the election of Israel and the terms of the covenant. The chapter is then closed off with a new section on destroying the nations and their religion. The same sandwich structure is also present in Deut 12, the text that first introduces the idea of the chosen place. It opens with the command to destroy the cult places of the nations whom they are about to dispossess. It then makes the contrast, "You shall not do thus to YHWH your God (לא תעשון כן ליהוה אלהיכם), but you shall seek the place which YHWH your God will choose…you shall go there, bringing there your burnt offerings…" (Deut 12:8–11).

---

12. See Pss 78:60, 67–71; 132:13. The idea that YHWH chose Shiloh and later chose Jerusalem is also present in Jer 7:12, and reflected in Jer 26.

13. There are two exceptions to this, Josh 9:27, discussed in Chapter 2, and Neh 1:9. The Nehemiah text is testimony to the willingness to let the place remain unnamed, an openness that Deuteronomy contains, and which may serve various ideological needs.

Deuteronomy 12:5–28 presents four different sections all detailing the various conditions that must be met for worship at the place which YHWH will choose. In vv. 4–7, the Israelites are commanded not to do such (as the nations) to YHWH their God, but they shall bring their sacrifices to the place. In v. 8, they are not to do as they are doing here, each what they think is right in their eyes, for they have not yet taken possession of the land. In other words, the ideal practice of the law is set in opposition to the situation now, on the other side of the Jordan. In v. 13, they are not to offer their sacrifices at any place, but only at "the place."

The idea of Israel as elected, separate from other people, different from the people of the land (the land that they are inheriting), has been firmly established in the chapters preceding this. The law about cultic activities, which must take place at "the place which YHWH will choose," is set in direct contrast to the cult of the "other" people, the anti-elect, one might call them, the ones that will be driven out of the land, or exterminated, the ones whose cult sites they are told to destroy, as the first command that they, the chosen people, are to carry out once they enter the land. Deuteronomy 12 closes off with warnings against following the gods of "the nations whom they are about to enter to dispossess them and live in their land," and both vv. 28 and 31–32 summarize that all these commands are the terms of the covenant that they must obey.

In a fairly subtle way, Deut 12 combines ideas that have already been joined together in previous passages about the election of Israel, with a new object of divine election, that is, the election of a place. The way that the same ideas appear, for example, the contrast with the anti-elect, both here and in Deut 7, which elaborates on the election of Israel, lends a dynamic authority to the idea of a divinely elected place.

In addition to the authority inherent in the idea of divine election, other rhetorical strategies add to the strength and unassailableness of the chosen place. For example, by never questioning it, and, rather, assuming it, taking it for granted, so to say, the idea of the chosen place becomes something that stands on its own authority. The idea of the chosen place for cultic activity is never justified or explained. No etiology is given, no rationale provided; it is simply stated. There is no real elaboration equivalent to what we find in 7:7–8 on the reasons for the election of Israel. There is no discussion of why sacrifices may only be offered at "the place." The way in which the rhetoric functions, the reader/listener is somehow co-opted into this attitude of not questioning. The chosen place is non-negotiable; there is no opening for questions. A further, even more subtle rhetorical strategy is that, as Helga Weippert has shown, the idea that YHWH will choose a place is never stated in a main clause, but always in a subordinate position. It is simply slipped in, but repeated so many times that it seems to become the core message.[14]

By being deftly woven into the cultic regulations, the idea of a divinely chosen place emerges as the core idea, the most important one, an idea that cannot be questioned, but which must simply be taken for granted. When the deity chooses something, this does not need explanation. This use of the principle of divine election functions as a powerful rhetorical strategy in the text, as we have seen from this survey of the ways in which the authority of divine election exhibits in the book of Deuteronomy.

The dynamic can be summarized in simple fashion in the following way: YHWH has chosen Israel, and YHWH will choose the place. And when this chosen people enters the land that they have been promised as their inheritance, they will worship YHWH, keep the festivals, and perform their holy duties at the place that he will choose. They will keep all of these commandments because they are a holy people who were chosen by YHWH, who rescued them from Egypt, from bondage. These ideas are woven tightly together, forming a highly persuasive document. To top it all off, they are also commanded to rejoice, as we read in 12:12, "And you shall rejoice before YHWH your God, you together with your sons and your daughters, your male and female slaves, and the Levites who reside in you towns (since they have no allotment or inheritance with you)."[15]

Divine Election in Other Parts of the Bible

In the exploration above, we have located the workings of divine election in Deuteronomy. Although focused mainly on the two main objects of election, Israel and "the place," Deuteronomy also mentions the election of the king (17:15) and of the tribe of Levi, to act as priests (18:5; 21:5).[16] In Deuteronomy, the election of the king is not developed in any

---

14. This was discussed also in Chapter 3. See Weippert, "Den Ort, den Jahwe erwählen wird."

15. J. W. Watts has developed a model for explaining how and why the book of Deuteronomy is so persuasive and effective rhetorically. He does not apply his analysis specifically to the laws about the "chosen place," but sets these laws into a larger context and rightly points out how the "lists" of laws have the purpose of mustering support for obedience to the law, in addition to communicating the content of the laws themselves; see Watts, "Rhetorical Strategy in the Composition of the Pentateuch," *JSOT* 68 (1995): 3–22, section 3.4.3; these ideas are developed further in Watts' 1999 monograph *Reading Law: The Rhetorical Shaping of the Pentateuch* (The Biblical Seminar 59; Sheffield: Sheffield Academic, 1999).

16. S. Norin makes a mistake when he claims that "when the word occurs with God as the subject, individual people or the people of Israel are most often the

way equivalent to what we have seen for Israel and "the place." The special status of the tribe of Levi is important in Deuteronomy. However, the idea that the Levites have been elected by YHWH for a specific task and special status is more straightforward than the idea of the chosen place or Israel as chosen, and does not involve the kind of subtle and persuasive argument as we have described above.

In the books of the Former Prophets, a reference to YHWH choosing a priest occurs only once, in 1 Sam 2:28, in an unnamed prophet's (man of God) oracle against Eli and his house. The text refers to the chosen one simply by the third person pronoun, but it is usually thought to be referring to Levi or Moses. This lengthy and detailed oracle prophesying a future "house" of a new family of priests foreshadows the demise of the "house" of Eli, and the rise of a new "house" of Zadok, in a way that parallels the fall of Saul and the rise of David. This narrative thread remains subordinate, however, to the narrative of the royal houses.

The Chosen King and the Chosen City
When we turn to Samuel and Kings, we find that the most ideologically prominent development of divine election concerns the connections spun around the chosen king and the chosen city, Jerusalem. There are three references to the king being chosen by YHWH in Samuel. In the first one, Samuel seems to be trying to garner support for Saul as the divinely sanctioned king (1 Sam 10:24). In the next instance, YHWH has rejected (מאס, an antonym for בחר) Saul, and Samuel is on a mission to find the next chosen one, David (1 Sam 16:6–13). In 2 Sam 6:21, after the episode where David has danced "before YHWH" when the ark is being brought into the City of David, David defends himself to Michal. She accuses him of behaving with vulgarity. In his speech to her, he says, "It was before YHWH, who chose me instead of your father…" The idea of YHWH electing a king thus plays a role in the rivalry between Saul and David, and in establishing the authority of the monarchy.

In 1 Kgs 8:16, the election of David is brought together with the election of the city. The idea of the election of a royal house or monarch and the election of a city, of Jerusalem, are brought together in Kings to

object" (my translation from the original German); see Norin, "'Die Stätte, die der Herr erwählt,'" in *La Cité de Dieu: Die Stadt Gottes, 3: Symposium Strasbourg, Tübingen, Uppsala 19.–23. September 1998 in Tübingen* (ed. M. Hengel et al.; WUNT 129; Tübingen: Mohr Siebeck, 2000), 99–118 (114). For a correct view on the relative prominence of the chosen "place" in Deuteronomy, see, e.g., K. Koch, "Zur Geschichte der Erwählungsvorstellung in Israel," *ZAW* 67 (1955): 205–26 (215–17).

form an ideological whole. The way that various threads of narrative that exist in Samuel are brought together in 1 Kings was discussed in Chapters 2 and 4 of this study. At this point, we will add one more perspective, which is the association of these motifs in some Psalms.

Psalm 78:67–71 is a text that reflects the connections between the election of David, his tribe, and Jerusalem (Zion):

> He rejected the tent of Joseph,
> he did not choose the tribe of Ephraim;
> but he chose the tribe of Judah,
> Mount Zion, which he loves.
> He built his sanctuary like the high heavens,
> like the earth, which he has founded forever.
> He chose David his servant,
> and took him from the sheepfolds;
> from tending the nursing ewes he brought him
> to be the shepherd of Jacob his people,
> of Israel his inheritance.

This psalm refers to itself as a teaching (תורה), a parable (משל). It devotes considerable space to recounting Israel's past, and dwells at length on the experiences in Egypt and the wilderness period, but does not mention the covenant at Sinai or the law, and does not even name Moses.[17] The point of interest to us is the explicit connection between the building of a sanctuary, the election of Zion, and the election of the tribe of David. In this case, the "house" of David as a royal house is not made explicit. Nevertheless, the association of these three—sanctuary (מקדש), Zion, and the tribe of David—forms a cluster that also underlies the association between these in the book of Kings.

Another text from the Psalms that brings together the privileged place of David and his house as the royal house, and the election of Jerusalem or Zion, is Ps 132:11–14:

> YHWH swore to David a sure oath
> from which he will not turn back:
> "One of the sons of your body
> I will set on your throne.
> If your sons keep my covenant
> and my decrees that I shall teach them,
> their sons also, forevermore
> shall sit on your throne."

---

17. For a study of this text and its proposed connections to Deuteronomy, see H. Junker, "Die Entstehungszeit des Ps. 78 und des Deuteronomiums," *Bib* 34 (1953): 487–500.

> For YHWH has chosen Zion;
> he has desired it for his habitation:
> "This is my resting place forever;
> here I will reside, for I have desired it.

This is a very illustrative text, displaying the logic that I think is there in the field of clusters around Zion/Jerusalem, David, and the promise of protection on condition that the commandments are kept. Although there are many psalms about Zion that do not refer to it as chosen, the idea of Zion is expressed in the language of election in some psalms.[18] The expression of these clusters in the poetry of the Psalms gives support to the connections we have identified in the books of Samuel and Kings, between the idea of a chosen royal dynasty (a house of David) and a chosen place of YHWH's protection where a house for YHWH, a sanctuary, will be built.[19]

Israel as Chosen

Israel is referred to as chosen only once in the Former Prophets. This is in 1 Kgs 3:8, in the dream where Solomon asks for wisdom. It might seem surprising, but the concept of the people as chosen does not seem to play a role in Kings. Israel is described as being rejected by YHWH in 2 Kgs 17:20, much like the chosen city is pronounced as rejected in 23:27 (see Chapter 2). The idea of a chosen people is found in the Pentateuch, in the Psalms, and is very prominent in Isa 40–66.[20]

Although Deuteronomy does not make a clear argument from the idea of Israel as chosen to the legitimacy of the "chosen place," we have seen that the authority of divine election plays a role in underpinning the authority of the concept of the "place." The authority associated with divine election is built up in the first third of the book of Deuteronomy, and therefore prepares for readers' smooth acceptance of the authority of

---

18. See, e.g., J. Levenson, "Zion Traditions," *ABD* 6:1098–102. For a recent study of Zion in the Psalms, see C. Körting, *Zion in den Psalmen* (FAT 48; Tübingen: Mohr Siebeck, 2006).

19. Observations similar to this are made by Melody D. Knowles in *Centrality Practiced: Jerusalem in the Religious Practice of Yehud and the Diaspora in the Persian Period* (SBL Archaeology and Biblical Studies 16; Atlanta: SBL, 2006), where she points out: "The idea that Yahweh had chosen a single sanctuary may rest on the tradition of Davidic election, widening Yahweh's exclusive choice of a certain royal family into a choice of the cult site under its control. Both the Ark Story (1 Sam 4–6; 2 Sam 6) and 2 Sam 24 witness to an old ideological connection between Yahweh's choice of the Davidic kingship and that of a sacred place" (p. 48).

20. Isa 14:1; 41:8, 9; 43:10; 44:1, 2; 49:7; Jer 33:24–26; Pss 33:12; 78:67, 68, 70 (David).

the "chosen place." In fact, yet another text from the Psalms shows that these ideas have been associated with each other in poetry. Psalm 135:4, 21, associates the idea of Israel as chosen with the idea of YHWH as present in Zion, "For YHWH has chosen Jacob for himself, Israel as his own possession (סגלה)... Blessed be YHWH from Zion, he who resides in Jerusalem, Praise YHWH (הללו־יה)!" It is not possible to conclude about the influence of one text on another, but this psalm is yet another illustration of the many subtle allusions that influence any reading of Deuteronomy.

Conclusion

In order to provide a secure foundation for the principle of one cult site, the book of Deuteronomy leans on the authority of several concepts. The authority of divine election is one of these, and it is developed in various ways within the book of Deuteronomy. As we saw above, the concept of Israel as chosen plays a significant role in putting an obligation on Israel to keep the law. Another coercive factor was the repeated reference to YHWH's rescue of Israel from Egypt. With the textual structure of chapters such as chs. 7 and 12, Israel's duty to serve YHWH is set in contrast to what they must do to the nations, the non-elect, those who will be exterminated. The authority that has been created regarding YHWH's choice of Israel is transposed onto the "chosen place," giving it also an unquestionable status.

In Samuel and Kings, the dynamic engendered around the divine election of the royal house and the city of Jerusalem works to shape readers' assumptions and interpretations. We have seen that some psalms also exhibit this dynamic. The probes undertaken in this chapter have helped to untangle some of this textual dynamic, to help us as readers better to understand why we read the text in certain ways; why, for example, Deuteronomy is so persuasive, and how the idea of Jerusalem as protected and privileged is constructed in the narratives of Samuel and Kings.

Chapter 8

KINGS REVISITED:
KINGSHIP IN DEUTERONOMY AND THE FORMER PROPHETS

In the course of this study it has come up several times that the view of kingship in Deuteronomy is in tension with what is said about kingship in the books of the Former Prophets and the ways in which kings are portrayed and evaluated.[1] This chapter will explore this subject in some detail. One reason for this is to provide a sort of counterpoint to the focus on the "chosen place," that has been at the center of this book. Like the concept of "chosen place," the law about the king is also something that distinguishes Deuteronomy from the rest of the legislative material in the Pentateuch. Further, the texts that concern the chosen city in Kings often

1. Studies comparing the law of the king in Deuteronomy with the narratives of the books of the Former Prophets have pointed to considerable differences, and various solutions have been proposed. Most recently, we may mention Knoppers, "Rethinking the Relationship," 393–415; "Solomon's Fall and Deuteronomy," in *The Age of Solomon: Scholarship at the Turn of the Millennium* (ed. L. K. Handy; Studies in the History of the Ancient Near East 11; Leiden: Brill, 1997), 392–410; "The Deuteronomist and the Deuteronomic Law of the King: A Reexamination of a Relationship," *ZAW* 108 (1996): 329–46; and Levinson, "The Reconceptualization of Kingship," 511–34.

E. Ben Zvi raises similar questions in "Josiah and the Prophetic Books: Some Observations," in Grabbe, ed., *Good Kings and Bad Kings*, 47–64 (54 n. 26). Other contributions include J. G. McConville, "King and Messiah in Deuteronomy and the Deuteronomistic History," in *King and Messiah in Israel and the Ancient Near East: Proceedings of the Oxford Old Testament Seminar* (ed. J. Day; JSOTSup 270; Sheffield: Sheffield Academic, 1998), 271–95; B. Halpern, *The Constitution of the Monarchy in Israel* (HSM 25; Chico, Calif.: Scholars Press, 1981).

See also N. Gos, "Deutéronome 17,18–19 et la Restauration de la Royauté au Retour de l'Exil," *BeO* 36, no. 3 (1994) : 129–38; A. Caquot, "Sur la 'Loi Royale' du Deutéronome," *Semitica* 9 (1959): 21–33; J.-M. Carrière, "Le cadre où se forme la decision politique: Lecture de Deutéronome 16,18–18,22," *NRT* 121 (1999): 529–42; U. Rütersworden, *Von der politischen Gemeinschaft zur Gemeinde: Studien zu Dt 16,18—18,22* (BBB 65; Frankfurt a.M.: Athenäum, 1987).

involve the monarchy and definitely involve kings as characters. This chapter will therefore add a look at the idea kingship as one more probe into the relationship between Deuteronomy and the Former Prophets.

Descriptions of Kings and Kingship in the Former Prophets

References to Kingship in "Premonarchic" Narratives

The first references to kings in the Former Prophets appear in the book of Judges, culminating in chs. 17–21, with the refrain "in those days there was no king in Israel" (17:6; 18:1; 19:1; 21:25). From these references, and the situation of chaos that seems to reign in this time as depicted in Judges, we get the impression that a king would have been the way to restore law and order in this dangerous and chaotic period. It would seem from these references that the author of Judges used the narrator to suggest that monarchy could be a remedy for the present situation of chaos, or at least that the absence of a king could explain the chaos of the time.

This voice of the narrator is in apparent tension with the story of Gideon. When the Israelites ask him to rule over them, he declines, saying it is YHWH who rules over them (Judg 8:22–23). The idea that a king could have secured order is also in conflict with the earlier report of Abimelech's tyrannical rule over the Shechemites, and his brother Jotham's indictment of the "lords of Shechem" for craving a ruler so badly that they would support such an obviously dangerous candidate for kingship. It is interesting that, if one were to compare the criteria of the Deuteronomic law of the king with the criteria whereby kings are actually judged in the book of Kings, this example is perhaps the one that comes closest to following the criteria of Deuteronomy. For example, the king is from "among their brothers" (Judg 9:3, 18).

The Establishment of the Monarchy in 1 Samuel

In Samuel the key texts that deal with the inauguration of the monarchy in Israel are found in 1 Sam 8–12 and in the special promise concerning the House of David in 2 Sam 7. In the opening verses of 1 Sam 8, we hear about the sons of Samuel not being fair leaders as judges. Because of this, the elders get together and demand "a king to judge (שפט) us, like all the other nations." Samuel does not like this (because his sons are criticized?), consults YHWH, and receives a highly ambiguous answer:

> Listen to the voice of the people in all that they say to you; for they have not rejected you, but they have rejected me from being king over them. Just as they have done (to me), from the day I brought them up out of Egypt to this day, forsaking me and serving other gods, so also they are

doing to you. Now then, listen to their voice only—you shall solemnly warn them, and show them the ways of the king who shall reign over them. (1 Sam 8:7–9)

When Samuel proceeds to "report all the words of YHWH," this warning includes specific mention of all the ways in which the king will oppress and make demands on the people, by demanding their children as soldiers, commanders, laborers, cooks, and bakers, by taxing their produce for the upkeep of the army and court, by taking slaves and animals. The narrator presents the "ways of the king," as reported in 8:11–17, as divine speech. But we as readers really have no way of knowing whether YHWH might have told Samuel these words and *we* are just not told, or whether Samuel is making it up. The speech concludes with a warning that YHWH will not hear their cry when they complain (1 Sam 8:11–18). But the people are adamant, they want a king, they want to be like other nations, they want a king to rule them (שפט), and to go out before them and fight their battles (8:20). Samuel reports this back to YHWH, who then tells him to set a king over the people.

This chapter seems to communicate two opposing views. A positive view is represented by the people, in which the positive arguments for a king include getting rid of unfair rulers, being ruled or judged by a monarch like the other nations, and having a king to lead them into battles. A negative view is represented by Samuel, though we never are quite sure why. He seeks the support of YHWH for his point of view, and by the divine word puts forward all the disadvantages of having a king and all the sacrifices it entails. In a curious way, the text manages to mediate these opposing views by having YHWH sanction the monarchy and commanding Samuel, the one who is most critical to it, to establish it. The stage is set for a divinely sanctioned, yet amply warned against, monarchy in Israel.

This ambivalence is further developed as the narrative proceeds to tell the story of the anointing of Saul, the first king of Israel. The narrative transitions directly to the story of Saul, introducing Saul and his house. Through a curious story of missing she-asses, the story of Saul crosses paths with the story of Samuel. The narrative shifts to relate the revelation that YHWH has given Samuel the day before he ends up in the same town as Saul, in which he is told that YHWH will send him a man that he will anoint ruler (נגיד) of Israel (1 Sam 9:16–17).[2] There is no sign of any negative attitude toward kingship in this text. On the contrary, YHWH

---

2. 1 Sam 9:17 uses the term עצר to denote the activity of ruling over the people. This usage of the word is very unusual. On the whole, a whole variety of terms are used in Samuel to denote the activity of ruing/judging/being king.

justifies the plan to anoint Saul by saying that he has seen the suffering of his people, and this king will save them from the hand of the Philistines. Here, the understanding of the role of the king as the one who fights the battles is consistent with what the people have demanded in the previous chapter.

There is still some tension about all of this, however, because Samuel does not reveal the divine plans to Saul until the day after he has met him, and then only in private. The narration of the actual anointing itself is completely unremarkable. Samuel simply pours oil on his head and says, "YHWH anoints you ruler over his own property (נחל)." The LXX gives more of a description of what the king will do in this verse, adding that he will rule over the people of YHWH and save them from the hand of the enemies.³ Even after Saul has returned back from this strange journey, has been secretly and privately anointed king by Samuel, has received a new heart from YHWH, has encountered a band of prophets and gone into a prophetic frenzy, and finally found the she-asses, he does not tell his family about the "matter of kingship" (את־דבר המלוכה, 1 Sam 10:16).

Samuel, on the other hand, gathers Israel in a formal assembly to present to them their king. He continues to be publicly against kingship, even though he has anointed Saul at YHWH's command already. He blames the people for their rejection of their God in their demand for a king (1 Sam 10:19). In a curious sort of lot-casting ceremony, the lot ends up falling on Saul, who, though the people do not know, has already been anointed king. Saul is presented to the people as the one that YHWH has chosen (אשר בחר־בו יהוה), his uniqueness is noted, and they shout "Live the king!" (1 Sam 10:24).

Then Samuel is described as expounding to the people the "ways of the kingdom" (משפט המלוכה), and writing this in a book that he places before YHWH. The contents of this book are not specified, but it seems right, in the context, to relate it to the warnings that Samuel gave the people in 1 Sam 8:11–17. This adds another ambiguity, since we have reason to be suspicious of Samuel as to his sincerity in rendering the word of YHWH in 8:11–17 because of his negative attitude to kingship, and his personal bias in the case on account of his sons. The scene ends with Samuel sending the assembly home, and a hint of things perhaps taking a turn for the worse with the mention of some men despising Saul and not trusting him (10:27).

This is still not the end of the complex and winding story of the beginning of the monarchy in Israel. First Samuel 11 goes on to relate

---

3. Most Western translations follow the LXX at this point.

the first battle that Saul fights, against the Ammonites, who have been oppressing the Reubenites and Gadites. With YHWH's spirit, Saul is successful. After this great success, some of the Israelites turn to Samuel and seek to kill those who had been suspicious of Saul. Samuel prevents this, appealing to how YHWH has brought deliverance to Israel. He does, however, initiate a ceremony at Gilgal to "renew" the kingship, and the people proceed to make Saul king (for the third time?), this time in a cultic ceremony also involving sacrifices (1 Sam 11:12–15).

Finally, in his farewell speech to the people, Samuel brings the people to realize that it was a sin to demand a king, and they ask him to pray for them because of this (1 Sam 12:19). Samuel makes it clear that the important thing is to follow YHWH, whether they have a king or not, even though, yes, it was wrong to demand a king.

The text of 2 Sam 7 was examined in Chapter 4, where the connections to the establishment of David's dynasty and his successor, Solomon, were identified. The connections between this text and the building of the temple in 1 Kings were also examined. In general, I pointed out how several distinct themes that are introduced in Samuel are brought together in Kings.

The conclusion from this superficial examination is an accumulated impression of ambivalence toward the monarchy as an institution.[4] The complex nature of the text simultaneously achieves a lot of room to maneuver. There is a lot of leeway in these stories; many outcomes are possible, many disparate details can be reconciled. There is also plenty of room for distributing blame for whatever may happen. YHWH warns against, but ultimately sanctions, the monarchy as an institution.

The Portrayal of Kings in Samuel and Kings
Moving on, how can the roles of biblical kings be described, based on what they are actually portrayed as *doing* in the Former Prophets? In the book of Samuel, we find the story of the first two kings of Israel, Saul and David. In the struggle between Saul and David, the main explanation for why David "wins" seems to be that the "spirit of YHWH" is taken away from Saul and given to David. In many ways, the portrayals of Saul and David are more like the portrayal of the judges than the kings that

---

4. For a detailed "close reading" of 1 Sam 8–12, see L. M. Eslinger, *Kingship of God in Crisis: A Close Reading in 1 Samuel 1–12* (Bible and Literature Series 10; Sheffield: Almond, 1985), 251–424; see also the review of scholarship on pp. 11–35. For a historical-critical reading that sees 1 Sam 8–12 as one literary unit, dated to early in the time of the exile, see S. L. McKenzie, "The Trouble with Kingship," in de Pury, Römer, and Macchi, eds., *Israel Constructs Its History*, 286–314.

follow Solomon. For example, the importance of the spirit of YHWH has been mentioned. In general, we can observe that the portrayal of kings corresponds fairly unproblematically to what was announced as the role of the king, which was to rule/judge, and to fight the battles for Israel (2 Sam 3:18). When David is anointed king, he is also likened to a shepherd of the people (2 Sam 5:2).

The promise to David, that his house and his kingdom shall be made sure forever, brings something new into the narrative in 2 Sam 7. As we also touched on in Chapter 4, the privileged position of the house of David becomes an important concept in the rest of the portrayal of the kings of Israel and Judah. In the book of Kings, David becomes the king against which other kings are measured, and YHWH's promise to the house of David becomes a commitment that in turn is referred to throughout the book of Kings.[5] As we also documented in Chapter 4, reference to Jerusalem, the city that YHWH has chosen, is step-by-step tied together with the reference to David and the promise of his protection. This promise turns out not to be unconditional, as is made clear to Solomon, both while he is building the temple, and after he has finished it. YHWH appears to him and lays out the conditions, which involve following YHWH and keeping his statutes and ordinances (1 Kgs 6:12–13; 9:2–9). As a kind of negative pole to the positive view of the house of David, the curse on the house of Jeroboam is apparent in a series of dynastic oracular curses (1 Kgs 14:7–14; 16:2–4; 21:20–24).

Next we turn to the portrayal of what kings actually do, according to Samuel and Kings. Most kings, except perhaps Solomon, are portrayed as doing battle. War fills much of the narrative, and is even sometimes commented on in the summaries of the reigns (e.g. "Now the rest of the acts Jeroboam, how he warred and how he reigned, are written in the Book of the Annals of the Kings of Israel," 1 Kgs 14:19). This activity is consistent with what was expected of a king according to 1 Sam 8.

From the warnings of Samuel, we might have expected reports about how the people suffered under the burdens that kings placed on them, but this is not usually the case in Samuel and Kings. The taking of laborers is mentioned in connection with Solomon's temple-building, but the information is contradictory, as I will point out below, and there is no mention of the people suffering until the convoluted story of the transition of power to Rehoboam and Jeroboam, and then only indirectly. Perhaps that part of Samuel's speech is a foreshadowing of the reign of Solomon specifically?

---

5. E.g. in 1 Kgs 6:12–13; 8:20, 25; 9:2–9; 11:12, 32; 15:4–5; 2 Kgs 8:19; 19:34; 20:6.

Next to warring, most attention is focused on relating the kings' cultic activity. This focus is closely related to the way in which kings are evaluated in the book of Kings. The stereotypical evaluation formula "King X did what was right/evil in the eyes of YHWH," is often followed by comments on the king's cultic activities. The kings are listed as either angering YHWH by their idols and worshiping at high places, or following YHWH (but not removing high places, e.g., Jehoash, 2 Kgs 12:2–3; Amaziah, 2 Kgs 14:3–4; Azariah, 2 Kgs 15:3–4; Jotham, 2 Kgs 15:34–35), or following YHWH and destroying high places. Jeroboam, the paradigmatic evil king (1 Kgs 12:26–33), is described as having established cult sites in Bethel and Dan and inaugurated a new cult, even though he is not actually judged as having "done evil in the eyes of YHWH." From the story of the reign of King Jehoash of Judah (2 Kgs 12), we get the impression that it was considered the duty of the priests to take care of the upkeep and repairs necessary at the temple. King Ahaz (2 Kgs 16) of Judah commands the building of an altar modeled on an altar he saw in Damascus. Second Kings 16:17–18 relates something of a reverse cultic reform, where the king oversees a dismantling of parts of the furniture and inventory of the sanctuary, "because of the king of Assyria." This justification is not clear, but could be a sign of appreciation that the Assyrian king Tiglath-pileser had rescued him from the king of Aram. King Hezekiah, as one of the two "better than good" kings, does what is right, and also removes high places. Manasseh reverses Hezekiah's actions by rebuilding the high places and also building altars for non-Yahwistic gods in the temple. And finally, of course, there are Josiah's reform actions. The book of Kings clearly see a cultic role for the king, whether it is positively or negatively evaluated.[6]

Kings are also portrayed as builders. The most famous builder is of course Solomon (1 Kgs 5–7), as perhaps David is the most famous warrior king. For his building activity, Solomon is said in one place to have conscripted forced labor from all Israel (1 Kgs 5:13–18). In another note, Solomon does not conscript forced labor from the Israelites, only from other nations whose descendants were living in the land (1 Kgs 9:15–22). Further, there is the information about the people complaining

---

6. There is a lot of literature on these formulas judging the kings. See, e.g., most recently, F. Blanco Wissman, *"Er tat das Rechte—": Beurteilungskriterien und Deuteronomismus in 1 Kön 12—2 Kön 25* (ATANT 93; Zurich: Theologischer Verlag Zürich, 2008). An influential study for the redaction-critical approach to Kings is H. Weippert, "Die 'deuteronomistischen' Beurteilungen der Könige von Israel und Juda und das Problem der Redaktion der Königsbücher," *Bib* 53 (1972): 301–39.

that Solomon had laid on them a heavy yoke (1 Kgs 12:4), though in this story it turns out that an even heavier yoke is promised by Rehoboam, something that serves to fulfill a divine prophecy. These comments on the forced labor might refer to the warnings of Samuel again, but it is not completely clear whether this disagrees with that warning or not.[7] Other "builder" kings include King Jeroboam who built Shechem and Pnuel (1 Kgs 12:25), King Asa (1 Kgs 15:23), King Omri who built Samaria (1 Kgs 16:24), Jehoash (2 Kgs 12:4–8), Hezekiah who is credited with building the pool and channel that brought water into the city (2 Kgs 20:20), and Josiah who makes repairs to the temple (2 Kgs 22:3–7).

Finally, kings also interact with prophets. Prophets come and speak words against the kings and give advice, which is usually unheeded. Ahab's interaction with Elijah is the most extended example. There is also the unnamed prophet who speaks against Jeroboam in 1 Kgs 13, the unnamed prophet who gives advice to Ahab in his war against Ben Hadad of Syria in 1 Kgs 20, Micaiah ben Imlah who speaks to Jehoshaphat of Judah, and Ahab who pronounces his death in 1 Kgs 22. There is Elisha and various kings, helping them win battles. There is also Hezekiah and Isaiah, during the threat from the Assyrians in 2 Kgs 18–20.

The Evaluation of Kings in Samuel and Kings

How are kings evaluated in the Former Prophets? This is a major question, and one that has been studied in various ways. For redaction critics, these evaluations have been seen as fundamental in assessing the redactors' point of view, and in establishing the Deuteronomists' understanding of kingship. According to Noth, the Deuteronomists blamed the monarchy for the downfall of the kingdoms.[8] Again, let us make a basic review of the material before we discuss and compare the findings with the view expressed in the book of Deuteronomy.

---

7. Samuel says that the king will take their slaves, and these could of course also be non-Israelites. Thus, it is not clear whether the narrative of 1 Kgs 9 is in tension with Samuel's warning or not. R. E. Clements thinks that the warnings of 1 Sam 8 are meant to recall Solomon (the typical oriental despot/tyrant/feudal tyrant); see Clements, "The Deuteronomistic Interpretation of the Founding of the Monarchy in 1 Sam. VIII," *VT* 24 (1974): 398–410 (404).

8. Noth, *The Deuteronomistic History*, 80–84, 133. The "double redaction" advocates (see Chapter 1) usually consider the first deuteronomistic redactor as positive toward the monarchy, whereas the second, exilic, redactor is considered more negative, thus accounting for the ambivalence in the material.

Saul, David, and Solomon
The first three kings, Saul, David, and Solomon are each portrayed uniquely and not according to the pattern that later establishes itself. The portrayal of Saul, as the above survey of 1 Sam 8–12 also showed, is complicated and contradictory. Saul is sanctioned as the first king, yet YHWH removes his favor from him and transfers it to David. Saul is chastised repeatedly by Samuel and is finally unable to get in touch with YHWH, even by the approved methods. The way in which Saul is judged has its own dynamic created by the narrative, one that is different from the more stereotypical patterns that we find in 1 and 2 Kings.[9]

The portrayal of David is also complicated and open to many interpretations. At the end of his reign, he is basically judged as a king who brought peace and firmly established the throne (1 Kgs 1:10–12, 33). This happens in spite of his "doing evil" in the affair with Bathsheba (2 Sam 11:27), later also referred to as "the matter of Uriah the Hittite" (1 Kgs 15:5, a phrase the LXX does not contain). In spite of what he might have done in his own career, David becomes the standard of comparison for how to evaluate all later kings. An interesting point about David is the contrasts in the portrayal of him in Samuel and 1 Kgs 1–2, and how he is referred to in the rest of Kings, as was observed in Chapter 4. For example, in 1 Kgs 11:38, David is posthumously held up before Jeroboam as the example that he should follow, and is explicitly judged as a king who did "what was right in the eyes of YHWH." In another oracle of judgment on Jeroboam, David is again held up as a contrast, and is again judged as the one who "kept [YHWH's] commandments and followed [him] with all his heart, doing only that which was right in [his] sight" (1 Kgs 14:8). Throughout the portrayal of the monarchy in the story of Solomon and the rest of the kings, David is referred to as the one with whom other kings are compared, sometimes favorably, as with Asa[10] (1 Kgs 15:11), sometimes unfavorably, as with Abijam (1 Kgs 15:3, 5) and Ahaz (2 Kgs 16:2), sometimes favorably but not measuring up completely, as with Amaziah (2 Kgs 14:3). David is also referred to as the one for whose sake YHWH does not destroy Jerusalem, or for whose sake YHWH "keeps a light burning in Jerusalem" in spite of the

---

9. For readings of the Saul narrative and commentary on how Saul has been judged, see D. M. Gunn, *The Fate of King Saul: An Interpretation of a Biblical Story* (JSOTSup 14; Sheffield: JSOT, 1980), and Miscall, *1 Samuel*.

10. King Asa actually also gets a reference similar to those usually reserved for David, when his son Jehoshaphat is said to have walked "in the way of his father Asa" (1 Kgs 22:43).

fact that he was also a "bad" king (e.g. 1 Kgs 15:4). In a sense, David becomes the symbol of the perfect king, even if this status does not accord with what he might deserve according to the actual portrayal of him.

Although he is remembered as the king who asked for wisdom (1 Kgs 3:10), and the one who built the temple, Solomon is actually evaluated once as "doing evil (רעה) in the eyes of YHWH" (1 Kgs 11:6) and once as "not walking in my ways, doing what is right (ישר) in my sight" (1 Kgs 11:33). These references are part of the narrative, and refer directly to specific actions, as with David and his affair. In both cases for Solomon, he is judged for following other gods, and this is also the reason why he is punished by having his kingdom split up. In the summary of his reign, Solomon is given no evaluation (1 Kgs 11:41–43). In the Josiah account, Solomon is associated with his apostasy and his building of altars to "foreign" gods.

Kings Who Do Evil
Jeroboam is actually never judged explicitly by the phrase "doing evil in the eyes of YHWH," despite becoming perhaps the paradigmatic evil king. He becomes the opposite of David, in being the one used as a comparison for the bad behavior of kings in such judgments as, "they did not turn from the sin of Jeroboam." However, it is telling of the symbolic role of Jeroboam that in the oracle against the royal house, the prophet Ahijah says of Abijah, the king's sick son, who is going to die, that "he alone of Jeroboam's family shall come to the grave, because in him there is found something pleasing to YHWH" (1 Kgs 14:13).

Ahab is judged three times as having done evil (1 Kgs 16:30; 21:20, 25). He also becomes a yardstick whereby other kings are judged as evil by their relationship to him. The king who perhaps receives the worst evaluation is Manasseh, in 2 Kgs 21:2–9. Jehu receives a very ambivalent judgment (2 Kgs 10:28–31). He eradicates Baal, but he continues to allow the calves in Bethel and Dan. In other words, he wipes out non-Yahwistic cult, but does not eliminate illicit Yahwistic cult. For this, he is promised that his sons will sit on the throne until the fourth generation. He received a delayed punishment, similar to Solomon.

Several other kings receive a mixed judgment. Whereas no Northern kings except Jehu have any kind of sympathetic judgment, some Southern kings, such as Jehoash (2 Kgs 12:2–3), Amaziah (2 Kgs 14:3), Azariah (Uzziah, 2 Kgs 15:3), and Jotham (2 Kgs 15:34), receive partially sympathetic judgment.

Kings Who Do Good: Hezekiah and Josiah

Hezekiah (2 Kgs 18:3–8) and Josiah are the only kings who measure up to David. Hezekiah and Josiah are both evaluated as unique, and seem to surpass even David (2 Kgs 18:5; 23:25). Hezekiah is contrasted with Solomon by being described as having "clung" (דבק) to YHWH and having not departed from him. The same verb is used of Solomon "clinging" to foreign women, the grounds for his apostasy. Hezekiah also self-professes to have done "good" (20:3). Both Hezekiah and Josiah's acts of dismantling wrongful cult are emphasized: their allegiance to YHWH, their following in the path of David, and their keeping of the commandment of Moses. In the case of Josiah, the *torah* of Moses is mentioned (2 Kgs 23:25), as it was also in David's speech to Solomon (1 Kgs 2:3).[11]

One conclusion from this superficial overview is that the cultic role of the king is very important in terms of how they are portrayed and how they are evaluated, especially in the book of Kings. In the critical texts in Samuel, the negative attitude toward the king has to do with the idea that having a king means a rejection of YHWH. The final, mediated, view is that as long as the people follow YHWH, it does not really make a difference whether or not they have a king. Thus, though the narratives do communicate a concern to show a negative stance toward monarchy as such, or at least to voice the idea that monarchy in itself could be bad, this is not the overall view that comes to the fore. Rather, it is a kind of ambivalent attitude; kingship itself is not wrong, but things will go wrong if they do not follow YHWH.

This view is somewhat different from the concern of the book of Kings to classify the kings in terms of their moral/cultic behavior and to assess how that had a say in their destiny. This logic is prepared for, however, in the passages where YHWH speaks to Solomon during his temple-building, where the promise concerning the throne of David is made contingent on the religious behavior of the king and his people. In this way, the concerns from 1 Sam 8–12 are tied together with the main thrust of the book of Kings, through the texts of 2 Sam 7 and the interaction between YHWH and Solomon in connection with the temple-building.

---

11. See the discussion of the role of "proper decorum" in the analysis of P. J. Botha, "'No King like Him...': Royal Etiquette According to the Deuteronomistic Historian," in *Past, Present, Future: The Deuteronomistic History and the Prophets* (ed. J. C. de Moor and H. F. Van Rooy; OTS 44; Leiden: Brill, 2000), 36–49.

The Law of the King in Deuteronomy 17:14–20

Now let us turn to examine briefly the law of the king in Deut 17:14–20. This text is found within a portion of Deuteronomy that is concerned with various types of positions of authority in Israel, such as the justice system, the priesthood, prophecy, and the monarchy (Deut 16:18–18:22).[12] The text begins with the introductory formula characteristic of the legal corpus of Deuteronomy, which is found dispersed throughout the legal material,[13] "When you have come into the land that YHWH your God is giving you, and have taken possession of it and settled in it, and you say, 'I will set a king over me, like all the nations that are around me,' you may indeed set over you a king whom YHWH our God will choose." The first piece of information is that the Israelites, when they enter the land, are permitted to have a king. The criteria for choosing this king are then listed: the king will be someone whom YHWH chooses, and he will be from among the people, that is, he must not be chosen from among those considered as foreigners. This seems clear and reflects the overall concern of Deuteronomy to keep the Israelites separate from the other nations.

Next follows further qualifications concerning the king. Introduced by the particle רק, a series of limitations is listed:

---

12. A significant amount of work has been done on this portion of Deuteronomy. For a summary, see U. Rüterswörden, "Der Verfassungsentwurf des Deuteronomiums in der neueren Diskussion: Ein Überblick," in *Altes Testament—Forschung und Wirkung: Festschrift für Henning Graf Reventlow* (ed. P. Mommer and W. Thiel; Bern: Lang, 1994), 313–28. See further, N. Lohfink, "Die Sicherung der Wirksamkeit des Gotteswortes durch das Prinzip der Schriftlichkeit der Tora und durch das Prinzip der Gewaltenteilung nach den Ämtergesetzen des Buches Deuteronomium (Dt 16,18–18,22)," in *Studien zum Deuteronomium und zur deuteronomistischen Literatur I* (ed. N. Lohfink; SBAB 8; Stuttgart: Katholisches Bibelwerk, 1990), 305–23 (this work was originally published in 1971); E. Otto, "Von der Gerichtsordnung zum Verfassungsentwurf: Deuteronomische Gestaltung und deuteronomistische Interpretation im 'Ämtergesetz' Dtn 16,18–18,22," in *"Wer ist wie du, HERR, unter den Göttern?" Studien zur Theologie und Religionsgeschichte Israels, für Otto Kaiser zum 70. Geburtstag* (ed. H.-M. Wahl et al.; Göttingen: Vandenhoeck & Ruprecht, 1994), 142–55; and, more recently, M. O'Brien, "Deuteronomy 16.18–18.22: Meeting the Challenge of Towns and Nations," *JSOT* 33 (2008): 155–72.

13. This introduction is found, e.g., in Deut 11:32, introducing the main corpus of the legal material in Deut 12–26. Another occurrence within the present unit is in 18:9.

> he must not acquire for himself (לא־ירבה־לו) many horses,
> he must not turn the people back to Egypt to acquire horses
> because YHWH has said to you, you shall not ever return on that road again
> he must not acquire for himself (לא־ירבה־לו) many wives,
> and not have his heart turn away (לא יסור לבבו),
> silver and gold he must not acquire for himself (לא־ירבה־לו) in great amounts.

These are the restrictions Deuteronomy places on the king. It is not easy to interpret this. Are the limitations on horses and wealth meant to refer to the king's private property, or is this a critique of the "ways of the king," such as that which is articulated in 1 Sam 8?[14] It does not seem as if Deuteronomy envisions a military role for the king, and in the laws on warfare in Deut 20, the king is given no role. This stands in striking contrast to the portrayal of kings in Samuel and Kings, and to the idea that kings would solve the problem of chaos, including war, in Judges. Could the limitations specified here be read as not necessarily forbidding keeping an army and a treasury for the kingdom, but simply urging restraint? The point about not acquiring wives at least seems to indicate that the reason is so that he will not stray off his task; but also this is unclear, and avoids any specific mention of straying from going after YHWH, for example, or being enticed to worshiping other gods.[15]

Finally, the text states the positive role of the king. The phrase "when he has taken the throne of his kingdom"—literally, "in his sitting on the seat of his kingdom"—refers to the time in the future when the people have set a king over themselves. When a monarchy has been established and a king is enthroned, "he shall write for himself a copy of this law (וכתב לו את־משנה התורה הזאת) in a book/scroll (על־ספר) before the Levitical priests." Is this text an instruction for the first king of Israel, or is every king supposed to write a copy of the law? This king is further instructed to read in this book "all the days of his life," and the reason given for this is that he may "learn to fear YHWH his God, and keep all the words of this torah, and these laws." This he should do so as not to

---

14. For this point of view, see E. Nicholson, "*Traditium* and *Traditio*: The Case of Deuteronomy 17:14–20," in *Scriptural Exegesis: The Shapes of Culture and the Religious Imagination: Essays in Honour of Michael Fishbane* (ed. D. A. Green and L. S. Lieber; Oxford: Oxford University Press, 2009), 46–61.

15. Whether these specifications are a critique of Solomon for letting his many wives influence his policy making (Knoppers, "The Deuteronomist and the Deuteronomic Law of the King," 343) or a warning against polygamy, not foreign wives, the allusions to Solomon's later apostasy where multiple wives led his heart to stray from YHWH, is difficult to ascertain.

"exalt himself above his brothers, and not turn from the commandments to the right or to the left, for the sake of lengthening the days of his kingdom, his and his children's, in (the middle of, בקרב) Israel."

This role of the king does not correspond to anything we have encountered in the historical books, at least not in terms of what kings are portrayed as actually doing. The establishment of the monarchy as portrayed in 1 Sam 8–12 does not correspond to this text in Deuteronomy when it comes to the ban on acquiring horses and riches. On this point, Samuel's warnings seem to deal precisely with an expectation of these things for the role of the king.

It is, however, said of Josiah that he "turned to YHWH...according to all the law of Moses" (2 Kgs 23:25), and that he "walked in the way of his father David, and did not turn aside to the right or to the left" (2 Kgs 22:2). There is, as such, some echo of the law of the king in the portrayal of Josiah. We could also mention that he reads the law, although this public reading is not mandated by Deuteronomy, but is rather supposed to be the job of a Levite. What is also the case is that Josiah too did much more than what the law of the king in Deuteronomy prescribes as the duty of the king.

The conclusion of this brief overview is that the law of the king seems not only to be *in tension with* the view in Samuel and Kings, but also silent on many particulars that are of crucial importance to these books. For example, we would have expected a prohibition on going after other gods and leading the people astray, and a command to refrain from worship on the *bamot*, and even perhaps a command to dismantle them.[16] Even though in Kings it is kings who are portrayed as leading the people either toward or away from YHWH, the command in Deuteronomy to dismantle the cult sites of the "people of the land" is given directly to the Israelites. In 2 Kgs 17, the *people* are judged for their actions, but most often and consistently, it is the king who is judged. Further, Deuteronomy does not seem to give the king a role in warfare, and does not really seem to be concerned with ruling, understood as *judging*, which is the primary concern in Samuel when the people demand a king for the first time. The law of the king (Deut 17:14–20) also does not coincide with any ancient Near Eastern royal ideology, whereas Samuel and Kings seem much closer to such ideologies, especially in connection with the promise to the House of David.

---

16. Deuteronomy is actually not concerned with the *bamot* at all, something that also is highly puzzling, and has been addressed elsewhere in this study (see, e.g., Chapters 5 and 6). Not even in Deut 12, which commands the Israelites to destroy the altars and *asherim*, and so on, are the *bamot* mentioned (see also Knoppers, "Solomon's Fall and Deuteronomy," 402–3).

Discussion of Kingship in Scholarly Debate:
An Illustration of the Problems

A first, simple question after this examination is to ask ourselves why it is a problem in the first place that Deuteronomy, on one hand, and Samuel and Kings, on the other hand, have different views as to the role of the king and how to assess the monarchy. There are other parts of the Bible that do not agree with each other about the same topic. The only reason it is seen as problematic could be the idea of the DH hypothesis.

As a general observation, in ways similar to the focus on the idea of "chosen place," this short investigation highlights the fact that it is difficult to see how the books of the Former Prophets could be said to be implementing the standards of Deuteronomy. The DH hypothesis does not help us in understanding the tensions in the view of kings and kingship. There would have to be a different explanation of why Deuteronomy has such a different understanding of kingship than the Former Prophets. If, as many have claimed, Deut 17:14–20 is a late addition, one would still have to ask the question of the relationship between a Deuteronomy that does not envision a king as a part of its society, and the books of Judges, Samuel, and Kings, so deeply concerned with the role of the king and the monarchy.

As the review of Chapter 1 showed, in spite of criticism and periodic refutations, the basic claim that some form of the core material of Deuteronomy predates the writing of the historical books of Joshua through 2 Kings and influenced the composition of these remains with us.[17] For most of this study we have been focusing on how the DH hypothesis in its various incarnations has impacted the understanding of the chosen place, the central cult site in Deuteronomy and the Former Prophets. In this chapter we have turned the focus to the idea of kingship. What do we do when the material is as disparate as what we have just been reviewing?

It is this question that Gary Knoppers takes up in several articles on the subject of kingship. He advocates a more complex relationship between Deuteronomy and the Deuteronomists[18] and shows that the Deuteronomists were independent writers, and that they were creative,

---

17. O. Kaiser, in his article reviewing scholarship on the Pentateuch and the DH, concludes that the theory of a unified DH has gradually been eroded; see Kaiser, "The Pentateuch and the Deuteronomistic History," 289–322.

18. Knoppers, "The Deuteronomist and the Deuteronomic Law of the King," 333; "Solomon's Fall and Deuteronomy," 394, 398, 401; "Rethinking the Relationship," 395.

even subversive in their use of deuteronomic material.[19] Knoppers develops his position by putting forward the type of explanation that Bernard Levinson has used to account for the hermeneutics of the writers of Deuteronomy themselves. This exegetical and hermeneutical strategy entails the notion that the writers of the present texts have drawn on earlier material in a way that completely transforms it, even to the point of having it speak against the material that it has appropriated.[20] Knoppers also proposes another possibility, namely that Deut 17:14–20 could stem from a deuteronomistic redaction/revision from a *different* editor than the editors of the DH.[21]

This second idea is further developed in his 2001 article, along with a critique of Noth, where Knoppers suggests that Deuteronomy and the DH do not necessary "stem from the same social milieu,"[22] opening up the possibility of a synchronic relationship. This is a very interesting idea. In fact, it should even be possible to imagine that the same writer could have more than one point of view of the same issue. The problem is that Knoppers does not seem to follow his own suggestion through to its logical conclusion.[23] He continues to claim that *Urdeuteronomium* is one of the influences on the DH, which seems to assume a diachronic relationship, but also posits that Noth's definition of what "Proto-Deuteronomy" was is wrong, and that there could have been distinct "deuteronomistic" redactions of Deuteronomy and the DH.[24]

Working under the "Cross" paradigm, Knoppers dates the first edition of the DH to the "time of Josiah," meaning that some form of Deuteronomy existed in the seventh century, and he seems to include Deut 17:14–20 in this edition of Deuteronomy. This brings us to Josiah's law book, the other scholarly constriction on our debate. The axiomatic identification of the law book found in the "time of Josiah" with Deuteronomy was discussed in Chapter 6. With respect to kingship, the dating of the book of Deuteronomy becomes the crucial question. Both Knoppers and

---

19. Knoppers, "The Deuteronomist and the Deuteronomic Law of the King," 344–45; "Solomon's Fall and Deuteronomy," 403–4; "Rethinking the Relationship," 413.
20. Levinson has identified this method mainly in legal material, particularly in his 1997 book *Deuteronomy and the Hermeneutics of Legal Innovation*.
21. Knoppers, "Solomon's Fall and Deuteronomy," 410.
22. Knoppers, "Rethinking the Relationship," 408. This is not a new idea at all, and in fact underlies both Cross's idea of two basic redactions, and the proposal by the "Göttingen school" of several, discrete, editors. The new element is the possibility that these are dated to the same time period.
23. Levinson, "The Reconceptualization of Kingship," 526–27 n. 41.
24. Knoppers, "Rethinking the Relationship," 413, 414–15.

Levinson follow Cross in dating some form of Deuteronomy to a time before Josiah. They date the first edition of the DH to the time of Josiah and identify the book found in 1 Kgs 22 with some form of Deuteronomy.[25]

Bernard M. Levinson begins with the observation that Deuteronomy seems to be at odds with the supposition that ancient Israel shared with the rest of the ancient Near East its understanding of monarchy and royal ideology. He describes what he calls the "double anomaly of Deuteronomy."[26] Deuteronomy's law of the king denies him a role in the justice system and in the cult, and the military. For Levinson, the methodological problem is the following:

> How is it that Deuteronomy, which scholarly consensus views as having been promulgated by King Josiah (2 Kings xxii–xxiii), could nonetheless be so usurping of royal power in its Law of the Kings (Deut. Xvii 14–20)? Equally, how is it that Josiah, however exemplary in his piety, would so easily participate in his own forced abdication from power?[27]

By asking these questions, Levinson is interrogating his own position from his 1997 book. The way he solves the problem is by proposing that Deuteronomy was written by scribes during the reign of Manasseh, as an ideal text. The writer of the first edition of the DH used Deuteronomy and wanted to impose its standards, but restored to the king the power taken from him in Deuteronomy. In this way, by having Josiah implement the cultic norms of Deuteronomy, the demands of the law are simultaneously brought into force, and also broken.[28]

For Levinson, the solution is dependent on his understanding of dating. For Knoppers, however, dating seems to get in his way and become a problem. I think many of Knoppers' observations are correct, including his critique of Noth. But it seems to me that Knoppers does not draw the

---

25. Knoppers, "The Deuteronomist and the Deuteronomic Law of the King," 331; "Solomon's Fall and Deuteronomy," 393; "Rethinking the Relationship," 395; Levinson, "The Reconceptualization of Kingship," 524. E. Otto also dates Deuteronomy to a pre-exilic date, but with criteria independent of 2 Kgs 22; however, he thinks that the law of the king is deuteronomistic, i.e., later; see E. Otto, "Treueid und Gesetz: Die Ursprünge des Deuteronomiums im Horizont neuassyrischen Vertragsrechts," *ZABR* 2 (1996): 1–52. A middle position is taken by Braulik, who worked out a five-stage development for Deuteronomy, where he dates the cult-centralization material to the time of Hezekiah, Deuteronomy as a covenant document to the time of Josiah, and later stages to the exilic and post-exilic period. Braulik dates Deut 16:18–18:22 to the exilic period.

26. Levinson, "The Reconceptualization of Kingship," 520–23.

27. Ibid., 524.

28. Ibid., 527–34.

full conclusion that his observations demand. In my opinion, they point toward the conclusion that Deuteronomy and the Former Prophets should be regarded as distinct works, and that we should stop calling the author/redactors "Deuteronomists." I suspect that what prevents him from doing so is his dating of some form of Deuteronomy to the seventh century and especially the connection to the "time of Josiah," even though he himself says that the problem is unrelated to dating.[29]

The above discussion illustrates how intimately tied up with the question of dating the discussion of the relationship between Deuteronomy and the rest of the so-called DH is. This is the case for the idea of a chosen place as well as for the concept of kingship. As claimed from the beginning of this study, the dating of Deuteronomy and the idea of a reform during the reign of King Josiah has shaped and continues to shape the way that the texts are understood and problems are explained. The lingering problem is that there are so many ways that this has been done and no agreement seems to be possible. The reason seems to be the nature of the texts—they simply elude an interpretation into any sort of DH hypothesis.

---

29. Knoppers, "Rethinking the Relationship," 414. Theoretically, he is right, but with the synchronic solution he has suggested, there should not be a problem with the disparity. As long as the idea of a Josianic edition or a pre-exilic *Urdeuteronomium* is upheld, however, the difficulty will remain, unless he is allowing for separate redactions from the time of Josiah.

Chapter 9

CONCLUSIONS

The goal of this book has been to approach the "chosen place" in the book of Deuteronomy, navigating through the texts without relying entirely on the maps provided by the past two hundred years of critical research. Thanks to this strategy we have been able to make a number of fresh textual observations relevant to the problem of the "chosen place." The first discovery, presented in Chapter 2, is the fact that the "chosen place" in Deuteronomy does not denote the same thing as the "chosen city" or "Jerusalem, the city that I have chosen" in Kings. In Deuteronomy, the "chosen place" denotes the idea of a divinely chosen place at which cultic activity will take place, and strongly suggests an idea of "centralization." In Kings, however, the "city that YHWH chose" denotes a privileged, divinely protected city that is intimately connected to the monarchy and the idea of the unique position of David. This finding is important because these concepts have often been conflated by scholars, especially once the idea of a DH became commonly accepted.

Once we become aware of the distinction between the two understandings of elected place, it also becomes easier to see that different sets of texts cluster around each of them, with different, though not totally unrelated, concerns. Deuteronomy's idea of "chosen place" is concerned with a place of cultic activity and worship. Kings is concerned with a city that is divinely protected and privileged. What ties these together is the use of the principle of divine election. This study began by following these various concerns through the relevant texts, and pointing out the complex and subtle links between them.

A close reading of Deut 12 then demonstrated some of the ways in which the "election phrase" brings the laws about the "chosen place" into focus and makes these laws seem so rhetorically powerful to readers. The various repetitions of the notion of the "chosen place" support the centralization command and formulate it from different angles, enumerating different religious duties associated with the place. The ways in which the centralization command is formulated contribute to defining the relationship between the Israelites and the nations in terms of the centering of their worship on the future "chosen place" in the land. Ultimately, all of these boundaries contribute to defining the relationship between YHWH and his people, all within the framework of cultic regulations. The effect is to create a new order of meaning. As such, Deuteronomy is a work that is always contemporary and always oriented toward the future. The reader who identifies with Israel will simultaneously find a prescriptive text that defines her relationship with its God, and an ethical vision of the future.

The mapping out of the construction of "Jerusalem" in the Former Prophets then provided a fascinating glimpse into the workings of narrative in Samuel and Kings, and also showed how subtly the idea of Jerusalem as chosen city is constructed throughout the course of various narratives. In 2 Samuel, Jerusalem is established as David's monarchic power base, as the place of the ark and as the place of a future "house of God." Bound up with this, the idea of a promise to the "house of David" is announced. In Kings, Jerusalem becomes further established as the seat of royal power and the place of the temple. Of the several ways that Jerusalem is constituted in Kings, the most significant is the elaboration of the idea of Jerusalem as chosen and the promises about the Davidic dynasty, ideas that are introduced in Samuel and brought together in 1 Kings. We saw that this is done quite subtly, and that the book of Chronicles makes these connections more explicit.

We also saw that in Kings, the idea that Jerusalem is chosen forms a rationale for the protection of the royal house, in spite of the monarchy's failure to uphold loyalty toward YHWH. From the outset this chosen city was under threat, and in the end YHWH decides to destroy it. Threats to Jerusalem were announced from the time the temple was built. Our survey showed that the idea of Jerusalem as chosen is a complex idea in Kings, and that there is no one understanding of this idea in the Former Prophets as a whole. Further, any imagined connection to the "chosen place" of Deuteronomy is not at all apparent. This fact provides further support for the findings of Chapter 2, namely that the "chosenness" of "place" in Deuteronomy and "city/Jerusalem" in Kings are quite distinct concepts in Deuteronomy and the Former Prophets.

In addition, the broad survey of the cultic context of Deuteronomy's chosen place within the Pentateuch showed that while it is true that Deuteronomy does not mention the sanctuary, it is concerned with the sacrificial cult and the festivals. The exploration also showed that the books of the Former Prophets have no one understanding of the role of cult and the cult place; rather, numerous views and concerns are represented. It was not possible to characterize any distinctly "deuteronomistic" view of cult in the Former Prophets. The individual books are too different. Kings is possibly the most "deuteronomistic." The centrality of the temple in Kings connects in many ways with the centrality of "place" in Deuteronomy. However, it also contrasts with the lack of interest in a sanctuary in Deuteronomy. In sum, the material surveyed provided the basis for the conclusion that scholarship has overemphasized the links and similarities between Deuteronomy and the books of the Former Prophets in terms of the "chosen place" theme, and has overemphasized the distinction of Deuteronomy from the rest of the Pentateuch. In general, this investigation showed that the many nuances in the cultic context of the "chosen place" need to be better appreciated. It also became clear that there are many links between Genesis–Numbers and the Former Prophets, and that the links between Deuteronomy and the Former Prophets need not be privileged in the way that they have been in the past. The survey thus provided a fuller picture of the relationship between the legislative material in the Pentateuch (including Deuteronomy) and the narratives of the Former Prophets.

The close reading of 2 Kgs 22–23, usually considered the central "proof text" for the DH hypothesis, showed that the significance of this narrative for the idea of centralization has been exaggerated. While it is possible to read the narrative as a story about discovering the book of Deuteronomy, or some form of it, and though it was read this way by early readers, modern scholars have identified this to mean that Josiah's reform was a reform of "centralization." However, this is not the only option, and definitely not the best. As we have seen, the reform is more clearly one of cultic cleansing and defiling. Most clearly, this narrative cannot carry the burden of being a proof text for the DH hypothesis. Although 2 Kgs 22–23 does demonstrate some of the many connections between the books of Kings and Deuteronomy, it also has profound connections with other parts of the Bible, for example, Leviticus, Joshua, Chronicles, Jeremiah, and Ezekiel.

I suggested in Chapter 6 that rather than read 2 Kgs 22–23 as a story that legitimizes the so-called deuteronomistic movement, or as the account of the implementation of a historical reform carried out in the late monarchic period, or as a "founding myth" of the deuteronomistic school, this story is best read primarily within the context of the book of Kings. In this context it a story about a royal attempt to reform the cult and cleanse it to an original, pristine state that ultimately failed to stave off the final disaster that befell the kingdom of Judah. This reading gives proper attention to the idea of destroying the "high places." Though they are not an issue at all in Deuteronomy, the "high places" have a crucial role in Kings, and in 2 Kgs 22–23 play a much more central role than the idea of cultic centralization. The essential issue in 2 Kgs 22–23 is the

9. Conclusions

drive to eliminate non-Yahwistic worship and illicit Yahwistic cultic activity.

The claim that Josiah (and Hezekiah) conducted reforms of cult centralization is based on a reading of these texts *in light of* "the law," whether one envisions the law to be Deuteronomy or the whole of the Torah. This is clearly the *effect achieved* by reading these narratives in light of the Torah or Deuteronomy, more specifically. But this does not mean that this effect is what the authors of Deuteronomy *intended*, or to say that 2 Kgs 22–23 was written with Deuteronomy in mind. When we keep in mind what scholars have normally assumed, and therefore expected, when they approach the Kings texts, we realize that 2 Kgs 22–23 in itself does not narrate a reform of centralization, a "deuteronomistic reform", or a "deuteronomistic passover."

Early on in this study I observed that the most obvious link between the idea of "chosen place" in Deuteronomy and "chosen city" in Kings is the use of the principle of election. The authority of divine election is a key concept that lends authority to the idea of the "chosen place." In Deuteronomy, the concept of Israel as chosen plays a significant role in putting an obligation on Israel to keep the law. Another persuasive factor is the repeated reference to YHWH's rescue of Israel from Egypt. Israel's duty to serve YHWH is set in contrast to what they must do to the nations, the non-elect, and those who will be exterminated, according to Deuteronomy. The authority that has been created regarding YHWH's choice of Israel is transposed onto the "chosen place," giving it also an unquestionable status.

In Samuel and Kings, the dynamics engendered around the divine election of the royal house and the city of Jerusalem also work together to shape readers' assumptions and interpretations, as I showed in Chapter 4. Some of the Psalms also exhibit this dynamic of assigning divine authority through the concept of election. The dynamic of divine election is one of the reasons for the persuasive power of Deuteronomy, as well as a key element in the construction of the idea that Jerusalem is protected and privileged, which we find in the narratives of Samuel and Kings.

Finally, our exploration of the idea of kingship in Deuteronomy and the Former Prophets showed the deep tension between the portrayal of kingship and the attitudes toward it in these works. By reviewing recent scholarly debate addressing this tension, I showed how the discussion of this subject depends on the positions scholars take on the issues of dating and the concerns arising from the DH hypothesis, as was also the case with most research on the "chosen place."

Final Thoughts

Deuteronomy and the books of the Former Prophets are distinct and need not be understood as belonging to a unified work of history. Yet, Deuteronomy and Kings, in particular, also intersect and are read in light of each other. And, to most readers, the book of Joshua obviously continues the story told in Genesis–Deuteronomy. The problem that has not been satisfactorily explained is how these books are related in terms of their compositional history. While I do not have a conclusion to this knotty problem, I have tried to highlight some points that have become buried or skewed by the most common explanations.

In general, I think we need to be satisfied with less precise answers than those that we have been positing for questions about the compositional and redactional history of Deuteronomy and the Former Prophets and the relationship between them. We have to accept that the biblical texts are anonymous and that they are the product of tradition, and that we really cannot reconstruct the process of their composition, although there is a lot to learn from trying.

This study has demonstrated that taking for granted scholarly constructs such as the idea of Josiah's "deuteronomistic" reform and the role of Deuteronomy in the "project of centralization" creates a problem for the production of knowledge. A hypothesis such as the DH is quite easily reductive and can quickly lead to overly simplified explanations that overlook many details. Or, because of all of the textual data that do not fit into a simple picture, it produces a body of secondary literature that can become impenetrable in its mass of detail, textual reconstruction, confusion of terminology, and systems of internal referencing between scholars working on the same issues. This impenetrable system blocks the effective transmission of new insights because it so dominates the grounds of the conversation that new voices might not find anyone to listen, or might find the language too difficult to learn.

There is nothing wrong, in theory, with positing a hypothetical writer or rewriter of Kings, for instance, whose language at times and whose ideas seem to overlap with those of Deuteronomy, and who for this reason is labelled Dtr, as long as we understand that this is a theory. The problems arise when it does not work. I think the ideas of redactors, historians, and authors have to be very flexible when talking about biblical texts. Too often, decisions are made about which texts were written by such and such a writer, and a whole diachronic history is set up which becomes rigid and is used again to determine the status of other texts. Another problem is the flattening of the discourse that occurs with the over-extension of models and their reduction in text books and other contexts in which the participants are not experts on the DH.

In fact, it is a huge and, as yet, unaddressed problem that many of the solutions offered about the diachronic history of texts are completely different from each other in terms of details. Sometimes, the exact same information is used to argue completely different points of view. Occasionally, the only consolation might be that the textual "evidence" is described in similar ways, but this only highlights the fact that we are constantly in a process of interpreting, and that textual "evidence" in itself is nothing.

Although other criteria are also used in order to underpin the concept of "deuteronomistic," such as a distinctive style and language, use of covenantal language and ideology, and so on, the idea of the "centralization" of the cult is most often cited as the most fundamental. Yet, many details do not fit into the various pictures that have been drawn. This is the case in spite of the claim, within a number of different paradigms of textual and historical reconstruction, that the demand for "centralization" is a deuteronomistic trait that distinguishes it from other books of the Pentateuch, and that it is reflected in the so-called DH.

Another area that needs revision is the degree to which centralization can be said to be "deuteronomistic." It is true that no other book explicitly demands cultic activity to be restricted to one place. But as we have pointed out and seen from the texts, the concept of centralization is assumed in the understanding of the sanctuary and cultic activity in what is commonly referred to as priestly material in the Pentateuch. Wellhausen, with his relative dating of the sources, made it clear that the P texts assumed centralization. This understanding of the chronology constituted an important component in his largely derogatory understanding of Judaism. With the recent reconsiderations of relative dates of Pentateuchal texts in mind, however, the whole idea of calling centralization "deuteronomistic" might have become misleading.

As this book has shown repeatedly, the affinities between Deuteronomy and Kings (and other books of the Former Prophets) are intriguing but elusive. Perhaps we can explain similarities and affinities by seeing these works that respond to some of the same challenges, each in a distinctive way? Deuteronomy, as law and as part of the Torah, provides a plan for the future; it is prescriptive. As an authoritative text for a community, it became a text that could become the basis for a new beginning, again and again. Moses speaks to the new generation, today, now. The Former Prophets succeed in salvaging a past that could become a treasure trove for the future. These books are descriptive, judgmental, and explanatory. At the same time, they form an identity-creating story, establishing a common past for those who identify with it. As a story of ultimate failure and collapse, the Former Prophets nonetheless provide a basis for a sense of origin and identity. King David continued to be an inspiration for the hopes of future generations, even though YHWH's promise to him failed to provide protection for Jerusalem.

I have begun to indulge in some speculation. Throughout, this study has spoken mostly of the inner-textual workings of the biblical texts. There has been some speculation about how texts may have read, and I have taken into account their ancient Near Eastern context, but I have refrained from any specific dating and from speaking of the intention of the writers. I will close this study, however, with some thoughts about a possible matrix to help us talk about the relationship between Deuteronomy and the book of Kings, as an example.

Even when we acknowledge that biblical texts have a long "history," it is likely that there has been a good deal of *parallel activity*. By that, I mean that biblical books were being written concurrently, most likely in related or identical environments. Coming to terms with the collapse of the kingdoms was one of the challenges after the fall of Jerusalem in 586. One solution was to judge most of the kings as failures, as the book of Kings does. With the king responsible for the cultic standard, they were also blamed for the fate of the nation. The kings did not do what was good in YHWH's eyes. For the kingdom of Judah, Manasseh receives most of the blame (2 Kgs 21; 23:26; 24:3–4; cf. Jer 15:4), but the downfall actually begins almost immediately, according to the narrator, due to the sins of Solomon. In the end, YHWH could not keep his promise of protecting Jerusalem. The city that YHWH chose, the king that YHWH chose, and the temple/house built for him were all destroyed by him. The ancient Near Eastern model of kingship failed. The success of David, God's promise to David, and the few kings who did "good," were not enough to save the kingdom. And yet the story does not end there. The ambivalence toward the monarchy in the biblical narratives leaves open the possibility of a reversal, a future restoration. This ambiguity is what has allowed scholars to hold such diverging opinions regarding the monarchy. Was it good or bad? Each reader will choose his/her emphasis. Both are supported by the text.[1]

---

1. A similar dynamic can be found in the book of Jeremiah. For an exploration of this, see my "Babylon in the Book of Jeremiah (MT): Negotiating a Power Shift," in *Prophecy in the Book of Jeremiah* (ed. H. M. Barstad and R. G. Kratz; BZAW 388; Berlin: de Gruyter, 2009), 187–232 (224–32).

9. Conclusions

Parallel to this "history"-writing, legislation for a future society is being written, based, as one would expect, on existing legal traditions. The legislation of the book of Deuteronomy formulates a role for the king, even though the monarchy no longer exists. It creates its own standard for judging the success of the kings of Israel, one that limits the powers and role of the king, at least in terms of those roles that are specified, and subordinates it to the law. In different ways, Deuteronomy and the books of the Former Prophets (also different individually) are works with different strategies for dealing with the same issues, and for facing some of the same challenges.

The books of Samuel and Kings offer a theodicy, an explanation for why the kingdoms of Israel and Judah were destroyed. It blames the kings, but also the people. It criticizes the monarchy, but simultaneously portrays it as divinely sanctioned. It allows a way to narrate the past, but is simultaneously open to the future, and does not close the book on kingship, so to say. The book of Deuteronomy provides a vision for the future; it is forward-looking, written from the point of view of looking to the future, introducing its laws with "when you enter the land…"

Scholars have used dating and redaction criticism to explain the tension between Deuteronomy and the Former Prophets (and within the Former Prophets), on kingship and on the idea of "chosen place." A synchronic reading of the books as a progressive narrative is what led to historical criticism in the first place. Because we read Deuteronomy as a book that prescribes law for the Israelite community *after* they settle in the land, we may be disturbed that the Former Prophets do not follow up on the agenda of Deuteronomy the way we might expect with regard to the "chosen place" or the king. However, dating and redaction-critical models have not solved the problems, as we have seen.

Readers tend to *harmonize*. By being placed before the *story* of Joshua through Kings, it might be that Deuteronomy succeeds in providing a different reading of the book of Kings than what would have been the case without it. On some points, this is very clear, on other points it is less so. Ambiguity is part of the result. Deuteronomic legislation on the king is not directly reflected in the narrative of the kings of Israel and Judah; in fact, it is sometimes flatly contradicted. But the fact that the Deuteronomic law of the king now precedes this narrative has influenced the reading of Kings.

Perhaps Deuteronomy functions to redeem the monarchy that is blamed in the story of Kings, by giving a role to the king which is subordinated to the law. It leaves the option open for the monarchy as an institution, but implicitly criticizes the way in which it has been exercised by completely disregarding the common ancient Near Eastern understanding of the role of the king. The role of the king is reduced to something similar to that in a constitutional monarchy. This might be a way of saying that "If we had had this law, the monarchy might not have failed." When we read the history in light of this law, it becomes clearer why disaster befell Israel and Judah. Each of the two works has its own logic. Read together, another, different, logic is possible.

BIBLIOGRAPHY

Albertz, R. *A History of Israelite Religion in the Old Testament Period, Volume I: From the Beginnings to the End of the Monarchy*. Translated by J. Bowden. OTL. Louisville, Ky.: Westminster John Knox, 1994.
———. "In Search of the Deuteronomists: A First Solution to a Historical Riddle." Pages 1–17 in Römer, ed., *The Future of the Deuteronomistic History*.
———. "Why a Reform Like Josiah's Must Have Happened." Pages 27–46 in Grabbe, ed., *Good Kings and Bad Kings*.
Albright, W. F. "The Judicial Reform of Jehoshaphat." Pages 62–69 in Lieberman, ed., *Alexander Marx Jubilee Volume*.
Assis, E. "The Position and Function of Jos 22 in the Book of Joshua." *ZAW* 116 (2004): 528–41.
Auld, A. G. "The Deuteronomists and the Former Prophets, or What Makes the Former Prophets Deuteronomistic?" Pages 116–26 in Schearing and McKenzie, eds., *Those Elusive Deuteronomists*.
———. *Kings without Privilege: David and Moses in the Story of the Bible's Kings*. Edinburgh: T. & T. Clark, 1994.
———. "Prophets Shared—But Recycled." Pages 19–28 in Römer, ed., *The Future of the Deuteronomistic History*.
Aurelius, E. *Zukuft jenseits des Gerichts: Eine redaktionsgeschichtliche Studie zum Enneateuch*. BZAW 318. Berlin: de Gruyter, 2003.
Barker, P. A. "The Theology of Deuteronomy 27." *TynBul* 49 (1998): 277–303.
Barrick, B. *The King and the Cemeteries: Toward a New Understanding of Josiah's Reform*. VTSup 88. Leiden: Brill, 2002.
Barstad, H. M. *History and the Hebrew Bible: Studies in Ancient Israelite and Ancient Near Eastern Historiography*. FAT 61. Tübingen: Mohr Siebeck, 2008.
———. *The Religious Polemics of Amos: Studies in the Preaching of Am 2, 7B–8; 4,1–13; 5,1–27; 6,4–7; 8,14*. VTSup 34. Leiden: Brill, 1984.
Baumgartner, W. "Der Kampf um das Deuteronomium." *ThR* NF 1 (1929): 7–25.
Beck, M., and U. Schorn, eds. *Auf dem Weg zur Endgestalt von Genesis bis II Regnum: Festschrift Hans-Christoph Schmitt zum 65. Geburtstag*. BZAW 370. Berlin: de Gruyter, 2006.
Begg, C. T. "1994: A Significant Anniversary in the History of Deuteronomy Research." Pages 1–11 in Martínez et al., eds., *Studies in Deuteronomy*.
Ben Dov, J. "Writing as Oracle and as Law: New Contexts for the Book-Find of King Josiah." *JBL* 127 (2008): 223–39.
Ben Zvi, E. "Imagining Josiah's Book and the Implications of Imagining it in early Persian Yehud." Pages 193–212 in *Berührungspunkte: Studien zur Sozial- und Religionsgeschichte Israels und seiner Umwelt: Festschrift für Rainer Albertz zu seinem 65. Geburtstag*. Edited by I. Kottsieper et al. AOAT 350. Münster: Ugarit, 2008.

———. "Josiah and the Prophetic Books: Some Observations." Pages 47–64 in Grabbe, ed., *Good Kings and Bad Kings*.

———. "Towards an Integrative Study of the Production of Authoritative Books in Ancient Israel." Pages 15–28 in *The Production of Prophecy: Constructing Prophecy and Prophets in Yehud*. Edited by D. V. Edelman and E. Ben Zvi. London: Equinox, 2009.

Berry, G. R. "The Code Found in the Temple." *JBL* 39 (1929): 44–51.

———. "The Date of Deuteronomy." *JBL* 59 (1940): 133–39.

Blum, E. *Studien zur Komposition des Pentateuch*. BZAW 189. Berlin: de Gruyter, 1990.

Botha, P. J. "'No King like Him…': Royal Etiquette According to the Deuteronomistic Historian." Pages 36–49 in *Past, Present, Future: The Deuteronomistic History and the Prophets*. Edited by J. C. de Moor and H. F. Van Rooy. OTS 44. Leiden: Brill, 2000.

Braulik, G., ed. *Bundesdokument und Gesetz: Studien zum Deuteronomium*. Herders biblische Studien 4. Freiburg: Herder, 1995.

———. "Die Abfolge der Gesetze in Deuteronomium 12–26 und der Dekalog." Pages 252–72 in Lohfink, ed., *Das Deuteronomium*.

———. "Die Ausdrücke für 'Gesetz' im Buch Deuteronomium." *Bib* 51 (1970): 39–66.

———. *Die deuteronomischen Gesetze und der Dekalog: Studien zum Aufbau von Deuteronomium 12–26*. SBS 145. Stuttgart: Katolisches Bibelwerk, 1991.

———. *Studien zum Deuteronomium und seiner Nachgeschichte*. SBAB 33. Stuttgart: Katholisches Bibelwerk, 2001.

———. ed., *Studien zum Pentateuch: Walter Kornfeld zum 60. Geburtstag*. Wien: Herder, 1977.

Brekelmans, C., and J. Lust, eds. *Pentateuchal and Deuteronomistic Studies: Papers Read at the 13th IOSOT Congress, Leuven 1989*. BETL 94. Leuven: Leuven University Press, 1990.

Brewer, J. A. "The Case for the Early Date of Deuteronomy." *JBL* 47 (1928): 305–21.

Budde, K. "Das Deuteronomium und die Reform König Josias." *ZAW* 44 (1926): 177–224.

Campbell, A. F. *2 Samuel*. FOTL 8. Grand Rapids: Eerdmans, 2005.

Caquot, A. "Sur la 'Loi Royale' du Deutéronome." *Sem* 9 (1959): 21–33.

Carrière, J.-M. "Le cadre où se forme la decision politique: Lecture de Deutéronome 16,18–18,22." *NRT* 121 (1999): 529–42.

Caton, J. E. "Temple and *bāmāh*: Some Considerations." Pages 150–65 in Holloway and Handy, eds., *The Pitcher is Broken*.

Childs, B. S. *Introduction to the Old Testament as Scripture*. Philadelphia: Fortress, 1979.

Clements, R. E. "The Deuteronomic Law of Centralisation and the Catastrophe of 587 B.C.E." Pages 5–25 in *After the Exile: Essays in Honour of Rex Mason*. Edited by J. Barton and D. J. Reimer. Macon, Ga.: Mercer University Press, 1996.

———. "The Deuteronomistic Interpretation of the Founding of the Monarchy in 1 Sam. VIII." *VT* 24 (1974): 398–410.

———. "Deuteronomy and the Jerusalem Cult Tradition." *VT* 15 (1965): 300–312.

———. "The Former Prophets and Deuteronomy—A Re-examination." Pages 83–95 in *God's Word for Our World*. Vol. 1, *Biblical Studies in Honor of Simon John De Vries*. Edited by J. H. Ellens et al. JSOTSup 388. London: T&T Clark International, 2004.

Cogan, M., and C. Tadmor. *II Kings: A New Translation with Introduction and Commentary*. AB 11. New York: Doubleday, 1988.

Coggins, R. "What Does 'Deuteronomistic' Mean?" Pages 22–35 in Schearing and McKenzie, eds., *Those Elusive Deuteronomists*.

Conroy, C. "Reflections on the Exegetical Task: Apropos of Recent Studies on 2 Kg 22–23." Pages 255–68 in Brekelmans and Lust, eds., *Pentateuchal and Deuteronomistic Studies*.

Cooper, A., and B. R. Goldstein. "The Festivals of Israel and Judah and the Literary History of the Pentateuch." *JAOS* 110 (1990): 19–31.

Cross, F. M. *Canaanite Myth and Hebrew Epic: Essays in the History of the Religion of Israel*. Cambridge, Mass.: Harvard University Press, 1973.

Dahl, G. "The Case for the Currently Accepted Date of Deuteronomy." *JBL* 47 (1928): 358–79.

Davies, P. R. "Josiah and the Law Book." Pages 65–77 in Grabbe, ed., *Good Kings and Bad Kings*.

De Wette, W. M. L. *Beiträge zur Einleitung in das Alte Testament:* I. *Kritischer Versuch über die Glaubwürdigkeit der Bücher und Gesetzgebung*. Halle, 1806; II. *Kritik der israelitischen Geschichte, Erster Teil: Kritik der mosaischen Geschichte*. Halle, 1807. Repr. in Darmstadt: Wissenschaftliche Buchgesellschaft, 1971.

———. *Dissertatio critico-exegetica qua Deuteronomium a prioribus Pentateuchi libris diversum, alius cuiusdam recentioris auctioris opus esse monstratur*. Diss. University of Jena, 1805. Repr. in Opuscula theologica. Berlin, 1830.

Dietrich, W. *Prophetie und Geschichte: Eine redaktionsgeschichtliche Untersuchung zum deuteronomistischen Geschichtswerk*. FRLANT 108. Göttingen: Vandenhoeck & Ruprecht, 1972.

Dozeman, T. B., and K. Schmid, eds. *A Farewell to the Yahwist? The Composition of the Pentateuch in Recent European Interpretation*. SBL Symposium Series 34. Atlanta: SBL, 2006.

Driver, S. R. *A Critical and Exegetical Commentary on Deuteronomy*. 3d ed. ICC. Edinburgh: T. & T. Clark, 1903. Repr. 1978.

———. *An Introduction to the Literature of the Old Testament*. Gloucester, Mass.: Meridien, 1956. Repr. 1972 by arrangement with World Publishing. First published 1897.

Duhm, B. *Das Buch Jeremia*. HAT 11. Tübingen: J. C. B. Mohr (Paul Siebeck), 1901.

Edelman, D. "Hezekiah's Alleged Cultic Centralization." *JSOT* 32 (2008): 395–434.

Eissfeldt, O. *The Old Testament: An Introduction: Including the Apocrypha and Pseudepigrapha, and Also the Works of Similar Type from Qumran: The History of the Formation of the Old Testament*. Translated by Peter R. Ackroyd, from the 3d German ed. New York: Harper & Row, 1965.

Ellens, J. H., and J. T. Greene, eds. "What Happened to the Yahwist? Reflections after Thirty Years: A Collegial Conversation between Rolf Rendtorff, David J. A. Clines, Allan Rosengren, and John Van Seters." Pages 39–66 in *Probing the Frontiers of Biblical Studies*. Princeton Theological Monograph Series. Eugene, Ore.: Pickwick, 2009.

Engnell, I. *Gamla testamentet: en traditionshistorisk inledning*, I. Stockholm: Svenska kyrkans diakonistyrelses bokförlag, 1945.

Eslinger, L. M. *House of God or House of David: The Rhetoric of 2 Samuel 7.* JSOTSup 164. Sheffield: JSOT, 1994.

———. *Kingship of God in Crisis: A Close Reading in 1 Samuel 1–12.* Bible and Literature Series 10. Sheffield: Almond/JSOT, 1985.

Eynikel, E. *The Reform of King Josiah and the Composition of the Deuteronomistic History.* OTS 33. Leiden: Brill, 1996.

Fensham, F. C. "The Burning of the Golden Calf and Ugarit." *IEJ* 16 (1966): 191–93.

Finkelstein, I., and N. A. Silberman, "Temple and Dynasty: Hezekiah, the Remaking of Judah and the Rise of the Pan-Israelite Ideology." *JSOT* 30 (2006): 259–85.

Fohrer, G. *Introduction to the Old Testament: Initiated by Ernst Sellin, Completely Revised and Rewritten by Georg Fohrer.* Translated by D. E. Green. Nashville: Abingdon, 1968.

Frankena, R. "The Vassal Treaties of Esarhaddon and the Dating of Deuteronomy." *OTS* 14 (1965): 122–54.

Fretheim, T. E. *First and Second Kings.* The Westminster Bible Companion. Louisville, Ky.: Westminster John Knox, 1999.

Fried, L. E. "The High Places (*BĀMÔT*) and the Reforms of Hezekiah and Josiah: An Archaeological Investigation." *JAOS* 122 (2002): 437–65.

Fritz, V. *Tempel und Zelt: Studien zum Tempelbau in Israel und zu dem Zeltheiligtum der Priesterschrift.* WMANT 47. Neukirchen-Vluyn: Neukirchener, 1977.

García López, F. "Deuteronomio 31, el Pentateuco y la Historia Deuteronomista." Pages 71–85 in *Deuteronomy and Deuteronomic Literature: Festschrift C. H. W. Brekelmans.* Edited by M. Vervenne and J. Lust. BETL 133. Leuven: Leuven University Press, 1997.

Geiger, M., *Gottesräume: Die literarische und theologische Konzeption von Raum im Deuteronomium.* BWANT 183. Stuttgart: Kohlhammer, 2010.

Geoghegan, J. C. *The Time, Place, and Purpose of the Deuteronomistic History: The Evidence of "Until This Day".* BJS 347. Providence, R.I.: Brown Judaic Studies, 2006.

Goodfriend, E. A. "Prostitution." *ABD* 5:505–10.

Gos, B. "Deutéronome 17,18–19 et la Restauration de la Royauté au Retour de l'Exil." *BeO* 36, no. 3 (1994): 129–38.

Grabbe, L. L., ed. *Good Kings and Bad Kings.* LHBOTS 393/European Seminar in Historical Methodology 5. London: T&T Clark International, 2005.

Graham, M. et al., eds. *The Chronicler as Historian.* JSOTSup 238. Sheffield: Sheffield Academic, 1997.

Gray, J. *I & II Kings: A Commentary.* 2d fully rev. ed. OTL. Philadelphia: Westminster, 1970.

Gross, W., ed. *Jeremia und die "deuteronomistische Bewegung."* BBB 98. Weinheim: Beltz Athenäum, 1995.

Gunn, D. M. *The Fate of King Saul: An Interpretation of a Biblical Story.* JSOTSup 14. Sheffield: JSOT, 1980.

———. *The Story of King David: Genre and Interpretation.* JSOTSup 8. Sheffield: JSOT, 1978.

Halpern, B. "The Centralization Formula in Deuteronomy." *VT* 31 (1981): 20–38.

———. *The Constitution of the Monarchy in Israel.* HSM 25. Chico, Calif.: Scholars Press, 1981.

Handy, L. K. "Hezekiah's Unlikely Reform." *ZAW* 100 (1988): 111–15.

———. "Historical Probability and the Narrative of Josiah's Reform in 2 Kings." Pages 252–75 in Holloway and Handy, eds., *The Pitcher is Broken*.

Hardmeier, Chr. "King Josiah in the Climax of the Deuteronomic History (2 Kings 22–23) and the Pre-Deuteronomic Document of a Cult Reform at the Place of Residence (23.4–15*): Criticism of Sources, Reconstruction of Literary Pre-Stages and the Theology of History in 2 Kings 22–23*." Pages 123–63 in Grabbe, ed., *Good Kings and Bad Kings*.

Hauge, M. R. *Descent from the Mountain: Narrative Patterns in Exodus 19–40*. JSOTSup 323. Sheffield: Sheffield Academic, 2001.

Hertzberg, H. W. *1 and 2 Samuel: A Commentary*. OTL. Philadelphia: Westminster, 1984.

Hjelm, I. *Jerusalem's Rise to Sovereignty: Zion and Gerizim in Competition*. JSOTSup 404; Copenhagen International Seminar 14. London: T&T Clark International, 2004.

Hobbs, T. R. *2 Kings*. WBC 13. Waco, Tex.: Word, 1985.

Hoffmann, H. D. *Reform und Reformen: Untersuchungen zu einem Grundthema der deuteronomistischen Geschichtsschreibung*. Zurich: Theologischer Verlag, 1980.

Hollenstein, H. "Literarkritische Erwägungen zum Bericht über die Reformmaßnahmen Josias 2 Kön. Xxiii 4ff." *VT* 27 (1977): 321–36.

Holloway, S. W., and L. K. Handy, eds. *The Pitcher is Broken: Memorial Essays for Gösta W. Ahlström*. JSOTSup 190. Sheffield: Sheffield Academic, 1995.

Hölscher, G. "Komposition und Ursprung des Deuteronomiums." *ZAW* 40 (1923): 161–255.

Hoppe, L. J. "Jerusalem in the Deuteronomistic History." Pages 107–10 in Lohfink, ed., *Das Deuteronomium*.

Houtman, C. *Der Pentateuch: Die Geschichte seiner Erforschung neben einer Auswertung*. Kampen: Kok Pharos, 1995.

Hurowitz, V. *I Have Built You An Exalted House: Temple Building in the Bible in Light of Mesopotamian and North-West Semitic Writings*. JSOTSup 115. JSOT/ASOR Monograph Series 5. Sheffield: JSOT, 1992.

Jepsen, A. *Die Quellen des Königsbuches*. Halle: Niewmeyer, 1953.

Jeremias, J., and L. Perlitt, eds. *Die Botschaft und die Boten: Festschrift für Hans Walter Wolff zum 70. Geburtstag*. Neukirchen–Vluyn: Neukirchener, 1981.

Jones, G. H. *1 and 2 Kings*, vol. 2. The NCB Commentary. Grand Rapids: Eerdmans, 1984.

Josephus. Translated by H. St. J. Thackeray et al. 10 vols. LCL. Cambridge, Mass.: Harvard University Press, 1926–65.

Junker, H. "Die Entstehungszeit des Ps. 78 und des Deuteronomiums." *Bib* 34 (1953): 487–500.

Kaiser, O. "The Pentateuch and the Deuteronomistic History." Pages 289–322 in *Text in Context: Essays by Members of the Society for Old Testament Study*. Edited by A. D. H. Mayes. Oxford: Oxford University Press, 2000.

Kaminsky, J. S. *Yet I Loved Jacob: Reclaiming the Biblical Concept of Election*. Nashville: Abingdon, 2007.

Kapelrud, A. S. "Temple Building: A Task for Gods and Kings." *Or* 32 (1963): 56–62.

Kartveit, M. *The Origin of the Samaritans*. VTSup 128. Leiden: Brill, 2009.

Kaufman, S. A. "The Stucture of the Deuteronomic Law." *Maarav* 1, no. 2 (1978–79): 105–58.
Keller, M. *Untersuchungen zur deuteronomisch-deuteronomistischen Namenstheologie*. BBB 105. Weinheim: Beltz Athenäum, 1996.
Knauf, E. A. "Does 'Deuteronomistic Historiography' (DtrH) Exist?" Pages 388–98 in de Pury, Römer, and Macchi, eds., *Israel Constructs Its History*.
———. "Observations on Judah's Social and Economic History and the Dating of the Laws in Deuteronomy." *The Journal of Hebrew Scriptures* 9 Article 18 (2009): 2–8.
Knoppers, G. N. "The Deuteronomist and the Deuteronomic Law of the King: A Reexamination of a Relationship." *ZAW* 108 (1996): 329–46.
———. "Rethinking the Relationship between Deuteronomy and the Deuteronomistic History: The Case of Kings." *CBQ* 63 (2001): 393–415.
———. "Solomon's Fall and Deuteronomy." Pages 392–410 in *The Age of Solomon: Scholarship at the Turn of the Millennium*. Edited by L. K. Handy. Studies in the History of the Ancient Near East 11. Leiden: Brill, 1997.
———. *Two Nations under God: The Deuteronomistic History of Solomon and the Dual Monarchies*. 2 vols. HSM 52–53. Atlanta: Scholars Press, 1993–1994.
Knoppers, G. N., and B. M. Levinson, eds. *The Pentateuch as Torah: New Models for Understanding Its Promulgation and Acceptance*. Winona Lake, Ind.: Eisenbrauns, 2007.
Knowles, M. D. *Centrality Practiced: Jerusalem in the Religious Practice of Yehud and the Diaspora in the Persian Period*. SBL Archaeology and Biblical Studies 16. Atlanta: SBL, 2006.
Koch, K. "Zur Geschichte der Erwählungsvorstellung in Israel." *ZAW* 67 (1955): 205–26.
Körting, C. *Zion in den Psalmen*. FAT 48. Tübingen: Mohr Siebeck, 2006.
Kratz, R. G. *Die Komposition der erzählenden Bücher des Alten Testaments*. Göttingen: Vandenhoeck & Ruprecht, 2000. ET *The Composition of the Narrative Books of the Old Testament*. Translated by J. Bowden. London: T&T Clark International, 2005.
Lasine, S. "'Everything Belongs to Me': Holiness, Danger, and Divine Kingship in the Post-Genesis World." *JSOT* 35 (2010): 31–62.
———. "Guest and Host in Judges 19: Lot's Hospitality in an Inverted World." *JSOT* 29 (1984): 37–59.
———. "Reading Jeroboam's Intentions: Intertextuality, Rhetoric and History in 1 Kings 12." Pages 133–52 in *Reading between Texts: Intertextuality and the Hebrew Bible*. Edited by Dana Nolan Fewell. Louisville, Ky.: Westminster John Knox, 1992.
Lenchak, T. A. *"Choose Life!" A Rhetorical-Critical Investigation of Deuteronomy 28,69–30,20*. AnBib 129. Rome: Editrice Pontificio Istituto Biblico, 1993.
Levenson, J. "Zion Traditions." In *ABD* 6:1098–1102.
Levin, C. "Das Deuteronomium und der Jahwist." Pages 121–36 in *Liebe und Gebot: Studien zum Deuteronomium: Festschrift zum 70. Geburtstag von Lothar Perlitt*. Edited by R. G. Kratz and H. Spieckermann. FRLANT 190. Göttingen: Vandenhoeck & Ruprecht, 2000.
———. "Joschija im deuteronomistischen Geschichtswerk." *ZAW* 96 (1984): 351–71.
Levinson, B. M. *Deuteronomy and the Hermeneutics of Legal Innovation*. New York: Oxford University Press, 1997.
———. "The Hermeneutics of Tradition in Deuteronomy: A Reply to J. G. McConville." *JBL* 199 (2000): 269–86.

───. "Is the Covenant Code an Exilic Composition? A Response to John Van Seters." Pages 272–325 in *In Search of Pre-exilic Israel: Proceedings of the Oxford Old Testament Seminar*. Edited by J. Day. London: T&T Clark International, 2004.

───. "The Reconceptualization of Kingship in Deuteronomy and the Deuteronomistic History's Transformation of Torah." *VT* 51 (2001): 511–34.

───, ed. *Theory and Method in Biblical and Cuneiform Law: Revision, Interpolation and Development*. JSOTSup 181. Sheffield: Sheffield Academic, 1994.

Lieberman, S., ed. *Alexander Marx Jubilee Volume on the Occasion of His Seventieth Birthday: English Section*. New York: Jewish Theological Seminary, 1950.

Lohfink, N. F. "Die Bundesurkunde des König Josias (Eine Frage an die Deuteronomiumsforschung)." *Bib* 44 (1963): 261–498.

───, ed. *Das Deuteronomium: Entstehung, Gestalt und Botschaft*. BETL 68. Leuven: Leuven University Press, 1985.

───. "Fortschreibung? Zur Technik von Rechtsrevisionen im deuteronomistischen Bereich, erörtet an Deuteronomium 12, Ex 21,2–11 und Dtn 15,12–18." Pages 127–71 in *Das Deuteronomium und seine Querbeziehungen*. Edited by T. Veijola. Schriften der Finnischen Exegetischen Gesellschaft 62. Helsinki/Göttingen: Finnische Exegetische Gesellschaft/Vandenhoeck & Ruprecht, 1996.

───. "Gab es eine deuteronomistische Bewegung?" Pages 313–82 in Gross, ed., *Jeremia und die "deuteronomistische Bewegung."*.

───. "Die Gattung der 'Historischen Kurtzgeschichte' in den letzten Jahren von Juda und in der Zeit des Babylonischen Exils." *ZAW* 90 (1978): 319–47.

───. "Opfer und Säkularisierung im Deuteronomium." Pages 15–43 in *Studien zu Opfer und Kult im Alten Testament mit einer Bibliographie 1969–1991 zum Opfer in der Bibel*. Edited A. Schenker. Tübingen: Mohr (Siebeck), 1992.

───. "Die Sicherung der Wirksamkeit des Gotteswortes durch das Prinzip der Schriftlichkeit der Tora und durch das Prinzip der Gewaltenteilung nach den Ämtergesetzen des Buches Deuteronomium (Dt 16,18–18,22)." Pages 305–23 in *Studien zum Deuteronomium und zur deuteronomistischen Literatur* I. Edited by N. F. Lohfink. SBAB 8. Stuttgart: Verlag Katholisches Bibelwerk, 1990.

───. "Die These vom "deuteronomischen" Dekaloganfang—ein fragwürdiges Ergebnis atomistischer Sprachstatistik." Pages 99–109 in Braulik, ed., *Studien zum Pentateuch*.

───. "Recent Discussion on 2 Kings 22–23: The State of the Question." Pages 36–61 in *A Song of Power and the Power of Song: Essays on the Book of Deuteronomy*. Edited by D. L. Christensen. Sources for Biblical and Theological Study. Winona Lake, Ind.: Eisenbrauns, 1993.

───. "Zur deuteronomischen Zentralisationsformel." *Bib* 65 (1984): 297–328.

Long, B. O. *2 Kings*. FOTL 10; Grand Rapids: Eerdmans, 1991.

Lundbom, J. R. "The Lawbook of the Josianic Reform." *CBQ* 38 (1976): 293–302.

Martínez, F. et al., eds. *Studies in Deuteronomy in Honour of C. J. Labuschagne on the Occasion of His 65th Birthday*. Leiden: Brill, 1994.

Mayes, A. D. H. "Deueteronomy 14 and the Deuteronomic World View." Pages 165–81 in Martínez et al., eds., *Studies in Deuteronomy*.

McCarter, P. K., Jr. *II Samuel: A New Translation with Introduction, Notes and Commentary*. AB 9. New York: Doubleday, 1984.

McConville, J. G. "Deuteronomy's Unification of Passover and Maṣṣot: A Response to Bernard M. Levinson." *JBL* 119 (2000): 47–58.

———. "King and Messiah in Deuteronomy and the Deuteronomistic History." Pages 271–95 in *King and Messiah in Israel and the Ancient Near East: Proceedings of the Oxford Old Testament Seminar*. Edited by J. Day. JSOTSup 270. Sheffield: Sheffield Academic, 1998.

———. "The Old Testament Historical books in Modern Scholarship." *Them* 22 (1997): 3–13.

———. "Time, Place and the Deuteronomic Altar Law," in McConville and Millar, *Time and Place in Deuteronomy*, 117–20.

McConville, J. G., and J. G. Millar. *Time and Place in Deuteronomy*. JSOTSup 179. Sheffield: Sheffield Academic, 1994.

McKenzie, S. L. "The Divided Kingdom in the Deuteronomistic History." Pages 135–45 in Römer, ed., *The Future of the Deuteronomistic History*.

———. "Postscript: The Laws of Physics and Pan-Deuteronomism." Pages 262–71 in Schearing and McKenzie, eds., *Those Elusive Deuteronomists*.

———. "The Trouble with Kingship." Pages 286–314 in de Pury, Römer, and Macchi, eds., *Israel Constructs Its History*.

———. *The Trouble with Kings: The Composition of the Books of Kings in the Deuteronomistic History*. VTSup 42. Leiden: Brill, 1991.

Mettinger, T. N. D. "The Name and the Glory: The Zion-Sabaoth Theology and Its Exilic Successors." *JNSL* 24 (1998): 1–24.

Milgrom, J. "The Alleged 'Demythologization and Secularization' in Deuteronomy." *IEJ* 23 (1973): 156–61.

———. *The JPS Torah Commentary: Numbers*. Philadelphia: JPS, 1990.

———. "Profane Slaughter and a Formulaic Key to the Composition of Deuteronomy." *HUCA* 47 (1976): 1–17.

Miller, P. D. *Deuteronomy*. Interpretation: A Bible Commentary for Teaching and Preaching. Louisville, Ky.: John Knox, 1990.

Miscall, P. D. *1 Samuel: A Literary Reading*. ISBL. Bloomington: Indiana University Press, 1986.

Montgomery, J. A., and H. S. Gehman, eds. *A Critical and Exegetical Commentary on the Book of Kings*. ICC. Repr. 1986. Edinburgh: T. & T. Clark, 1950.

Moran, W. L. "The Ancient Near Eastern Background of Love of God in Deuteronomy." *CBQ* 25 (1963): 77–87.

Mowinckel, S. *Zur Komposition des Buches Jeremia*. Videnskapsselskapets skrifter II. Hist.-filos. Klasse. 1913, no. 5. Kristiania: Jacob Dywad, 1914.

Na'aman, N. "The Law of the Altar in Deuteronomy and the Cultic Site near Shechem." Pages 141–64 in *Rethinking the Foundations: Historiography in the Ancient World and in the Bible, Essays in Honour of John Van Seters*. Edited by S. L. McKenzie and T. C. Römer. BZAW 294. Berlin: de Gruyter, 2000.

Nelson, R. D. *Deuteronomy: A Commentary*. OTL. Louisville, Ky.: Westminster John Knox, 2002.

———. *The Double Redaction of the Deuteronomistic History*. JSOTSup 18. Sheffield: JSOT, 1981.

———. "The Double Redaction of the Deuteronomistic History: The Case is Still Compelling." *JSOT* 29 (2005): 319–37.

The New Oxford Annotated Bible. 3d ed. Oxford: Oxford University Press, 2001.

Nicholson, E. "The Centralisation of the Cult in Deuteronomy." *VT* 13 (1963): 380–89.

———. *Deuteronomy and Tradition*. Philadelphia: Fortress, 1967.

―――. *The Pentateuch in the Twentieth Century: The Legacy of Julius Wellhausen.* Oxford: Oxford University Press, 1998.

―――. "*Traditium* and *Traditio*: The Case of Deuteronomy 17:14–20." Pages 46–61 in *Scriptural Exegesis: The Shapes of Culture and the Religious Imagination: Essays in Honour of Michael Fishbane.* Edited by D. A. Green and L. S. Lieber. Oxford: Oxford University Press, 2009.

Niehr, H. "Die Reform des Joschija: Methodische, historische und religionsgeschichtliche Aspekte." Pages 33–55 in Gross, ed., *Jeremia und die "deuteronomistische Bewegung."*

Nihan, C. "The Holiness Code between D and Some Comments on the Function and Significance of Leviticus 17–26 in the Composition of the Torah." Pages 81–122 in Otto and Achenbach, eds., *Das Deuteronomium zwischen Pentateuch.*

―――. "The Torah between Samaria and Judah: Shechem and Gerizim in Deuteronomy and Joshua." Pages 187–223 in Knoppers and Levinson, eds., *The Pentateuch as Torah.*

Noll, K. "Deuteronomistic History or Deuteronomic Debate? (A Thought Experiment)." *JSOT* 31 (2007): 311–45.

Norin, S. "'Die Stätte, die der Herr erwählt.'" Pages 99–118 in *La Cité de Dieu: Die Stadt Gottes, 3: Symposium Strasbourg, Tübingen, Uppsala 19.–23. September 1998 in Tübingen.* Edited by M. Hengel et al. WUNT 129. Tübingen: Mohr Siebeck, 2000.

Noth, M. *The Chronicler's History.* JSOTSup 50. Sheffield: JSOT, 1987. Translation of *Überlieferungsgeschichtliche Studien*, pp. 111ff. 2d ed. Tübingen: Max Niemeyer, 1957.

―――. *The Deuteronomistic History.* JSOTSup 15. 2d ed. Sheffield: JSOT, 1991. Translation of *Überlieferungsgeschichtliche Studien*, pp. 1–110. 2d ed. Tübingen: Max Niemeyer, 1957.

―――. *Überlieferungsgeschichtliche Studien.* Schriften der Königsberger Gelehrten Gesellschaft. Geisteswissenschaftliche Klasse 18. Königsberg: Wissenschaftliche Buchgesellschaft, 1943.

O'Brien, M. A. "The Book of Deuteronomy." *CRBS* 3 (1995): 95–128.

―――. *The Deuteronomistic History Hypothesis: A Reassessment.* OBO 92. Freiburg: Universitätsverlag Freiburg, 1989.

―――. "Deuteronomy 16.18–18.22: Meeting the Challenge of Towns and Nations." *JSOT* 33 (2008): 155–72.

Oestreicher, Th. *Das Deuteronomistische Grundgesetz.* BFCT 27/4. Gutersloh: Gutersloher Verlagshaus, 1923.

―――. "Dnt 12.13f im Licht von Dtn 23.16f." *ZAW* NF 2 (1925): 246–49.

Otto, E. *Das Deuteronomium: Politische Theologie und Rechtsreform in Juda und Assyrien.* BZAW 284. Berlin: de Gruyter, 1999.

―――. "The Pentateuch in Synchronical and Diachronical Perspective: Protorabbinic Scribal Erudition Mediating Between Deuteronomy and the Priestly Code." Pages 14–35 in Otto and Achenbach, eds., *Das Deuteronomium zwischen Pentateuch.*

―――. "Scribal Scholarship in the Formation of Torah and Prophets: A Postexilic Scribal Debate between Priestly Scholarship and Literary Prophecy—The Example of the Book of Jeremiah and Its Relation to the Pentateuch." Pages 171–84 in Knoppers and Levinson, eds., *The Pentateuch as Torah.*

———. "Treueid und Gesetz: Die Ursprünge des Deuteronomiums im Horizont neuassyrischen Vertragsrechts." *ZABR* 2 (1996): 1–52.

———. "Von der Gerichtsordnung zum Verfassungsentwurf: Deuteronomische Gestaltung und deuteronomistische Interpretation im 'Ämtergesetz' Dtn 16,18–18,22." Pages 142–55 in *"Wer ist wie du, HERR, unter den Göttern?" Studien zur Theologie und Religionsgeschichte Israels, für Otto Kaiser zum 70. Geburtstag*. Edited by H.-M. Wahl et al. Göttingen: Vandenhoeck & Ruprecht, 1994.

Otto, E., and R. Achenbach, eds. *Das Deuteronomium zwischen Pentateuch und deuteronomistischem Geschichtswerk*. FRLANT 206. Göttingen: Vandenhoeck & Ruprecht, 2004.

Paton, L. B. "The Case for the Post-Exilic Origin of Deuteronomy.'" *JBL* 47 (1928): 322–57.

Paul, J. M. *Het Archimedisch Punt van de Pentateuchkritiek: Een historisch en exegetish Onderzoek naar de Verhouding van Deuteronomium en de Reformatie van Koning Josia (2 Kon. 22–23)*. 's-Gravenhage: Uitgeverij Boekencentrum B. V., 1988.

———. "Hilkiah and the Law (2 Kings 22) in the 17th and 18th Centuries: Some Influences on W. M. L. de Wette." Pages 9–12 in Lohfink, ed., *Das Deuteronomium*.

Person, R. F., Jr. *The Deuteronomic School: History, Social Setting, and Literature*. Studies in Biblical Literature 2. Atlanta: SBL, 2002.

Pfeiffer, R. H. *Introduction to the Old Testament*. New York: Harper & Brothers Publishers, 1941/48.

Polzin, R. M. *David and the Deuteronomist: A Literary Study of the Deuteronomic History: Part III, 2 Samuel*. ISBL. Bloomington: Indiana University Press, 1993.

———. *Moses and the Deuteronomist: A Literary Study of the Deuteronomic History, Part 1: Deuteronomy, Joshua, Judges*. New York: Seabury, 1980.

Preuss, H. D. *Deuteronomium*. EdF 164. Darmstadt: Wissenschaftliche Buchgesellschaft, 1982.

Propp, W. H. C. *Exodus 19–40: A New Translation with Introduction and Commentary*. AB 2A. New York: Doubleday, 2006.

Provan, I. W. *1 and 2 Kings*. New International Biblical Commentary. Peabody, Mass.: Hendrickson, 1995.

Pummer, R. "The Samaritans and Their Pentateuch." Pages 237–69 in Knoppers and Levinson, eds., *The Pentateuch as Torah*.

Pury, A. de, T. C. Römer, and J.-D. Macchi, eds. *Israel Constructs Its History: Deuteronomistic Historiography in Recent Research*. JSOTSup 306. Sheffield: Sheffield Academic, 2000.

Rad, G. Von. *Deuteronomy: A Commentary*. Translated by Dorothea Barton. OTL. Philadelphia: Westminster, 1966.

———. "Deuteronomy's 'Name Theology' and the Priestly Document's 'Kabod' Theology." Pages 37–44 in *Studies in Deuteronomy*.

———. *Studies in Deuteronomy*. SBT 9. London: SCM, 1953 (repr. 1963). Translated by D. Stalker from the German *Deuteronomium-Studien*. Rev. ed. Göttingen: Vandenhoeck & Ruprecht, 1948.

Rendtorff, R. *Das Alte Testament: Eine Einfürung*. Neukirchen–Vluyn: Neukirchener, 1993.

———. "Die Erwählung Israels als Thema der deuteronomischen Theologie." Pages 75–86 in Jeremias and Perlitt, eds., *Die Botschaft und die Boten*.

———. *The Problem of the Process of Transmission in the Pentateuch.* Translated by J. J. Scullion. JSOTSup 89. JSOT, 1980.

———. *Theologie des Alten Testaments: Ein kanonischer Entwurf.* 2 vols. Neukirchen–Vluyn: Neukirchener, 1999–2001.

———. *Das überlieferungsgeschichtliche Problem des Pentateuch.* BZAW 147. Berlin: de Gruyter, 1977.

Reuter, R. *Kultzentralization: Entstehung und Theologie von Dtn 12.* BBB 87. Frankfurt: Anton Hain, 1993.

Richardson, H. N. "The Historical Reliability of Chronicles." *JBR* 26 (1958): 9–12.

Richter, S. *The Deuteronomistic History and the Name Theology:* l'shakken shemo sham *in the Bible and the Ancient Near East.* BZAW 318. Berlin: de Gruyter, 2002.

Riley, W. *King and Cultus in Chronicles: Worship and the Reinterpretation of History.* JSOTSup 1993. Sheffield: JSOT, 1993.

Rofé, A. "The Strata of the Law about the Centralization of Worship in Deuteronomy and the History of the Deuteronomic Movement." Pages 221–26 in *Congress Volume: Uppsala 1971.* Edited by P. A. H. de Boer. VTSup, 22. Leiden: Brill, 1972.

Rogerson, J. W. *W. M. L. de Wette: Founder of Modern Biblical Criticism: An Intellectual Biography.* JSOTSup 126. Sheffield: JSOT, 1992.

Römer, T. C. "Cult Centralization in Deuteronomy 12: Between Deuteronomistic History and Pentateuch." Pages 153–67 in Otto and Achenbach, eds., *Das Deuteronomium zwischen Pentateuch.*

———. "Deuteronomium 34 zwischen Pentateuch, Hexateuch und deuteronomistischem Geschichtswerk." *ZABR* 5 (1999): 167–78.

———, ed. *The Future of the Deuteronomistic History.* BETL 147. Leuven: Peeters, 2000.

———. *The So-Called Deuteronomistic History: A Sociological, Historical and Literary Introduction.* London: T&T Clark International, 2005.

Römer, T. C., and A. de Pury, "Deuteronomistic Historiography (DH): History of Research and Debated Issues." Pages 24–141 in de Pury, Römer, and Macchi, eds., *Israel Constructs Its History.*

Rose, M. *Deuteronomist und Jahwist: Untersuchungen zu den Berührungspunkten beider Literaturwerke.* ATANT 67. Zurich: Theologischer Verlag, 1981.

Rösel, H. L. "Does a Comprehensive 'Leitmotiv' Exist in the Deuteronomistic History?" Pages 195–211 in Römer, ed., *The Future of the Deuteronomistic History.*

———. "Why 2 Kings 17 Does Not Constitute a Chapter of Reflection in the 'Deuteronomistic History.'" *JBL* 128 (2009): 85–90.

Rowley, H. H. "Hezekiah's Reform and Rebellion." *BJRL* 44 (1961): 395–431.

Rüterswörden, U. *Von der politischen Gemeinschaft zur Gemeinde: Studien zu Dt 16,18—18,22.* BBB 65. Frankfurt a.M.: Athenäum, 1987.

———. "Der Verfassungsentwurf des Deuteronomiums in der neueren Diskussion: Ein Überblick." Pages 313–28 in *Altes Testament: Forschung und Wirkung: Festschrift für Henning Graf Reventlow.* Edited by P. Mommer and W. Thiel. Frankfurt aM: Lang, 1994.

Schearing, L. S., and S. L. McKenzie, eds. *Those Elusive Deuteronomists: The Phenomenon of Pan-Deuteronomism.* JSOTSup 268. Sheffield: Sheffield Academic, 1999.

Schley, D. G. *Shiloh: A Biblical City and Tradition and History.* JSOTSup 63. Sheffield: JSOT, 1989.

Schmid, H. H. *Der sogenannte Jahwist: Beobachtungen und Fragen zur Pentateuchforschung.* Zurich: Theologischer Verlag, 1976.

Schmid, K. "Buchtechnische und sachliche Prolegomena zur Enneateuchfrage." Pages 1–14 in Beck and Schorn, eds., *Auf dem Weg zur Endgestalt.*

Schmidt, W. H. "Die deuteronomistische Redaktion des Amosbuches: Zu den theologischen Unterschieden zwischen dem Prophetenwort und dem Sammler." *ZAW* 77 (1965): 168–93.

Schmitt, H.-C. "Dtn 34 als Verbindungsstück zwischen Tetrateuch und deuteronomistischen Geschichtswerk." Pages 180–92 in Otto and Achenbach, eds., *Das Deuteronomium zwischen Pentateuch.*

———. "Das Spätdeuteronomistische Geschichtwerk Genesis I—II Regnum XXV und seine theologische Intention." Pages 277–94 in *Theologie in Prophetie und Pentateuch: Gesammelte Schriften.* Edited by U. Schorn and M. Bütt. BZAW 310. Berlin: de Gruyter, 2001.

Shedletsky, L. "Josiah's Reform and the Dynamics of Defilement: A Phenomenological Approach to 2 Kings 23." Ph.D. diss., New York University, 2004.

Smend, R. *From Astruc to Zimmerli: Old Testament Scholarship in Three Centuries.* Translated by Margaret Kohl. Tübingen: Mohr Siebeck, 2007.

———. "Das Gesetz und die Völker: Ein Beitrag zur deuteronomistischen Redaktionsgeschichte." Pages 494–509 in *Probleme biblischer Theologie: G. von Rad zum 70. Geburtstag.* Edited by H. W. Wolff. Munich: Chr. Kaiser, 1971.

———. *Wilhelm Martin Leberecht de Wettes Arbeit am Alten und am Neuen Testament.* Basel: Helbing & Lichtenhahn, 1958.

Smyth, F. "When Josiah Has Done His Work or the King is Properly Buried: A Synchronic Reading of 2 Kings 22.1–23.28." Pages 343–58 in de Pury, Römer, and Macchi, eds., *Israel Constructs Its History.*

Soggin, J. A. *Introduction to the Old Testament: From Its Origins to the Closing of the Alexandrian Canon.* Translated by J. Bowden. Rev. ed. OTL. Philadelphia: Westminster, 1977.

Stackert, J. *Rewriting the Torah: Literary Revision in Deuteronomy and the Holiness Code.* FAT 52; Tübingen: Mohr Siebeck, 2007.

Staerk, W. *Das Deuteronomium: Sein Inhalt und seine literarische Form: Eine kritische Studie.* Leipzig: Hinrichs, 1894.

Steuernagel, C. *Der Rahmen des Deuteronomiums: Literar-kritische Untersuchung über seine Zusammensetzung und Entstehung.* Halle: Wischan & Wettengel, 1894.

Stott, K. "Finding the Lost Book of the Law: Re-reading the Story of 'The Book of the Law' (Deuteronomy–2 Kings) in Light of Classical Literature." *JSOT* 30 (2005): 153–69.

Suzuki, Y. "Deuteronomic Reformation in View of the Centralization of the Administration of Justice." *Annual of the Japanese Biblical Institute* 13 (1987): 22–58.

Sweeney, M. A. *I & II Kings: A Commentary.* OTL. Louisville, Ky.: Westminster John Knox, 2007.

———. "The Critique of Solomon in the Josianic Edition of the Deuteronomistic History," *JBL* 114 (1995): 607–22.

Thelle, R. I. *Ask God: Divine Consultation in the Literature of the Hebrew Bible.* BET 30. Frankfurt a.M.: Lang, 2002.

———. "Babylon in the Book of Jeremiah (MT): Negotiating a Power Shift." Pages 187–232 in *Prophecy in the Book of Jeremiah.* Edited by H. M. Barstad and R. G. Kratz. BZAW 388. Berlin: de Gruyter, 2009.

Thiel, W. *Die deuteronomistische Redaktion von Jeremia 1–25.* WMANT 41. Neukirchen–Vluyn: Neukirchener, 1973.

———. *Die deuteronomistische Redaktion von Jeremia 26–52.* WMANT 52. Neukirchen–Vluyn: Neukirchener, 1981.

Toorn, K. van der. "Cult Prostitution." *ABD* 1:510–13.

Uehlinger, Chr. "Was there a Cult Reform under King Josiah?" Pages 279–316 in Grabbe, ed., *Good Kings and Bad Kings.*

Van Seters, J. *Abraham in History and Tradition.* New Haven: Yale University Press, 1975.

———. "The Altar Law of Ex 20,24–26 in Critical Debate." Pages 157–74 in Beck and Schorn, eds., *Auf dem Weg zur Endgestalt.*

———. "The Formula *l^ešakkēn š^emô šām* and the Centralisation of Worship in Deuteronomy and DH." *JNSL* 30, no. 2 (2004): 1–18.

———. "The Future of the Deuteronomistic History: Can It Avoid Death by Redaction?" Pages 213–22 in Römer, ed., *The Future of the Deuteronomistic History.*

———. *In Search of History: Historiography in the Ancient World and the Origins of Biblical History.* New Haven: Yale University Press, 1983.

———. *A Law Book for the Diaspora.* Oxford: Oxford University Press, 2003.

Vaux, R. de. "Le lieu que Yahvé a choisi pour y établir son nom." Pages 219–28 in *Das Ferne und Nahe Wort: Festschrift Leonard Rost zur vollendung Seines 70. Lebensjahres...* Edited by R. Maas. Berlin: Töpelmann, 1967.

Veijola, T. "Deuteronomismusforschung zwischen Tradition und Innovation (I)." *ThR* 67 (2002): 273–327.

———. "Deuteronomismusforschung zwischen Tradition und Innovation (II)." *ThR* 67 (2002): 391–424.

———. "Deuteronomismusforschung zwischen Tradition und Innovation (III)." *ThR* 68 (2003): 1–44.

———. *Die ewige Dynastie: David und die Enstehung seiner Dynastie nach der deuteronomistischen Darstellung.* Toimituksia - Suomalaisen Tiedeakatemian, Annales Academiae Scientiarum Fennicae : Sarja-Ser. B, 193. Helsinki: Suomaleinen Tiedeakatemia, 1975.

———. "The History of the Passover in the Light of Deuteronomy 16,1–8." *ZABR* 2 (1996): 53–75.

Vogt, P. T. *Deuteronomic Theology and the Significance of Torah: A Reappraisal.* Winona Lake: Eisenbrauns, 2006.

Watts, J. W., *Reading Law: The Rhetorical Shaping of the Pentateuch.* The Biblical Seminar 59. Sheffield: Sheffield Academic, 1999.

———. "Rhetorical Strategy in the Composition of the Pentateuch." *JSOT* 68 (1995): 3–22.

Weinfeld, M. "Cult Centralization in Israel in the Light of a Neo-Babylonian Analogy." *JNES* 23 (1964): 202–12.

———. "Deuteronomy—The Present State of the Inquiry." *JBL* 86 (1967): 249–62.

———. *Deuteronomy 1–11: A New Translation with Introduction and Commentary.* AB 5. New York: Doubleday, 1991.

———. *Deuteronomy and the Deuteronomic School.* Oxford: Oxford University Press, 1972. Repr., Winona Lake, Ind.: Eisenbrauns, 1992.

———. "Deuteronomy's Theological Revolution." *BR* 12 (1996): 38–41, 44–45.

———. "On 'Demythologization and Secularization' in Deuteronomy." *IEJ* 23 (1973): 230–33.

———. "Pentateuch." Columns 232–63 in *Encyclopedia Judaica*, vol. 13. New York: Macmillan, 1971–1972.

Weippert, H. "'Den Ort, den Jahwe erwählen wird, um dort seinen Nahmen wohnen zu lassen': Die Geschichte einer alttestamentlichen Formel." *BZ* 24 (1980): 76–94.

———. "Das deuteronomistische Geschichtswerk: Sein Ziel und Ende in der neueren Forschung." *ThR* 50 (1985): 213–49.

———. "Die 'deuteronomistischen' Beurteilungen der Könige von Israel und Juda und das Problem der Redaktion der Königsbücher." *Bib* 53 (1972): 301–39.

Weiser, A. *Einleitung in das Alte Testament.* 6th improved ed. Göttingen: Vandenhoeck & Ruprecht, 1966.

Welch, A. C. *The Code of Deuteronomy: A New Theory of Its Origin.* London: J. Clarke, 1924.

———. "When Was the Worship of Israel Centralised at the Temple?" *ZAW* NF 2 (1925): 250–55.

Wellhausen, J. *Prolegomena zur Geschichte Israels.* 6th ed. Berlin: Druck und Verlag von G. Reimer, 1905.

Wenham, G. J. "The Date of Deuteronomy—Linchpin of Old Testament Criticism. Part One." *Them* 10, no. 3 (1985): 15–20.

———. "The Date of Deuteronomy—Linchpin of Old Testament Criticism. Part Two." *Them* 11, no. 1 (1985): 15–18.

———. "Deuteronomy and the Central Sanctuary." *TynBul* (1971): 103–18.

Westermann, C. *Die Geschichtsbücher des Alten Testaments: Gab es ein deuteronomistisches Geschichtswerk?* Theologische Bücherei 87. Altes Testament. Gütersloh: Kaiser Gütersloher Verlagshaus, 1994.

Weyde, K. W. *The Appointed Festivals of YHWH.* FAT 2/4. Tübingen: Mohr Siebeck, 2004.

Whybray, R. N. *The Making of the Pentateuch: A Methodological Study.* JSOTSup 53. Sheffield: JSOT, 1987. Repr. 1994.

Willis, T. M. *The Elders of the City: A Study of the Elders-Laws in Deuteronomy.* SBLMS 55. Atlanta: SBL, 2001.

Wilson, I. *Out of the Midst of the Fire: Divine Presence in Deuteronomy.* Atlanta: Scholars Press, 1995.

Wilson, R. R. "Israel's Judicial System in the Preexilic Period." *JQR* 74 (1983): 229–48.

———. "Who Was the Deuteronomist? (Who Was Not the Deuteronomist?): Reflections on Pan-Deuteronomism." Pages 64–82 in Schearing and McKenzie, eds., *Those Elusive Deuteronomists.*

Wissman, F. Blanco. *"Er tat das Rechte--": Beurteilungskriterien und Deuteronomismus in 1 Kön 12—2 Kön 25.* ATANT 93. Zurich: Theologischer Verlag, 2008.

Witte, M. et al. eds. *Die deuteronomistische Geschichtswerke: Redaktions- und religionsgeschichtliche Perspektiven zur "Deuteronomismus"-Diskussion in Tora und Forderen Propheten.* BZAW 365. Berlin: de Gruyter, 2006.

Wolff, H. W. *Joel und Amos.* BKAT 14 Neukirchen–Vluyn: Neukirchener, 1985.

Würthwein, E. *Die Bücher der Könige 1.Kön. 17–2.Kön. 25.* ATD 11/2. Göttingen: Vandenhoeck & Ruprecht, 1984.

———. "Die josianische Reform und das Deuteronomium." *ZAW* 73 (1976): 395–423.

———. "Erwägungen zum sog. deuteronomistischen Geschichtswerk: Eine Skizze." Pages 1–11 in *Studien zum deuteronomistischen Geschichtswerk*. Edited by E. Würthwein. BZAW 227. Berlin: de Gruyter, 1994.

Younger, K. L. *Ancient Conquest Accounts: A Study in Ancient Near Eastern and Biblical History Writing*. JSOTSup 98. Sheffield: JSOT, 1990.

INDEXES

INDEX OF REFERENCES

HEBREW BIBLE/
OLD TESTAMENT

Genesis
4	99
8:20	99
12:6	115
12:7	100
12:8	100
13:4	100
22	100
25:8	138
28:18–22	100, 118
31:44–54	100
33:18–20	115
33:18	116
35:29	138
49:29	139
50:25	116

Exodus
2	113
12–15	114
12–13	158, 159
12	109, 159, 164, 166
12:6	159
12:7	159
12:25	60
13:11	60
13:19	116
15:17	97
17:8–16	177
19:4–5	171
20	102, 106, 111, 112
20:1	178
20:8–11	110, 112
20:22–23:19	104
20:23–26	104
20:24–26	104, 105
20:24	105, 106
23:12	110, 112
23:14–19	104
23:14–17	109, 112, 157
23:23–24	111
23:25	111
24	101
24:1–11	104
24:4	101
24:7	156
25–40	25, 55, 66, 97, 106, 110, 127
25–31	98, 110, 125
25–27	97
25:8–9	97
25:8	97
25:16	106
26:1–14	98
27:1–8	105
28–29	98
29	100
29:46	178
31:11	101
31:12–17	110, 112
32	111, 153
32:20	147
33	98, 100
33:7–11	98
34	117
34:11–26	109
34:11–16	104
34:12–16	111
34:13	101
34:18–26	157
34:21	110, 112
35–40	98, 125
35	110
35:2–3	110, 112
36–38	97
36:8–19	98
38:1–7	105
39:1–31	98
40	98, 99, 108
40:2	98
40:6	98
40:18–19	98
40:19	98
40:20	106

Leviticus
1–7	66, 98, 108, 112
1	100
3–5	100
4	99, 109
7–9	100
8–9	99
8	99
8:6	108
9	99
9:23	108
11–26	98
11–15	108, 109
14	152
14:34	60

Index of References

17–26	22, 145, 152, 157	6	110	31:47	99
17	108	7:1	99	32	71
19:3	110	7:6–8	99	32:6–27	114
19:4	111	8	99	33	146
19:5–8	108	9	112, 160, 164	33:50–56	111, 117
19:11–13	108			33:51–53	145
19:23–25	109	9:1–15	158	33:52	145
19:23	60	9:1–14	109		
19:34	178	9:15	99	*Deuteronomy*	
19:36	178	10	55, 108	1:1–5	112
20:2–8	108	10:17	99	2–3	66
20:22–26	111	10:21	99	3:20	70
21–22	108	10:33–36	106	3:28	100
21:1–12	99	11	98	4–11	178
22:31–33	178	11:16–17	98	4–7	66
23	109, 111, 112, 160	11:24–26	98	4	175, 179
		12	98, 177	4:1–2	60
		12:1–8	98	4:5–6	60
23:3	110	14:44	106	4:9	60
23:4–8	158	15:1–31	108	4:15–28	111
23:40	67	15:2	60	4:15–24	175
23:43	178	15:18	60	4:20	175
24:46	112	15:41	178	4:25–31	175
25	108	16	99, 108	4:28	137
25:2	60	16:5	170	4:37–38	171, 172
25:38	178	16:7	170	4:37	175
25:55	178	17	99	4:40	60
26	112, 157	17:20	170	4:44–45	103
26:3–46	145	18	99	5:1	60, 103
26:11–13	178	19	108, 109, 152	5:6–10	111
26:13	178			5:6	178
26:30–33	145	19:13	99	5:12–15	110, 112
26:30	145	19:20	99	5:15	176
26:45	178	21:2	110	5:31–33	60
27	110	21:28	143	6	176
27:32	109	25	111	6:1–3	60
		26:31–32	116	6:6	60
Numbers		27:18–23	100	6:12	176
2	55	28–29	108	6:17	60
3:5–10	99	28:9–10	110	6:20–25	176
3:11–13	99	28:11–15	110	6:24–25	60
3:14–39	99	28:16–25	109, 158, 160	7	68, 111, 145, 146, 172, 176, 179, 180, 185
3:25	98				
3:44–50	99	28:29	109		
4	55	30	110		
4:1–49	99	31	106		
5:5–10	108	31:30	99	7:1–5	145, 173

Index of References

Deuteronomy (cont.)		12	16, 20, 24, 31, 32, 38, 39, 43, 54–60, 63, 65, 67, 69, 71, 73, 75, 76, 78–80, 85, 93, 111, 114, 129, 130, 143–46, 150, 152, 154–more-159, 166, 167, 173, 179, 180, 185, 199, 204	12:5	1, 27, 34–37, 65
7:5	101, 104, 143			12:6	65, 71, 103
7:6–16	173			12:7	66, 67, 72
7:6–7	172			12:8–12	68, 72, 76, 79
7:6	173			12:8–11	68, 179
7:7–8	180			12:8–9	68, 69
7:11	60			12:8	68, 75, 78, 180
7:12	143			12:9	76
7:13	143			12:10–14	59
7:17–26	173			12:10	69–71, 76, 85
8:1	60			12:11	1, 27, 36, 38, 57, 71
8:10	70				
8:11–20	176				
8:11	60				
8:14–16	176			12:12	67, 72, 75, 181
8:19–20	60, 176				
9	111, 153	12		12:13–28	72
9:21	147			12:13–19	73–75, 77, 79
9:23	70				
10	107, 179			12:13–18	73, 100
10:6–9	107				
10:8	107	12:1–16:17	30	12:13–14	73, 75, 76
10:12–13	60	12:1–7	60	12:13	13, 75, 180
10:15	173	12:1–3	151		
11	102, 176	12:1	61, 63, 76, 103	12:14	1, 27, 29, 34, 35, 57, 73
11:1	60				
11:4	145	12:2–7	65, 67, 68, 76	12:15–16	74, 76, 77
11:8	60				
11:13	60	12:2–3	62–67, 70, 79, 101, 111, 143	12:17–19	74
11:22	60			12:17–18	59, 76
11:26–28	60			12:17	75
11:29–30	101				
11:29	103	12:2	61, 62, 145	12:18	1, 27, 31, 57, 67
11:30–31	59				
11:31–12:1	60	12:3	65, 101, 104	12:19	73
11:31–32	59			12:20–28	76, 77
11:31	59, 69, 76	12:4–7	59, 64, 72, 79, 180	12:20–27	73, 79
11:32	197			12:20	76
12–26	30, 31, 59, 95, 101, 103, 110, 116, 130, 131, 171, 176, 197			12:21–25	77
		12:4–6	66	12:21	1, 27, 36, 37, 57, 59, 76–78
		12:4	57, 63, 64, 68, 75, 111		
				12:22–25	77, 78
		12:5–28	180	12:23–24	78
		12:5–7	64, 67, 68	12:26–27	59, 77
12–16	31, 146	12:5–6	65		

12:26	1, 27, 31, 57, 78	16:7	1, 27, 32	24:9	177		
		16:8	160	24:18	177		
12:27	40, 55, 66, 77, 100	16:9–12	57	24:22	177		
		16:11	1, 27, 39, 67	25:17–19	177		
				25:19	71		
12:28	78, 180	16:12	177	26	39, 103		
12:29–32	67	16:13–15	57	26:1–15	108		
12:29–31	78	16:14	67	26:1–2	57, 66, 75		
12:29	78	16:15	1, 27, 32, 67	26:1	60		
12:31–32	180			26:2	1, 27, 39		
13:6	177	16:16–17	57	26:3–4	108		
13:11	177	16:16	1, 27, 32	26:3	33, 96		
14	38, 39, 54, 57, 109, 154, 166	16:18–18:22	197, 202	26:5–11	177		
		16:21–22	66, 100, 101	26:8	177		
				26:10	177		
		17	25, 39, 125	26:11	67		
14:2	173, 174			26:17–19	103		
14:22–26	57, 75	17:1	108	27	29, 41, 101–104		
14:23	1, 27, 38	17:8–10	32, 33, 57				
14:24–25	109	17:8	1, 27	27:1–8	29, 102		
14:24	1, 27, 36, 38	17:10	1, 27	27:2–4	101		
		17:14–20	197, 199–202	27:2–3	101		
14:25	1, 27, 31			27:5–8	82		
14:26	67	17:14	60	27:5–7	101		
15	30, 39	17:15	181	27:7	67		
15:15	177	17:16	177	27:11–26	101		
15:19–20	57, 66, 75	17:17–18:22	30	27:15	137		
15:20	1, 27, 31	17:18	135	28	112, 131		
15:21–23	74, 108	17:19	139	28:9	174		
16	25, 32, 38, 39, 43, 57, 145, 154, 155, 158, 159, 164–67	18	39	28:11–26	115		
		18:5	35, 181	28:20	136		
		18:6–7	57	28:58	135		
		18:6	1, 27, 33	28:61	135		
		18:9	60	28:69	103		
		18:10–11	124	29	137, 138, 155		
		18:10	108				
16:1–17	109, 112	19–26	178	29:13	103		
16:1–8	160	19:1–13	30	29:18	103		
16:1–7	57, 158	19:15–20	30	29:20–21	137		
16:1	158, 159, 177	20	30, 111, 115, 198	29:20	35, 135		
				29:21	135, 157		
16:2	1, 27, 38	20:1	177	29:24	136		
16:3	177	21:1–9	30	29:25–27	137		
16:4	158, 159	21:5	181	29:27	135		
16:5	159	21:10–25:19	30	29:29	137		
16:6	1, 27, 39, 158, 159	22–23	25	30:10	135		
		23:17	171	30:19	171		

Deuteronomy (cont.)		18:1	41, 115, 116	8:33	119, 120
31	39			8:34–35	119
31:9–13	113	18:28	82	9	116, 120
31:9	107	20:7	116	9:3	187
31:10–11	57, 139	21:21	116	9:18	187
31:11	1, 27, 30, 31, 33	22	116, 117, 127	9:27	120
				9:46	120
31:14–15	100	22:19	97, 117	9:56	120
31:19	113	23:1–16	116	10:6–16	119, 136
31:21	113	23:6	135	11:1–12:7	120
31:24	113, 135	24	140	13–16	120
31:26	135	24:16–18	178	13:4–7	110
31:29	137	24:16	136	13:15–23	120
32–33	143	24:20	136	16:17	110
33:10	109, 112	24:26	97, 101, 135	17–21	187
33:18	67			17–18	120, 121
		24:32	116, 139	17:6	187
				17:7–13	120
Joshua		*Judges*		18:1	187
1–3	115	1	127	18:31	120
1:8	135	1:1	121	19	121, 122
1:15	71	1:7	82	19:1	187
2:10	178	1:8	82	19:10	82
3–4	107	1:21	82	20	121
4	82, 101, 114, 123	2:1–5	117	20:1	121
		2:1	178	20:18	121
5:11	161	2:3	119	20:27	121
6–12	115	2:6	118	20:37	121
6–8	115	2:12	136	20:47	121
6	107	2:13	136	20:48	121
7	115	2:20–3:6	127	21:2–4	121
8	41, 101, 107, 115	3:7	118, 119	21:5–12	121
		4:5	118	21:13–14	121
8:30–35	82, 101, 115	6	118	21:25	187
		6:8	178		
8:31	135	6:11–24	118	*1 Samuel*	
8:34	135	6:13	178	1–14	115
9–12	115	6:25–32	118	1:7	122
9:23	115	6:25–30	126	1:11	110
9:27	27, 40, 41, 82, 115, 117, 179	6:34	119	1:21	122
		7:15	119	1:22	110
		7:19–23	119	2:19	122
		7:22–23	119	2:27–36	122
15:8	82	7:24–27	119	2:28	35, 182
15:63	82	8:22–23	187	2:30	122
17:7	116	8:29–32	119	2:35	122
18–21	115	8:33–35	119	4–7	123

4–6	107, 184	16–31	124	10:14	87		
4:18	123	16:6–13	182	11:1	87		
5:5	87	17:54	82	11:12	87		
6:14–15	123	22:17–19	88	11:27	194		
7	123	28	88, 124	12:31	87		
7:1	123			14:23	87		
7:3–4	123	2 Samuel		14:28	87		
7:5–6	123	1:19	143	15	107		
7:8–10	123	1:25	143	15:7–10	124		
7:8	123	2:4	124	15:8	87		
7:12	123	3:18	191	15:11	87		
7:17	123	5	82, 83, 87	15:12	124		
8–12	123, 187, 190, 194, 196, 199	5:2	191	15:14	87		
		5:5	83, 86, 87, 91	15:24–29	124		
				15:29	87		
8	187, 193, 198	5:6–10	83	15:37	87		
		5:6	83, 87	16:3	87		
8:4–6	123	5:7	83	16:15	87		
8:7–9	188	5:8	83	17:20	87		
8:11–18	188	5:9	83, 84	19:20	87		
8:11–17	188, 189	5:11	87	19:26	87		
8:20	188	5:13	83	19:34	87		
9	123	6	82, 83, 86, 88, 107, 184	19:35	87		
9:16–17	188			20:2	87		
9:17	188			20:3	87		
10:5	123	6:12–19	124	20:7	87		
10:8	123	6:17	87	20:22	87		
10:9	123	6:21	182	21:16–17	124		
10:16	189	7	35, 49, 82, 85, 86, 88–91, 124, 187, 190, 191, 196	22:34	143		
10:17–27	123			24	184		
10:18	178			24:8	87		
10:19	189			24:16	87		
10:24	182, 189						
10:27	189			1 Kings			
11	189	7:1	86	1–2	15, 194		
11:12–15	190	7:2	83	1:10–12	194		
12:19	190	7:3	86	1:33	194		
13–15	123	7:4–16	85	2:3	135, 196		
13:8–15	87	7:5–16	86	2:10	83, 84		
13:8–14	123	7:10	85	2:11	91		
14:3	87	7:18–29	86	3–11	84		
14:18	87	8–24	82	3	143		
14:31–34	123	8–20	93, 124	3:1	92		
14:37	87	8	87	3:2–3	52		
14:51	87	8:7	87	3:2	143		
15	87, 122	9:13	87	3:4	52		
15:15–30	123	10–20	15	3:8	184		

Index of References   233

1 Kings (cont.)

3:10	195	9:24	84	14:13	195		
3:15	92	10:2	92	14:15	126		
4	194	10:26	92	14:21–24	126		
5–8	94	10:27	92	14:21	27, 35, 42, 44, 45, 90, 91, 144		
5–7	192	11–14	115				
5:1–6:37	89	11	35, 41, 43, 47, 52, 54, 89–91				
5:3–5	49, 50, 70			14:22–23	144		
5:3–4	85			14:25	92		
5:3	70	11:2	149	14:30	92		
5:13–18	192	11:6	195	15:2	91		
6–8	25	11:7	143, 149	15:3	194		
6–7	125	11:12	191	15:4–5	191		
6:1	48	11:13	27, 42–44, 90	15:4	195		
6:12–13	50, 191			15:5	194		
8	43, 45, 47–49, 52, 89–91, 108, 125, 129	11:27	84	15:6	92		
		11:31–39	44	15:7	92		
		11:31–32	43	15:10	91		
		11:32	27, 35, 42, 44, 45, 90, 191	15:11	194		
				15:13	126		
8:1	84, 92, 107			15:14	144		
				15:23	193		
8:15–21	89, 90	11:33	136, 195	15:44	144		
8:15–16	48, 50	11:34–36	44	16:2–4	191		
8:16	27, 35, 44, 51, 89, 182	11:36	27, 42, 44, 90	16:7	137, 138		
				16:24	193		
		11:37–38	44	16:30	195		
8:17	48	11:38	194	18	125		
8:20	191	11:39	44	18:18	137, 138		
8:22–54	48	11:40	44	18:19	126		
8:22–53	51	11:41–43	195	19:10	137		
8:23–53	51	11:42	91	19:14	137		
8:23	49	12–13	125	20	193		
8:25	191	12	116	21:20–24	191		
8:44–45	50	12:4	193	21:20	195		
8:44	27	12:25–13:33	151	21:25	195		
8:48–49	50	12:25	193	22	193, 202		
8:48	27	12:26–33	192	22:42	91		
8:56–61	51	13	143, 150, 153, 193	22:43	194		
9	193			22:44	144		
9:2–9	191	13:2	143				
9:3	53	14	42	*2 Kings*			
9:6–9	136, 138	14:7–16	126, 138	3	147		
9:15–22	192	14:7–14	191	8:17	91		
9:15	92	14:8	194	8:19	191		
9:19	92	14:9–10	138	8:26	91		

9–10	162	17:37	135	22:1	91
10:18–27	150	18–20	55, 193	22:2	199
10:28–31	195	18	92, 162	22:3–7	134, 193
10:31	135	18:1–12	114	22:3	141
11:17–19	150	18:2	91	22:8–10	9, 135
12	135, 162, 192	18:3–8	196	22:8	4, 131, 135, 162
		18:4	126, 141, 144		
12:2–3	192, 195			22:11	135
12:2	91	18:5	196	22:12	141
12:4–8	193	18:6	135	22:14–20	136
12:4	144	18:17	92	22:17	136
12:18–19	92	19	92	22:20	138
13:12	92	19:18	137	23	19, 47, 91, 126, 129, 130, 136, 139, 142, 146, 151, 152, 163
14:2	91	19:34	191		
14:3–4	192	20:6	191		
14:3	194, 195	20:20	193		
14:4	144	21	42, 45, 210		
14:6	135				
14:7	92	21:1	91		
14:8–14	92	21:2–9	195	23:1–3	139, 140
14:13	92	21:3–9	46	23:1	141
15:2	91	21:3	126, 144	23:2	156
15:3–4	192	21:4	46	23:3	125, 140
15:3	195	21:5	149	23:4–20	92, 140, 146, 152, 153, 166
15:4	144	21:7–8	44, 45, 90		
15:16–17	92	21:7	27, 35, 44, 46, 126	23:4–14	141, 150–52
15:33	91				
15:34–35	192				
15:34	195	21:11–15	46	23:4	141, 149
15:35	144	21:19–26	137	23:5	143, 148
16	192	21:19	91	23:6	141, 146, 147, 149
16:2–4	144	22–23	7, 9, 10, 55, 114, 128–30, 133, 134, 137, 141, 146, 151, 154, 162, 165–69, 202, 206, 207		
16:2	91, 194			23:8	143, 148
16:5	92			23:9	148
16:10–18	162			23:10	143, 148
16:17–18	192			23:12	141
17	144, 199			23:13–14	143
17:9	144			23:13	143, 148, 149
17:10	126				
17:11	144			23:15–20	144, 150, 151
17:13	135				
17:16	126, 137	22	5, 125, 129, 130, 132, 134, 136, 137, 141, 146, 202	23:15	143, 150
17:20	184			23:16–20	150
17:29	144			23:16–17	151
17:32	144			23:16	143, 148
17:34	135			23:19	143

2 Kings (cont.)

23:20	148
23:21–23	140, 153, 155, 156, 162
23:21–22	156
23:21	141
23:22	156, 161
23:25	196, 199
23:26	210
23:27	27, 42, 44, 47, 91, 165, 167, 184
23:31	91
23:36	91
24:3–4	210
24:8	91
24:10	92
24:14	92
24:15	92
24:18	91
25:1	92
25:8	92
25:9	92

1 Chronicles

9:17–32	156
9:22	156
10:13–14	124
13	107
15–16	107
17:1	85
21	88
22:1	88
22:19	97
28:10	97

2 Chronicles

3:1	88, 89
5–6	107
6:5	27
6:6	27, 89
6:34	27
6:38	27
7:1	108
7:12–16	53
7:12	27, 53
7:16	27, 53
12:13	27, 42, 44, 53
20:6	97
26:18	97
28:25	136
29–31	10
29:21	97
30:1–26	161
30:8	97
31:1	145
33:1–8	47
33:7	27, 44
33:12–20	47
34:14	156
34:15	156
34:30	156
35	154, 163, 165, 166
35:2–6	162
35:4	156, 163
35:6	157, 162, 163
35:7–9	163
35:10	163
35:12	157, 162
35:17	157
35:18	156, 164
35:30	156
36:17	98

Nehemiah

1:9	179
8–9	140
8:2	140

Psalms

33:12	184
60:6	116
78	115
78:54–55	97
78:59–60	97
78:60	179
78:67–72	97
78:67–71	179, 183
78:67	184
78:68	184
78:70	184
108:7	116
132	48, 59
132:11–14	183
132:13	179
135:4	185
135:21	185

Isaiah

2:8	137
14:1	184
30:22	148
37:19	137
40–55	172
41:8	184
41:9	184
43:10	184
44:1	184
44:2	184
49:7	184

Jeremiah

1:16	136, 137
7	59, 115
7:12	179
15:4	210
19:4	136
25:6	137
25:7	137
26	115, 179
32:30	137
33:24–26	184
41	115
44:5	136
44:8	136, 137
44:15	136

Ezekiel

5:11	148
6:3–5	148
8–9	148
9:7	148
40–48	125, 127

Hosea
10:5   142
14:4   137

Micah
5:12   137

Zephaniah
1:4   142

OTHER SOURCES
Josephus
Antiquities
4.305 102

INDEX OF AUTHORS

Albertz, R. 9, 19, 130
Albright, W. F. 10
Assis, E. 117
Auld, A. G. 19, 29, 165
Aurelius, E. 16

Barker, P. A. 102
Barrick, B. 131, 141, 150
Barstad, H. M. 11, 147
Baumgartner, W. 7
Begg, C. T. 63
Ben Dov, J. 136
Ben Zvi, E. 17, 138, 186
Berry, G. R. 7, 132
Blum, E. 16, 17
Botha, P. J. 196
Braulik, G. 58
Brewer, J. A. 7
Budde, K. 6

Campbell, A. F. 83
Caquot, A. 186
Carrière, J.-M. 186
Caton, J. E. 142
Childs, B. S. 6, 19
Clements, R. E. 8, 17, 18, 155, 174, 193
Cogan, M. 131, 134, 155
Coggins, R. 19
Conroy, C. 130
Cooper, A. 157
Cross, F. M. 14

Dahl, G. 7
Davies, P. R. 8, 133
De Wette, W. M. L. 3
Dietrich, W. 15
Dozeman, T. B. 17
Driver, S. R. 4, 6, 11, 96
Duhm, B. 11

Edelman, D. 10
Engnell, I. 12
Eissfeldt, O. 5, 11, 13, 15

Eslinger, L. M. 86, 190
Eynikel, E. 10, 19, 133, 162

Fensham, F. C. 147
Finkelstein, I. 10
Fohrer, G. 11, 13, 14
Frankena, R. 7
Fretheim, T. E. 132, 155
Fried, L. E. 131
Fritz, V. 98

García López, F. 16
Gehman, H. S. 5, 155
Geiger, M. 112
Geoghegan, J. C. 19
Goldstein, B. R. 157
Goodfriend, E. A. 147
Gos, B. 186
Graham, M. 165
Gray, J. 131, 155
Gunn, D. M. 87, 194

Halpern, B. 29, 34, 73, 186
Handy, L. K. 9, 10, 131
Hardmeier, C. 131
Hauge, M. R. 98, 125
Hertzberg, H. W. 88
Hjelm, I. 20, 103
Hobbs, T. R. 132, 134, 155, 162
Hoffmann, H. D. 141, 142, 147, 162
Hollenstein, H. 153
Hölscher, G. 7
Hoppe, L. J. 167
Houtman, C. 7
Hurowitz, V. 125

Jepsen, A. 12, 13
Jones, G. H. 132, 134, 155
Junker, H. 183

Kaiser, O. 16, 17, 200
Kaminsky, J. S. 170, 172, 175
Kapelrud, A. S. 125

Kartveit, M. 102
Kaufman, S. A. 58
Keller, M. 36
Knauf, E. A. 8, 19
Knoppers, G. N. 14, 167, 186, 198–203
Knowles, M. D. 184
Koch, K. 182
Körting, C. 184
Kratz, R. G. 8, 11, 16, 133

Lasine, S. 121, 126, 151
Lenchak, T. A. 58
Levenson, J. 184
Levin, C. 104, 131
Levinson, B. M. 1, 20, 33, 104, 105, 111, 157–59, 161, 186, 201, 202
Lieberman, S. 10
Lohfink, N. F. 8, 10, 19, 28, 67, 73, 132, 133, 141, 162, 174, 197
Long, B. O. 134, 138
Lundbom, J. R. 132

Mayes, A. D. H. 174
McCarter, P. K. 83, 85, 86
McConville, J. G. 13, 34, 59, 113, 159, 186
McKenzie, S. L. 15, 19, 190
Mettinger, T. N. D. 36
Milgrom, J. 36, 74, 106
Millar, J. G. 34, 113
Miller, P. D. 175
Miscall, P. D. 122, 194
Montgomery, J. A. 5
Moran, W. L. 12, 175
Mowinckel, S. 18

Na'aman, N. 1, 29, 102
Nelson, R. D. 4, 14, 19
Nicholson, E. 6, 17, 29, 198
Niehr, H. 131
Nihan, C. 22, 102, 103
Noll, K. 20
Norin, S. 182
Noth, M. 12, 13, 193

O'Brien, M. A. 10, 19, 197
Oestreicher, T. 7, 29, 34
Otto, E. 7, 17, 20, 197, 202

Paton, L. B. 7
Paul, J. M. 5

Person, R. F. Jr. 18
Pfeiffer, R. H. 11
Polzin, R. M. 1, 20, 86, 87
Preuss, H. D. 10
Propp, W. H. C. 97, 105
Provan, I. W. 134
Pummer, R. 103
Pury, A. de 11, 13–15

Rad, G. von 4, 29, 36, 58, 61, 102
Rendtorff, R. 14, 16, 174, 175
Reuter, R. 28, 34, 132
Richardson, H. N. 10
Richter, S. 37
Riley, W. 163, 164
Rofé, A. 70
Rogerson, J. W. 3, 131
Römer, T. 8, 9, 11, 13–17, 19, 20, 65, 73, 135
Rose, M. 16
Rösel, H. L. 18, 19
Rowley, H. H. 10
Rütersworden, U. 186, 197

Schley, D. G. 115
Schmid, H. H. 16
Schmid, K. 15–17
Schmidt, W. H. 12
Schmitt, H.-C. 16
Seebass, H. 29
Shedletsky, L. 148, 150, 152, 153
Silberman, N. A. 10
Smend, R. 3, 6, 14
Smyth, F. 141, 142
Soggin, J. A. 14
Stackert, J. 8
Staerk, W. 63
Steuernagel, C. 63
Stott, K. 135
Suzuki, Y. 33
Sweeney, M. A. 132–34, 155

Tadmor, C. 131, 134, 155
Thelle, R. I. 124, 136, 210
Thiel, W. 12
Toorn, K. van der 147

Uehlinger, C. 133, 142

Van Seters, J. 15, 16, 19, 37, 104

Vaux, R. de 37
Veijola, T. 13, 15, 20, 73, 157
Vogt, P. T. 2

Watts, J. W. 181
Weinfeld, M. 1, 5, 9, 36, 51, 61, 105, 106, 174
Weippert, H. 14, 24, 28, 29, 43, 71, 181, 192
Weiser, A. 18
Welch, A. C. 7, 29, 34
Wellhausen, J. 5, 22, 28
Wenham, G. J. 6, 29, 37, 132

Westermann, C. 15, 18
Weyde, K. W. 109, 157
Whybray, R. N. 6
Willis, T. M. 33
Wilson, I. 37
Wilson, R. R. 20, 33
Wissman, F. B. 192
Witte, M. 19
Wolff, H. W. 12
Würthwein, E. 18, 132–34, 153

Younger, K. L. 115